EDUCATION AND
MODERNIZATION
IN THE MIDDLE EAST

EDUCATION AND MODERNIZATION IN THE MIDDLE EAST

Joseph S. Szyliowicz

CORNELL UNIVERSITY PRESS

Ithaca and London

First published 1973 by Cornell University Press.
Published in the United Kingdom by Cornell University Press Ltd., 2–4 Brook Street, London W1Y 1AA.

International Standard Book Number 0–8014–0758–3
Library of Congress Catalog Card Number 72–12292

Printed in the United States of America by The Colonial Press Inc.

Librarians: Library of Congress cataloging information appears on the last page of the book.

TO IRENE, MICHAEL, AND DARA

Preface

Much has been written about the Middle East in recent years, and works on historical and contemporary aspects proliferate. Yet anyone who analyzes this output will become aware that many important topics have not received the attention they deserve. Rather surprisingly, education is one of these neglected subjects, even though the role that education plays in modernization has become a topic of concern to scholars and government officials alike. Despite its prominence and its importance in the political, social, economic, and cultural development of the Middle East, education has not been the topic of a regional study in any language for many years.

The extent to which education in the Middle East has been overlooked was brought home to me when I began to investigate various aspects of modernization related to educational processes, and I could find few detailed or analytical materials on either the historical or the contemporary role of education in the area. At this time, I had the good fortune to meet Professor Andreas Kazamias, whose own work on Turkey has provided us with a pioneering single-country study, and he encouraged me to undertake a study to fill the gap.

Because of my training and interests, I was naturally inclined to use the methodology of comparative analysis and to look at education, not in the formal structural way that characterized the work of so many educators until very recent times, but rather in terms of how education in the Middle East has functioned both as an object of change and as an agent of change. It is from this perspective that I have tried to examine education in historical and contemporary societies to demonstrate the relationship between education and modernization in the Middle East.

I have focused my attention on Turkey, Iran, and the Arab Republic of Egypt, three of the most important countries in the region. Although they share a common heritage, they have developed in different ways and have adopted different approaches to modernization. In dealing with each country I have, because of my concern with education as an agent and object of change, supplemented the detailed analysis of the development and functioning of educational processes with the kinds of materials required to place the analysis in appropriate context. In addition, I have discussed education in the Arab states from a regional perspective. I have not, however, included the Israeli case because of that country's unique heritage and characteristics.

All those persons who encouraged me and helped to crystallize my ideas and to sharpen the analysis deserve my appreciation, particularly several of my colleagues and students at the Graduate School of International Studies of the University of Denver. In parts of this book I have adapted materials from some of my earlier writings; I am grateful to the editors of *Comparative Education Review* and *Western Political Quarterly* for permission to do so and to the Publisher, Sage Publications, Inc., for permission to use portions of "A Political Analysis of Student Activism: The Turkish Case" by Joseph S. Szyliowicz, *Sage Professional Papers in Comparative Politics,* Volume 3, Number 01–034.

In addition, I must extend my thanks to the numerous persons in the Middle East who facilitated my research. Many scholars, administrators, librarians, and government officials generously gave their time and shared their knowledge and insights with me. Equally gracious were the representatives of UNESCO in Paris who kindly made available important materials of all sorts. I am also grateful to those institutions that provided the financial support that made my work possible. Part of the research was carried on while I enjoyed grants from the American Research Institute in Turkey, the Social Science Research Council, and the Graduate School of International Studies. Indeed, the GSIS supported my work in numerous ways, and I must extend my particular thanks to Dorothea Blair for her patience and cooperation. Nancy Miani and the late Jane Fischer were understanding typists throughout.

It is a pleasure to acknowledge the assistance of the staff at Cornell University Press, which provided perceptive and meticulous editorial advice. Finally, I must add that without the tolerance and cooperation of my wife and children this book would still be in the planning stage.

JOSEPH S. SZYLIOWICZ

Greenwood Village, Colorado

Contents

EDUCATION AND
MODERNIZATION
IN THE MIDDLE EAST

1

Education and
Its Environment

The Conceptual Overview

Change and innovation have always been a vital part of man's existence, yet only in the recent past has the process of change been transformed into the worldwide revolution of modernization. This revolution, of a scope and intensity unparalleled in human history, originated in Western Europe less than five hundred years ago and until quite recently was confined to that part of the world. But as Europe expanded outward, the process of modernization—or Westernization, to use the more limited and parochial term—became increasingly a universal experience and all regions were eventually affected by the impact of a dynamic Western culture upon relatively static societies. In few other parts of the world is this more evident than in the Middle East, a region whose major characteristic can be described in one word—change.

The changes in the Middle East during the last 150 years have disrupted the old society and culture. Conflict and reaction are evident everywhere as the interaction between the two cultures has led to the dislocation of value judgments and a fundamental unsettling of ancient ways. One scholar has described this process as follows: "the individual and his society are divided against themselves, suffering from feeling at the same time attracted and repelled when confronted with the nonchalant aggression of Western mentality." [1] Reinforcing the impact of this "nonchalant aggression" have been the attempts by various groups and governments to increase their power or that of the state by adopting Western technology and sponsoring policies of modernization.

[1] Gustav E. von Grunebaum, "Acculturation and Self-Realization," *The Contemporary Middle East,* B. Rivlin and J. Szyliowicz, eds. (New York: Random House, 1965), pp. 141–142.

As a result, ubiquitous, dynamic change has become an essential part of the Middle Eastern *Weltanschauung,* and in one country after another, the transformation of traditional society and culture is taking place, though at varying speeds and in different ways owing to differences in the timing, nature, and consequences of the Western impact. Symptomatic of the personal and social divisions caused by the disruption of traditional patterns are such factors as political instability, social tensions, psychological disorientations, and economic disequilibrium, one or more manifestations of which often make headlines in the world press. Even the tragic Arab-Israeli conflict, essentially a conflict between two nationalisms for the same territory, is part of the same phenomenon.

Education not only constitutes one of the major factors contributing to the changes that have already taken place in the Middle East but it is widely regarded as a powerful tool that will make possible the achievement of personal and societal goals. In the Middle East, as elsewhere in the Third World, such maxims as "education is the key to modernization" are encountered frequently in the speeches of United Nations and government officials, and education has acquired the prestige usually accorded to such symbols of modernity as atomic reactors and computing centers. Almost every political leader regards education as the basic component in nation-building and as the foundation for rapid economic development and social change. This faith stems from several sources, including the obvious fact that modern schools were an important channel of the new ideas and values which had a tremendous impact upon the traditional society of the Middle East, that reformers and modernizers have tended to be the products of these schools, and that these countries desperately need skilled and highly trained manpower which can come only from such institutions.

That education is an innovative force which can be used to further processes of change in any society is an idea that, though dating back to Plato, has received serious attention from scholars and decision-makers only in recent times. Historically, the learning process has emphasized the past rather than the present or the future, and the basic function of educational systems has usually been viewed as the preservation and transmission of traditional culture. Yet today schools are regarded as instruments of change and sizable investments in this area are, in fact, being made throughout the world. The belief in modern education is also shared by the peoples of the world. Everywhere education is correctly viewed as a channel of personal mobility, and demands for greater educational opportunities have created enormous pressures upon all governments. One scholar, writing about the Middle East, has summarized this phenomenon as follows:

In order to raise oneself above a certain standard of minimal life, the diplomas as well as personal initiatives are an inevitable necessity. That is, diplomas become more and more a *conditio sine qua non* for all high positions. . . . Whereas in former times the circumstances and especially the class to which one belonged determined the career that one would follow, now diplomas determine this. This does not exclude the importance of familial or personal relations. The "modernization" of the society, whether by the dislocation of traditional classes, whether by the rise of new "classes," has caused social mobility . . . we note simply the result; which is a veritable chase after diplomas.[2]

Paralleling the popular concern with education is the interest of scholars. Whereas once education was largely ignored as a serious field of inquiry by social scientists, increasing numbers have begun to focus upon the ways in which education is related to modernization. Economists have emphasized the need for investment in human resources and manpower development, political scientists the importance of education for nation-building and political development in general, and social scientists the role of education in transforming people's beliefs, attitudes, and values to render them consonant with the needs of a developing society.[3]

The fact that scholars are studying such disparate, though inter-

[2] Jean-Jacques Waardenburg, *Les Universités dans le monde arabe actuel* (Paris: Mouton, 1966), I, 4.

[3] The literature on this topic has expanded tremendously in recent years. For a useful bibliography, see Kenneth J. Rothman, "Attitude, Competence, and Education," in *Education and Political Development,* James Coleman, ed. (Princeton: Princeton University Press, 1965). The relationship between education and economic growth has also received widespread attention, and, in addition to the works cited in the notes, the books by Theodore Schultz, *The Economic Value of Education* (New York: Columbia University Press, 1963), and by Frederick Harbison and Charles Myers, *Education, Manpower, and Economic Growth* (New York: McGraw-Hill, 1964) deserve special mention.

related, phenomena indicates the breadth and generality of the concept of modernization. And, given so many different approaches and perspectives, it is not surprising that conceptual, terminological, and theoretical consensus remains elusive. Nevertheless there does appear to be general agreement that modernization involves such interrelated processes as industrialization, political development, and social and psychic mobility. In general terms modernization may be defined as a process that involves the transformation of man, his society, and his culture, and has at its core a fundamental belief in rationality and scientific thought. It is a process of unparalleled scope and intensity, involving the transformation of static, traditional societies into nations that can continuously generate, absorb, sustain, and process ubiquitous change.[4]

Implicit in this approach is the distinction between two ideal types, traditional and modern societies. To define traditional society is not easy, since the category usually includes simple folk organizations as well as complex empires. The ideal type of a folk society applies most appropriately to relatively small isolated tribal groups and is not really applicable to the actual situation existing now or in the past in most of the non-Western world. Accordingly, one scholar has suggested that a new construct, the "feudal society," may be more appropriate.[5] Essentially the feudal society is far more complex than the folk society and provides for a lower stratum composed largely of a peasant mass living in villages and utilizing a simple technology, plus some artisans and an urban-based ruling class consisting of bureaucrats, priests, scholars, landlords, and warriors in various combinations. The stratification pattern is a bifurcated one with the rulers separate and dis-

[4] Modernization has also become the subject of a vast literature. See, for example, the Studies in Political Development sponsored by the Committee on Comparative Politics, and such works as: Clifford Geertz, ed., *Old Societies and New States* (New York: The Free Press, 1963); Samuel P. Huntington, *Political Order in Changing Societies* (New Haven: Yale University Press, 1968); Dankwart A. Rustow, *A World of Nations* (Washington: Brookings Institution, 1967); C. E. Black, *The Dynamics of Modernization* (New York: Harper & Row, 1966): Myron Weiner, *Modernization* (New York: Basic Books, 1966); S. N. Eisenstadt, *Modernization: Protest and Change* (Englewood Cliffs, N.J.: Prentice-Hall, 1966).

[5] Gideon Sjoberg, "Folk and 'Feudal' Societies," in *Political Development and Social Change*, Jason L. Finkle and Richard W. Gable, eds. (New York: John Wiley, 1966), *passim.*

tinct in terms of appearance, language, and manners from the mass; hence social mobility between the two strata is minimal. The feudal society is also marked by the existence of highly developed administrative, religious, and educational institutions which are used by the ruling class to perpetuate its position within the social order. Important similarities with the folk society do exist; feudal societies, too, are static, sacred, and marked by a large degree of internal harmony. As we shall see, many states of the Middle East, the Abbasid and Ummayad empires of medieval times, the Ottoman Empire, and the Safavid state and its successors, conformed quite closely to this model.

Modern societies are completely different. They are characterized by egalitarianism and high degrees of social mobility. Their institutions are highly differentiated, specialized, and rational. Their economic, political, and social orders are continually processing change, and achievement criteria determine status. Perhaps the ultimate differentiation between the two types, however, is the dynamic nature of modern societies as contrasted to the relatively static character of the feudal type.

Such an analytical distinction should not be interpreted to mean that no change ever took place in non-Western societies. Obviously great empires rose and fell and important social and religious movements deeply affected large portions of mankind. However, the key point is that these traditional states were organized in such a way that any existing dynamism was limited to a particular sphere and, further, that these were closed societies that could not develop the capacity to absorb and process change in all sectors of their social order. This essential difference has been summarized as follows:

A traditional system thus differs from any modern system by its incapacity to deal with continuous systemic transformation: traditional societies were not faced continuously by system transforming demands and when, usually only after centuries, they were confronted by a particular challenge of this kind, they were capable of responding only by disintegrating or by creating a new closed system.[6]

---

[6] Manfred Halpern, "The Revolution of Modernization in National and International Society," *Nomos: Revolution,* American Society for Political and Legal Philosophy (New York: Atherton Press, 1966), p. 180.

Modern systems, on the other hand, possess the flexibility and adaptability to deal with rapid, self-sustaining changes in all sectors of the society.

Compounding the difficulties inherent in defining modernization are the great problems involved in conceptualizing how education is related to its achievement. Only in recent years have social scientists begun to investigate this relationship empirically and analytically, and, although there is widespread agreement that education contributes directly to modernization, no adequate body of theory is yet available that would permit the testing of specific hypotheses with data from the Middle East.

The complexities involved in delineating the precise relationship between education and modernization can best be illustrated by focusing upon the most universally sought—and conceptually most precise—strand of modernization: economic development. Practically every country in the world is seeking to achieve a rapid rate of economic growth, and underlying the huge investments being made in education is the belief that formal schooling is a major variable determining the rate and level of economic development. To some degree this faith has been empirically verified; in general, researchers have concluded that positive relationships do exist between the formation of human capital, in which education is a major component, and economic growth. Experts have calculated that much of the rise in the income of the United States between 1900 and 1956 was due to improvements in the educational qualifications of the workers. Besides the United States, the U.S.S.R. and Japan are often cited as proof of the relationship. All three countries possessed highly developed educational systems and a significant proportion of their population was literate before they began to undergo rapid development.[7] The complexities of the linkage, however, defy easy generalization because:

The relationship between levels of literacy and education and subsequent economic development is obviously much more complex than any two variable relationship statements would indicate. Identical rates of literacy or proportions enrolled in universities will have different consequences

---

[7] For a useful discussion of these studies, see Neil J. Smelser and Seymour Martin Lipset, eds., *Social Structure and Mobility in Economic Development* (Chicago: Aldine, 1966), pp. 29ff.

for societies with varying values, levels of economic development, types and quality of schooling, opportunities for educational mobility, and the like. Such factors do not appear in the national parameter statistics employed in most studies. . . .[8]

Not surprisingly, therefore, scholars disagree on the type and level of education that is most conducive to economic development. One study showed that twenty-one out of twenty-four countries with 90 per cent literacy rates had yearly per capita incomes of $500 or more; twenty-four out of twenty-five states with less than 30 per cent literacy had incomes of less than $200. In the intermediate category the relationship, though present, was weaker. Another sophisticated and extensive study found that in seventy-five countries economic development correlated more closely with higher education than with primary education or literacy rates, and this finding has been corroborated by a number of other studies.[9]

These results have recently been elaborated and refined by another scholar, who concluded that various levels of education are related to different stages of economic growth. Those countries whose primary schools enrolled more than 10 per cent of their total population in 1920 were the ones who subsequently achieved the highest per capita income. Secondary enrollments do not correlate with economic development until after about 8 to 10 per cent of the country's youngsters were receiving a primary education, and, similarly, enrollment ratios in higher education showed a marked relationship with per capita income only after primary education had become widespread. If these findings are valid the most effective allocation of resources to education takes the following form: emphasize primary education until the percentage of students enrolled exceeds 10 per cent of the population, then emphasize secondary enrollments until 2 per cent of the population is enrolled, and then shift once again to an expansion of university enrollments to about 0.3 per cent of the populace. While the emphasis of the effort changes, however, the expansion of the lower levels should be maintained.[10]

On a more general level, the relationship between education and

---

[8] *Ibid.,* p. 32.

[9] *Ibid.,* pp. 32ff.

[10] Alexander Paeslee, "Education's Role in Development," *Economic Development and Culture Change,* 17 (1968), 293–318.

economic growth would appear easy to demonstrate. Clearly, if rapid and self-sustaining growth is to be achieved, modern technology must be widely adopted and utilized, and in order to do so a wide range of skills which can be taught in modern schools is required. Developmental plans based on this reasoning usually include a more or less detailed analysis of the productive capacity of the educational system in terms of the projected demands for middle- and high-level manpower and projects designed to eliminate bottlenecks by increasing the supply of particular skills within the society.

Despite its apparently compelling nature this approach has been severely criticized by many scholars on both empirical and theoretical grounds, and their criticisms serve to demonstrate once again how complex are the linkages between education and economic development. They point first to the immense practical problems involved in preparing analyses of manpower supply and demand for any given society. Complex calculations are required but, as we shall see, the data that are available suffer to varying degrees from lack of comprehensiveness and reliability, thus rendering projections based on these figures highly suspect. Nevertheless such calculations have often served as the basis for the allocation of limited resources to different educational sectors. More importantly, skeptics point to the underlying assumptions and question such concepts as an optimum integration of schools and economy and the nonsubstitutability of skills. Not only can technical skills probably be more effectively provided through in-service training programs, but the emphasis upon specific technical preparation may prove inimical to the needs of a dynamic, developing society. Even if the proper number of persons with appropriate skills are trained it is likely that they will be far more mobile than anticipated and will not necessarily fill the particular needs envisaged by the planners. Hence even the manpower approach must be viewed within a broader framework than mere supply and demand calculations and must include consideration of the matrix within which schools operate. From the political, economic, social, and cultural milieu flows a reward structure that shapes the incentives, motivations, and aspirations of students as well as the specific career choices that graduates will make.[11] The failure of attempts to expand

[11] See Philip J. Foster, "The Vocational School Fallacy in Developmental Planning," *Education and Economic Development,* C. Arnold Anderson and

technical and vocational education in the Middle East, which we shall discuss later, is particularly instructive of the ways in which the intentions of planners can be subverted by individual orientations and nonsupportive and nonreinforcing environmental factors.

In recent years most economists have, in fact, become increasingly aware of the importance of social, cultural, and political considerations in development and include such noneconomic variables as institutions, organizations, motivations, and values in their growth models. Though all of these factors are interrelated and represent necessary but not sufficient causes for modernization, many experts emphasize the pivotal importance of attitudes and values. One scholar has made this point in the following words:

The state of a people's politico-economic development, together with its rate and direction, depends largely upon what is in the minds of its members, and above all upon the content of the minds of its elites. The content of men's minds is looked upon as the potentially dynamic element, as the source whence issue change and novelty, in a world or universe that is otherwise essentially passive. Accordingly, transformation of an underdeveloped society into a developed one entails transformation of the contents of the minds of elites who direct and of the men who man such underdeveloped society.[12]

Later, when we discuss the relationship between education and the political strand of modernization, we shall return to the crucial role of leadership. First, however, it is necessary to elucidate the general relationship between the "content of men's minds," education, and modernization because this relationship, which we regard as preeminent, will serve as a major focus for the analysis of education and modernization in the Middle East.

Mary Jean Bowman, eds. (Chicago: Aldine, 1965), pp. 142–166; Hla Myint, *The Economics of the Developing Countries* (New York: Praeger, 1964), pp. 173ff; C. Arnold Anderson, "Education and Human Resources Development: Recommendations for the Implementation of the International Education Act," mimeo. (June 1967), *passim.*

[12] Joseph J. Spengler, "Theory, Ideology, Non-Economic Values, and Politico-Economic Development," *Tradition, Values, and Socio-Economic Development,* Ralph Braibanti and Joseph J. Spengler, eds. (Durham, N.C.: Duke University Press), p. 5. For a systematic elaboration of the role of social factors in economic development see Wilbert E. Moore, "The Social Frame-work of Economic Development," *ibid.,* pp. 57–82.

Since Max Weber's classic exposition of the relevance of the "Protestant ethic," many scholars have focused upon the importance of particular value orientations for modernization and upon the psychological and other factors that lead to the emergence of innovative personalities or individuals with an achievement orientation. E. H. Hagen has argued that social change and economic development occurred when a group underwent a "withdrawal of status respect," thus creating a rejected group whose members became deviants with innovative and creative personalities.[13] Closely related is the work of David McClelland, who believes that the personality variable "need for achievement" is the critical antecedent for entrepreneurship and hence for economic development. He has found that children in Turkey seem to acquire a higher achievement orientation than children in Iran and argues that this factor accounts for the differential rates of economic growth evidenced by the two countries. He attributes the different orientations to the school system since the other socializing agencies are very similar. Because of such findings McClelland has concluded that although both education and achievement orientations spur economic growth, "motivation plus knowledge has a significantly greater effect than motivation or knowledge alone." [14]

Another recent study also underlines the critical role of education in forming and strengthening the specific behavioral and attitudinal traits that it identified as characteristic of modern man. This sophisticated multinational project revealed that the same attitudes, values, and ways of acting comprise a syndrome that distinguishes modern from traditional man in all nationalities and occupational groups studied and that education was the major influence in changing men's minds from traditional to modern. The principal elements of the modern-man syndrome include:

[13] E. H. Hagen, *On the Theory of Social Change* (Homewood, Ill.: Dorsey Press, 1962).

[14] Cited in Smelser and Lipset, *op. cit.*, p. 45. McClelland's study was published as *The Achieving Society* (Princeton: Van Nostrand, 1961). For a critical evaluation of this analysis see A. Kazamias, *Education and the Quest for Modernity in Turkey* (Chicago: University of Chicago Press, 1966), pp. 197–199. Subsequently McClelland tested his theory empirically and through psychological training programs increased the achievement motivation of businessmen in the United States and India. These results are presented in David C. McClelland and David G. Winter, *Motivating Economic Achievement* (New York: Free Press, 1969).

(1) Openness to new experience, both with people and with new ways of doing things such as attempting to control births; (2) the assertion of increasing independence from the authority of traditional figures like parents and priests and a shift of allegiance to leaders of government, public affairs, trade unions, cooperatives, and the like; (3) belief in the efficacy of science and medicine, and a general abandonment of passivity and fatalism in the face of life's difficulties; and (4) ambition for one's self and one's children to achieve high occupational and educational goals. Men who manifest these characteristics (5) like people to be on time and show an interest in carefully planning their affairs in advance. It is also part of this syndrome (6) to show interest and take an active part in civic and community affairs and local politics; (7) to strive energetically to keep up with the news, and within this effort to prefer news of national and international import over items dealing with sports, religion, or purely local affairs.[15]

Although a complex of forces—urbanization, mass communications, modern enterprises, political mobilization—are involved in the transformation of a traditional man into a person with these characteristics, the educational process when conceptualized as involving not merely formal curricula but also the inculcation of values in an informal and often unarticulated fashion remains the most significant.[16]

Thus the degree to which the educational system does, in fact, produce graduates with modern orientations can be considered a vital dimension of any country's effort to modernize and appears to be of more fundamental importance than attempts to establish a balance between supply and demand for particular skills. Accordingly, the first dimension of the relationship between education and modernization that we shall focus upon in our study of educational systems in the Middle East is the degree to which these systems inculcate, both formally and informally, the behavioral traits and attributes of modern man. Though detailed empirical studies are practically nonexistent, we shall supplement our concern with the effectiveness of manpower planning by assessing the functioning of schools from this perspective.

Even if creative and innovative individuals who are able to adapt to the requirements of change are trained, however, important ques-

---

[15] Alex Inkeles, "Making Men Modern: On the Causes and Consequences of Individual Change in Six Developing Countries," *American Journal of Sociology,* 75 (1969), 210.

[16] *Ibid.,* p. 211.

tions of absorption and productive utilization remain. We have already emphasized the importance of societal variables and could cite examples of states that do not provide adequate support for such persons, absorbing them in traditional settings where they can not adequately apply their skills and orientations or simply not generating an effective demand to absorb the talent that is in fact trained. Hence the role of education in modernization must be viewed in a broader setting than the training of manpower with particular skills or even with modern orientations and attitudes. The ways in which such persons are utilized become critical, and variations in the social, cultural, and political patterns of any society will determine the degree to which modern men are produced and utilized appropriately. In fact, such variables will probably play a larger role in determining the degree to which education is consonant with the requirements of a modernizing society than any specific educational experience.

From this perspective the character of the political system and especially of its elites becomes a critical variable. Though there is an obvious interaction between politics and other segments of the social order and one must consider the particular configurations of forces within any society as more or less rigid constraints upon the ability of any leader to adopt particular policies, it is through political choice and political action that economic, educational, social, and, for that matter, political institutions themselves are fundamentally shaped. Educational policies are directly related to broader questions of policy-making within any society, and the specific decisions taken on such issues as who shall gain access to the schools, what they will learn while enrolled, and how they will be utilized will inevitably reflect the distribution of power, the kinds of support that any particular regime possesses, its ideological orientation, its level of political development, and the like.

Moreover, political decisions are clearly required if an educational system is to be structured in such a way as to be consonant with national goals and if environmental structures are to be appropriately supportive and reinforcing; but, as we shall see, not all societies possess leadership that is willing and able to adopt and successfully implement the kinds of policies that are required. Nevertheless decision-makers in practically every developing society have recognized the potential of education as an integrative and socializing force and have sought to utilize it in this manner. The formal educational system is expected to serve, not only as a means of achieving economic growth, but also as a socializing agency into modernity and nationhood. The many diverse groups that comprise the state are to be integrated into a common sense of nationality, and political and ideological themes are to be found more or less explicitly articulated in every curriculum. Yet, despite the importance accorded to the expansion of education as a means of promoting nation-building, little is known about how education will in fact affect the many cleavages that characterize the new states, and some scholars have warned that the results may well be dysfunctional, at least in the short run. As more and more people become educated they will become increasingly aware of their specific ethnic, religious, and racial identities, thus exacerbating rather than bridging existing gaps and creating potential new sources of unrest. Furthermore, it is likely that higher levels of education will lead to greater demands upon political systems that may well prove incapable of processing them adequately, resulting in stagnation or decay.[17]

Different political systems will respond in different ways to such demands, and whether development or decay occurs will ultimately be determined by the quality and character of the leadership. Hence, although political socialization and political integration are important issues, we shall focus primarily upon the analysis of groups with power and influence. By so doing we can investigate comparatively the relationship between education and the polity, while viewing education both as a dependent and an independent variable. Clearly all contemporary societies are characterized by new groups that have emerged from the modern schools and which are either competing for power or have already gained access to it, and by examining this process over time in the Middle East we can assess the ways in which education has affected various polities. On the other hand, political decisions have also clearly shaped the educational opportunities available to different groups. Although the linkage between elite status and a high level of modern education is evident everywhere—

---

[17] For a discussion of the relationship between education and the political system see Coleman, *op. cit., passim.* For an analysis that focuses upon nation-building see Trevor Coombe, "Education in the Building of Nations" (Ph.D. diss., Harvard University, 1963).

a factor which has served to enhance the great social demand for education and its political saliency referred to earlier—the degree to which entry into the higher reaches of the educational system or into certain selected schools is restricted varies from society to society and is reflected in and determined by the composition and character of particular social groups.

If we are to explore such relationships adequately it is necessary to conceptualize the social system. In our view any society, be it feudal, modern, or some mixture thereof, contains three primary components: a social core group, functional elites, and a mass. The first component of our model, the unifying, exemplary, and directing center of a society, has seldom been conceptualized adequately, although such phrases as "ruling class," "power elite," "ruling elite" and the like do in fact refer to specific patterns which a social core group may take.[18] The second important component, elites, may be defined as "functional, mainly occupational groups which have a high status (for whatever reason) in a society." [19] Our third component consists of the remainder of the populace. The term "class" will be used to refer to the stratum from which the members of any social core group or elite are recruited.

The concept of the social core group was developed by Suzanne Keller in an insightful elaboration of the functional role of elites in society. In her analysis she carefully distinguished between the social core group and elites and identified five kinds of social core groups —ruling caste, aristocracy, first estate, ruling class, and strategic elites. The first four, however, are really variations common to the feudal society model discussed earlier, the last to modern societies.[20] Hence this theoretical construct is not applicable to most countries of the non-Western world which are characterized by a different kind of social core group, the political elite. This distinction has been noted by another scholar, T. B. Bottomore, who has also contributed greatly to conceptual clarification. Carefully defining his terms, he concluded that one must distinguish between three types of societies, those with

[18] Suzanne Keller, *Beyond the Ruling Class* (New York: Random House, 1963), pp. 29ff.

[19] T. B. Bottomore, *Elites and Society* (Baltimore: Penguin, 1964), p. 14.

[20] Keller, *op. cit.,* pp. 54ff.

a ruling class, and at the same time elites which represent particular aspects of its interests; societies in which there is no ruling class, but a political elite which founds its power upon the control of the administration, or upon military force, rather than upon property ownership and inheritance; and societies in which there exists a multiplicity of elites.[21]

The differences between these three patterns are many. Firstly, there can be only one ruling class but many strategic elites within any society. Patterns of recruitment also differ markedly. Achievement criteria are of little importance in a ruling-class social core group but they dominate the selection process for strategic elites. A political elite falls somewhere between these two poles. Such other variables as the basis of power, the range and domain of authority, the character of the power distribution within the society, the basis of legitimacy and the like can also be differentiated for each of these types as is evidenced in Chart 1.

Chart 1. Characterization of social core groups

	Ruling class	*Political elite*	*Strategic elites*
Importance of achievement criteria for recruitment	Low	Medium	High
Hereditary continuity	High	Medium	Low
Basis of power	Ownership of property	Control of institutions of political power	Skill and competence of members
Range of authority	Wide	Wide	Narrow
Domain of authority	Diffuse	Diffuse	Specific
Cultural bonds	Class membership	Common ideology	Professional culture
Accessibility	Relatively closed	Relatively restricted	Relatively open
Character of power distribution	Monopolistic	Monopolistic	Oligopolistic
Basis of legitimacy	Cultural ideology	Political ideology	Professional ideology
Social and cultural attributes	High homogeneity	Medium homogeneity	Low homogeneity

Such distinctions provide us with a model with which to analyze the consequences of the introduction and establishment of modern educational systems in the Middle East on a comparative basis. Specifically, we shall attempt to answer the following kinds of questions which are suggested by our conceptualization:

(1) What were the characteristics of the social core groups and of elites in the traditional Middle Eastern states? By what criteria was

[21] Bottomore, *op. cit.,* p. 44.

membership attained and maintained? What were the patterns of recruitment and advancement? Specifically, what were the educational, social, and economic backgrounds of their members?

(2) What educational institutions existed within the traditional Middle East? What was the structure and functioning of the educational system? What educational opportunities were available to different segments of society?

(3) What changes occurred in these patterns as a result of the Western impact? What was the effect of modern education upon patterns of recruitment into the social core group and particular elites? What influence did the graduates of the new schools have upon the affairs of empire and nation-state? To be specific, what positions did the graduates hold, and what career patterns emerged?

(4) What conflicts were engendered within the ranks of the social core group, among elites, and within the state as a whole? To what extent can they be attributed to differences in educational background and to the kinds of educational institutions existing within the society?

Answers to questions such as these, however, can provide only a partial insight into the relationship between education and modernization for the questions focus upon the impact of education and do not deal with the second vital dimension of the relationship that we have identified, the ways in which education is shaped by the political system. Of particular relevance in this regard is the character of the social core group, for the specific configuration of a society's core possesses important and fundamental implications for the educational process within that state. Empirical support for this position has recently been provided by a team of scholars who tentatively concluded from a study of education in a diversified sample of ten states that "variations in the nature of the societal center in general will be systematically related to the variation in the pattern of educational demand, in the patterns of responses . . . to these demands and in the impact of the educational process on the change-oriented behavior of the educatees." [22]

This perspective provides the basis for the last dimension of our conceptualization. Heretofore we have dealt with the manner in which

[22] L. Aran, S. N. Eisenstadt, and C. Adler, "The Effectiveness of Educational Systems in the Process of Modernization," *Comparative Education Review,* 16 (February 1972), 40.

educational developments affect society. Now we turn specifically to an examination of the broader framework and, viewing education as the dependent variable, analyze the ways in which the structure and functioning of educational systems are influenced by particular social-core-group and elite configurations. We shall attempt to determine what uniformities, if any, characterize educational policies of different kinds of states and the degree to which systemic political changes affect educational policy.

In our analysis we shall utilize a typological approach. Although this approach can often be misleading because we are forced to label countries neatly when in fact some of their empirical characteristics do not conform to the ideal type, the classification of political systems remains a useful basis for comparison and analysis. Accordingly we shall combine our earlier conceptualization of social core groups with a second variable that emerges from our concern with modernization, orientation toward change and innovation, in order to create a typology relevant for our purposes and applicable to the states of the Middle East, historically and comparatively.

To conceptualize the dimension of change is no simple matter, though one might suggest that such variables as the area in which change occurs, the intensity of the change, and the orientation of the change are subjects for analysis. For our purposes, however, it is adequate to identify three general orientations toward change and innovation. The first involves a total commitment by the regime to modernization as evidenced by its willingness to restructure all aspects of the society, patterns of stratification, resource allocation, basic values, and institutional structures to achieve modernity. A second orientation is characterized by a regime's willingness to allow changes in some areas of the social order, even permitting the organization of new groups and the redistribution of resources so as to bring about change in the position of hitherto ignored segments. The regime promotes change only insofar as no threat is posed to fundamental societal goals and values. The third orientation seeks to minimize the amount of change that occurs within the society. Little or no shift in the usually regressive pattern of resource allocation occurs; few innovations are permitted in any area, and those that cannot be avoided are either isolated or integrated into traditional patterns to the largest possible extent.

By combining the ideas in our earlier discussion of social core groups with these attitudes toward modernization we can create a nine-cell matrix—three different social core groups, each possessing one of three orientations toward change. Retaining the essence of this approach, we can simplify it by combining some of the nine types and reducing them to four fundamental ones. We do so because important parameters are imposed by the configuration of any social core group. Few if any ruling-class societies, for example, have been willing to adopt innovations and to promote change in every aspect of the society. Rather, they have sought to prevent the adoption of innovations that would threaten fundamental authority and value patterns. Furthermore, the implementation of a similar orientation toward modernization by two different social core groups results in similar institutional and attitudinal pressures and requirements. Accordingly, we shall utilize a typology consisting of four ideal types of political systems: the radical, the reformist, the adaptive, and the competitive.[23]

The radical system is characterized by a willingness to transform every aspect of the society. The entire society and culture is examined from a new perspective—that of modernization—and whatever changes are necessary to achieve that goal are inaugurated. Perhaps not surprisingly, such regimes are to be found in those countries where the social core group consists of a political elite composed of modern elements who have achieved power through a coup or a struggle against a colonial power. Legitimacy is based, not on traditional considerations, but on ideology and charisma. Efforts are often made to mobilize the mass of the populace in the drive for modernization, and egalitarianism is an important ideological strand.

A reformist government is one that is willing to promote reform and change, but only if traditional institutions, relationships, and values can be maintained. Power is vested in a ruling class or in a political elite representing conservative groups, but co-optation of new elements is common. The aim is essentially to reorganize traditional groups' structures and the relations between them from ethnic, tribal, or religious bases to those found in a modern state but to do

[23] For a similar typology with only three categories see Iliya Harik, "An Approach to the Study of Middle Eastern Politics," *Middle East Studies Association Bulletin*, 4 (Feb. 15, 1970) 30ff.

so without affecting the primacy of the ruling group or of the values that legitimize its position. Change is not introduced in every aspect of the society and culture, and the regime's legitimacy remains based on traditional factors. In many ways, all colonial regimes fall into this category, as do traditional societies that have embarked upon reform programs. The dangers of such a policy are, of course, exemplified by the overthrow of colonial regimes; it is difficult to contain modernizing elements once they have been introduced into the society to such a degree.

The third type, the adaptive polity, is characterized by an unwillingness to change. The fundamental goal of the ruler, usually a traditional monarch, is to preserve the existing system, although he is usually willing to accept infrastructural improvements in such areas as technology and economic affairs. The society is characterized by a ruling class, and political roles are filled by the members of this class. Ascriptive criteria predominate and other traditional values prevail throughout the society. Indeed, every effort is made to maintain traditional structures, values, beliefs, and patterns of interaction, and required innovations tend to be integrated into the social order so as to minimize any possible dislocations in the existing way of life. Such a policy is typical of many feudal societies.

The competitive system is one that has achieved a certain level of modernity and in which politics are structured along democratic lines. The society is characterized by specialized, functional elites, recruitment into which is determined largely by achievement criteria. Power tends to be dispersed between these elites, who compete for power both among themselves and with more traditional elites. The ideological thrust, however, is not directly toward modernization. Governments tend to represent many different factions and to change according to established constitutional procedures, and a considerable degree of opposition is tolerated within the system.

Each of these categories is, of course, an ideal type, and any state will possess characteristics that will not fit any one model. Even though modern elements seize power through revolutionary means, for example, the political elite may well devote more attention to the rhetoric of rapid development than to the adoption of the necessary measures to achieve it. In other cases a political elite seeking to implement its modernizing aspirations may be prevented from achieving any significant rate of change through various internal or even international pressures. Nevertheless the use of this typology has an important advantage: It permits us to combine a historical and comparative perspective so that we can order data concerning several societies over extensive periods of time. Using this framework we can not only categorize contemporary political systems but also discuss changes within one country over time and compare rulers in different time periods, for example, Ataturk and Nasser or Reza Shah and Mohammed Ali. In this way we shall examine the relationship between a particular political system and the structure and functioning of the schools. We shall discuss educational developments within their political context and outline briefly, at each appropriate point, the relevant characteristics of the polity in terms of the ideal types discussed above.

Thus we approach the study of education and modernization in the Middle East from three perspectives. First, we regard the educational system as an agent of change and, using the societal model outlined earlier, focus upon the ways in which the introduction of modern education has affected Middle Eastern society by looking at how social core groups and elites have changed over time and at the role of education in this process. Second, we view the educational system as an object of change in order to assess the relationship between particular political systems and the structure and functioning of their schools. Finally, we shall discuss the contemporary educational systems of the region in terms of the degree to which they are meeting societal needs, specifically the extent to which they are producing graduates who possess the attributes we have identified as characterizing modern man.

Unfortunately much of the data necessary for such an analysis are simply not available. Despite the area's long exposure to modernity and its significance as a potential case study with wide-ranging application to the problems of the new states in Asia and Africa, few specific studies on such topics as stratification patterns, the rise and decline of social groups, the development of specific educational institutions, or their actual functioning have so far been undertaken.

Even accurate statistical information is often lacking. In discussing the problems of gathering reliable data for the Arab countries a 1970 UNESCO report noted:

The assembling of statistical information . . . has proved to be very difficult; in some cases the data supplied by government departments are not in agreement with the facts as known from other sources; in other cases, the use of unprecise terms varying from one country to another makes it impossible to determine the true proportions between different types and levels of training; lastly, in all cases, the most recent official figures available for consultation relate to situations as they existed in 1966 or, at best, in 1967.[24]

These difficulties are compounded by the fact that the data provided by some countries is far more reliable than for other states, that comparable data for the same categories are not always available, and that in some cases information can be obtained only for one particular year. For such reasons even the most systematic study requires "estimates which can at best be regarded as approximations." [25]

Nevertheless, a considerable amount of information has been generated in recent years by scholars, governmental agencies, and international organizations, particularly UNESCO. Hence despite the serious limitations imposed by the type and character of the available data it is possible to describe the development and present condition of education in the Middle East and to study, though only in a preliminary way, the relationship between education and modernization in that region as outlined above.

Rather than attempt to deal with every state in appropriate detail, however, we shall concentrate our attention on Turkey, Iran, and the Arab Republic of Egypt, three important countries that represent major subareas within the region and can serve as case studies of different approaches to modernization. Though each has developed along different lines they share a common heritage; Chapter II describes traditional societal and educational patterns. Chapter III examines the impact of the introduction of modern educational practices in the region. Chapter IV discusses the development and functioning of education in the interwar period, and Chapters V–VII contain a detailed examination of the current structure and functioning of each

---

[24] "Trends in General, Technical, and Vocational Education in the Arab States," prepared for the Third Regional Conference of Ministers of Education and Ministers Responsible for Economic Planning in the Arab States, Marrakesh, 12–20 January 1970, mimeo. (Paris: UNESCO/MINED/ARAB STATES/4, 1970), p. 36; hereafter referred to as "Trends."

[25] *Ibid.*, p. 2.

country's educational system. To provide some insights into the character of education in other Arab states, Chapters IV and VII include a brief regional overview.

Earlier we emphasized the close relationship between educational systems and their environment. Accordingly we begin with a discussion of the ways in which contemporary social, economic, political, and cultural patterns affect and are affected by the functioning of educational institutions in the Middle East today.

Economy, Society, and Culture

No part of traditional Middle Eastern life has been immune to the impact of the West, not even its core, Islam, the last of the three great monotheistic faiths to emerge in the area.[26] Ninety-five per cent of the population is Muslim, the remainder Christian and Jewish.

As the belief system shared by the great majority of the population, Islam is obviously a vital contemporary social force. "Islam" literally means "submission," and a Muslim is one who has submitted to the will of God, Allah, and who acknowledges Mohammed as his messenger. Submission is not limited either temporally or functionally; all is sacred, so that Islam determines and sanctions all aspects of life —private and public, political, social, economic, and educational, as well as religious beliefs and activities. Accordingly, any change or innovation tends to be resisted as being against sanctified tradition, and adapting Islam to the requirements of the modern world is one of the basic problems confronting all Muslims.

This challenge has created new divisions within the Middle East, and the specific manner in which this basic question will be resolved —a challenge which has, of course, confronted every other major religion at various times—remains unclear, for no definite consensus has yet emerged. A wide range of attitudes exist, but they can be divided into three basic categories: secularism, reformism, and traditionalism. The outstanding exemplar of the secularist approach is Ataturk, who, believing that the influence of Islam had to be eliminated if Turkey was to become a strong, modern nation, placed rigid controls over religious orders and practices, and disestablished Islam. Despite this example, few leaders in the Middle East are working to

---

[26] A more detailed treatment of the themes presented in this section is to be found in Rivlin and Szyliowicz, *op. cit.*

establish secular states, and very few would openly admit to these leanings. Diametrically opposed to the secularists are the traditionalists, who insist upon strict adherence to Islamic practices. They believe that Islam is valid for all times and that changing conditions do not constitute a sufficient reason for not adhering strictly to all the precepts of Islam. Most of the Middle Eastern leaders, however, are neither secularists nor traditionalists but reformists who argue that Islam must be made to relate to contemporary conditions, that it is possible to do so without destroying the essence of the faith, and that, indeed, only in this way can Islam remain the vital force that it has been for centuries.

Apart from Saudi Arabia, most of the countries of the Middle East are, in fact, attempting to relate religious practices to the demands of development and social change, a most complex task which leads almost inevitably to controversy. The problems inherent in reinterpreting ancient beliefs are evidenced by the controversy over the Fast of Ramadan, which requires Muslims to abstain from food and drink from sunup to sundown during an entire month. President Bourguiba of Tunisia, concerned with the waste and inefficiencies caused by the fast, feels that a developing country with meager resources, like Tunisia, cannot afford to continue the practice. He argues: "There are good grounds today for not observing the Fast of Ramadan. . . . At a time when we are fighting against poverty . . . when the recovery of this Muslim nation depends upon strenuous work; I urge you to make use of a dispensation [and not fast during Ramadan]." [27] This attitude is diametrically opposed to that of the traditionalists, and when a member of the faculty of the famous Al-Azhar University in Cairo adopted a position similar to that of President Bourguiba, a violent controversy ensued, following which the offender was barred from teaching.[28] Similar examples of the problem of reconciling Islam with modernity can be given in many other fields, including marriage, banking, inheritance, women's rights, and indeed, the very basis of political organization.

From an educational perspective, this burning question presents two basic sets of problems. The first involves the fundamental question

[27] Habib Bourguiba, "For Ramadan Reform," in Rivlin and Szyliowicz, *op. cit.,* p. 172.
[28] Rivlin and Szyliowicz, *op. cit.,* p. 174.

of secular versus religious schools, and the place of religious schools in the national life of any particular country: Should religious schools be abolished entirely? Should they be brought under the control of the Ministry of Education? Should their curricula be coordinated with those of the secular schools, and if so, to what extent? The second dimension of the religious issue in education revolves around the role of religion within secular schools: How much and what kind of religious instruction should be provided at all levels of the educational system? Such an issue can, of course, be divisive in any society, but this question is rendered even more complex here by the existence of a large number of religious groups even within Islam in all the countries of the region. As a result of such considerations, no con- sensus has yet emerged on the question of how much time should be devoted to religion and related subjects in the schools of the Arab world, and wide variations exist.

Nevertheless a close relationship can be discerned between the type of political system and the resolution of these two questions in any society. Adaptive systems tend to emphasize religious instruction to a far greater degree than radical regimes and accord a sizable proportion of the primary school curriculum to religious education. Overall the average is 12 per cent, but in Saudi Arabia 36 per cent of the primary school curriculum is taken up with this subject as compared to 2 per cent in Algeria and 11 per cent in Egypt.[29] A similar distinction can be found in the attitudes toward religious schools evidenced by different kinds of political systems. The tra- ditional bifurcation between religious and secular schools continues to hinder efforts at nation-building and development through the dis- semination of non-modern orientations, attitudes, and values and the perpetuation of a major societal cleavage between traditional and

[29] "Survey of Educational Progress Achieved in Arab States since Ministers and Directors of Education met in Beirut in February 1960," paper prepared for the Conference of Ministers of Education and Ministers Responsible for Economic Planning in Arab States, Tripoli, Libya, March 5–10, 1966, mimeo. (Paris: UNESCO/MINED/ARAB STATES/8, 1966), Table 14, p. 19; here- after referred to as "Survey." Some of the information in this study was pub- lished by Abdel A. H. El Koussy, "Recent Trends and Developments in Primary and Secondary Education in the Arab World," *International Review of Educa- tion,* 21 (1967), 198–211.

modern groups. Ataturk abolished religious schools entirely and, although few leaders in the Arab world share his orientation, this bifurcation has been tackled in a serious manner primarily by radical regimes. Only after Nasser came to power in Egypt, for example, was the notorious dual system of separate and parallel secular and religious institutions reformed and the famous Al-Azhar university reorganized to emphasize modern approaches and values. We shall trace this issue in detail later but it is important to emphasize the dysfunctional consequences of this type of educational system for modernization; it served to divide and fragment Egyptian society and culture and to greatly retard the political, social, and economic development of the country.

Change and conflict are not limited to this aspect of the social order, and perhaps the most serious issue area in terms of education and modernization is the demographic anarchy caused by the rapid increase in modern medical practices. Improved health and sanitation measures have led to drastic declines in death rates while birth rates have remained high, with the result that almost every country in the Middle East is experiencing a rapid population increase—about 2.8 per cent a year, as compared to a world average of 1.8 per cent— with resultant strains upon the society, economy, and polity. Since death rates are likely to continue to decline even more, the demographic explosion will continue; in the Arab world the growth rate in the seventies is expected to exceed 3 per cent a year.[30]

To describe this situation as critical is no exaggeration. The ever-increasing numbers of citizens to be housed, educated, and fed demands that a large percentage of available capital be devoted to social investments just to maintain existing standards, so that fewer resources are available for developmental projects. The educational implications are readily apparent from a study of population growth in Turkey which estimated that although the second five-year plan provides for a 13 per cent annual increase in education expenditures, over 80 per cent of the increased allocations will have to be utilized to provide facilities for new students so that the amount of resources available

[30] Mohammed A. El-Ghannam, *Education in the Arab Region Viewed from the 1970 Marrakesh Conference,* Educational Studies and Documents, no. 1 (Paris: UNESCO, 1971), p. 7.

for qualitative improvements will grow by less than 3 per cent per year.[31] How differences in population growth rates affect investments in education is graphically illustrated by Table 1, which contains estimates of the different educational expenditures that will be required if the Turkish population grows at 2, 2.6, or 3 per cent annually.

Table 1. Alternative educational expenditures required, Turkey, 1987 and 2000 (in billions of Turkish liras)

| Population growth rate | 1987 | | | 2000 | | |
	Primary education	Secondary education	Total	Primary education	Secondary education	Total
2.0%	3.8	6.8	10.6	7.0	17.0	24.0
2.6%	4.1	7.5	11.6	8.2	19.6	27.8
3.0%	4.4	8.0	12.4	9.0	21.5	30.5

Source: Baran Tüncer, *The Impact of Population Growth on the Turkish Economy* (Ankara: Hacettepe University, 1968), p. 48.

The problem confronting the other Middle Eastern countries is identical. In the mid-sixties estimates indicated that the population of the Arab countries was doubling every twenty-five years and that the figure of 10 million students enrolled at that time in primary schools would increase by 24 million by 1980 if existing trends continued and if every child were to be enrolled. Merely to accommodate this increase without taking qualitative considerations into account would require a rise in educational investments of 350 per cent. More recent estimates suggest that there will be 47 million children in this age group by 1980 so that even greater educational expenditures will be required.[32]

These problems are compounded by the extremely young age structure which results from rapid population increases and high fertility rates. In the Arab world (except for Kuwait) more than 42 per cent of the population is under fifteen years of age. In Turkey about 42 per cent are in this category, and in Iran about 55 per cent of the population is under twenty years of age.[33] Such an age structure is

[31] Baran Tüncer, *The Impact of Population Growth in the Turkish Economy* (Ankara: Hacettepe University, 1968), pp. 46–47.

[32] "Survey," p. 8; El-Ghannam, *op. cit.*, p. 9.

[33] The data for the Arab world are derived from *ibid.*, p. 8; for Turkey, from the *Second Five Year Development Plan, 1968–1972* (Ankara: State Planning Organization, 1969), p. 54; and for Iran, from the *Fourth National Develop-*

related to development in two ways: a large percentage of the population is economically nonproductive and there are relatively few persons in the working age group which must generate the capital needed for investment. Because of such considerations, the seriousness of the population explosion for the Middle East cannot be overestimated. Eugene Black, an expert on development, has warned that, "Unless the demographic expansion is checked we may have to give up, at least for this generation, the hope that the overpopulated areas of the Middle East can develop." [34] Some countries, notably Turkey, Egypt, and Tunisia, have initiated family planning programs to deal with this problem but no major breakthroughs have yet been achieved.

Closely connected with this problem is the entire array of social relations—perhaps the most sensitive area of any culture. Here, too, great changes are taking place. The patriarchal family is slowly being replaced by the conjugal unit, women are being emancipated and gaining a new legal and social status, polygamy is declining, and family ties are being loosened. Each of these changes clearly creates serious conflicts at all levels of society, the controversy over the position of women being particularly relevant in terms of educational development.

Traditionally, the role of women was limited to procreation and child-raising, but many of the leaders of the Middle East argue that this is no longer adequate, that all the human resources of the country must be mobilized if development is to take place. President Bourguiba has been particularly outspoken on this issue. Wishing to utilize women in the fight for the modernization of Tunisia, he has argued: "Women must first of all enlarge the world in which they live. . . . Then they must be able to work. . . . Only in this way will they become aware of playing a part in society in the same way as men." [35] President Bourguiba's views run counter to those held by traditionalists whose position is vividly illustrated by a book appropriately en-

---

ment Plan, 1968–1972 (Teheran: Plan Organization, 1968), p. 3. The latter two works are hereafter referred to as *Second Plan* and *Fourth Plan.*

[34] Eugene Black, president of the International Bank for Reconstruction and Development, in his report to the Social and Economics Council of the United Nations, April 24, 1961, as published in *Le Commerce du Levant* (Beirut, 1961).

[35] Habib Bourguiba, "A New Role For Women," in Rivlin and Szyliowicz, *op. cit.,* p. 352.

titled *Defense of the Veil.* In the words of the author: "The purpose in writing this treatise is . . . to show that the world furnishes brilliant proofs and clear arguments for those who believe in the veil . . . woman in origin, creation, body, propriety of conduct, opinion, intelligence, and action is inferior to man." [36] Although this book was published in 1926, its philosophy has remained very much alive as evidenced by the riots that occurred in several Iranian cities in June 1963 as a protest against the emancipation of women.

As a result of such attitudes, the education of women poses a special problem in the Middle East and hinders its development, though in such countries as Turkey and Egypt women are beginning to play a meaningful role in all aspects of societal activity. Nevertheless much remains to be done. In the field of health, for example, thousands of nurses are desperately needed, but this profession was not traditionally considered respectable. Hence nursing education was sadly neglected, the first nursing school being established in Egypt only in the mid-fifties, and in Iraq only in the early sixties.

Most Arab leaders are aware of the importance of increasing educational opportunities for girls, and in 1964 a UNESCO-sponsored conference on this subject in Algeria emphasized the need for appropriate measures to accomplish this end. It recommended that clauses guaranteeing equal rights of women to schooling be included in constitutions and legislation, that Ministries of Education cooperate with religious authorities to eliminate misunderstandings and prejudices which hinder the provision of educational opportunities to women, that the scope of women's technical education be expanded, that the number of women teachers be increased, and that curricula of the girls' schools be made more relevant.[37] Similar resolutions have been passed at

[36] Hajji Shaykh Yusuf, "In Defense of the Veil," in Rivlin and Szyliowicz, *op. cit.,* p. 356. Excerpts from the book were translated by Charles R. Pittman and published as "In Defense of the Veil," *Muslim World,* 33 (July 1943).

[37] "Regional Co-operation for Educational Development in Arab Member States," paper prepared for Conference of Ministers of Education and Ministers Responsible for Economic Planning in Arab States, Tripoli, Libya, March 5–10, 1966, mimeo. (Paris: UNESCO/MINED/ARAB STATES/14B), pp. 3–4; hereafter referred to as "Regional Cooperation"; "Expert Meeting on the Access of Girls and Women to Technical and Vocational Education in the Arab States," paper prepared for the Third Regional Conference of Ministers of Education, *op. cit.,* Ref. 3, Jan. 8, 1970, pp. 3–4; hereafter referred to as "Access."

subsequent conferences but the gap between male and female education in the Arab countries remains extremely wide. That much remains to be done before this problem is resolved is indicated by the fact that in 1960–1961 female students accounted for 33.8 per cent of enrollments at the primary level, 25 per cent at the first cycle of the secondary level, and 18.5 per cent at the second cycle of the secondary level. In 1967–1968 they represented 35.7 per cent, 28.2 per cent and 21.8 per cent of enrollments at these levels. Not only was the increase extremely small but this situation compares most unfavorably with the world average of 44, 43.4, and 36.6 per cent, respectively. Literacy rates reveal a similar pattern. In 1960 the illiteracy rate in the Arab world for young women (15–24 years old) stood at 85 per cent, for men in the same age group at 70 per cent. By the end of the decade the illiteracy rate for women had declined to 70 per cent but that for young men had dropped precipitously to 35 per cent. These figures indicate not only that literacy is increasing much more rapidly among men than women but also that the discrepancy between the sexes is growing markedly.[38]

The importance of this situation cannot be exaggerated, for studies in many countries have testified to the importance of women's education in shaping the psychological, cultural, and social character of the home. Among other things, the educated wife and mother determines consumption and achievement patterns for the family, spurs educational aspirations among children, and motivates the husband to achieve a higher income—values that constitute a vital dimension of the developmental orientation. A study carried out among Egyptian high school students, for example, revealed that the most important factor affecting the attitudes of boys toward women's emancipation was the educational level of the mother. In general, if the mother had not received formal schooling her son was opposed, if she was highly educated then he strongly favored the emancipation of women.[39] Another study conducted in Egypt indicated a similar relationship be-

[38] "Trends," pp. 4, 5, 8.
[39] Peter C. Dodd, "Youth and Women's Emancipation in the United Arab Republic," *Middle East Journal,* 22 (Spring, 1968), 169. See also "Problems of Children and Youth in National Planning and Development," paper presented to the Third Regional Conference of Ministers of Education and Ministers Responsible for Economic Planning in the Arab States, *op. cit.,* Ref. 5, *passim.;* hereafter "Problems of Children."

tween the educational attainment of the mother and the number of children in the family. Mothers who were illiterate had an average of 8.1 living children, but this figure declined dramatically as the educational level of the mother rose: 6.9 living children for a primary-educated mother, 5.7 for a middle-school-educated mother, 5.1 for a high school graduate, and 3.9 for a college graduate.[40]

This finding strongly emphasizes the critical need to expand educational opportunities for women. More educated women will mean a lower birth rate and thus contribute greatly to the solution of one of the major problems confronting the region. In addition, one calculation shows that if Egypt raises the compulsory education requirement from 12 to 15 years (thus providing a new stimulus for the expansion of women's education) the number of births will drop by 2,300,000 between 1970 and 1974, leading to an estimated saving of 165,000,-000 Egyptian pounds per year in education, health, and social services.[41]

Since well over half of the population of the Middle East lives in rural areas (60 per cent in the Arab countries, 57 per cent in Iran, 70 per cent in Turkey),[42] it is obvious that significant decreases in population growth are dependent upon fundamental changes in village life. To persuade village women to adopt such a radical innovation as birth control, however, is no simple matter, for in many instances the peasant's way of life has changed but little over the centuries. Many still live in isolated villages and adhere to traditional customs and beliefs. There is a high mortality rate, especially among infants, and disease, illiteracy, and drudgery are the daily lot of many villagers while parochialism, inertia, and fatalism still constitute powerful forces inhibiting change.

Practically all governments, however, are attempting to transform this depressing picture and are paying increased emphasis to rural development. Many measures, including a shift toward cash crops such as cotton, fruits, and vegetables, the application of new high-yield cereals, increased dissemination of fertilizers, improved irrigation, and the mechanization of agriculture, are being implemented in an effort to intensify production. Moreover the peasantry is, in every

[40] "Survey," p. 8.
[41] *Idem.*
[42] El-Ghannam, *op. cit.*, p. 8; *Second Plan,* p. 28; *Fourth Plan,* p. 28.

country, becoming increasingly integrated into the national life as modern transportation and communication systems replace dirt roads and gossip. The development of a modern highway network in Turkey, for example, made it possible for the rural inhabitants to migrate easily and freely within the country with important economic, social, and political consequences.

In addition, questions of land reform and rural development have received increased attention everywhere. Extensive land reform programs have been undertaken in Iran (1963), Egypt (1952), and Syria and Iraq (1958), and ambitious efforts have been launched to provide the new tenants with the necessary skills and infrastructure to raise output. In Iran and Egypt these reforms have led to increased production; in Syria, and especially in Iraq, production has fallen owing to inadequate preparation and political instability.[43] Throughout the region, however, the ancient problem of powerful absentee landlords maintaining a semifeudal relationship with the peasantry has been largely eliminated.

Despite all the changes that have been inaugurated the agricultural sector still is not characterized by the kind of efficiency required for self-sustaining growth. Most Middle Eastern countries are not self-sufficient in foodstuffs since living standards have improved and population growth has outpaced increases in output. Some countries have witnessed an actual decline in per capita production as population pressures upon the land have increased. Hence, despite many efforts, agricultural productivity remains low and unemployment and underemployment is common. The importance of agriculture for modernization cannot be exaggerated. Firstly, a valuable resource that could and must be used to generate capital for investment in developmental and industrial projects of all sorts remains underutilized. Secondly, the large increases in population create an urgent need for jobs that cannot be supplied by the industrial sector which possesses a low absorptive capacity owing to modern capital-intensive techniques and rising productivity per capita. Thus, employment for the numerous newcomers to the labor force will have to be found in a modernized agricultural sector utilizing such techniques as labor-absorptive crops.[44]

[43] Charles Issawi, "Growth and Structural Change in the Middle East," *Middle East Journal,* 25 (Summer 1971), 317–318.

[44] *Ibid.,* pp. 323–324.

Finally, rural development is obviously necessary if the great urban-rural gap which continues to characterize every state, to a greater or lesser degree, is to be overcome and processes of nation-building and political integration furthered.

Problems of absorption may be eased in some countries through the expansion of arable land but, overall, although only about 5 per cent of the total area of the Middle East is presently cultivated owing to the lack of water in other parts, it is not likely that the use of irrigation techniques can increase the cultivable land by much more than a third, unless radical breakthroughs in desalinization technology occur in the near future. And, even if economic processes for transforming sea water into sweet water were developed, the costs involved in pumping and transporting this water to uncultivated areas would be immense. Nor is irrigation a panacea, since the addition of water to hitherto arid areas may not only disturb the existing ecological balance but might also induce chemical changes that would transform land which was at first productive into saline and sterile soil. Despite this danger, practically every country—notably Turkey, Egypt, Iran, Morocco, Lebanon, and the Sudan—is implementing extensive irrigation schemes. Millions of new acres will thus become available for agriculture, and Iraq, Syria, and the Sudan, with their extremely low population densities, possess considerable potential for increasing their cultivable acreage greatly, but the long-term implications deserve and have not yet received very careful analysis. One ecologist, for example, has suggested that the "new Aswan High Dam [which] is designed to bring another million acres of land under irrigation . . . may well prove to be the ultimate disaster for Egypt." [45]

Regardless of the specific problems involved in the modernization of agriculture in different parts of the region, every state confronts a gigantic task: the transformation of peasants into farmers. Unless this can be achieved—and in this effort education has a vital role to play—no genuine rural development can take place.

A wide range of human skills, from technicians to agricultural scientists developing new hybrids, will be needed, and these will have to be acquired through formal training. Yet the existing schools are capable of turning out only a small fraction of the personnel needed

[45] Lamont C. Cole, "Can the World Be Saved?" *New York Times Magazine,* March 31, 1968, p. 106.

to transform rural life; one UNESCO expert has concluded that all their graduates would not even suffice to maintain equipment and infrastructures in rural areas.[46] The problem of training adequate numbers of experts is complicated by the fact that not all graduates enter the agricultural sector. In many cases, the former village youths, having been exposed to the attractiveness of urban life, no longer wish to return to the rural areas to educate their fellow countrymen and resort to a variety of strategies to obtain white-collar positions in towns and cities.

Such attitudes are even more prevalent among university graduates. Few are concerned with problems of rural development or wish to engage in manual labor of any kind. One American professor, for example, who sought to make students at the Agricultural College of Teheran University undertake practical activities quickly learned that many of them had no intention of entering into agricultural occupations but had selected this area because they could not gain admission to the faculty of their choice. Further, most graduates obtained positions in government or industry, and few actually entered upon an agricultural career.[47]

Nor is the problem limited to the training of specialists; peasants must also acquire a wide range of skills. Yet everywhere much remains to be done if educational processes in the rural areas of the Middle East are to become supportive of agricultural development. In all countries, fewer village children than urban ones attend school; schools, which are usually limited to the lower grades, tend to be in poorer condition than their urban counterparts, their teachers less well prepared than those in towns and cities. Furthermore, the curricula utilized in the rural areas often tend to be totally unrelated to the conditions and needs of the inhabitants, and few teachers are equipped to relate the subject matter to the students' immediate problems in a meaningful way. One result of this lack of communication is a very high dropout rate; for most young peasants education,

[46] "Literacy and Development in the Arab Countries," paper prepared for The Conference of Ministers of Education and Ministers Responsible for Economic Planning in Arab States, Tripoli, Libya, March 5–10, 1966, mimeo. (Paris: UNESCO/MINED/ARAB STATES/13, 1966), p. 6; hereafter "Literacy."

[47] Gaylord P. Harnwell, *Educational Voyaging in Iran* (Philadelphia: University of Pennsylvania Press, 1962), p. 39.

at best, consists of a few years of some exposure to an educational institution that is not functionally related to the community of which it is a part. Even if the student graduates from a rural school, his chances of continuing education are usually nonexistent. The common result is that within a few years, most graduates have forgotten most of what they have learned and lapse back into illiteracy. Hence it is generally agreed that "the school system in rural areas is seriously inadequate in relation to the needs of rural society." [48]

Moreover those students who do stay in school and continue into the higher levels tend to be diverted away from agriculture into urban centers. As a recent UNESCO report pointed out:

At present the school system as a whole can by no means provide the rural sector with the highly qualified personnel and the skilled labour required for development. Young people . . . even those who are farmers, refuse to go in for agricultural occupations. . . . School education as it is today . . . would seem to accentuate that trend.[49]

The results are twofold: first, large numbers of youngsters with an elementary or secondary education migrate to the cities where they quickly learn that despite their educational background they do not possess any marketable skills; second, the best-equipped persons flow steadily away from rural life.

To help deal with this problem the UN cooperated in establishing the Regional Rural Functional Literacy Center for the Arab States (ASFEC) at Sirs-el-Layyan in Egypt in 1952. Originally designed to promote fundamental education, it was reorganized in 1960 into a community development center and in 1968 its focus was changed to functional literacy in an effort to more precisely define its activities. Its major programs include research and training, the preparation and distribution of materials, and the provision of advisory services when requested. It provides both regular, six-month courses in functional literacy and specialized training in specific aspects of literacy programs. The center also organizes special courses and workshops. Between 1960 and 1968, 983 persons attended courses at the Center. In 1969 a UNESCO evaluating team visited ASFEC and recommended that the center become more truly regional in scope, increase

[48] "Problems of Children," p. 9.
[49] "Literacy," p. 6.

the number of trainees, and move toward a more rigorous method-ological approach in its training.[50]

One reason for the growing attention to rural development is that urbanization has become a matter of increasing concern everywhere. In recent years, the urban centers of the Middle East have acted as irresistible magnets drawing the most ambitious and talented persons away from the rural areas. Metropolitan populations have climbed sharply; today such cities as Cairo, Teheran, Istanbul, Alexandria, and Baghdad have populations well over a million, while Ankara, Algiers, Casablanca, Tunis, Aleppo, Beirut, and Damascus have 500,000 or more, and about twenty other cities have more than 100,000 inhabitants. The flood of peasants to town and city has been due both to pressures within rural areas, especially overpopulation and hidden unemployment, and to the attraction of the cities with their promise of glamour, excitement, and luxury.

Since cities require a high investment in infrastructure—the provision of water, gas, electricity, transportation, sewage disposal, and the like—the rapid influx of villagers into urban areas complicates the task of economic development by increasing the pressures upon government to divert resources into such services and away from developmental projects. Furthermore, migrants tend to congregate in shantytowns on the edges of the metropolis where they soon find that the illusion of city life does not translate easily into reality. There are few jobs for illiterates and untrained laborers, living conditions are often no better than in the village, educational, medical, and sanitation facilities are seldom available, and the middle-class way of life so evident around them usually remains unattainable. The resulting frustrations make the "urban peasantry" a potentially explosive force in all cities of the region, and street mobs composed of slum dwellers have often been mobilized for riots and demonstrations of various kinds. Thus, there are at least two types of urban dwellers: the middle and upper classes who have been Westernized and who dominate the national life, and the lower class, including the "urban peasants," who still retain, to a large extent, traditional outlook and values. The task of transforming these attitudes, of providing migrants

---

[50] "Report of the Committee on the Evaluation of UNESCO-Operated or Aided Regional Institutions in the Arab Countries," paper submitted to Third Regional Conference of Ministers of Education, *op. cit.*, Ref. 4, pp. 17–27.

with new skills and integrating them into the national life in a productive way, poses a particular educational challenge and remains a serious problem everywhere.

Another important group that must also be integrated into the national life is the nomads, those legendary figures who have been romanticized in literature and who still typify the Middle East for many. Nomads have been equally affected by developments in communication, transportation, and rural development, and the image of the desert bedouin riding his camel across sandy wastes still corresponds somewhat to reality, although less so each year. More and more tribesmen have become settled farmers or have migrated to urban areas as less and less land has remained available for pasture, owing to increases in the cultivated area or to such abuses as overgrazing.

Friction between tribesmen and governments has been perennial and has often amounted to rebellion and warfare. No government enjoys having to deal with powerful autonomous enclaves within its territory or having large groups of people wander freely across national boundaries, and with the advent of such machines as helicopters, radios and telephones, trucks and jeeps, governments have seized the opportunity to expand their authority over hitherto remote and inaccessible areas inhabited by tribesmen. Although they have lost most of their former power there are still well over a million nomads in central Arabia, the Sahara, Iran, and Turkey.

To work out a pattern of educational opportunity for these peoples is obviously not a simple task, and until very recently they have had almost no educational opportunities. In recent years, however, Iran has inaugurated a promising experiment, the "White Tent" project whereby the school teacher, usually a tribesman himself, accompanies the nomads on their wanderings and pitches his school tent wherever the tribe settles. Yet this program (which we shall discuss in detail later) reaches only a small percentage of Iranian nomads and the problem of educational opportunity for these peoples remains a major one throughout the region.

If the growing aspirations of nomad, peasant, and townsman and the goals of the countries themselves are to be met, large investments in education will be required, and such investments are possible only if a rapid rate of economic development is achieved. The degree to which these two elements are related has been vividly demonstrated by UNESCO experts who, using a sophisticated model, have calculated the increases in educational costs that will be required during the seventies. For the Arab states total costs will increase from $1,247,227,000 in 1970 to $2,865,169,000 in 1980. Recurring costs comprise $1,040,571,000 and $2,349,380,000, respectively, capital costs, $206,656,000 and $515,789,000. Whether such large expenditures can actually be financed will depend on the rate of economic development: the greater the annual growth in gross national product, the lower the burden. If a growth rate of 5 per cent is achieved the cost of educational expansion will rise from about 4 per cent of GNP in the late sixties to 6.18 per cent of GNP in 1980, whereas if the growth rate is 6 per cent the increase is only from 4.2 per cent to 5.36 per cent, and if a growth rate of 7 per cent per annum is achieved the rise is even less, to 4.65 per cent.[51]

For economic development capital formation is essential and many countries of the Middle East are fortunate to possess extensive deposits of oil and natural gas. Over two-thirds of the world's known oil reserves are located here and the world's great producers include Kuwait, Saudi Arabia, Iran, Libya, Algeria, and Iraq. Recent indications suggest that Egypt may also possess quite extensive oil resources. Other important resources include chrome in Turkey, phosphates in Morocco and Tunisia, and deposits of copper, lead, zinc, turquoise, iron ore, and coal throughout the region.

To date, however, these resources have not been fully exploited and the level of industrialization is not high though output has grown rapidly in recent years (about 10 per cent annually between 1960 and 1967). In overall terms manufacturing and mining (exclusive of the oil industry) account for between 15 and 20 per cent of GNP. Comparatively the level is about the same as Asia, above that of Africa which is about 10 per cent, and below that of Latin America which ranges between 15 and 30 per cent. Wide variations exist within the region. Manufacturing and mining account for about 25 per cent of GNP in Egypt and about 15 per cent in Turkey, Syria, Iran (excluding oil), and Lebanon.[52] Little industrialization has taken place elsewhere. The most prevalent form of industrial development is light

[51] El-Ghannam, *op. cit.,* pp. 31–32.
[52] Issawi, *op. cit.,* pp. 316–318.

industry geared to the domestic market. Iron and steel mills have been established in some countries (Turkey, Egypt, Iran) and others have plans for their development, but most industrialization has taken place in such areas as textiles, food processing, building materials, and consumer goods.

Almost every country of the area, however, is concentrating its efforts upon the expansion of its industrial plant as a means of achieving rapid economic growth. Education must play a central role if such growth is to occur but the existing educational systems in most countries are not geared to the needs inherent in industrialization. As we have stressed, the schools must turn out graduates who possess problem-solving, entrepreneurial orientations but everywhere much remains to be done before this goal is achieved. For example, primary education in the Arab countries still emphasizes such traditional subjects as religion, Arabic, and the humanities, leading a UNESCO study to conclude: "Surely science, mathematics and practical activities must be given more importance." [53]

Another indication of existing weaknesses is the serious imbalances which characterize education throughout the region. Despite attempts to improve and expand vocational and technical education, this field remains a serious problem, as evidenced by the following figures: while the percentage of pupils in general secondary education in the Arab world rose from 81 per cent to 86 per cent between 1960–1961 and 1967–1968, the percentage of students enrolled in technical and vocation schools at this level dropped from 15.2 per cent to 11.1 per cent.[54] Several important factors account for this dismal situation especially the identification of vocational schools with the lower classes, the traditional preference for white-collar administrative positions with high prestige and economic security, and the concomitant distaste for manual labor by the educated. A recent study in Egypt, for example, revealed that a large percentage of secondary school and university graduates rejected manual labor, which they considered

---

[53] "Survey," p. 19. See also "Regional Workshop on Pre-Service and In-Service Primary Teacher Training in the Arabic-Speaking Member States," report presented to the Third Regional Conference of Ministers of Education, *op. cit.*, Ref. 1, 1969, Appendix II, p. 13; hereafter referred to as "Regional Workshop."

[54] "Trends," p. 19.

"undignified and not worthy socially." [55] Nor can problems of irrelevancy and quality be ignored. A marked dissonance exists between the training provided and the needs of industry, leading a group of experts to conclude, in 1969, that "vocational training in the Arab countries requires a fundamental revision." [56] As we shall see later the situation in Turkey and Iran is essentially the same.

As a result of such factors, nearly every country in the Middle East faces critical shortages of middle-level manpower. This category includes such subprofessional positions as nurses, technicians, and agriculturists, and it has been estimated that if one doctor or engineer is to perform at his fullest capacity, three or four persons with middle-level skills are needed to assist him. Although pre-employment training in formal technical and vocational schools is only one way to provide such manpower little attention is being paid to in-service training and auxiliary institutions. Even less attention has been accorded to changing the situational context so as to provide the kinds of incentives and rewards that would motivate individuals to follow manual and technical careers.

The situation at the higher levels is essentially the same. University education still means, for thousands of students, a focus upon law, the humanities, and the social sciences, and most states already confront serious shortages of high-level manpower that are expected to become even more acute. Here, too, environmental factors have not received adequate attention so that thousand of trained technical and scientific personnel migrate to developed countries each year. Accompanying this shortage is an oversupply of graduates in non-technical fields whose absorption represents a serious problem everywhere. In such disparate countries as Tunisia, Algeria, and Kuwait the situation has become so noticeable as to be deemed worthy of reports in U.S. newspapers under such headlines as: "Youths Worry Tunisia and Algeria" and "Kuwait Finds Money Isn't Everything; Idle College Graduates Pose Problems." [57] The question of how to

[55] D. K. Wheeler, "Educational Problems of Arab Countries," *International Review of Education,* 12 (1966), 307. The study referred to was published as *Research Project on Employment and Unemployment among the Educated* (Cairo: Institute of National Planning, 1963)

[56] "Problems of Children," p. 11.

[57] *New York Times,* July 25, 1971, Aug. 28, 1971.

provide satisfactory positions for an ever-growing number of youths with formal academic training and high expectations remains a potentially politically explosive issue throughout the area. As we shall see, discontented youths have been a problem even in Egypt, which has made the most determined efforts to transform its educational system from one with a predominantly literary character to one oriented toward technical and vocational education.

Politics and Ideology

Because of such problems and the continuing interplay of traditional and modernizing forces the area is marked by great political instability and is groping toward a political system consonant with the social and economic changes that are taking place. Doctrines and discussions fill the airwaves as leaders attempt to formulate an ideology that will make possible the achievement of national goals. Within the Arab world, the debate rages over the specific content of Arab nationalism, which holds that all the Arabs should be united in one state. The concept of Arab unity has a powerful hold on the imagination of these peoples, and no Arab leader is strong enough to ignore its appeal. In the bitter rivalries which deeply divide the region, each leader justifies himself in terms of his devotion to this ideal and accuses his opponents of its betrayal.

Nationalism, too, is a result of the Western impact. While difficult to define, consisting of a complex of many attitudes, the crux of nationalism involves a conglomeration of emotions based on love of homeland, pride of common descent, common language, and common religion. Essentially it is a psychological phenomenon, a feeling of identity among a group of people. Although similar feelings have existed for centuries, not until the arrival of modern Western influences were they transformed into the credo that each community should constitute an independent polity and that each people had the right to self-determination. Such attitudes, however, could not be superimposed neatly upon a society marked by isolated, independent, and highly integrated communities, each with its own distinct social and cultural characteristics. Not only is Middle Eastern society divided into a wide variety of ethnic, linguistic, and religious groupings, but the mosaic pattern is to be found within almost every country of the area as well, with the result that nation-building remains an important problem confronting all governments.

In the Arab world, however, the situation is aggravated by the fact that existing boundary lines bear little relation to ethnic, religious, or linguistic realities; they were drawn by colonial powers and great pressures exist for their abolition. Yet, though originally artificial, the recent course of history has shown that nations are being created in such countries as Iraq, Syria, and Lebanon which have developed unique institutions and patterns of loyalties that make for viable independence. Furthermore, powerful groups within each state want to maintain their position and not disappear within a larger unit. Thus there is a conflict of an overall versus a particular nationalism, of Arab versus Arab, and President Nasser, who proclaimed himself the leader of the Arab nationalist movement, ran into much opposition from rulers of other states who were unwilling to accept his claim to hegemony.

In their efforts at nation-building every government now has at its disposal institutions—including educational systems—and structures of power that were not available to its predecessors. Each country is being linked together by developments in education, industry, communication, and transportation, and the importance of traditional centers of power such as the tribal leader and the landowner is receding rapidly. Accompanying this process is a redefinition of the relationship between state and society. Until fairly recent times, the government was conceived as being primarily responsible for defense against foreign enemies and the maintenance of internal stability. Almost every individual need was met by religious, social, or economic groups, and the ideal for most persons was to avoid contact with the administration whenever possible. Today this fear of government action is being transformed everywhere as governments have assumed responsibility for and are actually filling these needs to a greater degree each year.

The same factors that have made for increasing penetration and integration have also led to an increase in the capability of governments who today possess unprecedented capacities to make and implement decisions. This trend is also a result of the impact of modernity, especially the development of modern educational facilities through which new groups have acquired the technical skills necessary to fill the new administrative, military, and technological roles that have emerged. Membership in this new technocratic elite is determined largely by achievement criteria and by exposure to modern higher education, though in some cases, notably in the more traditional regimes, ascriptive criteria still play an important role in determining who gains access to the training required for such positions. In other cases, notably in Egypt, Iraq, Syria, and Libya, these groups, often spearheaded by military leaders of non-ruling-class background have come to power and established radical regimes.

Not surprisingly, therefore, although all governments in the Middle East have been affected by similar developments, they have reacted in different ways. Nationalism represents but one of the many ideologies that have swept across the Middle East, and conflicting perspectives on modernization exist throughout the Arab world. President Nasser, for years the dominant personality in the region, espoused an ideology whose mainsprings were revolution and socialism. In a typical speech he argued: "Revolution is the only means by which the Arab nation can free itself of its shackles, and rid itself of the dark heritage which burdened it. . . . Revolution is the only way to overcome under-development, forced on the Arab nation through suppression and exploitation." [58]

Such views (and many more radical voices could be cited) make for further conflict within the region and have greatly hampered the drive for Arab unity. Most simply the Arab states can be divided into "radical" and "adaptive" regimes. The monarchs of the Arab world, whether in Saudi Arabia, Jordan, or Morocco, view ideologies of revolution and reform with great suspicion and have often made common cause despite longstanding rivalries and feuds among themselves against the more radical leaders. Cleavages also exist among radical states, and even when their leaders loudly voice their devotion to common ideals, little cooperation is apparent. The attempt to establish the United Arab Republic broke up in 1962 when Syria seceded; the ascendancy of the Baath party, which is also characterized by radical perspectives, did not change the situation. Similarly the traditional rivalry between Iraq and Egypt continued unabated after

[58] Gamal Abdel Nasser, "Revolution and Socialism," in Rivlin and Szyliowicz, *op. cit.,* pp. 433–434.

the overthrow of King Faisal in 1958 and the establishment of a radical government there. Whether the newly formed Federation of Arab Republics represents a departure from this pattern remains to be seen.

Though Arab nationalism has a long history, not until many Arab states achieved their independence after World War II could institutional arrangements be made to further the goal of unity. The League of Arab States was founded in 1946 but its stormy history has reflected the difficulties inherent in achieving cooperation when member states are divided by bitter rivalries. Such an environment has, of course, greatly complicated the Arab states' avowed desire to harmonize their educational and cultural developments and to use the school as an agency for the promotion of Arab nationalism. The treaty setting up the Arab League provided for cultural cooperation through such means as the exchange of teachers and the standardization of diplomas, and Article 12 called for the inclusion in all curricula of materials dealing with Arab history, geography, and literature.

To implement these objectives and to coordinate and unify their educational systems, the ministers of education, soon after the formation of the League, began an active round of conferences. The first, held in Lebanon, had as its goal the elimination of fundamental differences between the various educational systems, the simplification of Arabic instruction, and the revision of primary-level history and geography courses. In 1950 a second conference, in Egypt, agreed to unify the objectives of secondary and higher education. The 1955 meeting, attended by representatives of UNESCO, accepted the need for universal primary education. In 1960 the ministers of education and ministers concerned with economic planning met, in cooperation with UNESCO, to discuss common educational problems and to identify areas which required joint action. This was followed by a series of specialized seminars on general secondary education, educational statistics, girls' access to education, educational television, and the planning and organization of literacy programs.[59]

The second Conference of Ministers of Education and Ministers Concerned with Economic Planning met in Tripoli in 1966, and in 1970 a third conference was convened in Marrakesh. As their pred-

---

[59] "Regional Cooperation," *passim.*

ecessors had done, the participants sought to draw up a general set of guidelines for future action and generally reaffirmed the resolutions of the Tripoli conference which had called for the achievement of compulsory primary education by 1980 and greater efforts to achieve educational quality. The 1970 conference considered the degree to which these resolutions had been implemented and again devoted much attention to the issue of quality. The delegates focused upon such problem areas as vocational and technical education, particularly for girls, adult illiteracy, planning and research, the educational needs of such groups as nomads, villagers, and the children of Palestinian refugees, and national and international cooperation, especially among the Arab states themselves.[60]

Whether the renewed commitment to higher standards will lead to actual changes in educational practice remains to be seen, but the record of past conferences is not encouraging. Much of what goes on at these meetings is clearly motivated by political and bureaucratic considerations, and not infrequently the countless resolutions merely gather dust in numerous files. This tendency is apparent in such fields as curriculum reform and technical and vocational education, but perhaps the most glaring example is provided by the fundamental issue of quality. At the 1966 Tripoli conference the delegates had stressed the need to devote more attention to qualitative factors and specifically noted that quality had often been ignored in favor of quantity. This concern, however, produced few appreciable results; three years later UNESCO experts discreetly pointed out that "a remarkable anomaly still exists" because quality was still being sacrificed for quantity.[61]

At the heart of the issue of achieving meaningful agreement on educational cooperation lie the bitter divisions and rivalries that we have described and the conflicting demands posed by internal political considerations and the desire for greater unity. How greatly these factors affect educational policy is reflected in the decision taken by many countries to Arabize their curricula. Of all the ties that bind the Arab peoples together and make for feelings of unity the strongest is their language. Arabic has been the language of their religion, their art, and their history, and has, in fact, become such an integral part

[60] El-Ghannam, op. cit., pp. 21ff.
[61] "Trends," p. 17.

of the culture that it exercises a unique and almost mystical influence over their minds. They are intoxicated by its very sound and regard it as "a God-given language unique in beauty and majesty, the best equipped and the most eloquent of all languages for expressing thought and emotions." [62]

From the earliest days of the Arab nationalist movement Arabic was considered the core of the ideology and it has maintained this position to the present, so that it has become a symbol of national pride and a dominant component of Arab nationalism. It is not surprising that upon achieving independence the Arab countries immediately took steps to eliminate the dominance of the language of the colonial power and to Arabize their educational systems. They agreed to promote the ideal of unity through the use of a common language and Arabic instruction occupies an important position in all primary school curricula ranging from 23 per cent in Lebanon to 37 per cent in Libya and Aden.[63]

Such a decision creates many serious educational problems, for it involves, in effect, the formulation and implementation of a completely new educational philosophy. The many difficulties involved are clearly illustrated by Morocco which, upon achieving independence from the French in 1956, decided to nationalize and Arabize the limited educational system which it inherited. Nationalization involved the rewriting of such courses as literature, history, geography, and art, with all the attendant difficulties in terms of finding qualified people to write new curricula and textbooks, as well as compounding an existing teacher shortage by the policy of replacing French teachers with natives. Similar problems were encountered in Algeria where the policy of Arabicization was also adopted and determinedly pursued. By 1969 the first two years and part of the third of primary education were taught in Arabic but these changes were carried out at the cost of major teacher supply and training problems since most of the better trained teachers were French-speaking, most of the least qualified, Arabic-speaking.[64]

In the case of Morocco the decision to make Arabic the medium

---

[62] Anwar G. Chejne, "Arabic: Significance in Arab-Muslim Society," *Middle East Journal*, 19 (Autumn, 1965), 449.

[63] "Survey," Table 14, p. 19.

[64] "Regional Workshop," Appendix II, p. 15.

of instruction has been described as "the last straw that in fact weighed as heavily as all the other problems put together," because not only did texts have to be translated and teachers trained, but Arabic itself was unsuitable for the educational needs of the country. Although Moroccan Arabic was the common language, it was, in fact, "an ungrammatical deformation of classical Arabic into a confusing richness of dialects in which both sedentation and nomadic life have destroyed standardized meanings. The spoken language is no closer to the written language than French is to Latin." [65]

The difficulties with Arabic, however, extend far beyond the confusing richness of classical, vernacular, and dialectical forms, for in any of its varieties Arabic suffers from serious deficiencies as a language suitable for any country wishing to achieve rapid development. One problem is the lack of vowel signs; there are only three, and even these are often omitted from ordinary texts. In effect, Arabic represents an excellent form of shorthand, but it is extremely difficult to teach reading for that very reason. A second, and perhaps more basic difficulty, stems from its rich heritage. A language of the past, it enables a speaker to discuss with refined nuances the most esoteric aspects of bedouin life, but does not contain the vocabulary to describe the contemporary technological world, leading many to believe that Arabic cannot be utilized to teach modern science; as we shall see later, controversy on this point continues to agitate Egyptian scholars especially.

Despite such disadvantages, the ideological dimension has proven irresistible and Arabicization has become accepted policy everywhere. Nevertheless, many important issues remain to be settled. Should this policy be implemented at all levels of the educational system or only for some? Should all subjects be taught in Arabic or should some (the sciences, for example) be excluded? Should Arabic serve only as a medium of instruction or should it also be the language of books and examinations? On a more general level, a policy of Arabicization reflects the drive for Arab unity and involves such dimensions as the inclusion of courses on Arab civilization, history, geography, and

---

[65] I. William Zartman, "Problems of Arabization in Moroccan Education," in Rivlin and Szyliowicz, *op. cit.,* pp. 333, 334.

culture in the curriculum and the reliance solely upon teachers of Arab nationality.[66]

Such issues are, of course, essentially political because they are but a manifestation of the conflict between the powerful and appealing goal of Arab unity and the drive for nation-building by particular states which we have already described. A policy of Arabization can easily come into conflict with the requirements of nation-building, with the desire of national leaders to strengthen the feelings of loyalty that have developed in the new states that were established in the interwar period and after. Thus all Arab states are faced with difficult decisions in terms of reconciling their desires for the Arabization of their educational systems with their goals of "Lebanization" or "Jordanization." On the one hand, all countries are using the schools to socialize the young into feelings of loyalty to the particular nation and are emphasizing their own unique characteristics, culturally, historically, and ideologically. On the other, all are deeply affected by feelings of Arab nationalism and support efforts at educational harmonization.

Despite this dilemma, nationalism remains of fundamental importance and vitally affects the educational system of every Arab state. As one knowledgeable observer has remarked:

Of all the factors which influence education in the Arab countries nationalism is the major ideological factor in the education of children. The Arabic language and its potential are emphasized, the past, notably after the coming of Islam, is taught and the mind is directed towards national ends. The creative force of Islam in history is demonstrated in many ways. Even when teaching subjects as far removed from politics as biology or psychology the spirit is stamped with this nationalist Arab fervor.[67]

Clearly, education in the Arab world has been deeply influenced by the political dynamics of the region. However, education has also contributed greatly to shaping these dynamics and it is to an examination of the specific role of education in the modernization of the Middle East that we now turn. In the following chapters we shall,

[66] "Survey," p. 39.
[67] Waardenburg, op. cit., p. 35.

using the conceptual scheme outlined earlier, focus upon educational developments in Turkey, Iran, and Egypt, the three largest and most important countries in the Middle East; each represents a different example of the impact of the West, and of patterns and levels of development.

Turkey was born out of the dissolution of that great state, the Ottoman Empire, in the crucible of World War I. Originally marked by great dynamism the Empire became increasingly resistant to change and innovation. By the end of the nineteenth century the need for change could no longer be denied and the following decades were marked by great and significant reforms. Subsequently, under the leadership of Ataturk, Turkey embarked upon a program of radical change and development that made it a model radical political system. After World War II, a multiparty system was established which, except for a brief interregnum in 1960, has endured to the present, so that the country truly can be classified as a competitive political system.

Iran, too, has a long history of independence, although for years it was a buffer zone over which the British and the Russians were constantly trying to exert their influence. Under these conditions it remained essentially a feudal society until the early 1920's. Many superficial similarities exist between the policies followed by Reza Shah, the father of the present ruler, who assumed power in 1923, and those of his contemporary, Ataturk, to whom he has often been compared. As we shall show later, however, Reza Shah was never willing to undertake the same kinds of fundamental reforms as Ataturk, and Iran since the twenties may best be classified as a reformist system. Significant changes have occurred in the country since 1950 but Mohammed Reza Shah is attempting, essentially like his father, to achieve a powerful modern state while preserving existing cultural and authority patterns.

Egypt alone experienced a considerable amount of colonial rule. Nominally a part of the Ottoman Empire since the sixteenth century, Egypt had, by the nineteenth century, become almost completely independent but was still subject to a considerable degree of European influence. In 1872 the British undertook a "temporary" occupation which lasted for several decades—Egypt, in fact, did not become fully independent until after the 1952 revolution which overthrew

Table 2. Levels of socioeconomic development of Middle Eastern states

	Population 1968 (millions)	Gross domestic product (total mil. $)	Per capita (dollars)	Average annual rate of growth 1960–67 (%)	Agri-cultural production 1968 (1963 = 100)	Industrial production 1968 (1963 = 100)	Infant mortality rate 1968 (per 1,000 live births)	Life expectancy (years)	Rate of annual natural increase (%)	1,000 inhabi-tants per physician; c. 1966	Literate adult popu-lation (%)
Algeria	12.9	3,192	255	−1.5	103		86	35	3.1	8.9	15
Egypt	31.7	5,733	187	3.9	110	131	119	53	2.2	2.2	20
Iran	27.3	7,881	300	7.8	127	186			3.0	3.7	23
Iraq	8.6	2,381	273	5.8	157				1.5	4.0	20
Israel	2.7	4,031	1,510	7.3	145	159	23	71.5	1.9	0.4	84
Jordan	2.1	544	267	10.0	127		28	52	3.1	4.0	32
Kuwait	0.5	2,442	3,757	6.1			36		5.5	0.8	47
Lebanon	2.6	1,220	484	3.1					2.4	1.4	86
Libya	1.8	2,218	1,276	30.0	162			38	3.3	3.1	22
Morocco	14.6	2,688	190	2.9	139	98		47	2.7	12.1	14
People's Dem. Rep. of Yemen	5.7	230	200	8.7			80	35	2.3	2.1	
Saudi Arabia	7.1	3,201	458	4.1	111			40	3.3	13.1	
Sudan	14.8	1,568	109	7.8	96		94	40	2.9	24.6	12
Syria	5.7	1,177	211	3.7	87	171			2.1	5.1	29
Tunisia	1.8	1,011	210			(1966)	110			8.3	30
Turkey	33.5	11,522	352	4.2	119	170	155	54	2.7	2.8	
Yemen	5.0	550	110					35		62.5	10

Sources: World Economic Survey 1969–1970 (New York: United Nations, 1971); Statistical Yearbook, 1969 (New York: United Nations, 1970).

the regime of King Farouk and brought President Nasser, who established a radical political system, to power.

These three countries also represent different subcultures within the Middle East—Arab, Turkish, Persian. Egypt is very homogeneous; its population is almost entirely Arab; 90 percent are Sunni Muslims, the remainder being largely Christian Copts. Turkey, too, possesses few minorities; Turks make up 94 per cent of the population; the remainder are largely Kurds. Seventeen per cent of the population, however, are Shiite Muslims. Iran is the most fragmented country. Persians make up 81 per cent of the populace, but there are sizable minorities of Turks (15 per cent) and Kurds (4 per cent). Shiism is the official religion practiced by about 88 per cent of the population. Socially and economically, Turkey, Egypt, and Iran suffer to a greater or lesser degree from all of the problems discussed in this chapter, and they confront the same challenges. Where each stands in relation to the other and to the other states of the Middle East can be seen in Table 2, which indicates how various countries compare on specific indices of social and economic development.

Because of their different backgrounds and patterns of development, Turkey, Iran, and Egypt are now attempting to reconcile the old and the new in different ways: Egypt for over a decade under a dynamic charismatic leader, Turkey through democratic processes, and Iran under the leadership of a reformist monarch. Thus each of the countries provides a different model for development and for the study of the role of education in modernization, but we begin with an examination of their common educational heritage.

II

Traditional Educational Systems

Within the space of a few short decades after the death of Mohammed, the inhabitants of Arabia burst forth into other parts of the Middle East and not only conquered vast territories but sowed the seeds of what was to become a great civilization. Within one hundred years, the Arab armies reached deep into France, and the lands controlled by the Umayyad dynasty, with its new capital at Damascus, extended from Spain into Central Asia. The displacement of the Ummayads by the Abbasids further spurred the geographical and cultural explosion of Islam, and by the eighth century, when Harun al-Rashid of *Thousand and One Nights* fame was ruling in Baghdad (786–809), the Middle East enjoyed a civilization culturally far superior to that of Western Europe. Altogether this civilization endured for about five hundred years, from the eighth to the thirteenth century, and witnessed intellectual, artistic, scientific, and cultural achievements that were to deeply influence world culture. Yet in the end, this rich and complex culture became ossified, the high achievements in science, literature, medicine, and the fine arts became dim memories, and pedantism and obscurantism replaced the thirst for knowledge and intellectual activity. Similarly, the educational system that had once produced savants and scholars, statesmen and administrators, now became an agency of conservatism and reaction.

With the fading of the great Islamic civilization a new force burst onto the scene in the Middle East—the Turks, who first established the Seljuk Empire and later the great Ottoman Empire which was to last until the end of World War I. At its zenith, the Ottoman Empire stretched over all of the Middle East and North Africa, and across Europe up to the gates of Vienna. The only country in the Middle East that remained independent from Ottoman power was Persia (Egypt fell under Ottoman domination in 1531) which, under the

51

great Safavid dynasty, adopted Shiism as the state religion and successfully created a powerful state which, though retaining its independence, also declined greatly in subsequent centuries.

In the development and expansion of the Ottoman state, the educational system was to play a leading role, and in fact, a unique institution, the palace schools (which we shall discuss below), was established to provide the state with well-trained leaders chosen on the basis of achievement criteria. During its greatest days of glory, the Ottoman Empire reached new heights of intellectual achievement, but it too, like the Umayyad and Abbasid empires, was to decline rapidly, and eventually be destroyed. One of the reasons for this decline was the failure of the educational system to continue to produce the kinds of imaginative and resourceful leaders that had characterized the earlier period of Ottoman greatness—a system which in the heyday of Ottoman civilization had produced savants of great intellectual and scholarly achievement. It now atrophied and became resistant to change and innovation with lasting consequences for the society.

Not only did the Umayyad, Abbasid, Safavid, and Ottoman empires meet the same historical fate, but the structure and functioning of their educational systems were similar, as well as the role that education played in each society. In fact, whether one examines the type of schools that were to be found in Baghdad in the eleventh century, or in Istanbul in the sixteenth, or in Cairo in the seventeenth, or in Tabriz in the eighteenth, one is struck by the extent to which Islamic society created a unique educational system that prevailed in all parts of the Middle East from the seventh century onward. This system, which has lasted more than a thousand years, has bequeathed an educational legacy to the states of the region that must be analyzed and understood if we are to comprehend contemporary educational issues. And not only has this heritage deeply affected the modern schools but, as we shall show later, many parts of the traditional educational system are still functioning in various states of the Middle East. Accordingly, it is necessary to examine the ways in which this system developed and its major characteristics, as well as the ways in which it related functionally to the society.

The Medieval Islamic System

In view of the religious basis of Islamic society, it is not surprising that the mosque was, from the earliest day of the era, the hub of the community, and that in addition to its religious and even social role, it soon acquired an educational function—it became the earliest school in Islam. Here scholars would meet to discuss the Koran, and before long, they began to teach the religious sciences, especially the study of Hadith (tradition), since devout Muslims were deeply interested in learning all they could about the prophet Mohammed. As the realm of Islam expanded, mosques, where instruction in the basic rules and precepts of the faith was provided, were quickly established in the newly conquered territories; these served a most important socializing and unifying function for the emerging polity and society and proliferated rapidly. Within three centuries Baghdad possessed 3,000 mosques, and in the fourteenth century an estimated 14,000 were to be found in Alexandria.[1]

Before long, many acquired fame as centers of learning and scholarship, developing into important institutions with large libraries and thousands of students. Here students learned to read and recite the Koran, and lectures on such subjects as the Koran, law, tradition, Arabic philology, history, and sometimes even medicine were given to large audiences comprised of young students, mature townspeople, and travelers passing through.

Almost simultaneously a system of elementary schools was established to supplement the educational opportunities available in the mosques. This very early and rapid development of elementary education with its emphasis upon religious training can be explained in two ways. First, Islam has always placed a high value upon education as is indicated by numerous traditions. One of these, for example, attributed to Mohammed himself, states that a father can confer upon his child no more valuable gift than a good education. In fact, respect for education was such an ingrained value that there are accounts of able pupils being paraded through the streets of Baghdad on camelback while passers-by tossed almonds at them as a sign of praise and encouragement.[2]

The early and rapid development of elementary education with its emphasis upon religious training can also be explained in terms of the value structure of the society and its urgent need to socialize large

[1] Mehdi Nakosteen, *History of Islamic Origins of Western Education, AD 800–1350* (Boulder: University of Colorado Press, 1964), p. 47.

[2] James Hastings, ed., *Encyclopedia of Religion and Ethics,* V (New York: Charles Scribner's Sons, 1912), 199.

numbers of newly conquered converts and thus create a universal and cohesive social order. To do so it was obviously vital to educate children in Islamic teaching and beliefs, and by the end of the Umayyad period, a system of elementary education had been established in all Muslim lands, new and old alike, which was to flourish for centuries. Koranic schools known as mekteps or kuttabs provided remarkably similar training, both in terms of subject matter and educational practices, to the youngsters of Baghdad, Istanbul, and Cairo. The importance of these schools cannot be overestimated, for not only did they socialize many different peoples and ethnic groups into a universal Islamic faith, but they also provided the foundation for all further education. Whether the student was to pursue a military, administrative, religious, or commercial career, his early training was in these schools.

The high degree of respect accorded to the Koran was a noted characteristic of Islamic civilization, and it is accordingly not difficult to appreciate how elementary education revolved around that sacred book which was considered the basis of all knowledge. From the time that a child began school at six or seven years of age, his main preoccupation was to memorize the Koran as perfectly as possible in the three or four years that he attended the school. When learning to write, children usually copied passages from secular works, "as the act of wiping inspired words from the tablets seemed to cast dishonor upon the sacred book"; when verses from the Koran were copied elaborate precautions were taken to safeguard the holy writ from being defiled.[3] Besides memorization of the holy Koran, the elementary curriculum usually included the learning of fundamental religious practices such as prayers in the mosque and the different ways in which ablutions were performed, the rudiments of arithmetic, and reading and writing. Often selections from well-known poets were also taught but these were carefully screened to avoid the inclusion of erotic passages.[4]

Classes were held mainly in mosques or in buildings attached to them; only occasionally were they held elsewhere, usually in shops or the teacher's home. Nor is it a coincidence that the founding of a

---

[3] A. S. Tritton, "Muslim Education in the Middle Ages, Circa 600–800 A.H.," *The Muslim World*, 43 (April 1953), 85.

[4] Hastings, *op. cit.*, p. 201.

school was considered a good deed and that large numbers of pious persons throughout the Islamic world provided endowments for such institutions, or that great efforts were made through the frequent provisions of food, clothing, and allowance for the students to make such education, as far as possible, a universal experience for young Muslims.

Paradoxically, despite the high regard for education, primary school teachers held a rather low status, being considered the equals of such despised trades and professions as weavers and bloodletters.[5] One reason for this attitude may have been that teachers were generally regarded as being rather stupid. And it is true that most were quite ignorant, the ability to read the Koran and to explain its contents in a simple manner sufficing to qualify a prospective teacher. In some schools, of course, high standards were maintained, and the teachers were chosen on the basis of their knowledge of the subject matter and their competence. In the Ottoman Empire this was especially true of primary schools attached to major institutions of higher learning in Istanbul which, though in theory open to all, tended to attract the sons of the better families. Nevertheless, depending upon the conditions of the endowment, orphans and indigents were often enrolled side by side with the children of high religious and civil administrators.[6] Institutions such as these, however, tended to be the exceptions, and the low quality of most teachers is attested to by popular sayings such as: "How can one look for sagacity in one who is beside his wife in the evening and in the early morning goes back to the society of little children?" One scholar with low regard for teachers analyzed their stupidity in the following way: "The rationality of women (who are universally regarded as . . . deficient in rationality and religion) equals that of 70 weavers; that of a weaver equals that of 70 schoolmasters." Such mockery, however, was not universal and many individuals defended the maligned schoolteacher in their writings.[7] Furthermore this attitude did not extend to established scholars or to professors teaching at more advanced levels.

[5] *Idem.*

[6] Robert Mantran, *La Vie quotidienne à Constantinople au temps de Soliman le Magnifique et de ses successeurs (XVIe et XVIIe siècles)* (Paris: Hachette, 1965), p. 225.

[7] Hastings, *op. cit.*, pp. 201, 202.

Some scholars have argued that this contemptuous attitude toward elementary teachers was a reflection of the "haughtiness inherent in the Arabic race," [8] others attribute it to the fact that large numbers of the early teachers were Christians and converts, while others have pointed out that many ancient societies held teachers in similar low regard. Perhaps the fundamental reason for the low estimate of schoolteachers, however, was a religious one, namely that paying teachers to instruct children in the holy writ deeply agitated many Islamic theologians. The question of payment was vigorously debated for many decades, during which the poor teacher was not only maligned and held in disrepute but was also poorly paid. Nor did his financial position improve even after Islamic law had come to recognize the legitimacy of providing an income for this profession. It is true that some scholars demanded and received large fees for their services, but these were persons with established reputations; seldom, if ever, could the ordinary teacher qualify for such largess. Some teachers were subsidized by an endowment; the income of most was provided by the local inhabitants in whose eyes the teacher was an important personage who also performed other valuable duties by serving as a public scribe or religious functionary.[9]

Despite the opprobrium attached to teaching and its poor remuneration, teachers in early Islam were expected to maintain high standards, both in their personal lives and in their professional capacity. They were expected to be honorable, chaste, and trustworthy, to know the Koran by heart, to have good handwriting, and to know arithmetic. They were not to advertise their schools in any way, and when inviting parents to attend school festivals should not couch invitations in flattery.[10]

In his classroom, the teacher possessed much authority, and not only had the right to administer corporal punishment whenever necessary, but was expected to use the rod frequently. One rule specified that "a boy must be beaten for bad manners, insulting speech, and other breaches of the law such as playing with dice and eggs, backgammon, and any gambling games." However, the manner and degree

---

[8] *Idem.*

[9] Ahmad Shalaby, *History of Muslim Education* (Beirut: Khayats, 1954), p. 127, pp. 202ff.

[10] Hastings, *op. cit.,* p. 204.

of punishment was strictly controlled in order to protect students from their teachers. "Beatings must not be done with a stick thick enough to break bones nor thin enough to harm the body, but with a medium one." Furthermore, only students who had reached the age of ten could be punished in this manner and they could only be given between three and ten strokes. As a further safeguard, the town inspector visited the schools to ensure that children were not beaten too severely.[11]

These precautions, however, were in time abandoned, and severe physical punishment was universally regarded as essential if children were to develop suitable character. One indication of this trend is to be found in Iran, where the emphasis upon physical punishment was of relatively late origin; only after the thirteenth century did such celebrated poets and philosophers as Sadi and Nasr-ed-Din teach that use of the rod was essential, as it was impossible to correct an "evil nature" by education alone.[12] In Egypt, by contrast, philosophers had emphasized for centuries the value of the teachers' rod and this viewpoint was pursued with great enthusiasm in the mektep as well. "If Prince Tahuti [c. 1500 B.C.] reminisced about receiving a flogging about as regularly as he received his lunch, his successors in the kuttab used to receive it about as regularly as they took their breaths." [13]

Only slight differences existed in terms of atmosphere, organization, facilities, or curricula throughout the Islamic world. Everywhere children received an education that was extremely restricted in scope, consisting basically of memorizing most or all of the Koran complemented usually by instruction in reading, writing, and arithmetic, though sometimes, as in Egypt, arithmetic was omitted from the curriculum. In Iran, the curriculum was apparently far more comprehensive than elsewhere, and also included calligraphy, Islamic history, and the teaching of works by classical Iranian poets and authors.[14]

[11] G. E. von Grunebaum, *Medieval Islam* (Chicago: University of Chicago Press, 1946), p. 218; Hastings, *op. cit.*, p. 204; Reuben Levy, *A Baghdad Chronicle* (Cambridge: Cambridge University Press, 1929), p. 197.

[12] Ali Mohammed Kardan, *L'Organisation scolaire en Iran* (Geneva: Imprimerie Reggiam et Jacond, 1957), p. 27.

[13] Abn Al-Fatouh Ahmad Radwan, *Old and New Forces in Egyptian Education* (New York: Teachers College, Columbia University, 1951), p. 62.

[14] *Idem.;* Kardan, *op. cit.*, p. 26.

In the mekteps of the Turkish parts of the Ottoman Empire, elementary education was particularly inadequate because Turkish students had to memorize a holy book written in a foreign language that, although sharing a common alphabet and to some extent a common vocabulary, possessed a totally different grammatical and syntactical structure from Turkish. In the Arab parts of the Empire students were at least memorizing a work written in a variant of their native tongue, but Turkish students were, in effect, merely exercising their memories. Learning to recite the verses of the Koran without any possible comprehension of its contents was an exercise that, from an educational viewpoint, although possibly not from a religious one, cannot be considered as particularly productive. The same situation obtained in Iran, but since the curriculum there had been broadened to include native works, the educational process appears to have been slightly more meaningful.

Girls, of course, were not subject to the rules and procedures discussed above. Their education was considered in a totally different light, and although it was thought important to provide women with moral and religious instruction, since their role "centers in the spindle" no other training was required. Particularly condemned was teaching women to write: "He, the teacher, must not instruct any woman or female slave in the arts of writing, for thereby would accrue to them only an increase of depravity." An early saying read that "a woman who is taught to write is like a serpent who is given poison to drink." This orthodox view was generally ignored by wealthy families whose daughters were often tutored privately in the home.[15]

It is difficult, if not impossible, to assess the extent to which schools were distributed throughout the Middle East, but judging from the sparse data available there were about 300 schools in Istanbul alone in the seventeenth century;[16] in Iran every town had several schools, and it has been estimated that from one-fourth to one-third of the

---

[15] Hastings, *op. cit.,* p. 205; Mantran, *op. cit.,* p. 221.

[16] Richard Maynard, "The Lise and Its Curriculum in the Turkish Educational System" (Ph.D. diss., University of Chicago, 1961), p. 3. According to H. A. R. Gibb and Harold Bowen, *Islamic Society and the West* (London: Oxford University Press, 1950, 1957), Vol. I, Pt. II, p. 143, n. 1, there were about 200 schools in Istanbul still existing at the beginning of the twentieth century.

populace of Cairo was literate.[17] In other words, it would appear that opportunities for elementary education were readily available (at least in towns and cities) to children who wished to take advantage of them.

Qualitatively, as we have seen, these schools possessed serious deficiencies. In addition to restricted curriculum and poorly trained teachers, there was no provision for control or inspection. Any person able to read the Koran could open his own school, and little or no supervision of the actual conduct of instruction ever took place. Only in rare cases where the founder of an endowment took a personal interest in the school—carefully choosing the teacher and supervising his activities—was a fairly high educational level maintained. Yet even with the most careful supervision, given the nature of the curriculum and the emphasis upon discipline, memorization, and repetition, it is hard to see how an individual student could benefit greatly from his experience in the school.

Later writers have almost universally condemned this unintegrated and undifferentiated system, but it should be emphasized that it also possessed positive aspects. Through these schools, those for whom this was a terminal education were socialized into the Islamic way of life, and those students who would continue their education were provided with appropriate and necessary training since memorization characterized the higher levels of the system as well.

For persons wishing to continue their studies, the possibilities in early Islam were limited. One was to attend the lectures of a scholar in the mosque which were given regularly to audiences that varied in size depending upon the ability and personality of the teacher. Classes of 30,000 were not unusual, and one class is reputed to have consisted of 100,000 and required the help of many assistants who repeated the scholar's words to the students on the fringe of the audience.[18]

A second possibility were the famous circles (*Halka*) that had emerged by the second half of the first century A.H., whereby a group

---

[17] A. S. Tritton, *Materials on Muslim Education in the Middle Ages* (London: Luzac and Co., 1957), p. 198; J. Heyworth-Dunne, *An Introduction to the History of Education in Modern Egypt* (London: Luzac and Co., 1938), p. 10.
[18] Tritton, *Materials,* pp. 35–36.

of persons would meet with a scholar in a mosque to discuss some aspect of the Koran. In time, this institution became more formal; the great mosques came to possess several chairs known by the subject matter taught to the circle or by the name of the incumbent who was appointed by the caliph, usually for life. Besides teaching, the professor would provide legal opinions, preach sermons, and hold discussions on legal matters for students and visitors, and sometimes the townspeople.

Basically, the curriculum consisted of the Koran and all the disciplines related to it, such as law, tradition, exegesis, drama, and literature. Subjects considered heretical, such as Greek philosophy, were usually ignored, though such topics as mathematics, science, and medicine were also studied. Law was an important subject and all four legal codes which were accepted as orthodox were represented. By the eleventh century differences over which traditions were genuine and the relative importance of the other accepted sources of law (analogy, consensus, private opinion) had led to the emergence of four separate codes of legal practice, the Hanafite, Malikite, Shafiite, and Hanbalite. Despite the importance of this subject, however, classes (or circles) in law, being more specialized, were never as popular as those on tradition. Besides subject matter, the ability, reputation, and personality of the scholar all determined the size of the circle, which varied greatly.

A third possibility was for a student to apprentice himself to a learned man and spend varying amounts of time with him until he had learned as much as he desired. Some persons devoted themselves completely to one teacher, becoming an integral part of his household, sometimes marrying his daughter and carrying on his work. Others spent a few years with one teacher, then attached themselves to another scholar noted for his knowledge of a different subject, often in a very distant part of the Islamic world, until they had mastered the new topic. The willingness to travel long distances to study with learned men was commonplace, and this tradition was an important supplement to other institutional arrangements that were designed to further the unity and cohesion of the far-flung lands of the Islamic world. With time, this highly informal system of higher education became somewhat more structured and a system of certificates evolved as evidence of a student's training and ability. One early example of such a diploma reads as follows:

The most eminent, unique, learned lawyer . . . read with me the whole of *al-muhadh'dhab* in law with all proofs from the Koran and Sunna and, where there are no proofs, the meaning, correct reading, and implications of the text, the agreement, the adductions and extension of it so that he is worthy that advantage may be taken of him and may be handed on by his teaching.

Such certificates soon became extremely elaborate and were often written in verse.[19]

Two other institutions performed an educational function: the book shop and the literary salon. The growth of Islamic civilization, especially under the Abbasids, and the great emphasis upon translations, led inevitably to the growth of bookstores in all the great Muslim cities; there were one hundred in one Baghdad street alone.[20] Many of these contained a rich selection of books on varied subjects and scholars would congregate here, thus making these stores centers of intellectual activity. Literary salons where the cultural elite would gather privately to discuss intellectual topics also flourished in Abbasid times, often sponsored by the caliph himself. Attendance was restricted to a favored few—scholars and selected members of the ruling class—and protocol was carefully delineated: guests were required to wear certain clothes, sit in a reserved place, refrain from interrupting, and come and leave at a predetermined time.[21]

All these educational institutions made up a relatively informal, undifferentiated, and simple system of higher education which soon proved inadequate for the needs of the rapidly developing society. As Islam continued to expand and absorb new territories and peoples, the complex problems of administration and political integration which had to be resolved created ever growing needs for trained manpower and for institutions to defend and propagate political and religious doctrines. Furthermore there was a growing demand for increased educational opportunities from various groups. Among the new converts were many persons who were familiar with the rich

[19] *Ibid.,* p. 42.
[20] Philip K. Hitti, *History of the Arabs* (London: Macmillan, 1956), p. 414.
[21] Nakosteen, *op. cit.,* pp. 47–48.

heritage of pre-Islamic learning and wished to pursue scholarly work. Similarly, many persons who had completed their elementary education and wished to continue their studies to become religious leaders and teachers could not be absorbed by the existing system. When to these pressures is added the fact that the ever growing number of students increasingly disturbed and distracted the regular worshipers in the mosques the development of new institutional arrangements was inevitable.

The first of these was, in effect, a research center. These were established either by persons with a love of learning who wished to promote scholarship or by rulers seeking to disseminate and propagate certain religious or political doctrines. In these institutions, which often had a library or observatory attached, discussions were frequently held on various aspects of law or theology and courses on sundry subjects were sometimes given. Among the best known are the Dar-al Ilim in Cairo that taught Fatimite doctrine, the Shiite Dar Abdawa in Aleppo, and the Sunni Bayt al-Hikmah in Baghdad. Although both the mosque schools and this type of institution were often subsidized by a ruler or other important official, it should be noted that the scholar in the former labored in a far freer intellectual environment than he who occupied a position in the latter. This was especially true in a Fatimite center where he was expected merely to serve as a propagandist for the official doctrine.[22]

Various types of colleges formed the other category of higher educational institution that developed: the *madrasa* (college of law), the *mesjid* (mosque college), and the *meshed* (shrine college). The differences among them, especially between the first two, are still debated by scholars.[23] However it appears that although both the madrasas and the *mesjid*s were institutions where the law of a particular school was taught, the *mesjid* was also a place of worship. Endowments for the latter provided only for staff salaries, whereas those of the former also included student fellowships. Although there is no distinction between religion and culture in Islam, one can illuminate these differences by suggesting that the *mesjid* emphasized re-

[22] Jacques Waardenburg, "Some Institutional Aspects of Muslim Higher Education and Their Relation to Islam," *Numen*, 12 (April 1965), 99.
[23] George Makdisi, "Muslim Institutions of Learning in Eleventh-Century Baghdad," *BSOS* (*Bulletin of the School of Oriental Studies*), 24 (1961), 48ff.

ligious aspects, the madrasa cultural ones. The shrine colleges were often merely madrasas built next to the tomb of a holy man which had become a center of pilgrimage.

The similarities between the three types of colleges were far more important than these subtle differences. They all specialized in legal instructions and aimed primarily at producing experts in one of the four schools of Islamic law. To attend classes, the student had to be a member of the school whose law was taught in the college, so that a Hanbali student would attend a Hanbali college, a Shafii student a Shafii college. Each person could, of course, choose which school of law he wished to study. Upon completing the course, the graduates became members of the ulema, the legal experts of the community— its teachers, judges, and administrators. Some persons, however, chose not to engage in a profession, but to devote themselves to a life of religious learning, asceticism, or mysticism.

These colleges, too, were endowed by rich merchants or government officials or even scholars as evidence of their piety. The founder chose the professor who was to occupy the sole chair and often entrusted the administration of the endowment to him also. Tenure was for life, and the scholar would choose one of his disciples, often his son, if he had one who had become a scholar in his own right, to inherit the position.

Although madrasas may have been founded as early as the ninth century, the first real college was established in Naisabur, Iran, early in the eleventh.[24] But the most famous madrasa, which in time became the model for the whole madrasa system of education, was founded in 1057 by the Nizam-al-Mulk in Baghdad. Known as the Nizamiye, it achieved widespread renown and stimulated the growth of similar institutions elsewhere. In the words of the *Encyclopedia of Islam*:

The enthusiasm and energy of the Nizam-al-Mulk meant the beginning of the new period of brilliance for medresses. The Sultan and men of high rank were now interested in it, and the type evolved by the Nizam-al-Mulk in which students were boarded, became the prevailing one after his time.[25]

Although the impact of this institution is universally accepted, there is disagreement among scholars as to the specific reasons for the

[24] Bayard Dodge, *Muslim Education in Medieval Times* (Washington: Middle East Institute, 1962), p. 19.
[25] *Encyclopedia of Islam* (4 vols.; Leiden: E. J. Brill, 1913–1938), III, 354.

founding of this madrasa, as well as the eight others that the Nizam-al-Mulk established. Some have argued that the fundamental impetus came from the desire of this able grand vizier to the Turkish Seljuk sultans who had made themselves masters of the Middle East to promote Sunni Islam and to influence the public against Shii doctrine; others that they were established to meet the need for qualified personnel to staff a growing and reorganized bureaucracy; still others that the Nizam-al-Mulk needed institutional means to harness the potential power of the religious leaders to influence public opinion and feeling.[26] Which of these motives or combination of motives was uppermost in the Grand Vizier's mind remains unclear but it does appear that he felt the need for new institutions to supply the kinds of trained manpower that could enable him to achieve his political goals.

To ensure that the madrasa would attract the kind of students and faculty he wished, the Nizam-al-Mulk greatly strengthened the resources available to each. Professors who taught there received excellent salaries and could thus support themselves solely by their intellectual activities. Until now support for intellectuals had come for a fortunate few in the form of patronage by rulers and rich merchants, but the majority of scholars were forced to engage in such non-intellectual occupations as making shirts, dyes, or fans, or selling silk or soap. From the students' viewpoint, too, the Nizamiye, with its generous scholarships, was most attractive. Traditionally, the would-be scholar had to struggle through long, lean years to become a member of the intellectual class. Some indication of what it meant for a person who did not have a patron or an independent source of income to be a student can be derived from the following excerpt from a seventeenth-century autobiography:

He attended the college daily till noon for instruction and discussion and on returning to his lodging was so hungry that in default of any better food he used to collect the melon skins cast aside on the ground, wipe off the dust and eat what fragments of edible matter remained. One day he came upon his companion similarly employed. Each had tried to conceal from the other the shifts to which he was reduced for food, but now they joined forces and collected and washed their melon skins in company.

[26] Nakosteen, *op. cit.*, pp. 38ff.; A. L. Tibawi, "Origin and Character of Al-Madrasah," *BSOS*, 25 (1962), 225–231; Makdisi, *op. cit.*, pp. 52ff.

Being unable to afford lamps or candles, they learned by heart the texts they were studying . . . on moonlight nights, and on the dark nights repeated them by heart so as not to forget them.[27]

Under these conditions the average student preferred to enroll in an institution that could subsidize his studies and, since any good Muslim could choose any of the four orthodox schools of law, he would select that madrasa which provided fellowships, in this case the Shafiite school. In this manner, the Nizam-al-Mulk secured a constant flow of able students into his institution and, to ensure that they would receive appropriate training, he made a second important innovation; unlike all the other contemporary institutions, the professors at the Nizamiye were not appointed for life but were hired and fired at the will of the Nizam-al-Mulk and his successors.[28]

The madrasa's primary orientation was upon religious training, although other subjects were also included. The subjects taught were divided into two branches of knowledge: the physical sciences (*ulum tabiiya*), which had their roots in ancient times and, being "based on observation by the senses and deduction . . . are therefore also called *falsafiya* (philosophical) or *aqliya* (rational)," and the communicated sciences (*ulum nakliya*), which had developed in connection with Islam and which "therefore comprise all branches of knowledge which owe their existence to Islam." Important subjects included the Koran, traditions, law and "theology, which is *naqliya* (communicated) in as much as it is really a further development of *iman* (faith) which comes under the head of religious duties, but is *aqliya* (rational) in its nature since it is entirely based on abstract proof." [29]

A vivid picture of the actual conduct of classes in the Nizamiye has been provided by a contemporary traveler, Ibn Jubayr, who visited the college in 1184. He wrote:

When the class was assembled, the lecturer mounted a platform or pulpit and the students, sitting on stools in front of him, read out, or rather intoned, the Koran. The Sheik delivered an address interpreting a section of the Koran with a wealth of learning, and the application of pertinent traditions of the Prophet. The teacher was then assailed by showers

[27] Quoted in Nakosteen, *op. cit.*, p. 59.
[28] Makdisi, *op. cit.*, pp. 52ff.
[29] *Encyclopedia of Islam*, III, 362.

of all questions from all parts of the room, and, when he had answered them, with great elaboration and facility, he received a number of written questions with which he dealt. By the time he had answered all these, evening prayers were due, and the class dispersed.[30]

The founding of the Nizamiye provided a great impetus for the creation of other madrasas, and soon there were more than seventy-five in Cairo and fifty-one in Damascus; between 1155 and 1260 the number of colleges in Aleppo increased from six to forty-four. In the fourteenth century there were fifty-one in Aleppo and eighty-six in Damascus.[31] This rapid expansion of the network of colleges had but little impact upon established intellectual institutions. Teaching continued to be carried on as before, and many scholars still had to earn their livelihood through commerce or handicrafts.

In the Ottoman Empire the system of madrasas reached its zenith. Beginning in 1331 the Ottoman sultans began to carry on the tradition of their Seljuk predecessors by endowing new institutions in ever increasing numbers. Each succeeding ruler devoted himself to this task, and soon numerous madrasas were found in every town of the Empire; by the eighteenth century, there were at least 275 in Istanbul alone.[32] These institutions were organized in a hierarchical system with the elite madrasas of Istanbul (the ones founded by Suleiman the Magnificent, Mehmed the Conqueror, and Beyazit II) at the apex of the hierarchy; slightly below these were the others of Istanbul and those of Bursa and Adrianople, the first two capitals of the Empire.

The great madrasas were large and imposing complexes; that of Mehmed the Conqueror was described as follows:

To the right and to the left of the great exterior gate of the mosque, there are to the north and to the south eight medresses . . . which were constructed for the acquisition and the veneration of religious sciences and, for the honor and exaltation of their occupants. . . . At the foot of the . . . door of the great gateway, a school to teach the Koran to Muslim children has been built, and to the southeast of these medresses has been built a hospital. . . . To the north and to the south of these eight medresses are to be found the buildings for the students: one counts in

---

[30] Levy, *op. cit.*, p. 197.

[31] Dodge, *op. cit.*, p. 25; N. A. Ziadeh, *Urban Life in Syria under the Early Mamluks* (Beirut: American University of Beirut, 1953), p. 155.

[32] Gibb and Bowen, *op. cit.*, p. 145.

all three hundred rooms. In each room live four or five students of religious sciences; there are servants for each room; as for the *Ulema* they live in a building where they can also take their meals. There is also a kitchen with seventy cupola and twice a day meals are served to rich and to poor, to the miserable and to the indigent. Close by there is a caravansaray as well as a stable for the beasts of the travellers big enough to contain 3,000 animals.[33]

In these colleges the curriculum was broader than elsewhere, and though the emphasis remained upon the Koran, the traditions, and Islamic law, such subjects as logic, mathematics, geometry, astronomy, music, the natural sciences, medicine, literature, rhetoric, and grammar were also taught, especially in the great days of the Empire. Teaching was by lecture, and the works of Arab authors, which had usually been translated into Turkish, constituted the basic text.[34]

From the middle of the sixteenth century onward, however, the quality of these institutions declined rapidly. Many ulema had always looked upon the teaching of nonreligious subjects with suspicion and hostility so that before long the study of these topics decreased progressively and the curriculum became restricted to the religious sciences. We shall discuss the reasons for this development later in this chapter, when we analyze the functional role of madrasas in the Ottoman Empire.

Iran, too, was the site of many early madrasas and their number multiplied until the thirteenth century, when the battle between these Sunni institutions and the Sufi *khanegahs* resulted in the victory and proliferation of the latter owing to their better adaptation to the ideological current of the time.[35] A second development that deeply affected intellectual life in Iran followed the establishment of the Safavid dynasty in the fifteenth century. Shiism was propagated as the state religion in order to unify the country and to bolster it against threats from its Sunni neighbors, the Ottoman and the Uzbek Turks. As a result the madrasas were completely transformed from Sunni to Shiite institutions and their curriculum became more limited than

---

[33] Mantran, *op. cit.,* p. 228. The Turkish word for the college of law is *medrese,* but for consistency I have used the more common Arabic form, *madrasa,* throughout.

[34] Gibb and Bowen, *op. cit.,* p. 148; Mantran, *op. cit.,* p. 228.

[35] Kardan, *op. cit.,* pp. 29, 34.

ever; now study in the madrasas was restricted to Islamic law, the Koran, and closely related subjects, while the study of such fields as sciences and mathematics was actively discouraged.

Education in the Sufi *khanegah* (also called *ribat* or *ziwaya*) was based on an entirely different philosophy, which emphasized an individual's mystical development. The stress was upon memorization of the names of Allah, various Koranic texts, and mystic lyric poems by Sufi poets, through repeatedly chanting the work in chorus, with rhythmic cadences and modulations and bodily movements, the goals being not only to learn but to achieve a mystical trance as well. What this orientation meant for the development of Sufi intellectual life and for Islamic culture in general is unclear. Despite its importance, Sufi education has been largely neglected and little is known concerning the functioning and impact of these institutions. One scholar, for example, has concluded:

these Sufi intellectuals were far from being the equals of the scholar-jurists. They probably restricted themselves to mystical theology and its subordinate studies, sometimes with a philosophical basis, but neglected other aspects of Islam, such as natural science and history. Thus their world view was never a complete one, and they never were able to dominate Islamic higher education, even if one or two men . . . obtained considerable influence.[36]

To what extent the curriculum was in fact so restricted deserves further study, for it is well known that many of the wisest men in Islam, including Ibn Khaldun, al-Farabi, and Avicenna, received a Sufi education. Similar problems arise when one seeks to assess the contribution of these institutions to Islam, which one expert has described as follows:

Coming also from the East, side by side with the madrasas, the *ribats* have had a less spectacular, but not less important function in medieval Islamic society, for Sufism has developed a spiritual force of which society by its own nature is deprived. Moreover, if the madrasas consolidated orthodox Islam, these ribats appear to have contributed to the spread of Islam in the East as well as in the West. Where Islam took a mystical form, ribats were the places of instruction; where it remained

---

[36] W. Montgomery Watt, *Islam and the Integration of Society* (Evanston: Northwestern University Press, 1961), p. 248.

orthodox, higher teaching took place in mosque (masjid, jami) and madrasa.[37]

Whether this was indeed the sum of the contribution that Sufism made is another topic that requires further investigation, for it may well be that the numerous Sufi orders which came to count large numbers of adherents played important roles even in those areas where orthodox Islam held sway by maintaining the vitality of the traditional Islamic education despite the stultification of Sufism itself.

One institution which maintained its vitality for centuries was the pride of Egyptian higher education, the famous Al-Azhar. Many other madrasas were to be found throughout Egypt although there is some disagreement as to the number. One scholar has estimated that only five or six towns possessed such colleges but another has suggested that about twenty towns each had from one to seven such institutions.[38] Descriptions of the functioning of Al-Azhar are fortunately quite plentiful, one of the most eloquent being that of Taha Hussein, the famous Egyptian scholar. During his days there,

The Azar was still in that happy period when work days and rest days were not meticulously marked out either for students or for lecturers. There was no rigid timetable to enforce attendance daily and hourly without fail. Everything was flexible and easy. The rector would fix the official date of return, but lecturers were free to return when it suited them and students might come to lectures as soon as they wished or found it convenient.

When they did come,

the students listened to the lectures with the same quiet languor with which it was given. There was a striking contrast between the different tones that the sheiks used at the early morning and midday lectures. At dawn their voices were calm and gentle, with traces of drowsiness in them, at noon they were strong and harsh but fraught, too, with a certain sluggishness induced by the lunch they had just eaten, the baked beans and pickles and so on which made up the usual fare of an azharite at this time.

Hussein did not possess a particularly high opinion of the institution:

---

[37] Waardenburg, *op. cit.,* pp. 101–102.

[38] Radwan, *op. cit.,* p. 63, n.16; Heyworth-Dunne, *op. cit.,* pp. 19–20; Gibb and Bowen, *op. cit.,* p. 155.

There was not a single thing in all that he heard said to give him a good opinion of either lecturers or students and the longer he listened, the less he thought of either. It is true that now and again a good word was said for the intelligence of one of the sheiks, either junior or senior, but innumerable were the reproaches poured upon old and young alike for every kind of failing in character, morals, and even confidence.[39]

This low evaluation of the quality of Al-Azhar is not surprising in view of the many serious deficiencies that institutions of this type possessed. There is, of course, no question that Al-Azhar or the Ottoman madrasa or the Persian *khanegah* possessed many positive factors, perhaps the most important being that these institutions were open to any interested students, rich or poor, and hence served as important channels of social mobility. But it must also be pointed out that the relatively informal character of Muslim institutions of higher learning placed severe limitations upon the educational process. Anyone could become a student; there were no entrance requirements, no academic standards, no attendance requirements, no required courses, examinations, or formal graduation, and there was even very little distinction between students and faculty since a talented and ambitious person could often teach one subject while studying a second.[40] As a result the quality of most students was very poor and many persons enrolled merely in order to obtain the privileges of receiving free meals. The quality of the faculty was often equally unsatisfactory. Many persons were appointed as teachers solely because of family connections, and teachers often devoted little time to their scholarly responsibilities. Kinship considerations also meant more to many teachers than performance or ability so that qualitative criteria seldom prevailed in the training of the students.[41]

Education and Culture

Perhaps the single most important factor responsible for intellectual and educational stagnation and decay was the Islamic definition of acceptable knowledge. Although knowledge was highly valued and its quest always considered important, factors which permitted Islam

[39] Taha Hussein, *The Stream of Days: A Student at the Azhar,* trans. Hilary Wayment (2d ed.; London: Longmans, Green, 1948), pp. 50, 95.

[40] Dodge, *op. cit.,* p. 25.

[41] Gibb and Bowen, *op. cit.,* II, 159.

to make unique contributions to world civilization, its very importance led quickly to precise definition and the view that what lay beyond was not proper for inquiry.[42] Freedom of thought was never a central value of Muslim society and culture; rather, the emphasis lay upon acquiring as much of the accepted wisdom as possible.

The very origins and character of the educational system reflected this point. The higher level consisted of institutions that were created for purposes of sectarian education or for political ends; the system was founded, not out of any desire to further the cause of knowledge or intellectual activity, but to defend and disseminate a particular body of knowledge and to meet religious, bureaucratic, or political needs. Education was viewed from a purely utilitarian viewpoint—a tendency that was strengthened if not made inevitable by the Islamic concept of the role of the individual and society. G. E. von Grunebaum has summarized this point as follows:

Inquiry into the surrounding world was dictated by the needs of the community . . . anything that goes beyond these manifest (and religiously justifiable) needs can and in fact ought to be dispensed with. No matter how important the contribution Muslim scholars were able to make to natural sciences and no matter how great the interest with which at certain periods the leading classes and the government itself followed and supported their researchers, those sciences (and their technological application) had no root in the fundamental needs and aspirations of their civilization. . . . The research had nothing to give to their community which the community could accept as an essential enrichment of their lives.

Hence, it is not surprising that the great Muslim accomplishments in mathematics and medicine occurred only when "the elite were willing to go beyond, and possibly against, the basic strain of orthodox thought and feeling." [43]

Such a philosophy led naturally to a view that the essence of education was to memorize as much of the "truth" as possible. In elementary school the child memorized the Koran; in the mosque the students memorized the teachers' notes. As a result, many scholars

[42] Franz Rosenthal, *Knowledge Triumphant* (Leiden: E. J. Brill, 1970), pp. 340–341.

[43] G. E. von Grunebaum, *Islam: Essays in the Nature and Growth of a Cultural Tradition* (London: Routledge and Kegan Paul, 1961), pp. 113–114.

developed fantastic memories, one of whom recited 30,000 traditions with only three mistakes,[44] but few individuals developed the ability to search for originality or produce new ideas. Not only were inquisitive minds not valued by the culture, but the functioning of the educational system itself ensured that imitation and orthodoxy would become commonplace for it produced

scholars with an immense range of information within the closed structure of "learning," but this information consisted mainly of facts linked to one another in a traditional sequence. . . . The grinding effort of assimilation rendered them incapable of independent investigation into the organic relations of the facts to one another and to the structure as a whole.[45]

Thus before long the vital intellectual traditions of earlier decades became but a dim memory and it is possible to understand how, as we shall show later, the orthodox religious leaders, once Sunnism had more or less come to terms with Shiism and Sufism, were able to utilize these unstructured, decentralized educational institutions, not only to counteract the remaining vitality of Sufism and Shiism, but also to strengthen their own position within the society. Hence they were able to corrupt first themselves, then the educational process, and ultimately the society as well.

Yet, when evaluating this educational process, one should also remember that in a sense the educational system was genuinely functional for the society in terms of its cultural values and its manifest and latent requirements, for, as H. A. R. Gibb has also pointed out:

We must bear in mind that it ministered to the deepest needs of a society which was founded upon and held together by a religious culture, and which had been cut off from external cultural contacts since the later Middle Ages. It sustained a tradition and an ideal of learning which was not only of value in keeping alive the conception of intellectual attainment as a good in itself and a necessity of social life, but which also preserved from decay the two elements with which were bound up the history, the ideals, and even the existence of the race: the Arabic language and Islam. For it is with his language that the self-consciousness and

[44] Dodge, op. cit., p. 25.
[45] H. A. R. Gibb, "University in the Arab-Muslim World," in The University Outside Europe, E. Bradby, ed. (London: Oxford University Press, 1939), pp. 282–283.

emotional life of the Arab is most intimately linked; and it is in and through Islam that he and it have attained to fullness of self-expression and have made their mark on the history of mankind.[46]

Education and Society

Despite the unity imposed by Islam, Middle Eastern society was deeply fragmented and relatively unintegrated, consisting of a large number of small social groups that were almost entirely autonomous and self-governing. In other words, the social pattern was marked by deep horizontal and vertical cleavages; the former consisted of the general differentiation between elite and mass, the latter of the distinction between Muslim and non-Muslim and of differentiation within the Muslim community itself. In our analysis of the relationship between education and society we shall examine, first, the manner in which the horizontal cleavages were related to the educational system and, second, the linkage between vertical cleavages and educational processes.

Although differentiations based on wealth, power, and status did, of course, exist in the Middle East, these were to be found within each of the numerous ethnic and religious groups and were never as rigid as those obtaining in Western Europe. Islamic society was a relatively unintegrated and open society in which talented and able individuals, regardless of their origin, could rise to the top. In this respect it tends to differ from the feudal society model discussed earlier. The subtle interplay of the factors that determined the pattern of horizontal stratification has been well described in the following words:

Position might be owed to membership in an aristocratic family of Arabic or perhaps Persian, or even Jewish or Turkish background. Money, though deprecated by the moralist, played its customary part. Education opened the doors of the great to the ambitious poor, and it was a prerequisite for public office, although princely whim did not always stoop to scrutinize a favorite's qualifications. Political influence, military power, administrative rank, wealth, birth and schooling in every possible combination strengthened or counteracted one another in assigning a given individual his place in society.[47]

---

[46] *Ibid.*, p. 283.
[47] Von Grunebaum, "Islam," p. 211.

While mobility was possible, and in fact occurred not at all infrequently, it would be wrong to exaggerate the degree of fluidity within the society and to minimize the gap between upper and lower strata; the former possessed wealth and political power, the latter consisted of artisans, peasants, and tribesmen. Relations between these two strata were limited owing partly to the urbanized character of medieval Islamic society. City life was favored by the Koran and migration into towns encouraged. On the other hand, migration to a rural environment was frowned upon and there were almost no ties, apart from an economic one, between town and country. The degree of social, cultural, and economic differentiation between these two sectors of society was so great that it has been described as "a contrast in civilizations." [48]

In this environment education was almost exclusively an urban phenomenon and very few village children or tribesmen received any formal schooling. The normal pattern, as in any traditional society, was for the son to follow in his father's footsteps. The boy would learn from his father, the girl from her mother. Nevertheless, geographic and social mobility was possible and Islamic history is studded with examples of poor village children who migrated to urban centers, acquired an advanced education, and became noted scholars.

Besides the self-sufficient and almost totally isolated peasants and tribesmen, the lower elements of Islamic society included many urban dwellers whose ranks and occupations were also usually based on ascriptive criteria. Depending upon their position within this stratum and the type of autonomous group to which they belonged, their children received more or less formal education, though it is unlikely that many sons of poor artisans and craftsmen received extensive formal schooling. Skills were handed down to apprentices who spent many years under the guidance of a master craftsman. Usually, however, a child would be apprenticed only after graduating from the local school, so that in major cities such as Cairo, merchants, shopkeepers, and artisans comprised a large percentage of the literates.[49]

The moderately well-to-do and rich urban dwellers probably made up the audiences of circles and lectures in mosques; they patronized the bookshops and provided the financial support for many elemen-

[48] Gibb and Bowen, *op. cit.*, Vol. I, Pt. I, p. 276.
[49] Heyworth-Dunne, *op. cit.*, p. 10.

tary institutions as acts of piety. Often wealthy merchants would have their children instructed at home by private tutors, but the instruction they received did not differ very greatly from that available in the schools.[50] The ruling class, of course, were even better patrons of the educational system, and most of the institutions were probably founded by its members. There is little doubt that, especially in Abbasid times, the court was a center of learning and intellect where the greatest scholars, poets, and artisans were to be found. Scholarship was honored and patronized and the most distinguished scholars were recruited to serve as tutors for the many royal princes. This was especially true of the great Abbasid ruler of *Thousand and One Nights* fame, Harun al-Rashid, who, always concerned with education, carefully selected teachers of grammar and poetry for his children.[51]

The education provided in special schools such as this was by and large the same as in the public institutions, although the content of the curriculum was specified by the ruler and was as narrow or as broad as he wished. Often the tutor would live in the palace and become a member of the royal entourage. Usually instruction continued long after the pupils had passed elementary age.[52]

The educational level of the ruling class in medieval Islamic society and the fact that even women could receive a high level of education is reflected in the story of Tawaddud in the *Thousand and One Nights*. Skeptical of the girl's claim that she knows grammar, poetry, the Koran, law, the tradition, music, mathematics, philosophy, logic, rhetoric, and is an accomplished musician and singer, the caliph has her examined by a group of scholars. Naturally she astounds everyone by her knowledge, which may be considered as accurately reflecting the state of learning in twelfth-century Islam. She knew, for example, that man was

compounded of the four elements of water, earth, fire, and air . . . anatomically and physiologically, man is made up of 365 veins, 240 bones, and the three spirits, the vital, the animal, and the natural. . . . There

---

[50] Gibb and Bowen, *op. cit.*, Pt. II, p. 139.

[51] Nabia Abbott, *Two Queens of Baghdad: Mother and Wife of Harun al-Rashid* (Chicago: University of Chicago Press, 1946), p. 7.

[52] Henri Lammens, *Etude sur le siècle des Omayyades* (Beirut: Imprimerie Catholique, 1930), pp. 160ff.

are the five senses and the corresponding organs; the heart is in the left part of the chest with the stomach in front of it while the lungs are ventilators to the heart. . . . In the field of astronomy, the girl shows acquaintance with 28 stations of the moon which are equivalent to 12 divisions of the zodiacs. She knows . . . the seven planets . . . Sun, Moon, Mercury, Venus, Mars, Jupiter, and Saturn and what the astrological qualities are, as well as the length of the occupation of each division of the zodiac. . . . On the whole, the standard is a high one [and] may fairly be applied to the attainment of a citizen of Baghdad in the twelfth century.[53]

Ottoman Palace Schools

It was in the training of the ruling elite that the Ottoman Turks made their greatest contributions to educational practice. Mehmed the Conqueror founded a network of palace schools to train the top administrators and officials—a dramatic innovation in educational practice because of its unique base of recruitment and its integrated curriculum combining religious, physical, academic, and vocational training designed to prepare students for a wide range of careers, including the highest posts in the Empire—through the eighteenth century seventy-nine grand viziers were graduates of this system.[54]

Although Mehmed the Conqueror held education in high regard, he probably founded the system to meet growing demands for civil and military officials in a rapidly expanding empire, especially after the conquest of Constantinople, and to overcome the sultan's dissatisfaction with the training of officials through apprenticeship and practical experience. In effect, this remarkable institution was an innovative solution to a fundamental problem faced by the ruler of any such empire: to create institutions with power without endangering his own position. Not only was it important that the administration be subservient to the ruler's will, but its officials also had to be highly trained if they were to form an effective instrument in the accomplishment of his policy. The palace schools and the system of recruitment were designed to fill these requirements. In their success lies a fundamental reason for much of the glory of the Ottoman Empire; in their decay, its decline.

[53] Levy, *op. cit.*, pp. 248–251.
[54] Başgöz and Wilson, *op. cit.*, p. 15.

Admission to the schools and hence to the highest position in the Ottoman Empire was open only to non-Muslim slaves recruited through periodic levies of non-Muslim boys aged from ten to twenty. They became, in effect, the "slaves" of the sultan, a position that implied little if any social inferiority and carried with it other outstanding advantages, especially that the highest positions within the Empire were now open to them if they possessed talent and ability. The sultan, in turn, was provided with a body of totally dependent officials who owed their allegiance and loyalty only to him and whose relations with other groups were almost nonexistent. Thus, he did not have to rely upon established groups within the Empire to meet his manpower needs. He possessed a unique and safe way of concentrating political power since any "slave," however powerful he might become, always remained at his mercy, did not possess any hereditary privileges, and thus could never represent a threat to his power.

The palace schools consisted of several preparatory and vocational schools, which formed an integrated and hierarchic educational system. Students were selected on the basis of physical and mental ability and would be assigned either to the Inner Service, that sector concerned primarily with palace affairs, or to the Outer Service. In either case they would undergo thorough and rigorous training that combined practical experience with formal education. They attended daily classes and heard periodic lectures from the ulema, visiting scholars, and other experts and also participated actively in the palace routine. Since the purpose of the educational process was to socialize the students as Ottoman gentlemen and potential members of the ruling elite, they received instruction, in addition to religious subjects, which constituted an important part of the curriculum, in such fields as Turkish, Arabic, Persian, Turkish and Arabic literature, Turkish history, and music and mathematics. Physical training and such sports as riding, weight lifting, wrestling, javelin throwing, and archery were also emphasized. Their vocational training included such skills as sewing, bookbinding, calligraphy, goldsmithing, and inlaying.[55]

The palace schools played a leading role in the development of the Ottoman Empire and trained the achitects, the sculptors, the cal-

[55] On the functioning of the schools, see also Barnette Miller, *Beyond the Sublime Porte: The Grand Seraglio of Stamboul* (New Haven: Yale University Press, 1931).

ligraphers, the painters, the cannon-founders, the naval architects, and the builders of the Empire. As one scholar has noted:

During the two centuries which succeeded its organization . . . the majority of the officials of the court and government, the officers as well as the rank and file of the regular cavalry of the Sublime Porte . . . the superior officers of the Navy, and for a time, the chiefs of the Janissary corps, were the products of its training.[56]

In time, however, achievement criteria were replaced by ascriptive considerations, and the system declined greatly. This was both result and cause of the decay of the Empire itself, and it is therefore important to analyze the factors involved. Perhaps the most fundamental is the nature of the institution. Its dependence upon the sultan and lack of autonomy ensured that when the sultan retired from active leadership the palace schools would be unable to function as before. As the influence of the harem and, to some extent, of the court personnel increased, the sultan came to accept the advice of "persons unfit to proffer it" and to promote to high offices "persons unfit to fill them." [57] Recruitment into the top civil, religious, and military positions of the Empire became subject to the intrigues of the harem, court cliques, page factions, and army groups, and the school could no longer perform its former function. Before long, ascriptive criteria came to dominate here too; the system of recruitment by levies was first compromised, then abolished completely.

This shift in the composition of the nonreligious elements of the social core group has often been identified as one of the major reasons for the decay of the Ottoman Empire. In essence, as weak personages became rulers, their control declined and the "slave meritocracy" achieved autonomy, displaced its goals away from a service orientation toward self-aggrandizement, and was transformed into an aristocracy of free Muslims. This process and its consequences have been summarized as follows:

The Ruling Institution had thus, by the eighteenth century, undergone as complete a transformation as was compatible with the maintenance of most of its original forms. Instead of being manned almost exclusively by slave converts, it was now manned entirely by free Moslems. Instead of

[56] *Ibid.*, pp. 6–7.
[57] Gibb and Bowen, *ibid.*, p. 177.

inspiring its members to earn merit by the exercise of talent and virtue, it taught them that they must look to corruption for advancement, and might safely neglect the duties that should have been concomitant with their privileges. Finally, instead of providing the Sultans with an efficient instrument for the preservation of their power, it was now scarcely strong enough to maintain their authority at home, and had become an engine of feeble tyranny over those of their subjects that were unable to combine against it.[58]

Recent research, however, has demonstrated that this analysis based on a rigid division between a "ruling institution" composed of slaves and a "religious institution" staffed by Muslims is an oversimplification of the classical pattern and of subsequent developments. Although the social core group was composed largely of the sultan's slaves, free-born Muslims were always to be found in important posts, particularly in the administration, and religious origin was never an absolutely determining criterion in either institution. Many of the eighteenth-century grand viziers were not born Muslims, and many persons who occupied important financial positions in the sixteenth and seventeenth centuries were of Muslim origin. Conversely, persons of non-Muslim origin were to be found within the religious institution as well.[59]

From our viewpoint, however, the important consideration is that patterns of recruitment and training did change within the Empire and that the previous meritocratic pattern was replaced by one based on ascriptive factors. As a result, the power structure of the state changed drastically. The independence and power of core elites increased steadily, and in time the social core group came to consist of a ruling class. We shall discuss this process and its significance for later developments in the next chapter. Suffice it here to point out that it is not difficult to see why any sultan who wished to adopt new policies could seldom do so, or why it became essential for reforming sultans to centralize power into their hands and to reestablish control over the instruments of power.

Another consequence of the corruption of the palace school system was that the madrasas now constituted the only remaining channel from which could come the intellectual leadership necessary for the

[58] *Ibid.,* p. 199; see also pp. 173ff.

[59] Norman Itzkowitz, "18th-Century Ottoman Realities," *Studia Islamica,* 16 (1962), 82–83.

continuing development of the Empire, but these institutions did not, and indeed could not, produce this type of innovative, creative, skilled, or even well-rounded manpower. On the contrary, they produced the type of people who were most committed to the maintenance of the status quo, a status quo that before long was to threaten the very existence of the state. To understand this development fully it is necessary to examine the vertical cleavages within Islamic society and the role of the ulema as an integrating force therein.

The Ulema: Integration and Decay

Perhaps the most striking characteristic of Islamic society was its fragmentation into a large number of autonomous groups organized along religious or ethnic lines. The most obvious and also the most basic vertical cleavage was the one between Muslims and non-Muslims. Although Jews and Christians were known as "people of the book" and were granted a privileged position within Islam, their position was below that of the Muslims. Nevertheless, despite their second-class citizenship, Christians and Jews were granted a significant degree of autonomy, and were, by and large, left free to conduct their affairs as they wished. This concept reached its zenith in the Ottoman Empire where it was institutionalized as the *millet* system. At the head of each autonomous religious community was an elected leader who was confirmed in his position by the sultan, and who was considered responsible for the administration of the community. Education remained the responsibility of each group, so that Jews and Christians organized their own schools and did not participate in the system we have described. By and large, however, these educational patterns were also very religiously oriented and aimed at socializing the child into the culture of the particular community.

Ethnic divisions within Islam marked a second great vertical fissure within Muslim society. Because of the historical development of Islam, the Arabs considered themselves the leaders of the Muslim world—a view that was not warmly received by the many Persians, Turks, Greeks, and others who accepted Islam. At first these converts had to affiliate themselves with Arab tribes and were know as *mawali* ("clients"), but they were never regarded as equals of the Arabs, although many of them were wealthy, educated, and the heirs to a far richer civilization than the Arabs. The displacement of the Umayyads by the Abbasids eliminated much of the discrimination against this group, but the Arabs continued to look upon them with contempt.

These ethnic differentiations had important consequences for cultural and religious developments. For one thing, the assimilation of large numbers of educated urban dwellers who were familiar with the rich pre-Islamic heritage gave a direct impetus to the growth and development of Islamic civilization and, as we have suggested, to the development of higher educational institutions. Within the new frontiers of Islam were now to be found Persian, Christian, and Jewish centers of learning, and it was inevitable that sooner or later there would be an interaction between traditional Muslim scholarship and the knowledge contained in these institutions. This interaction actually took place within a short span of time as the relative inattention of the Umayyad rulers, whose primary concern had been the construction of a new Islamic society, was replaced by a great flood of translations sponsored by the Abbasid caliphs.[60]

Numerous Greek works on medicine, philosophy, mathematics, astronomy, and other scientific fields became available to Muslim scholars and the intellectual life of the Middle East was transformed. One reason for the sudden attention by Muslims to the great pre-Islamic sciences and philosophy was that the very success of the Umayyads in establishing an Islamic state enabled the Abbasids to concentrate on cultural matters. This factor, however, does not explain the high priority the Abbasids assigned this effort. One scholar has suggested that religious considerations played a prominent role, and in view of the fundamental religious ethos of medieval Muslim civilization it is plausible to argue that

by this time the Muslims had come into contact with Jewish and Christian religious authorities who were defending the tenets of their faith, and also attacking those of Islam by appealing to arguments drawn from Aristotelian logic and philosophy of which the Muslims were ignorant. . . . Most likely it was in order to supply Islamic faith with intellectual armor of a similar kind and thereby to preserve the power of the Sharia upon which their own authority depended that the Caliphs spent so much effort to have philosophic and scientific work translated into Arabic.[61]

[60] Sayyed Hossein Nasr, *Three Muslim Sages* (Cambridge: Harvard University Press, 1964), pp. 5–6.

[61] *Ibid.*, p. 5.

The relationship between the different ethnic groups which comprised the new Islamic state was also to have serious repercussions in the functioning of the educational system. The identification of Islam with its small ruling group of Arabs led almost inevitably to the opposition of all their adversaries to the orthodox Arab view of Islam, and to the adoption of sectarian interpretations. Thus, the rapid spread of Islam was accompanied by an equally rapid religious division, which resulted in the third great vertical fissure within the society. The first challenge to othodoxy came from Shiism, but the Sunni ulema proved flexible enough to successfully incorporate their opponents within their own structure.[62]

Threats to the orthodox establishment continued to be nourished by the stratification pattern of the society and, before long, the Sufi orders had supplanted the Shiite appeal to the lower classes. Once again, the Sunni ulema tried to come to terms with Sufism; Sufi methods were recognized as valid in return for Sufi acceptance of Sunni rights and teaching. Nevertheless, Sufism continued to flourish and soon it had created an independent rival organization with its own theology and institutional arrangements, including the Sufi colleges (*khanegah*s) discussed earlier.

All these cleavages were reflected in the fragmented character of urban life. Cities were divided into quarters, most of which were, in effect, the real communities to which people owed their allegiances. These quarters were inhabited by persons with a common occupation, a common religious faith (Jews or Christians), an ethnic or racial bond (Persians or Turks), or by a particular sect or religious group (the Hanbalis in Shafii Damascus). However, there was almost no relationship between these groups or between the quarters of a city, which was "an uncoordinated mosaic of many sections." In such a context, it is perhaps not surprising that municipal administration was almost totally unknown, and that no Arabic equivalent of "citizen" existed.[63]

Only one group in medieval Islam could forge bonds to transcend local quarters, to integrate such communities with their rural hinterland, and to bind the entire society into a coherent unit. This was the

---

[62] Gibb and Bowen, *op. cit.*, Pt. II, pp. 70ff.

[63] Walter J. Fischel, "The City in Islam," *Middle Eastern Affairs*, 7 (1956), 229–230.

ulema, who, in addition to their religious role, also comprised an administrative and social elite whose membership represented all the horizontal divisions within Islamic society.

Since Islam is an all-encompassing religion, civil affairs are also regulated by religious law; thus the ulema were responsible for administering a wide range of activities, ranging from the regulation of businesses to the administration of legal and educational institutions. In other words,

the Ulema were judges, lawyers, professional witnesses and servants attached to the legal profession and functionary to the state bureaucracy, market inspectors, supervisors of Waqfs, and treasury offices. They were the literate and professional elite of the cities. All realms of public affairs were an intrinsic part of the duties of this multi-competent undifferentiated, and unspecialized communal elite.[64]

Nor could the ulema be considered a separate social class, but rather a group of persons who permeated the entire society from the highest to the lowest levels. They possessed close ties with the ruling elite, the bureaucrats, the merchants, and the craftsmen, as well as with the common people, since it was possible for ulema to make careers for themselves as merchants or bureaucrats and for the craftsmen and merchants to become members of the intellectual and religious elite.

This tendency was reinforced by the fluidity of Muslim society which made it possible for persons of ability to utilize the educational process as a means of social mobility. Thus merchants would often combine a journey to distant places with study there and upon returning home would teach what they had learned to other interested persons in the mosque. Similarly, craftsmen and artisans would acquire knowledge about Islam and thus become eligible for membership in a law school and recognition as a member of the ulema.

Ties with the many groups in society were also established through the educational institutions themselves. The circle headed by a distinguished scholar meeting to discuss religious, philosophical, and social matters would consist not only of local merchants and artisans,

[64] Ira Lapidus, *Muslim Cities in the Later Middle Ages* (Cambridge: Harvard University Press, 1967), p. 108.

but also of other ulema, students, and wealthy patrons who came to study with a learned scholar. Similar clienteles were formed by the ulema in their administrative, judicial, and religious roles. Whether as judges or religious functionaries, the ulema would gather around them large numbers of students, deputies, and subordinates who were responsible for various duties.

The major institution that bound together the ulema and, consequently, all the groups which focused around them was the law school. Here students, teachers, judges, and scholars gathered together to study and elaborate the practices and teachings of Islam according to one of the four recognized versions of the Sharia. Not only did every member of the ulema, rich merchant and poor craftsman alike, belong to one of these schools, but every good Muslim was also associated with a school, either as patron or follower. Membership was often inherited or determined by the practice of the local community, but rich and poor, educated and ignorant alike turned to the school and its scholars for guidance on many aspects of daily life, ranging from interpretation of appropriate religious behavior to the settlement of local disputes. For this reason the vitality of the society was dependent to a significant extent upon the degree to which religious norms and values continued to command general acceptance and the degree to which the ulema themselves were respected by the populace. Thus, the law schools were far more than scholarly institutions; they also helped bridge the elite-mass gap and served as channels through which the ulema could disseminate their views and opinions, thus extending and propagating their influence. Similarly, control of the educational system was of fundamental importance to the ulema, who maintained, during the early centuries of Islam, a long, bitter, and finally successful struggle to dominate the educational process.

Yet their very success determined that while medieval Muslim society would retain its traditional value orientation and internal equilibrium, its golden age would not, and indeed could not endure, since control of the intellectual life had come to rest in a group that was to resist change and innovation. The factors responsible for this phenomenon are as yet not fully understood, but one scholar has recently argued that four causes must be taken into account. Two of these, the static view of knowledge inherent in the Islamic view of the world and the preoccupation of intellectuals with scholasticism, we have already discussed in detail. The other two spring from the role of the ulema in society: namely, that the ulema became bureaucratized, professionalized, and ultimately concerned with their own self-aggrandizement, and that the relationship of the ulema to the ruling elite became increasingly one of dependency and, hence, weakness.[65]

Not surprisingly, Muslim rulers quickly came to recognize the power and importance of the ulema and, implicitly or explicitly, attempted to establish a positive relationship with them. They sought to maintain their good will by endowments for the support of mosques and madrasas and by the avoidance of unorthodox religious practices. At the same time, they endeavored to establish control over the ulema through payments to judges and other officials. In the early days of Islam, many scholars scrupulously refused such emoluments, but by the time of the Abbasids a majority of the ulema had succumbed to the temptation, thus becoming financially dependent on the government and hence susceptible to pressure. The bureaucratization and professionalization of the ulema inevitably ensued. Hastening this development was the subsequent expansion of educational opportunities and the opening of new schools and colleges, for students increasingly came to expect an official position upon graduation.[66] In other words, the golden age of medieval Islam could not endure because the position of the intellectuals in society changed to one of dependence upon the ruler. Such a situation could favor either scholasticism or free inquiry depending upon his orientation, but in most cases, the kind of leadership that was necessary to maintain or restore intellectual vitality was not forthcoming. Indeed, as the ulema became increasingly bureaucratized and institutionalized, the possibility of reform and change within that institution became ever more difficult to realize. And their control of the educational system ensured that scholasticism would be the norm and that its graduates would not only be unequipped to challenge the status quo, but would possess

[65] W. M. Watt, *Muslim Intellectual* (Edinburgh: Edinburgh University Press, 1963), pp. 161–162.

[66] *Ibid.*, pp. 102–103.

a vested interest in the maintenance and protection of traditional values and beliefs.

The Ottoman Case

This process was to be largely repeated in the Ottoman Empire, where the ulema also bound together many autonomous groups by providing them with a common bond and loyalty that overlay their primary loyalties. Similarly, the ulema were able to perform this vital socializing and integrating function because of their linkages with all sectors of the society; there were, for example, many ulema who engaged in craft or business or industry, and ulema of humble origin. The educational system constituted the main tool utilized by the ulema in their attempt to socialize all these groups into an acceptance of their values and ideals.

Just as the functional role of the ulema in these societies was similar, so in time, did the religious elites of both cultures come to develop many of the characteristics that were responsible for the decay of medieval Islamic civilization and hence contributed greatly to the ossification of society. During the great days of the Empire, however, the religious elite, like the secular one, was marked by an emphasis upon ability and achievement, and its educational system, centered around the madrasas, can be considered the functional equivalent of the palace schools. Both these educational systems represented an organized and institutionalized means of recruiting persons on an achievement basis to the highest levels of the religious and secular hierarchies of the Empire, a fact which goes far to explain the success and glory of the Ottoman state during its golden era.

As we have already seen, the madrasa comprised a complex, hierarchical educational system. Every important town had at least one, but if a person wished to achieve important office he had to attend the madrasa in one of the three major cities: Bursa, Adrianople, and Istanbul. For highest office he had to be a graduate of one of the great Istanbul institutions.

Although no fixed course of study existed in these schools, an ulema aspiring to a high post had to pass both as a student and as a teacher through twelve grades. After preliminary instruction in the first six grades, the student would proceed to studies of those branches of law and theology he favored under the principal sheikhs, or possibly teach the lower classes what he had already learned. After graduating from each stage, the student would obtain a certificate stating that he could teach the particular book that was taught at that level. Furthermore, the student desirous of achieving high office had not only to pass successfully through all or most of these twelve grades, but he also had to repeat at least nine of them. Not many students possessed the ability and the determination or enjoyed the support necessary to gain admission into an elite madrasa and to survive the rigorous academic training. The course of study was so long and demanding that the graduates tended to be forty or forty-five years old, and the majority dropped out at various stages to fill the numerous lower- and middle-level positions of the religious institutions and become clerks, secretaries, imams, cadis, and muftis.[67] Before long, influence as well as academic expertise became a major criterion for appointment to such posts, and this factor became increasingly important after the reign of Suleiman the Magnificent, as the high ulema began to ensure that their children could follow in their footsteps. Thus the position of the father became increasingly important and the religious elite began to perpetuate itself and to form a closed circle. In time the ulema began to procure for their children and followers the diplomas that rendered them eligible for appointment regardless of merit or training. In this manner the pattern of the ruling institution was soon followed, and once again the disposal of posts by nepotism was only a step removed from their disposal by sale.

The corruption and deterioration of the madrasa system soon ensued as irregular practices also came to characterize the hiring and firing of faculty and educational matters in general. Not only did students who proceeded slowly through the various stages receive an inferior education (even in traditional terms), but they began to find that the positions to which they aspired were more and more frequently being given to rivals who had not passed through such arduous training but who possessed the appropriate personal connections. The extent to which the leading ulema families had en-

---

[67] Mantran, *op. cit.*, p. 229.

trenched themselves by the eighteenth century has been described by one European observer:

> The men of the law can attain no office without having first gone through a course of studies in Turkish academies. After having filled the post of Muderis . . . then that of Nazib and of Mollah or judge . . . the prescribed procedure would be to ascend successively the various steps of the judicature . . . to arrive finally to the supreme rank of Mufti.
>
> But the noble and rich families of the core of the Ulema, . . . in which the offices are in some sort hereditary, are often dispensed by dint of the particular favors bestowed on them from passing through the degrees of the judicature of which we have spoken. They are, nevertheless, obliged to equip themselves with all the diplomas certifying that they have successively passed through these stages. This malpractice which has been introduced some years ago makes talented people languish in poverty and crawl in sloth to the greatest prejudice of Turkish literature.[68]

The emergence of these families was facilitated by the withdrawal of the sultan into the palace which also allowed the ulema complete control over the contents of the curriculum. As was the case in Abbasid and Umayyad times, the ulema were not noted for their liberalism in terms of subject matter, and they had always been hostile to attempts by various sultans to support creative individuals and to sponsor the diffusion of new ideas. The corruption of the ulema ensured that antagonism to creative learning and new ideas would be greater than ever before, since any modification in existing practice would be viewed as a direct threat to their position in society. Thus, it is not surprising that, although "rational" as well as "religious" sciences were taught to some extent during the reign of Suleiman the Magnificent, the former soon disappeared from the curriculum. Some individuals continued to study the rational sciences, but only for personal rather than professional reasons. Inevitably, the study of such subjects lapsed almost completely, and the educational process was marked once again by a closed conception of knowledge and an emphasis upon scholasticism.[69]

---

[68] Toderini, quoted in Şerif Mardin, "Some Notes on an Early Phase in the Modernization of Communications in Turkey," *Comparative Studies in Society and History*, 3 (1961), 253.

[69] Gibb and Bowen, *op. cit.*, Pt. II, p. 147.

Thus in Umayyad, Abbasid, and Ottoman times the relationship between education and change was very similar. In each case the educational system proved unable to break out of a narrow conception of its function as a transmitter of knowledge and culture for integrative ends. The reasons for this were always the same: the Islamic view of knowledge and the consequent emphasis upon scholasticism. Under these conditions it is not surprising that intellectual vitality did not endure long or that decay and stagnation ensued. And, as the ulema became bureaucratized, institutionalized, and self-perpetuating, they became more and more conservative and determined to prevent change in educational processes under their control. Given their steadily growing political power, only when caliphs or sultans were willing and able to exercise strong leadership could new ideas penetrate into the educational system or new fields open up for study. When caliphs or sultans were weak and retreated from affairs of state, the ulema were left in complete control of the educational process. And, as we have emphasized, their philosophical orientation and their role in society led them inexorably to regard education in highly traditional terms.

The critical importance of the ruler's role is reinforced by developments in the Ottoman Empire which proved unable to avoid the fate of the Umayyad and Abbasid empires even though it possessed a separate, functionally oriented educational system designed to supply the state with rigorously selected and trained civil and military elites. And, as long as powerful and able sultans ruled, key civil and military posts were filled by "slave" graduates who achieved their positions by dint of ability and perseverance. During this golden age, the high posts in the religious institutions, too, were filled on the same basis, and the training that the ulema received was relatively broad and flexible.

But when weak sultans retreated into the harem, the pattern of administrative and military corruption was repeated and the religious institution and its educational system were equally and similarly affected. The consequence was unavoidable: intellectual decay and stagnation. And, though the corruption of the educational system resulted from political factors, by producing men who were not only totally ignorant, except in rare cases, of the progress in the West, but regarded their own society and way of life as inherently superior, the schools accelerated and perpetuated the decay. The lack of able leadership led to the ossification of educational systems, to artistic and intellectual stagnation, and, most significantly, to a society relatively impervious to change and innovation.

III

The Introduction of Modern Education

While intellectual life was ossifying and stagnating in the Middle East, Europe emerged out of medieval times to undergo the Renaissance, the Reformation, and the Industrial Revolution in rapid succession. As a result, the balance of power and of intellectual vitality shifted rapidly and decisively away from the Middle East, whose moribund educational system ensured that the region would remain unaware of Western European developments and secure in the superiority of its own way of life. This feeling, which served as an important factor in isolating the Middle East from European influences, was founded on the great disparities which had, in fact, existed between the two cultures in earlier times when Charlemagne was a contemporary of Harun al-Rashid, the great Abbasid caliph. The attitude of Muslims toward Europe at that time is vividly illustrated by the following excerpt from an eleventh-century work in which the author ranked the countries of the world according to their scientific achievements. Europeans were placed on the level with Berbers and Sudanese but lower than Chinese or Turks:

As for the rest of this category which cultivated no sciences, they are more like animals than human beings. Those of them who live deep in the north —between the end of the seven climates and the confines of the habitable world—have been so affected by the extreme distance from the sun from the Zenith above their heads, resulting in cold climate and thick atmosphere, that their temperaments have become chilly and their humors rude. Consequently their bodies are huge, their color is pale and their hair long. For the same reason they lack keenness in intelligence and perspicacity, are characterized by ignorance and stupidity. Folly and mental blindness prevail among them as among Slavs, Bulgars, and other neighboring peoples.[1]

While this feeling may originally have been justified, Middle Eastern superiority was not to endure for very long. By the time of the Crusades, the two regions were equally powerful—even though the Europeans had much to learn in the fields of science, medicine, mathematics, and astronomy—and the balance of power continued to swing away form the Middle East. Even the Ottomans, who at first overwhelmed the Europeans with their power and might, found their advance halted at the gates of Vienna in 1529, and from then on the frontiers of the Empire inexorably receded as successive Sultans suffered defeat after defeat at the hands of the infidels. Despite such practical demonstrations, the conceit of the inherent inferiority of the West continued to be widely accepted by all the peoples of the Middle East, a state of affairs to which the prevailing educational patterns contributed greatly.

This fallacious belief was to have important consequences for Middle Eastern societies by creating a practically impenetrable barrier to the introduction of European values and techniques. One scholar has analyzed this attitude and its consequences as follows:

the Muslim Arabs' belief in the perfection of the religious principles underlying their political and social institutions and in the sacredness of their language, as well as the memory of their "glorious past" and of their military conquests in the early days of Islam, had developed in them a feeling of "Arab" superiority. This "superiority complex" had rendered them aloof and, therefore, unwilling to change their ideas and their way of life for what they considered to be new-fangled and heretical innovations originating in non-Muslim lands.[2]

We shall discuss later the extent to which similar beliefs were dominant in Iran and the Ottoman Empire.

What is especially striking about the Ottoman case, however, was that the Turk, in contrast to Arab and Persian, had enjoyed very

---

[1] Said al-Andalusi, *Kitab Tabaqat al-Uman*, L. Cheikho, ed. (Beirut: al-Matba'ah al-Kathulikiyah, 1912), pp. 8–9, cited in Philip K. Hitti, *Islam and the West* (Princeton: Van Nostrand, 1962), p. 166.

[2] Zeine N. Zeine, *The Emergence of Arab Nationalism* (Beirut: Khayats, 1958), pp. 17–18.

extensive contacts with Europe for many decades. The Ottoman state had been a European power since its earliest days (the Ottomans entered Europe as early as 1354; within a hundred years they entrenched themselves throughout the Balkans) and had borrowed very freely from European states, especially in the field of military technology. Nor were appropriations limited to practical matters; Mehmed the Conqueror, for example, had invited Italian scholars and artists to Constantinople after the capture of that city in 1453.

But as the Empire decayed, such contacts became more and more limited and opposition to change became more and more deep-seated. One factor for this attitudinal retrogression must have been the ossification of the educational system discussed earlier. As obscurantism became the norm within madrasas and palace schools, students were increasingly taught to accept a body of infallible and eternal truths. The earlier skepticism and flexibility that had marked Ottoman education disappeared, and with it the willingness by the graduates who occupied the highest posts in the religious and administrative institutions to question accepted values and beliefs or to tolerate any innovation that might conceivably endanger the existing way of life or their position within the state.

The decline of Ottoman power had many causes, including the economic crises resulting from the expansion of Europe and the subsequent disruption of Ottoman trade and finance, and the exhaustion of fresh sources of revenue as the limits of empire were reached. Nor can one overlook noneconomic factors such as the corruption and weakness of many rulers due, to a significant extent, to the ways in which future sultans were selected and raised. And, as we have already stressed, once inept leadership came to rule, various institutional arrangements such as patterns of recruitment and educational preparation for high office inevitably decayed. Paralleling the corruption of the secular institutions was the bureaucratization of the ulema, which led to the deterioration of the religious institution and thus of the educational system itself, so that, as we have seen, a reinforcing cycle of corruption and decay was established.[3]

Regardless of the causes, this decay, against which various re-

[3] For an excellent analysis of the causes of Ottoman decay see Bernard Lewis, *The Emergence of Modern Turkey* (London: Oxford University Press, 1961), pp. 21ff.

formers and statesmen had warned since the days of Suleiman the Magnificent, meant the gradual and steady erosion of the Empire's frontiers as the central administration proved unable to maintain effective control in the outlying territories. Many of these provinces gained a position of almost total autonomy or else fell under the influence of European states, and rebellion became commonplace.

In the European provinces, in North Africa, and in the Levant, local dynasties came to power which, while nominally recognizing the suzerainty of the Porte, pursued almost completely independent policies. These local rulers, whether in Egypt, Iraq, Jerusalem, or Aleppo, engaged in rivalries with one another, often maintaining private armies, and except for token gestures refused to recognize the authority of Constantinople, even going as far as to enter into independent diplomatic negotiations with various European states.

The nature of the Ottoman system, which by and large delegated administration to local leaders and which made no attempt to "Turkify" the peoples of the Empire, not only facilitated these developments but actually established a shield behind which life could go on much as it always had. Thus when one adds the prevailing concept of superiority to this static isolation, it is possible to understand the extent to which the Arab world, in the shadow of Ottoman power, remained isolated from foreign influences for almost four hundred years, its somnolence shaken only by the rise and fall of local rulers such as the Mani dynasty which established its independence in the sixteenth century and rapidly extended its authority over much of the Levant before it, too, decayed into history.

Isolation, however, is not synonymous with deprivation, and despite widespread beliefs and writings to the contrary, it does not appear that the Arabs suffered culturally, socially, or economically from Ottoman rule. In fact, the evidence seems to suggest that at least some regions benefited greatly, and that the most important factors making for intellectual stagnation in the Arab provinces were domestic rivalries and the Arab "superiority complex." Such an argument has been convincingly presented by one scholar in the following words:

There is no historical evidence to support the popular view, current in the twentieth century, that the Turks were mainly responsible for Arab "backwardness" and cultural retardation for four hundred years. On the contrary, the Arab lands seem to have profited from the Turkish occupation. . . . Generally speaking, up until the middle of the nineteenth century, the Arabs seem to have suffered more from their own feudal lords, their feuds and rivalries and their conflicts with the Pashas, than from the central authority at Constantinople. Their internal dissensions, their tribal organizations and feudal institutions, their dynastic rivalries and their extreme individualism continued to keep them divided and weak.[4]

While the Ottoman Empire was losing control, first of its European provinces, then later of its Arab territories, European states were steadily increasing their influence within the Empire. European rivalries were translated into conflicting attempts to sway the Ottoman government and to gain control of its lands, thus giving birth to the "Eastern Question" as Russia, England, Austria, and France adopted conflicting policies toward the "sick man" of Europe. Some countries, such as Austria and Russia, were interested in expanding their boundaries at the expense of the Ottomans; some, especially France, were concerned with increasing their trade, commerce, and cultural influence, and with gaining control of the routes to the Far East; others, like England, strove to protect the integrity of the Ottoman Empire in order to check the growth of control and influence by their rivals, especially Russian expansion into the Mediterranean, or French control of routes to the Far East. Thus, throughout the nineteenth century, England encouraged the Porte to adopt various reforms designed to strengthen the Empire and prevent its collapse.

These became known as the Tanzimat and marked a major channel through which Western values and technology were introduced to the Middle East. The Tanzimat however had deep roots within Ottoman society and cannot be attributed solely to external pressures for reform. As early as the seventeenth century, Ottoman reformers were sponsoring systematic attempts to remedy weaknesses and abuses within the Empire. Yet their attempts to do so were inevitably rendered ineffective by the cultural limitations on change and innovation imposed by the continuing belief in an inherent Ottoman supremacy.

[4] Zeine, op. cit., p. 17. See also P. M. Holt, Egypt and the Fertile Crescent (Ithaca: Cornell University Press, 1966), p. 256.

Because weakness and decline were attributed to the decay of particular Ottoman institutions rather than European superiority, seldom did reformers recognize the need to go beyond efforts to revitalize traditional practices and prove willing to adopt a particular Western institution, especially one that might affect the fabric of their society; even more rarely did any appreciate the fundamental power imbalance of the Empire vis-à-vis Europe. The result of this attitude was to preserve traditional patterns throughout the Middle East and to render ineffectual the early Ottoman attempts to adjust to the realities of the new power factors. As long as the "myth of the Ottoman way" remained dominant, all attempts at reform were bound to be ineffectual since the essential causes of Ottoman weakness could not be tackled effectively.[5]

Reality could not be denied permanently in view of the continuing demonstrations of European superiority during the eighteenth century, and the legend was amended to include the belief that the basis of Europe's superiority was its military strength and that the balance of power could once again be redressed in favor of the Ottomans with the revitalization of the military establishment. Hence, by the time of Selim III (1789–1807) usually regarded as the first great reformer, there was widespread agreement on the need to reform the army, and Selim did, in fact, create a new military group, the Nizam-i Cedid, equipped with new weapons and trained in modern methods of warfare. This change, however, was essentially no different from earlier attempts at reform, and the creation of a new military unit was bound to be ineffective unless accompanied by the systematic reorganization of the entire military structure. Such a drastic move, however, could not be contemplated unless appropriate leadership were forthcoming to transform the Empire into a reformist polity.

A major blow was required to create the necessary dynamic conditions from which such leadership could emerge, and it came from a totally unexpected source, Napoleon Bonaparte, and occurred in a

---

[5] Stanford Shaw, "Some Aspects of the Aims and Achievements of the Nineteenth-Century Ottoman Reformers," in *Beginnings of Modernization in the Middle East*, William R. Polk and Richard L. Chambers, eds. (Chicago: University of Chicago Press, 1968), pp. 29ff.; see also Lewis, *op. cit.*, pp. 34–35.

totally unexpected place, Egypt, which at that time was one of the most isolated and backward parts of the Empire. Traditionally, Egypt had been among the richest and most important provinces of the Empire, providing foodstuffs for its populace, men for its army, and gold for its treasury. But as Ottoman power decayed, so did control over the province, and this was soon accompanied by decreasing benefits. Egypt suffered, too, for as the country became increasingly independent, it fell prey to power rivalries between various local factions with the result that the country's stability came to an end and its prosperity declined.[6]

Thus, by the end of the eighteenth century, when Egypt was almost completely independent, internal conditions were far less satisfactory than after the Ottoman conquest. Furthermore, Egypt enjoyed virtually no contacts with the outside world, since the discovery of the Cape route had meant the loss of transit trade, and as time went on the country gradually slipped into a sort of forgotten, half-ignored existence.

It took a crushing blow to transform Egypt from a backwater into a center of European activity and this was provided by the arrival of Napoleon off the coast of Alexandria in 1798. His subsequent occupation, carried out with surprising ease, finally dramatized as no other event could have the extent to which all the peoples of the Middle East—Arab, Persian and Turk alike—had deluded themselves with their arrogant notions of self-sufficiency and inherent superiority. Thus July 3, 1798, has often been selected as the date marking the beginnings of the modern era in this region.

Napoleon's invasion and its aftermath unleashed forces destined to transform the entire area, and it therefore represents the second major channel for the introduction of modernity. One of its important consequences was the placement, more strongly than ever before, of the Middle East within the orbit of European rivalries, and the nineteenth century witnessed a tremendous growth in the number of Europeans living and working in the region. As European power increased, the diplomats of various states emerged as major

[6] Stanford Shaw, *Ottoman Egypt in the 18th Century*, Harvard Middle Eastern Monograph Series, no. 7 (Cambridge: Harvard University Press, 1962), pp. 3–5.

actors in the region, and embassies and consulates became key centers of influence. Closely attached to these were various minority groups with certificates of protection granting them many prerogatives. These special privileges represented, in effect, extraterritorial rights and were an outgrowth of the capitulations originally granted by Suleiman the Magnificent to King Francis I of France in 1535 to promote trade between the two countries. In those days the balance of power had been very different indeed, and by the eighteenth century the once-limited rights of foreign nationals who lived and worked within the Empire had been greatly expanded. A particularly large percentage of the minorities enjoyed such advantages in the Levant, where, for example, Catholics were protected by France and the Greek Orthodox by Russia. The activities of the powers and their agents and nationals especially among these groups made the Levant a third route for the introduction of Western ideas into the Middle East.

In short, European influences were to flow into the region through three main channels: the Ottoman Porte, the Levant, and Egypt. Iran, as we shall see, continued in a state of relative isolation from the resulting changes, including what was to prove perhaps the most significant of all from the perspective of this study, the introduction of European concepts of education. In sharp contrast to existing educational systems which had served a highly conservative function by socializing students at all levels into an unquestioning acceptance of traditional beliefs and values, the new schools were to serve as radical agencies for change and innovation by exposing students to all aspects of European life and culture.

Egypt

The French Occupation

At the time of Napoleon's victory, Egyptian social structure corresponded closely to the feudal society model and was characterized by a wide gap between elite and mass. The social core group had traditionally consisted of a ruling class comprising Ottoman officials headed by an Ottoman governor who, as representative of the Porte, was the equivalent of the sultan. Under his supervision were the military establishment and the bureaucracy, especially the Treasury, which was responsible for maintaining the country's prosperity and collecting the appropriate revenues for the sultan. The religious hierarchy, the ulema, was responsible, as in Constantinople, for the application of Islamic law and for the administration and operation of the educational system. By the time of Napoleon's invasion, however, the composition of the ruling class had changed drastically. Its membership, which had previously consisted of Ottoman officials, was now made up of former slaves, the Mamelukes, who by the eighteenth century had emerged as the real rulers of Egypt. They were organized in "houses" which competed for power and influence, not only militarily, but also by attempting to place as many of their own men within the Ottoman hierarchy as possible. By this time, they had infiltrated the military and administration so effectively that the Ottoman governor remained the only loyal servant of the sultan— and he was almost totally powerless except insofar as he was able to utilize Mameluke divisions and rivalries to maintain the sultan's authority.[7]

Thus, when Napoleon landed, Egypt, though nominally a part of the Ottoman Empire, was actually ruled by the Mameluke beys, each of whom controlled a particular part of the country from which he extracted the resources necessary to maintain himself and his supporters. In contrast to the feudal system in Europe, however, the Mamelukes did not exercise judicial or social powers; these remained the province of Ottoman administration.[8] The real ruler of the country was the leader of the strongest Mameluke house. Beneath this Turco-Circassian ruling class was the ruled stratum—the native Egyptians. As in the other Middle Eastern states, there was almost no contact between these two groups, the leaders of the people being found among the ulema.

Into this society Napoleon arrived with his army and his corps of savants. Since he planned a permanent occupation, he brought with him engineers, doctors, archaeologists, and other scientists to advise

[7] Stanford Shaw, *Ottoman Egypt in the Age of the French Revolution* (Cambridge: Harvard Middle Eastern Monograph no. 11, 1964), pp. 3ff.

[8] Nadav Safran, *Egypt in Search of Political Community* (Cambridge: Harvard University Press, 1961), pp. 27–28.

on ways of perpetuating French rule, to aid in exploiting Egypt's resources for the needs of his expedition, and to help pass on the high French culture to the local inhabitants. Workshops of all kinds were established, a printing press was put into operation, and before long teams of scholars were studying the country's agriculture, its taxation, its administrative system, its public health facilities, and its archaeological heritage, discovering the Rosetta stone in the process. They mapped the country, investigated the possibility of a Suez canal, and in general introduced modern technology and ideas into Egypt.

It is difficult, however, to assess precisely the contribution of the French occupation to Egyptian life. It is known that in the course of the three years administrative and judicial reforms were inaugurated; that scientists and soldiers engaged in more or less limited contacts with various segments of the populace; that frequent proclamations involving the symbols and values of the French Revolution, specifically such concepts as republic, liberty, and equality, were promulgated; and that the laboratories and library of the French scientists were visited by many interested Egyptians. These myriad activities undoubtedly affected Egyptian society and culture, but the overall result of these contacts was probably far less than is usually assumed and should not be exaggerated. The potential impact was limited owing to the relatively short period of time, but more importantly because the value orientations and belief systems of the French and the Egyptians were vastly different. One indication of this cleavage is that even al-Jabarti, the great contemporary chronicler who admired many of the French innovations, fully realized the inherent threat posed by French culture to Egyptian society and described the French occupation as "the beginning of a reversal of the natural order and the corruption or destruction of all things." [9]

This sentiment was shared by other members of the ulema elite. Though impressed by the French military prowess and the efficient administration, they reacted unfavorably to the new sciences and especially to the symbols and values of the French Revolution. At best they were viewed as irrelevant to the needs of their society; at worst they were considered destructive of fundamental Islamic values.

[9] A. H. Hourani, *Arabic Thought in the Liberal Age, 1798–1939* (London: Oxford University Press, 1962), p. 51.

The only notable exception was Sheikh al-Attar, who traded Arabic lessons for " 'the arts of their countries.' He would come away from these lessons with heart and mind brimful of the new learning. 'Our countries must change,' he was accustomed to say, 'and we must take from Europe all the sciences which do not exist here.' " However, he was young and apparently of little influence at this time, though he later became rector of Al-Azhar.[10]

The real significance of the French expedition for Egypt, therefore, lay not in the values or knowledge transmitted, but in its political and social consequences. Not only did it bring Egypt into the forefront of European rivalries, opening the door wide to Westernization, but it undermined the existing social and political structure, thus making possible the emergence of new leaders who eagerly accepted Western science and technology in an effort to strengthen their power.

Obviously the French possessed neither the manpower nor the understanding of the society necessary to administer the country by themselves; they had to rely upon native Egyptians who were suddenly exposed to all aspects of a modern European bureaucracy. This was particularly true of the two basic fields of finance and administration where the Ottoman personnel who had fled were replaced by Coptic and Muslim intendants working with Frenchmen. Similarly, in the religious and judicial spheres the Turkish-speaking judges were replaced by members of the ulema who had until then been limited to the less important positions in the judicial hierarchy. The ulema also came to be the major source of representatives to the local and provincial organs and soon identified themselves with the popular will, thus achieving for a brief period, "a position and influence far exceeding anything they had dreamt of since the Ottomans had come to Egypt." [11] Hence the basic consequence of the French occupation was felt, not in the field of cultural change, but in the political arena. The destruction of the sources of power of the existing ruling class

[10] Jamal Mohammed Ahmed, *The Intellectual Origins of Egyptian Nationalism* (London: Oxford University Press, 1960), p. 5.

[11] Shaw, *Ottoman Egypt in the Age of the French Revolution*, p. 29. See also Afaf Loutfi el Sayed, "The Role of the Ulama in Egypt during the Early 19th Century," *Political and Social Change in Modern Egypt*, P. M. Holt, ed. (London: Oxford University Press, 1968), pp. 264–280.

and the placement of French and native Egyptian officials into high positions enabled a man without any ties to the previous oligarchy to assume power.

Mohammed Ali's Educational Policy
And Its Consequences

That man was Mohammed Ali, a clever, able, and ambitious military officer of Albanian origin. His path to power was made difficult by other individuals and groups who were determined to retain their positions within the country, but in the end Mohammed Ali emerged victorious. From the outset he realized that Egypt was now an important force in the international system, that events in Egypt would be watched carefully in all the chancelleries of Europe, and most carefully of all in the capital of the Ottoman Empire, whose sultan was determined to retain Egypt as part of his dominions. Hence, if Mohammed Ali were to achieve his objective of establishing hereditary rule in Egypt, he had to consolidate his own power and establish Egypt as an independent force, a truly formidable task. Egypt had a population of only about two million and, despite the shock of Napoleon's invasion, still conformed closely to the model of a traditional society.

Since the basis of power was a strong military establishment, Mohammed Ali set out to create a modern army. In so doing he was to transform the entire country, for his military ambitions could be realized only within the framework of a modern administration, economy, and society. His first requirement was for skilled manpower, and he turned to education as the prime source of officers trained in European ways.

As early as 1809 he sent a student mission abroad, and in 1816 he opened the first modern school where, in addition to the Koran and reading and writing, foreign languages (Turkish, Persian, Italian) and military subjects were taught. Before long other schools were opened, each designed to meet a specific need perceived by Mohammed Ali, particularly in the military field where schools for infantry, cavalry, artillery, and navy officers were established. A second area of concern was to produce trained personnel for the auxiliary services required by a modern military organization, and between 1827 and 1834 he opened such institutions as a medical school, a school of pharmacy, one of veterinary medicine, an engineering school, a signal school, and even a school of music to train buglers and trumpeters.[12] Besides his military aims, Mohammed Ali also wished to build up an administrative structure totally dependent upon and loyal exclusively to him, and to do so he had to replace the Copts who dominated various branches of the existing administration with his own followers. Hence he established a school of accounting (1826), civil school (1829), and a school of administration (1834). To provide manpower for his industrial and agricultural enterprises, he opened an industrial school and a school of irrigation in 1831 and a school of agriculture three years later.

Thus Mohammed Ali established an extensive network of higher technical schools of various types, each designed to provide trained manpower for a specific field. This early attempt at relating education functionally to the perceived manpower needs of the society served above all to emphasize the need for coordinated educational planning among the various parts of an educational system and the complex problems involved in attempting to establish modern educational institutions in a traditional setting.

The first difficulty was finding instructors for the schools. At the beginning the only solution was to employ large numbers of Europeans, since few Egyptians were trained in the subjects that Mohammed Ali wanted taught. This remedy soon proved costly and inefficient. Not only were the Europeans of uneven quality, but they commanded large salaries, and since few knew Arabic, interpreters (and qualified ones were extremely scarce) had to be utilized, which increased the cost of foreign teachers and the inefficiency of this method. From Mohammed Ali's viewpoint, however, the most serious weakness in using such instructors was their independence; he was unwilling to tolerate in key positions persons whose loyalty was doubtful and over whom he had no control.

For these reasons, the decision was soon made to train native Egyptians as teachers, and students were sent to Europe for this purpose. The first mission left Egypt in 1809, and by 1826 twenty-eight Egyptians were being educated in Europe. As the need became ever more apparent, their numbers increased dramatically. By 1849, an

[12] J. Heyworth-Dunne, *An Introduction to the History of Education in Modern Egypt* (London: Luzac, 1938), pp. 117ff.

additional 321 Egyptians were in Europe studying military subjects and medicine, as well as industrial arts, engineering, administration, agriculture, and science.[13]

The second problem was to find qualified students, since no modern schools existed at the lower levels of the educational system. Recourse was perforce to the graduates of traditional institutions, with obvious consequences for the quality of the new schools. Even this remedy, however, soon proved unfeasible because many parents preferred to deny their children a traditional education rather than make them eligible for enrollment in the colleges which were rightly regarded as sources of manpower for the hated military. To be a student was to be a member of the army and to be treated as such. This was the experience of the famous educator Ali Mubarak, who after gaining admission to one of the new preparatory schools in 1836 found that the quality of the institution was low, that the accommodations and the food were of poor quality, that pupils were treated harshly, and that most of the instruction consisted of military drill.[14] The easiest way for a parent to save his son from such a future was not to enroll him in any school at all, and enrollments declined accordingly.

The strength of the traditional schools was further undermined when Mohammed Ali confiscated all revenues and properties of the pious foundations which subsidized them. By 1833 the traditional educational system was so badly attended that not even poorly qualified students could be recruited, and Mohammed Ali ordered the creation of ten primary schools in upper Egypt to provide freshmen for his higher institutes. To increase the attractiveness of his colleges and to overcome existing apathy, he also provided generous subsidies of food, clothing, lodging, and an allowance.[15] These measures proved successful, enticing an adequate flow of students into the colleges, and in time the popular attitude toward modern schools changed dramatically. As it became obvious that the new system comprised an important channel of social mobility, and that graduation from its higher levels ensured a position in the bureaucracy with a guaranteed

[13] *Ibid.,* pp. 104–106; 221–222; 243ff.
[14] Lorne M. Kenny, "Ali Mubarak: Nineteenth-Century Egyptian Educator and Administrator," *Middle East Journal,* 21 (Autumn 1967), 37.
[15] Heyworth-Dunne, *op. cit.,* pp. 155–156.

income and high prestige, the number of applicants soon came to greatly exceed available spaces.

A third problem area was the absence of suitable instructional materials. European texts had to be translated, so Mohammed Ali, in his typical manner, launched a massive project using whatever translators were available. Here too, however, the Egyptian leader's ambition clearly outpaced his resources. Few translators of any kind were available, and the good ones tended to be engaged in a wide variety of other related occupations. Nor could anyone provide the quick results that the impatient ruler demanded. Characteristically he is reputed to have sliced a work on geography into three sections and assigned each part to a different translator.[16]

Such uncoordinated though determined efforts merely served to demonstrate the need to institutionalize the translation of European works in a more effective way, and in 1835 he established a school of translation within which was located a bureau of translation. It has been estimated that in the next thirteen years, this bureau, which became the focal point for all translation activities, produced over 2,000 books. This flood of European works represented a major channel for the introduction of new ideas and thus spurred the growth of an Egyptian national consciousness.[17]

The educational difficulties inherent in attempting to run a modern school without qualified teachers, students, and instructional materials are best illustrated by the following description of the medical school:

It was a most curious situation. A hundred Egyptian students from al-Azhar who knew only Arabic and who had never received any training but in Arabic grammar, Koranic exegesis, Fikh, etc., were gathered together in order to be trained in medical subjects of which they had not the slightest idea by a number of European teachers who did not know the language of their students and who themselves were not even homogeneous.

To remedy the inadequate preparation of the pupils, a special two-year preparatory course was introduced to teach the future doctors such modern subjects as French, mathematics, history, and geog-

[16] Ahmed, *op. cit.*, p. 10.
[17] *Idem.*

raphy. But even this reform was not sufficient to raise the quality of education. In the words of one commentator, "there was far too much haste about turning out men who had not learnt enough . . . there is far too much evidence to show that [the student] was [merely] . . . a miserable failure when it came to a question of practical work." [18]

These criticisms, however, should not blind us to the fact that all the students were native Egyptians—the members of the upper class, the Turks and Circassians, did not deign to attend any institution that was not designed to produce military officers (although many of the medical school graduates did serve with the Army)—thus facilitating Mohammed Ali's policy of recruiting native Egyptians into his service. This factor was to have a fundamental impact upon the stratification of Egyptian society, a point to which we shall return later.

It soon became apparent that such expedients as sending students abroad and using foreign teachers constituted merely a temporary palliative, and that it was necessary—even for the limited utilitarian educational aims of Mohammed Ali—to coordinate and diversify the educational system that had developed. By the early 1830's, the modern educational institution consisted of primary schools in every province and a large number of specialized colleges with but one preparatory school between the higher and lower levels.

The weaknesses of this unplanned, fragmented, and uncoordinated system led to the establishment in about 1834 of a commission of investigation. The commission's report recommended the total reorganization and restructuring of education. The system was to be divided into primary, secondary, and higher levels and would consist of fifty primary schools with 5,500 pupils and two secondary schools —one in Cairo with 1,500 students and one in Alexandria with 500.[19] However, because of Mohammed Ali's opposition to this scheme— whether he was too impatient to implement it or was averse to the idea of spreading education among the people is unclear—nothing much was done to change the educational system during the remainder of his reign. His able and gifted son, Ibrahim, did approve a

[18] Heyworth-Dunne, *op. cit.,* pp. 126–127, 130–131.
[19] Mohammed Ahmad El-Ghannam, "Egyptian Public School Administration: An Historical Analysis and Appraisal" (Ph.D. diss., Columbia University, 1958), pp. 60ff. See also Heyworth-Dunne, *op. cit.,* pp. 186–187.

project in 1847 to introduce Western methods, but after the death of both father and son the following year it was abandoned.

There is some disagreement among scholars concerning the extent to which Mohammed Ali's interest in education was based exclusively upon military considerations. Some have argued that when he was forced by the European powers to limit his army to 18,000 men and hence had no more use for large numbers of trained officers, he dismantled the educational system that had been so laboriously built up. That a retrenchment took place at this time is widely acknowledged, but the size of the educational enterprise that he bequeathed to his successor, Abbas I (1848–1854), is unclear. Some scholars have argued that Abbas inherited an ongoing system which he practically destroyed; others that Abbas, owing to his financial difficulties, only further limited an already small enterprise.[20]

In any event, the principles that underlay the educational system during Mohammed Ali's reign and the characteristics that the schools developed during this brief period forced the Egyptian educational system into a unique mold that was to endure for many decades. Most obvious was its extreme centralization. To some extent, this may be attributed to the pervasive French influence which made it extremely likely that the French model of centralization would be adopted.[21] Equally important, however, is that this model was extremely congenial to Mohammed Ali's philosophy of government. An autocrat who concentrated all power into his own hands so that he could supervise and control every administrative detail, he naturally organized his educational enterprise in this manner as well. Furthermore, since the entire system was geared toward filling his perceived needs for trained manpower, it is quite natural that the Egyptian leader should have taken a direct and personal interest in every aspect of the educational system. Thus were the foundations for a totally centralized educational system established.[22]

[20] See Kenny, *op. cit.*, pp. 39–40.

[21] This point is stressed by Russell Galt, *The Effects of Centralization on Education in Modern Egypt* (Cairo: Dept. of Education, American University at Cairo, 1936), pp. 37ff.

[22] For a discussion of the importance of these factors, see El-Ghannam, *op. cit.*, pp. 65ff.

Second, given Mohammed Ali's aim of producing the skilled personnel needed to carry out his policies, he naturally concentrated most of his efforts upon higher institutions which were designed specifically to train officials and officers. Thus the educational system constituted a pipeline into government service, and the notion that higher education represented preparation for an administrative career and, indeed, that such training entitled an individual to these positions, was also soon firmly established.

Third, the modern system was strongly elitist in character, a feature that was reinforced by the neglect of the lower levels. Even when Mohammed Ali realized that other schools were essential if qualified students were to be recruited, he opened only a limited number and discriminated against them. Regardless of whether this was owing to Mohammed Ali's concern for rapid results or to a fear of the consequences of a people exposed to modern ideas, the result was that the traditional schools remained the only source of education available to the mass of the populace.

Fourth, Mohammed Ali made a conscious decision to bypass the existing schools and not to attempt to create a modern system for all. Many observers have subsequently severely criticized this decision, but others have emphasized the numerous difficulties inherent in any attempt to create an integrated system.[23] There was, in fact, little reason for Mohammed Ali to have adopted such a policy, for he was not interested in educational reform per se and his needs could be met by the new system. Moreover, he was concerned with power factors and knew that any attempt to abolish the duality would antagonize the ulema. In the last days of Mameluke rule, they had acquired a new prominence and represented a potentially dangerous opposition which Mohammed Ali promptly sought to weaken and to neutralize by expropriating the pious foundations and other sources of their wealth, exploiting rivalries, and, when necessary, exiling or imprisoning a particular recalcitrant. As a result, not only did the power of the ulema elite decline but they became even more conservative than heretofore and, unlike their brethren in the Ottoman Empire,

---

[23] Afaf Lutfi al-Sayyid Marsot, "Modernization among the Rectors of the Al-Azhar, 1798–1879," in Polk and Chambers, *op. cit.*, pp. 276ff. See also Sadek H. Samaan, *Value Reconstruction and Egyptian Education* (New York: Teachers College, Columbia University, 1955), p. 86.

opposed all reforms. We have already noted that the French occupation had little impact upon this group, which remained committed to medieval scholasticism; now they "entrenched themselves in their citadel [Al-Azhar] and clung to the status quo, for any change became identified with the new order of things and implied a hidden menace." [24] As long as the ulema elite did not oppose him, Mohammed Ali found such a situation acceptable and saw no reason to provoke hostility and opposition by promoting reforms that affected their educational institutions.

In any event, two separate and parallel systems of education, the modern and the traditional, emerged within the country, each committed to radically different value-orientations. In this manner, an institutionalized cleavage was created that was to have important consequences for Egypt's future development: the elite-mass gap was to be perpetuated and the intellectuals of the country were to be divided between those who had graduated from the religious schools and those who were the products of the modern institutions.

Perhaps the most significant legacy that Mohammed Ali bequeathed to Egypt was the transformation of the social core group. Until his reign, Egyptian society consisted of a Turco-Circassian ruling class and an indigenous mass, with the ulema linking these two strata. We have already seen how he moved quickly and positively to consolidate his position against possible opponents by neutralizing the ulema elite and, in effect, isolating them from the political mainstream. To realize his ambitious plan of founding a hereditary monarchy, Mohammed Ali also had to create a new core pattern.[25] He achieved this goal by displacing the Copts, by integrating the Turco-Circassian community into Egyptian society, and by utilizing the modern educational system as a channel of mobility through which native Egyptians could, for the first time, achieve positions of power and influence. Members of the existing ruling class were encouraged to settle in rural areas through generous land grants, a temptation to which many succumbed even though it meant moving away from Cairo, the center of power and influence. Most yielded simply because the eco-

---

[24] Marsot, *op. cit.*, p. 272.

[25] For an analysis of this change see Ibrahim Abu-Lughod, "The Transformation of the Egyptian Elite: Prelude to the Urabi Revolt," *Middle East Journal*, 21 (Summer 1967), *passim*.

nomic basis of their power could be maintained, and in any case the chances of successfully defying Mohammed Ali were minimal. At the same time, native Egyptians were recruited into important administrative positions, including the many new economic enterprises. The position of this new elite which had been trained in the modern schools was strengthened by the liberal financial emoluments attached to high office. These were usually in the form of land grants so that both the older Turco-Circassian group and the new Egyptian administrative elite shared a common economic interest that was to serve as a powerful factor in the emergence of a new integrated ruling class.

Mohammed Ali's school system also contributed to this integration in another way, because Arabic was the medium of instruction. The decision to use Arabic in the schools was, in fact, based upon the simple consideration that the majority of students knew only that language, but the consequences were far-reaching, for the existing dichotomy of language and culture was destroyed. Until now, communications between the ruling class, which spoke Ottoman Turkish, and the Egyptians, who spoke Arabic, had been severely limited, thus maintaining societal cleavages and restricting the opportunities for mobility. Now the foundations were laid for the emergence of Arabic as the national language and, in time, for the cultural integration of the society. Moreover, the increasing use of Arabic in the higher levels of the administration was a precise indicator of the degree to which Egyptians were gaining membership in the administrative elite. Before long, Arabic as well as Turkish had to be utilized as the graduates came increasingly to occupy governmental posts. As early as 1840, the extent to which Arabic was used in the administration was noticed by foreign observers; in 1858 it was decreed that all official correspondence be conducted in Arabic.[26] Within a few decades, Arabic completely replaced Turkish, thus signifying that a circulation of elites had taken place within the Egyptian bureaucracy. Now the traditional cleavage between an Ottoman-Circassian elite and Egyptians in lower ranks was to be found only in the military. There the high posts remained the preserve of the Ottoman-Circassian group, and the discontent of the junior Egyptian officers with this situation was

[26] Gabriel Baer, "Social Change in Egypt, 1800–1914," in Holt, op. cit., p. 150.

one of the factors that provoked the nationalist revolt led by Colonel Arabi in 1881.

Abbas, Said, Ismail, and Tewfik

The reign of the next two rulers, Abbas I (1848–1854) and Said (1854–1863), was a period of neglect and regression as far as education was concerned. With the failure of a project in 1854 to establish a modern school system, no educational reforms took place until Ismail assumed the throne in 1864. To a significant extent this ruler's concern for education was the result of a fundamental change in popular attitudes toward the schools. Whereas the populace, during the early years of Mohammed Ali's reign, had been apathetic and even hostile toward the idea of a modern education, its utility had become so visible by the end of his reign that public opinion shifted drastically, and the demand for a modern education—especially in institutions that did not possess the oppressive features of Mohammed Ali's schools—spread rapidly among the Egyptian people. The strength of this feeling is indicated by the fact that among the reasons given by the parents who signed petitions supporting the abortive 1854 reform was their approval of the voluntary nature of the project.[27]

One of the factors that influenced public opinion was the success of the various types of foreign schools established in Egypt during this period. The first type was the missionary school, supported and operated by French Catholic and, later, British, German, and American orders. Here a European education was available, though accompanied by a conservative educational philosophy and an emphasis upon religious teaching. The second type of foreign school were the *écoles libres gratuites et universelles,* nondenominational institutions sponsored by Frenchmen living in Egypt, open to Egyptian and foreign students alike. A third type was the minority school, organized and run by the local Greek, Jewish, or Armenian community. Particularly important in terms of demonstrable effects were the Jewish institutions which systematically attempted, after 1840, to provide quality training in European languages and culture. They produced highly Westernized graduates who entered the professions, business,

---

[27] Fritz Steppat, "National Education Projects in Egypt before the British Occupation," in Polk and Chambers, *op. cit.,* p. 282, no. 5.

and government service and achieved great success in their vocations.[28]

Before long, the initial reluctance of Muslim parents to send their children to foreign-sponsored schools was somewhat lessened and the number of these institutions grew rapidly from 59 in 1863 to 146 in 1878, with 12,539 students, 1,139 of whom were Muslims. The importance of these schools can readily be appreciated when it is realized that in 1878 there were in the whole of Egypt only thirty government primary schools with 5,500 students.[29] Nevertheless, many Muslim families, while convinced of the desirability of a modern education, remained reluctant to enroll their children in the foreign schools, thus increasing the pressure upon the state to open more schools.

Besides the model provided by these institutions, other more basic factors served to increase the demand for education and, indeed, accounted for the attractiveness of such schools. In these years the country fell within the orbit of European imperialism and was greatly affected by European values, knowledge, and technology. Foreign influences on all aspects of Egyptian life grew markedly and a great influx of Europeans occurred in these years, particularly after the start of construction on the Suez Canal and the outbreak of the civil war in the United States which forced Europe to look elsewhere for cotton. During Mohammed Ali's reign there were 10,000 Europeans living in Egypt. By 1863 their numbers had more than tripled to 33,000, and in the next two years the influx became a flood—in 1865, 80,000 foreigners were living there and Cairo and Alexandria became almost European cities. Before long these newcomers had gained prominence in commercial, financial, and industrial circles, an eminence due not only to the special privileges accorded them by the Capitulations, but also to their educational background. Further spurring the awareness of the importance of a modern education were the attempts by the upper class to imitate and assimilate Western ways; the obvious fact that the graduates of the modern schools established

---

[28] For a useful discussion of the foreign schools, with special emphasis upon those of the Jewish community, see Jacob M. Landau, "The Beginnings of Modernization in Education: The Jewish Community in Egypt as a Case Study," in Polk and Chambers, *op. cit.,* pp. 299–312.

[29] Steppat, *op. cit.,* pp. 283, 293–294.

by Mohammed Ali had prospered and achieved elite status; and the growing awareness by many reformers and nationalists that education had to serve as the basis for the development of Egypt and the achievement of economic independence.[30]

When Ismail came to the throne, therefore, he promptly reactivated the Department of Education (which had been closed in 1854), established some primary and secondary schools, and began planning a new educational policy. The result was the first organic law devoted to education, the Law of 10 Rajab 1284 (November 7, 1867), which provided for the total reorganization of education. The statute sought to end the duality that characterized the educational system by reforming the kuttabs and integrating them with the modern schools. Such a step had been discussed for some time by reformers, but the very size of the traditional educational establishment and the delicate political, religious, and social issues involved had served to prevent its adoption. The new law emphasized the reform of a relatively small number of traditional schools—the larger ones (those with more than seventy students) located in the major cities. Their curriculum was to be totally reorganized to include courses in economics, history, geography, and a foreign language. The majority of the kuttabs, however, were largely neglected, though they were also to be brought under the state's control for the first time. The only changes in these institutions was the addition of mathematics to the curriculum, the requirement that a teacher possess a diploma, and a provision that they be encouraged to expand into the larger, more modern type of school. Finally the law provided that the government would help to establish eight "central schools" (below the secondary level) in the provincial capitals where graduates of the larger kuttabs could enroll to study such subjects as zoology, botany, and agriculture. Since the government was financially hard-pressed, the funds to implement this law were to be derived largely from private sources, including existing pious foundations, school fees paid by parents (an innovation for government schools), and public donations. By charging fees (which soon became the practice in all state schools except the higher ones, which continued to train persons for the bureaucracy) the authors of the law hoped not only to spare the treasury new obligations which it

---

[30] Steppat, *op. cit.,* pp. 283–284; Baer, *op. cit.,* p. 158.

could not fulfill, but also to further arouse public interest in education through the financing of their children's schooling.[31]

This act, however, was never fully implemented, owing to administrative and especially financial difficulties. A few new schools were opened and the quality of a number of the larger traditional institutions did improve, but most kuttabs continued to function as they had for centuries. The attempt to bring them under government supervision, to modernize their curricula, was not particularly successful.

Leading administrators, especially Ali Mubarak, were aware of these failures. In 1871 he drew up another reform program for provincial education and, convinced that reform was dependent above all upon finding qualified teachers, founded the House of Science (Dar al-Ulum) in 1871 where students from Al-Azhar who were planning to become teachers could attend lectures on modern and traditional subjects. The following year a regular teachers' college was established there and fifty students were recruited from Al-Azhar. The curriculum included both traditional subjects—Arabic language and literature, Koranic exegesis and law—as well as mathematics, science, history, and geography. The impact of the school, however, was not particularly great. Only fifty students graduated between 1873 and 1881 and they proved indistinguishable in style from the other teachers, so that, not surprisingly, the atmosphere in most schools continued to be one of traditional pedanticism.[32]

This period also witnessed an attempt to reform Al-Azhar. With Khedive Ismail's support a comprehensive and thorough reform program was drawn up. Before long, however, Ismail decided not to promote the project, perhaps because he weighed the political consequences and felt it important to maintain the support of the ulema who naturally were opposed, perhaps because he felt it would be more rewarding to create a new institution to train teachers and judges and to concentrate his resources upon the establishment of the Dar al-Ulum. In any case, this episode emphasizes once again the crucial role of strong leadership in bringing about change in an educational system, for his withdrawal of support proved, of course, fatal to the project. In 1872, however, a reform was successfully introduced

---

[31] For details of this act and its consequences see Steppat, *op. cit.,* pp. 289–290.

[32] *Ibid.,* p. 294.

whereby students had to pass a final examination in eleven fields before graduating. Given our earlier discussion of the ulema mentality, it should not be surprising that conditions were now worse than before —within a short span of time only those eleven subjects came to be offered instead of the previous twenty-one, so that students were now exposed to only half of the badly taught curriculum they had studied before.[33]

Public interest in, and governmental concern with, education continued to increase while the country's financial situation continued to deteriorate. Ismail was an extravagant ruler who borrowed money freely at usurious rates from European banks (during his reign Egypt's debt grew from about seven million pounds in 1863 to almost 100 million pounds thirteen years later). Finally, in 1879, England and France intervened to secure his deposition, and his son, Tewfik, acceded to the throne. These events spurred the growth of nationalist sentiment and soon the nationalists, led by Colonel Ahmed Arabi, an Egyptian of peasant stock, were represented in the government, which determinedly initiated a renewed effort to resolve the country's educational problems. In that year a report was prepared which criticized the neglect of the rural populace and the poor quality of primary and secondary schools. A commission was subsequently established to draw up a plan for the complete reorganization of the educational system. The dual system was to be abolished; religious schools were to be gradually replaced by new primary schools, and additional secondary schools and colleges were to be opened. The government moved promptly to implement the scheme, opening up a new teachers' college and several primary schools, but the Arabi revolt and the subsequent British occupation made the entire question of education in Egypt a matter to be decided by the colonial power.[34]

Thus, between Mohammed Ali's reign and the British occupation, significant developments took place in the field of education and in turn, as we have seen, these educational developments had important consequences for Egyptian society. Perhaps most importantly, a keen awareness of the country's educational problems had been created

[33] Marsot, *op. cit.*, pp. 277ff; for the history of Al-Azhar see Bayard Dodge, *Al-Azhar: A Millennium of Muslim Learning* (Washington: Middle East Institute, 1961).

[34] Steppat, *op. cit.*, pp. 295–296.

among many people and projects to overcome the weaknesses in education had been discussed and inaugurated. Unfortunately, the results were limited owing to inadequate financial resources and often inadequate planning, so that when the British landed the Egyptian educational system remained bifurcated and elitist—the few modern schools both public and private being the domain of the urban dwellers, the traditional schools that of the mass of people. Most schools retained their authoritarian character and continued to be marked by an emphasis upon harsh discipline, the memorizing of texts in order to pass examinations, and adherence to inflexible rules and regulations handed down from Cairo. Yet the continuing efforts of the reformers to promote a more appropriate educational system and to improve the quality of teachers and of the administrative structure in general had begun to produce significant results. Indeed, the government was on the verge of abolishing the most glaring weakness of the system, the duality between the traditional and the modern schools. Unfortunately, the "temporary" British occupation prevented the implementation of this and other proposed reforms, and cemented the many existing weaknesses even more firmly into the structure and process of Egyptian education.

The Levant: Education and the Rise of Arab Nationalism

Another channel for the transmission of Western ideas into the Middle East was the activities of Europeans, especially missionaries, in the Levant. That they were able to establish themselves so firmly here may be credited to Mohammed Ali, whose ambition left an enduring heritage, not only within Egypt itself, but also upon Syria and Lebanon. Following the example of Napoleon, he sent his armies, under the leadership of his able son, marching into Syria, but unlike the great Frenchman, Ibrahim soon established his control over the region. Ibrahim was a wise and tolerant governor whose policies provided such an impetus to education that, though he was soon forced out, the area became, within half a century, a major center of cultural life in the Arab world.

Missionary activity in the Levant can be traced as far back as the twelfth century and educational activities by French missionaries, especially Jesuits, to the seventeenth century, but the effectiveness of these efforts was severely limited by the hostility of the Muslim population.[35] As a result the orders were able to minister only to the Catholic minorities, and their impact on the region was very small. Under Ibrahim's benign rule this pattern changed drastically. By attempting to eliminate discrimination against Christians and Jews, Ibrahim created a climate within which missionary activity was to flourish. Expanded activity led to vigorous competition, since the first American Protestant missionaries who had arrived in Beirut in 1823 had, in the absence of any Protestant community, turned their attention toward other Christian groups. The result of these proselytizing efforts was a renewal of French missionary fervor, but within a few years the emphasis of most missionaries had turned toward the wider goal of education.

The first modern school had been established in the village of Ayn-Tura in 1734 by the Jesuits, and though their order was suppressed in 1773, the Lazareths continued their work; the boys' school they opened in Damascus in 1755 is still functioning. In 1831 the Jesuits, stimulated by the American endeavors, were permitted to return by Ibrahim, and within a few years had opened a large number of educational institutions. In 1848 they founded a seminary at Ghazir that became the famous and influential University of St. Joseph in 1874. Schools on all levels were opened by all the Catholic orders, including, in 1846, a girls' school, which provided the first opportunity for women in the area to acquire a modern education. These efforts were matched by the Americans who also opened many excellent schools in Beirut, Jerusalem, and throughout the Lebanon; by 1860 their thirty-three schools enrolled 1,000 students, almost 200 of whom were girls.[36] In 1866 the renowned American University of Beirut opened its doors under the name of the Syrian Protestant College, and though its beginnings were humble—"We commenced our first class in a hired dwelling house of six or seven rooms, badly situated and poorly ventilated, where we continued for two years suffering many inconveniences and subject to the derisions of our enemies" [37]—it rapidly

---

[35] Philip K. Hitti, "The Impact of the West on Syria and Lebanon in the Nineteenth Century," *Journal of World History*, 2 (1955), 611–612.

[36] *Ibid.*, p. 612; George Antonius, *The Arab Awakening* (London: Hamish Hamilton, 1938), p. 42.

[37] Cited in Elie Kedourie, "The American University of Beirut," *Middle Eastern Studies*, 3 (1966), 75.

became a leading educational institution and, together with the French university, had a significant impact upon the region.

Ibrahim's influence upon local education was not limited to his tolerant attitude toward religious minorities. He was, like his father, concerned with the development of an educational enterprise that would produce the human resources he needed for his army, and he established several primary schools and three military colleges where students were subsidized at government expense and trained as army officers. The impact of these schools was not great since they functioned only between 1834 and 1840, when the Egyptians were forced to retreat from Syria, but they did spur the development of other schools since many parents wished their children to receive an education but did not wish to see them trained as Egyptian army officers. Far more significant were the literary consequences of the occupation. Numerous books on a wide variety of subjects, printed in Cairo, now became readily available in the area and were purchased by a large number of persons in different walks of life.[38]

The renewed intellectual life produced a new generation that created, first, an Arabic cultural revival and, by the end of the century, a philosophy of Arab nationalism that was to have repercussions throughout the region. However, it is easy to overemphasize the missionaries' contribution to these developments, and many who have written on this subject have done so. One writer argues succinctly, for example, that "it was through these [educational] institutions that modern Western ways of thought penetrated Syria. The most potent of these new ideas were nationalism and democracy."[39] This view, though commonplace, is at best an oversimplification of a complex phenomenon, and the role of Western educational institutions in shaping the nationalist movement deserves a detailed reappraisal. Such an analysis would distinguish between the different schools and attempt to find answers to questions such as: What types of students entered these schools? How many graduates were there? What did they learn? What types of extracurricular activities did they engage in? What po-

[38] A. L. Tibawi, *A Modern History of Syria* (London: Macmillan, 1969) p. 88. For more details see his *American Interests in Syria, 1800–1901* (Oxford: Clarendon Press, 1966), pp. 68ff.

[39] J. B. Glubb, *Syria, Lebanon, Jordan* (New York: Walker, 1967), p. 117.

sitions did the graduates occupy? What was the role of the graduates in the Arab nationalist movement specifically?

At present the data available to answer these questions are extremely limited, but certain tentative conclusions can be drawn. It is necessary, first, to distinguish between the impact of the French and the American institutions. Although the Syrian Protestant College and St. Joseph's University were founded by missionaries at about the same time as an outgrowth of their religious rivalries, the two institutions from the outset possessed very different characteristics stemming from the varied orientations of the founders. St. Joseph's always emphasized religious training and attachment to French culture. The Syrian Protestant College, on the other hand, viewed Protestantism not as an end in itself but as a means of improving the life of its graduates and came to define religion in very liberal terms. These differences were reflected in the actual functioning of the institutions, the French one emphasizing traditional ideas, the American proving far more innovative and receptive to concepts with radical implications. For this reason, the impact of the two institutions upon the local communities was very dissimilar. This generally neglected distinction has been described in the following words:

True to its Protestant-American tradition of freedom of thought and propagation of individual and social welfare, AUB became a fertile ground for radical ideas such as Arab nationalism and anti-imperialism which were not welcomed by the Turks nor by the French after them. In contrast USJ had a different development. In political attitudes it remained largely subservient to French interests, the same interests which gave it protection. Instead of producing radicals and nationalists its graduates turned out to be (at least until World War II) outstanding theologians, orientalists, and professionals.[40]

In broader terms the existence of these two institutions, each with its own cultural orientation, contributed greatly to the division of Lebanese life by socializing their students into particular values and orientations which often had more relevance to America and France than

[40] Munir Antonios Basashur, "The Role of Two Western Institutions in the National Life of Lebanon and the Middle East: A Comparative Study of the American University of Beirut and the University of St. Joseph" (Ph.D. diss., University of Chicago, 1964), p. 59.

to the local situation. On the other hand, it has also been suggested that the results of this fragmentation may have proved helpful to the development of a pluralistic society in Lebanon.[41]

Although this distinction between the French and the American schools is useful and necessary, the extent to which the latter was in fact a "fertile ground for radical ideas such as Arab nationalism and anti-imperialism," especially during the late nineteenth and early twentieth centuries, remains unclear. In its early days the American missionaries emphasized conversions and their proselytizing zeal repelled almost every Muslim with whom they came into contact. The philosophy of these schools, which was reflected in the commonplace requirement that students attend services daily and that teachers pass a religious test, is clearly illustrated by the refusal of the Syrian Protestant College in 1887 to modify its regulations for the benefit of Muslim and Jewish students on the grounds that "we are far more anxious to establish a Christian college than we are to increase the number of our students." As late as 1909 the trustees refused to compromise when Muslim and Jewish students went on strike in protest over this issue.[42] In such an environment few young Arabs were likely to develop nationalistic feelings. Nor was the usual diet of courses in religion, language, literature, and mathematics calculated to arouse their ideological imaginations. Another factor in assessing the impact of these schools is the relatively small number of persons whom they actually trained. In 1879, for example, only five students graduated from the Syrian Protestant College.[43]

Under these conditions it is impossible to accept the claim advanced by George Antonius in his influential book, *The Arab Awakening,* that the Syrian Protestant College's influence on the Arab revival, *at any rate in its earlier stage* [my emphasis], was greater than that of any other institution." Similar reservations apply to his assessment of the impact of the publications sponsored by the American missionaries:

The educational activities of the American missionaries had, among many virtues, one outstanding merit; they gave pride of place to Arabic, and,

[41] *Ibid.,* pp. 311–312.
[42] Kedourie, *op. cit.,* pp. 84, 87ff.; see also Zeine, *op. cit.,* pp. 46ff. The quote is from Kedourie, p. 83.
[43] Zeine, *op. cit.,* pp. 50–51.

once they had committed themselves to teaching in it, put their shoulders with vigour to the task of providing an adequate literature. In that, they were the pioneers; and because of that, the intellectual effervescence which marked the first stirrings of the Arab revival owes most to their labours.[44]

There is no doubt that the decision of the Americans under Eli Smith to produce their own textbooks did have important consequences. Until then Arabic newspapers were nonexistent, no bookseller was to be found in Damascus or Aleppo, and the output of the presses that had been established in Istanbul and Cairo in 1816 and 1822 was seldom available in the Levant. Now a printing press was established locally and a publication program which included a translation of the Bible undertaken. The Jesuits soon followed suit, the Catholic Press being established in 1853, and they too turned out many important scientific, cultural, and historical works.[45] Nevertheless the above claim, which one scholar has labeled "a fiction," [46] cannot be substantiated. Moreover it is important to keep the work of the missionaries in perspective and not to overlook the many activities sponsored by Muslims themselves. As one scholar who undertook a detailed study of this question has pointed out:

Unfortunately both the character and the forces that contributed to the rise of the [great educational and literary] movement have long been obscured by partisan or uncritical presentation. By some writers the rise and development of the movement is ascribed exclusively to Protestant or more particularly American missionary effort; by others to Catholic missions, by most to Christians to the exclusion of Muslims, but by none to a combination of native development and foreign efforts. . . . the claim . . . that the missionaries were instrumental in the "rediscovery" of the Arabic literary heritage, is untenable.[47]

Such a reappraisal places the profound impact of missionary activities in a more appropriate context, for it is not necessary to exaggerate their contributions to recognize the important role they have played in the region. Missionary schools did serve as important models for local governments to emulate, they did represent benchmarks of educational quality, they did introduce many important sub-

[44] Antonius, *op. cit.*, p. 43.
[45] *Ibid.*, p. 38.
[46] Kedourie, *op. cit.*, p. 87.
[47] Tibawi, *Modern History of Syria*, pp. 140–141, 145.

jects including medicine, dentistry, and engineering, they did pioneer in the field of women's education, and, over the years, they trained many persons who came to occupy important administrative, political, and cultural posts.[48]

The British Occupation of Egypt

It can be argued that colonialism is inherently conservative since, in order to maximize economic benefits and minimize political instability, it desires to maintain and even strengthen the existing system. Such an orientation does not give education a high priority, and it is not surprising that education was usually neglected in colonial areas —as embittered nationalists often point out—except insofar as its conservative tendencies could be utilized to help maintain the status quo. In the long run, such policies, which were not completely motivated by the selfish interests of the colonial powers, proved to be dysfunctional both in maintaining colonial rule and later in postcolonial attempts at modernization. This was particularly the case in Egypt, where the British, explicitly viewing the occupation as a period of tutelage during which they should not make basic changes in the local society, could therefore sponsor no fundamental reforms in education. Buttressing this philosophical orientation was the fear of Lord Cromer (the British agent and consul general who actually ruled the country), based on the Indian experience, that educational reform and expansion would lead to the development of a nationalist, anti-British elite, and his belief that education was not, in any case, a governmental responsibility. Hence previous educational expansion not only came to an almost complete halt, which was justified in British eyes by the need to eliminate the large Egyptian debt and restore financial stability to the country, but various steps were taken to minimize the politically destabilizing potential of the existing educational system.

Since fiscal relief was accorded the highest priority, Lord Cromer drastically reduced expenditures for education and sought to make the system largely self-supporting by eliminating fellowships and increasing tuition fees. In 1881, 70 per cent of the students had received

[48] Hitti, "Impart of the West," pp. 616–617.

some sort of subsidy from the government; by 1892, 73 per cent of the students were paying all their own expenses. This policy certainly eliminated a drain upon the treasury—throughout most of this period only about 1 per cent of the budget was devoted to education—but ignorance and illiteracy were also fostered.[49] Such a policy also meant that only those who could afford an education would receive one and that the existing upper class would monopolize all the high-level positions within the society. In other words, the modern schools would no longer serve as a channel of upward mobility; rather they were to freeze the existing social structure.

To make education a largely self-supporting affair, Cromer not only increased the revenues provided by the students, but also moved to reduce governmental expenditures. He consolidated some and abolished other higher institutes and reduced enrollments at primary and secondary levels. By 1892, the only higher schools that remained were law, medicine, and engineering, and training schools for police, military officers, and teachers. The total number of students enrolled in primary and secondary schools in 1890 was 5,761 and 734, respectively.[50]

Cromer, however, was motivated by considerations other than fiscal requirements. His own philosophical bias stressed individualism, and he believed that the elite of a country had to be self-reliant. Education, too, was a private and not a governmental responsibility and members of the upper class ought to value it sufficiently to be willing to pay for it. On a more pragmatic level, Cromer regarded tuition charges as a useful means of controlling inputs into the system. Though he might not be able to control the popular demand for education, he was able, by raising fees, to limit the numbers who could acquire a modern education and hence be eligible for governmental positions. In this manner economic considerations meshed neatly with political goals, since the British wished to create an efficient adminis-

[49] For an excellent discussion of British educational policies in Egypt see Robert Tignor, *Modernization and British Colonial Rule in Egypt, 1882–1914* (Princeton: Princeton University Press, 1966), pp. 319–348. The figure on subsidies is cited on p. 324. The budget figure is taken from Roderick Matthews and Matta Akrawi, *Education in Arab Countries of the Near East* (Washington: American Council on Education, 1949), p. 16.

[50] Tignor, *op. cit.*, pp. 322–323.

trative structure that would serve as an effective instrument for the implementation of their policies. They were concerned with the need to prepare Egyptians for administrative careers, but such preparation was to be limited in two ways. First, the number to be trained should not exceed the capacity of the administration and of the economy to absorb them. Second, they should be trained to fill only the middle and lower levels of the bureaucracy, since the high-level posts were reserved for Europeans, especially Englishmen. By not providing a university education, the British hoped to prevent the creation of an educated group that might provide leadership for a nationalist movement, and by limiting the output of other schools they sought to prevent an oversupply of frustrated and alienated graduates unable to find satisfactory employment to swell the ranks of such a movement. By providing some sort of rudimentary education for the masses in the traditional kuttabs, they hoped to socialize them toward accepting the status quo. These goals were described officially as "to spread as widely as possible, amongst both the male and female population, a simple form of education consisting of an elementary knowledge of the Arabic language and of arithmetic. In the second place [the government] has wished to form a highly educated class suitable for the requirements of the government service." [51]

The implementation of these policies meant that the modern educational system was more than ever a pipeline into government employment, and Cromer linked education and administration even more tightly together when he divided the bureaucracy into two levels and decreed that primary and secondary school certificates were required for appointment. In technical fields, too, a diploma was viewed as a passport to government service. In the words of one contemporary observer:

Government service was indeed the haven which all schoolboys tried sooner or later to reach. Even the candidates from primary schools were employed on the lowest rungs of the clerical ladder, at a meagre salary of a few pounds a month, secondary school boys receiving slightly higher pay: while those who graduated successfully from the Higher Colleges were assured of employment in the junior ranks of the technical services,

---

[51] Cited in Charles Issawi, *Egypt at Mid-Century* (London: Oxford University Press, 1954), p. 50.

being allotted to the departments—Health, Justice, Public Works, and so on—to which their qualifications entitled them.[52]

To obtain the passport was no easy matter. A rigorous examination system was utilized to maintain high standards and to limit the number of applicants to the higher levels. Only students who passed these examinations could obtain the certificates that entitled them to occupy an administrative post and the number who were able to do so was very small; usually far less than 50 per cent of the candidates taking the primary and secondary examinations passed.[53]

The combination of high fees and harsh examinations led naturally to a high dropout rate so that very few of the limited numbers of students who entered a school ever reached the point where they would be eligible to attend the examinations. Of the 201 students who entered the first year of secondary school in 1887, only seventy enrolled in the fourth-year class and many of these probably failed the final examination and did not graduate; the rate for the school of agriculture was ten graduates for forty students who entered.[54]

The examination and all other aspects of education were controlled by the Department of Public Instruction. In reality, one man was responsible for education in Egypt; Douglas Dunlop, the British advisor who administered the programs designed by Cromer, controlled Egyptian education until after World War I. Dunlop, a Scot martinet and a devout believer in centralization and strict adherence to rules, shaped the school system into a rigid, inflexible mold that made learning a stultifying experience. Regulations, syllabi, timetables, and teaching methods were all determined by him, and his decisions had to be followed rigorously in all parts of the country. The conclusion of a person who knew him was that

his aim was to produce in the schools of the Egyptian Government efficiency based on rigid uniformity and iron discipline. Efficiency of a sort there undoubtedly was, but there was a complete lack of elasticity in the system. Originality and initiative on the part of the British staff were not encouraged; if an Egyptian dared to show them he was regarded with

---

[52] Humphrey Bowman, *Middle East Window* (London: Longmans, Green, 1942), p. 53.

[53] Abn A. A. Radwan, *Old and New Forces in Egyptian Education* (New York: Teachers College, Columbia University, 1951), p. 96.

[54] *Ibid.*, p. 97.

positive disfavour. Headmasters and assistants alike were ruled by an iron Code of Regulations drawn up by Dunlop himself, a breach of which was visited by stringent penalties.[55]

Since the goal of education was to pass the dreaded examinations, the efforts of students and teachers alike were directed toward memorizing a specific body of knowledge so that the ethos of Al-Azhar, always strong within the system, came to dominate educational practices even more. The emphasis was upon rote learning, and any tendency to the cultivation of intelligence, sensitivity, and awareness that might have emerged in the schools in the years after Mohammed Ali were ruthlessly squelched. One observer has described this situation as follows:

The notes were learned by heart at their leisure time, and it was a painful but daily experience to see a crowd of boys walking up and down the courtyards or playgrounds of the school, in the intervals between lessons, the boys reconning their notebooks, and repeating the script in an audible murmur over and over again to themselves.[56]

The nature of the teaching staff and of the teaching materials also contributed to this atmosphere. The language of instruction was English, but most of the students had no contact with English outside of the classroom and little of what they learned could be properly digested. Nor were adequate textbooks available; those that did exist were badly written and boring. Most of the teachers were poorly prepared for their task. Many teachers had an Al-Azhar background and most were not even graduates of the existing teacher training institutions whose output was too small to serve the needs of the country, so that recourse was often to whoever was willing to accept a position. Teaching was held in such low regard that the government was compelled to attract students by offering them fellowships. Nor was the quality of the many English teachers any higher. Most of them were of lower-class origin who were looked down upon by Englishmen in other departments and who regarded their appointment as a preparatory step to a better post elsewhere. They were not particularly concerned with their educational responsibilities; they usually viewed the students condescendingly and took no pains to become acquainted

---

[55] Bowman, *op. cit.*, p. 42.
[56] *Ibid.*, p. 56.

with them or to make the classroom experience a fruitful one. For them, as for the Egyptian teachers, teaching involved the inculcation of feelings of obedience and discipline and the memorization of curricula drawn up in Cairo.

Discipline and obedience were the very characteristics the British desired in the Egyptians who entered the administration since the overwhelming majority were restricted to routine clerical tasks. Nor were the few Egyptians who did achieve responsible positions expected to display any initiative and leadership; such qualities were not encouraged among Egyptians at any level.

The obvious result of such socialization was that subservience and passivity became the hallmark of the Egyptian bureaucrat. As one Englishman acidly observed, "throughout his long tenure of office Lord Cromer had sedulously depressed and kept down every independent Egyptian and had filled all the high posts with cyphers with the result that the natural leaders of the people had no opportunity of leading the people." Such a policy created an administration where: "No words can express [the Egyptian official's] ineptitude, his laziness, his helplessness, his dread of responsibility, his maddening redtape formalism. His panacea in every unexpected case is the same. 'It must be put in writing; I must ask for instructions.' " The significance of such a bureaucracy for the country's development is obvious.[57]

While the modern part of the educational system was recruiting and socializing persons from the middle and upper classes in this manner, the great majority could attend only traditional kuttabs. In 1898, when additional funds became available, the British attempted to bring these autonomous schools under central government control in order to create a system that could achieve Cromer's educational goal for the mass, "the three r's in the vernacular language, nothing more." Financial support was to be provided to those schools whose curriculum was to be expanded to include courses in reading, writing, and arithmetic. The number of such kuttabs rose from 301 with 7,536 students in 1898 to 4,432 with 156,542 students in 1906.[58] Although this is an impressive increase, only a small proportion of all the kuttabs within Egypt were in fact brought under this program and, even

[57] Morroe Berger, *Bureaucracy and Society in Modern Egypt* (Princeton: Princeton University Press, 1957), p. 26; Radwan, *op. cit.,* p. 103

[58] Tignor, *op. cit.,* p. 330

in these, little change took place owing to the ancient problem of finding qualified teachers of the new subjects. Most schools were staffed by a person who could recite the Koran, and the attempt to provide well-trained instructors through the opening of two teacher training institutes was totally inadequate.

How dismally this program failed is evidenced by the Report of the Elementary Education Commission, established after World War I, which concluded that the problem of elementary education could not possibly be solved in this manner. Its analysis of the 600 kuttabs which were under government supervision revealed that "no adequate expansion of elementary education seems possible on present lines or within the limits of existing legislation." Of the other 7,000 schools it wrote:

The vast majority . . . have little educational value and are insusceptible of much real improvement. . . . The buildings are often mere hovels; the children are huddled together under the most insanitary conditions; over 95% of the children are suffering from ophthalmia; the teachers are ignorant and incompetent; sometimes they are themselves illiterate; the simplest requirements as regards equipment are generally lacking; the instruction is frequently limited to memorizing the Qur'an, work is carried on amidst a deafening babel.[59]

The attempt to expand educational opportunities for the mass entailed a diversion of resources from what most intellectuals considered a basic necessity, the establishment of a university. In 1900, Egypt still possessed only a few higher colleges whose limited focus produced, at best, narrow technicians. In the words of Mohammed Abdu:

The only schools which represent higher education in Egypt are the Schools of Law and Medicine and the Polytechnic. Of all the other sciences of which human knowledge is composed, the Egyptian may sometimes obtain a superficial notion at the preparatory schools, but it is almost impossible for him to study them thoroughly, and often he is compelled to ignore them. The result is that we possess judges and lawyers, physicians and engineers more or less capable of exercising their professions; but amongst the educated classes one looks in vain for the investigator, the thinker, the philosopher, the scholar, the man in fact of open

[59] Galt, *op. cit.*, pp. 13, 14.

mind, fine spirit, generous sentiments, whose whole life is found devoted to the ideal.[60]

Cromer never appreciated the symbolic significance of the drive for an Egyptian university, which was finally established (through public subscription) in 1908, a few months after his departure. Actually it was a university in name only and operated on a very limited scale; in 1908 the faculty consisted of two Egyptians and three Europeans. In 1910 the faculty was increased to four Egyptians and seven Europeans; altogether 107 students were enrolled, of whom 82 were Egyptians. No women were included, though special lectures were occasionally given for them.[61]

Although opportunities for higher education were extremely restricted during the British occupation, the upper class ensured that their children would receive appropriate training by sending them abroad when necessary. If a scion of an established family failed to qualify for admission to the law school, the most prestigious institution, or the medical school, he would obtain the necessary training in Europe and then return home to practice his specialty.

Some students were sponsored by the government, and the number of Egyptians studying abroad increased during these decades. The majority, however, were sent abroad privately and if the rapid population growth is taken into account, the proportion of students declined in comparison with earlier periods. Two other trends occurred during this era—a shift in interest from the study of technical subjects to the humanities, and a diversion of students from France to Britain as the most favored country for overseas study.[62]

The foreign schools in Egypt provided another means whereby the upper class could ensure their children's education. These existed at all levels—there was even a private French-run law school. Most active were the French and American missionaries whose educational standards were quite high, but even their schools tended to replicate the characteristics of the government ones and suffered from many of

[60] Cited in Tignor, *op. cit.,* p. 337

[61] H. A. R. Gibb, "University in the Arab-Muslim World," in *The University Outside Europe,* E. Bradby, ed. (London: Oxford University Press, 1939), pp. 285–286.

[62] Issawi, *op. cit.,* p. 51.

the same weaknesses. The other private schools ranged widely in quality, but the majority tended to be inferior to the public institutions, suffering from the same defects only more so. Nevertheless, the private system played a major role in Egyptian education and enrolled more students than the government schools.

The most notable contribution of the private schools was in the field of women's education. Under Ismail several girls' schools had been opened and the issue of education for women had rapidly gained the support of the intelligentsia so that by the beginning of the twentieth century the position of upper-class women within Egyptian society had changed considerably. Though sympathetic to this movement, the British were reluctant to sponsor reform in so sensitive an area of the culture and little was accomplished apart from a small expansion of educational opportunities at the primary level and the preparation of women as primary teachers. On the other hand, fellowships that had been available to girls wishing to enter primary schools were soon replaced by a fee system and upon graduation it was almost impossible for a girl to continue her education. No government secondary schools for girls existed at this time, nor did the atmosphere in the primary schools contribute very greatly to a change in the status of women; traditional attitudes were strictly enforced; in at least one school girls were required to wear veils on reaching the age of twelve. Under these circumstances it was the private and not the government schools that furthered the cause of women's emancipation in the country. In 1914, 786 girls were enrolled in public schools, whereas 5,517 attended American institutions.[63]

The philosophy of transitory, indirect rule, which was in large measure responsible for British reluctance to transform the fabric of Egyptian society, also meant that religion and religious institutions would not be subject to change so that the religious schools remained insulated from developments within the country. Al-Azhar continued to function as it had for centuries and became increasingly separated from the modern system. Previous attempts during the nineteenth century to reform this institution had been sporadic and limited in effectiveness, partly because Mohammed Ali's decision to establish a separate system had diverted the attention of reformers away from the

---

[63] Tignor, *op. cit.,* p. 343.

traditional institutions for many decades, so that Al-Azhar was largely ignored except as a source of supply for students and teachers in the new schools. The greatest pressures for change had come during Ismail's reign. At that time the noted reformer and Pan-Islamist Jamal al-din al-Afghani had lectured at Al-Azhar, but his criticism of the school had, as we have seen, little immediate effect, because of Ismail's decision not to support reform in the face of strong faculty opposition. Nevertheless, Afghani's radical ideas were implemented to a limited degree for Mohammed Abdu, who had studied with Afghani at Al-Azhar, inherited his teacher's principles, and as part of his efforts to reconcile Islam with modernity, moved to reform many of the existing practices while on the faculty there. He endeavored to change the teaching methods; he revised the curriculum to include such modern subjects as mathematics, Islamic history, literature, and geography; he improved the physical and sanitary facilities by reorganizing the library, introducing gaslighting and clean water, and improving the food, clothing, and health care available to the students. These changes, though useful, dealt only with peripheral problems and did not affect fundamental issues. No other significant reforms were undertaken during the British occupation because many Egyptian reformers, including Abdu, feared that Cromer's offers of assistance were a mask for a British policy aimed at gaining control of the existing Islamic institutions in order to perpetuate British rule. Thus Egyptian distrust and British reluctance combined to maintain the status quo within Al-Azhar, which remained a medieval institution, isolated from the mainstream of Egyptian life.[64]

As we have seen, the results of Cromer's policies in the field of education were disastrous for Egypt. Apparently he sincerely believed in the utility of education, attached great importance to it, and was even aware of how little had actually been accomplished during his term. In his memoirs he argues that, in view of the great difficulties confronting him, "it may well be a matter for surprise, not that so little, but that so much progress . . . has been made in so short a

[64] *Ibid.,* pp. 344–345; see also Dodge, *op. cit.,* pp. 70ff.; Jacques Waardenburg, "Some Institutional Aspects of Muslim Higher Education and Their Relation to Islam," *Numen,* 12 (April 1965), 114; Christina Phelps Harris, *Nationalism and Revolution in Egypt* (The Hague: Mouton, for the Hoover Institution on War, Revolution and Peace, 1964), pp. 122–123.

time." [65] But this claim is not really valid. Certainly his primary concern, the need to save the country from bankruptcy, meant that few funds would be available for education, but even when the financial crisis had been resolved only limited additional resources were diverted to the schools. The total expenditures on education between 1907 and 1912 never rose above 3.4 per cent, and between a third and a half of this sum was raised through fees.[66] It is therefore impossible to avoid a conclusion that extreme parsimony remained the rule in educational matters, even when change was possible. Similarly the other difficulties cited by Cromer, the problems of "Pashadom" and the legal nature of the British occupation, are prevarications—legally and practically the British always had the power to enforce a consistent educational policy. Obviously the real factors determining British educational policy in Egypt were not those articulated by Cromer, but rather the political and philosophical ones discussed above.

Regardless of the reasons, the British left behind a small, fragmented educational system in which some of the worst aspects of the earlier system were thoroughly consolidated and new dysfunctional features assimilated. There now existed two deeply embedded and conflicting systems of education—a traditional one for the mass and a modern one for the elite, neither of which provided the kind of training that was functional in terms of development. The condition of education was so bad that an investigatory British subcommittee concluded in 1920 that "no true social, economic, or political progress can be looked for without a complete revision of the educational system in Egypt." [67]

Nor did these policies even further British interests by promoting stability within the country. Fears concerning the link between education and nationalism proved well founded as the drive for independence was spearheaded by the educated elements. Though the first few years of the British occupation were relatively quiet, the nationalist feelings manifested in the abortive Arabi revolt remained

---

[65] Lord Cromer, *Modern Egypt* (2 vols.; London: Macmillan, 1908), II, 526.
[66] Tignor, *op. cit.*, pp. 346–347.
[67] Cited in Malcolm Kerr, "Egypt," in *Education and Political Development*, James S. Coleman, ed. (Princeton: Princeton University Press, 1965), p. 173.

dormant, and when new leadership emerged, the movement sprang into life once again. That leadership was provided by the French-educated lawyer, Mustafa Kamil, who believed strongly in education as the basis of a strong and independent Egypt and advocated many important reforms including universal free education. Students, in particular, responded to his appeal, and soon student activism—the first strike was staged in 1906 by law students—became a major factor in Egyptian political life. Students in the secular institutions were quickly joined by the Azharites who, after a strike in 1909 over curricular changes, also participated in the nationalist struggle. Mustafa Kamil's untimely death in 1908 did not mark the end of the National Party, but its importance was to be surpassed by other parties that sprang up in these turbulent years, notably the Wafd party under the leadership of Saad Zaglul.[68]

Essentially, support for the nationalist movement was provided by graduates of the modern schools—lawyers, teachers, bureaucrats, journalists, and writers—but as the tide of nationalism engulfed the country they successfully mobilized all segments of the society. They even forced such groups as the new industrialists and the landowning elite that had also emerged in the nineteenth century and that had benefited from British rule into an alliance with them. The appeal of nationalism continued to grow, and Lord Milner, who headed the commission that arrived in Egypt in 1919 to investigate the situation, reported:

Nationalism has . . . established complete dominance over all that is vocal and articulate in Egypt. From the Princes of the Sultan's family down to the children of the primary schools, the men of property, the professional men, the religious teachers (of al-Azhar), the *literati,* the journalists, the students and school-boys have all, more or less willingly, been swept into the Nationalist movement. Most serious of all, perhaps, it now permeates the official class and the upper ranks of the army.[69]

Such widespread opposition to British rule did not lead immediately to independence. The outbreak of World War I permitted postponement of an unpalatable decision, and it took several years of intense

---

[68] See Harris, *op. cit.,* pp. 67ff.
[69] *Ibid.,* p. 94.

and sometimes violent struggle by the nationalists before the British government finally terminated the protectorate in March 1922.

The Ottoman Empire

The Great Reformers

The impact of Napoleon and the threat posed by Mohammed Ali's successes in Egypt to the very existence of the Ottoman state forced a fundamental reappraisal of Ottoman perspectives and attitudes toward the West. The reforms of Selim III, usually considered the first of the great reformers, particularly his establishment of a new military unit (Nizam-i Cedid) in 1792–1793, unleashed forces that were to culminate in the fundamental reforms of Mahmud II. One reason is that Selim, a far abler ruler than many of his predecessors, understood fully the need to establish military schools if he were to successfully strengthen the Ottoman military establishment. Like his predecessors, Selim turned to France for help in organizing these schools, and the French, as before, were eager to assist him.[70] Hence, the first modern military schools, which became the precursors of a growing number of army and naval schools designed to train officers in European methods of warfare, date from his reign. These schools proved to be a most important channel for the transmission of Western technology and values into the Ottoman Empire; not only did they create a group of officers who knew French and were familiar with Western ways,

[70] For a unique and insightful analysis of the relationship between educational developments and the political and social changes that occurred during the nineteenth century and after, see Andreas Kazamias, *Education and the Quest for Modernity in Turkey* (Chicago: University of Chicago Press, 1966). These reforms are also discussed in such general historical works as Bernard Lewis, *op. cit.*, Niyazi Berkes, *The Development of Secularism in Turkey* (Montreal: McGill University Press, 1964), and Roderic H. Davison, *Reform in the Ottoman Empire, 1856–1876* (Princeton: Princeton University Press, 1963). Much important information is contained in such Turkish sources as Osman Ergin, *Maarif Tarihi* (5 vols.; Istanbul, Osmanbey Matbaası, 1939–1943), Nevzad Ayas, *Türkiye Cumhuriyeti Milli Eğitimi: Kuruluşlar ve Tarihceler* (Ankara: Milli Eğitim Basimevi, 1948), and also Faik Reşit Unat, *Türkiye Eğitim Sisteminin Gelişmesine Tarihine Bir Bakiş* (Ankara: Milli Eğitim Basimevi, 1964). This work includes appendixes listing all ministers of education through 1960, the structure of the educational system from 1857 to 1924, and a chronology of important cultural and educational events from 1727 to 1924.

but they also greatly influenced the nature of subsequent educational developments since the civilian schools benefited greatly from their experience.

Military reform, though conceived initially in a relatively narrow sense, was soon perceived by the officers and reformers who participated in Selim's Nizam-i Cedid to involve changes in the entire military structure of the Empire. The reforms of Mahmud II included the destruction in 1826 of the Janissaries, the centuries-old corps which had opposed all previous efforts at military reform in a desperate attempt to preserve its own position. Hence a fundamental distinction must be drawn between the empire of Selim III, an adaptive polity, and the empire of Mahmud II and his successors, a reformist polity.

Throughout these decades, the main goal of Mahmud II (1808–1839) was to strengthen his own position by eliminating potential sources of opposition, and to preserve the Empire from external threat, especially from Mohammed Ali, who almost overthrew the Ottoman dynasty and would have done so except for European intervention. Thus the military received the greatest emphasis, and following the destruction of the Janissaries, Mahmud II moved rapidly to build a modern army. To do so, however, was not a simple task. Recruits could be procured easily enough, but qualified officers were in extremely short supply. Only two institutions, the naval and the military engineering schools, dating back to 1776 and 1793 respectively, could produce the kind of modern officers Mahmud II needed, and their output was totally inadequate to meet the existing needs. As one expedient, Mahmud II copied Mohammed Ali and decided to send military and naval cadets in 1827 to various European capitals. At the same time, one military school after another was established to train Ottomans in the many specialities required by a modern army; in 1827 a medical school to provide doctors for the army, in 1831 the Imperial Music School whose function has been rather tartly described as being "to provide the new army with drummers and trumpeters to match its tunics and britches," [71] and in 1846 the renowned military academy, the Harbiye, was formed by the amalgamation of several existing schools. At first the Harbiye was a very small institution, about twenty-five officers graduating annually in the 1840's, but

[71] Lewis, *op. cit.*, p. 83.

the demands of the military for modern officers proved insatiable and by the 1870's the annual average had quadrupled. Within another thirty years this new total had again quintupled, about 500 cadets graduating annually in the early years of the twentieth century.[72] These graduates were to have a major impact upon Ottoman society, as we shall show later.

These institutions, in which modern subjects were taught, profoundly affected subsequent educational and political developments. As in Egypt, these colleges encountered serious problems of staffing, textbooks, and students. European instructors could be recruited, but here too this soon proved awkward and expensive and efforts were made to have native instructors trained abroad. Textbooks were translated from European languages and published by the schools themselves. This translation activity, which was later broadened and systematized, marked the first time that European works were available to Turkish students who, since no lower schools existed, were at best ill prepared and often totally illiterate. Usually the colleges had to provide their own preparatory classes; in the naval academy, for example, half the students were learning how to read and write.[73]

Nevertheless, the contribution of these schools should not be underestimated. A visitor to the engineering school in the 1780's reported that the teachers knew European languages and that the best European works and marine instruments were used. In later years most of the teaching was done by Turks and a knowledge of French was required of all students who also took courses in mathematics and military subjects in their four years at the school. According to a European observer in the early 1800's:

In their school of engineers, we find Turks engaged in mathematical studies; also a library, with all our best treatises on such subjects; instruments of geometry and astronomy, and all the details of fortifications, within and without the body of a place. . . . The school of engineers and miners contains 40 pupils who devote a number of years to the

---

[72] J. C. Hurewitz, "The Beginnings of Military Modernization in the Middle East: A Comparative Analysis," *Middle East Journal*, 22 (Spring 1968), 151, reprinted in a slightly revised form in his *Middle East Politics: The Military Dimension* (New York: Praeger, 1969), pp. 28–46.

[73] Roderic H. Davison, "Westernized Education in Ottoman Turkey," *Middle East Journal* 15 (Summer 1961), 295.

acquisition of skill in their occupation. They learn mechanics, elementary mathematics, fortification, the theory of mining, and the drawing of maps, of which they have a collection indifferently well executed.[74]

In addition to their contribution to military reforms, these schools also had an impact in a wider sense. Their graduates formed the nucleus of a small group of secular intellectuals who began to write and publish treatises on nonmilitary subjects, sometimes utilizing the printing presses attached to these institutions, which thus came to be important channels for the introduction of European science into the Ottoman Empire.[75]

Under Mahmud II, the administration was reorganized along functional lines beginning in the 1820's. His attempts to centralize power, to bind the sprawling and decentralized Empire together, led to a series of administrative and legal reforms which were to transform Ottoman life. In the short term they inevitably spurred educational change, since the madrasa system could provide neither the expert manpower to staff the new differentiated ministries nor graduates with the reformist outlook and mentality that were necessary if needed reforms were to be implemented. This lesson was slowly and painfully learned, as many projects, including the famous Gülhane Charter of 1839 with its affirmation of equality and justice for all Ottomans, could not be carried through because of opposition by entrenched elements within and without the administration.

Of all the skills required by the bureaucracy, one of the most crucial was a knowledge of a foreign language. To meet this need, Mahmud II established the well-known Translation Office (Tercume Odasi), which soon became one of the most important schools in the Empire. Located in the department concerned with foreign affairs, its employees were expected to handle the rapidly increasing flow of correspondence from foreign states. Formerly this had been the job of the interpreter of the Imperial Divan, a position monopolized by a few Phanariote Greek families, and his assistants, but the Greek revolt of 1821 made it desirable to utilize Muslim Turks for this task. Nor could the ever-increasing workload be handled efficiently in the traditional manner. Hence it became necessary to create a new office to

---

[74] Cited in Berkes, *op. cit.*, p. 76; see also p. 60.
[75] *Ibid.*, pp. 79–80.

handle relations with European powers and to train Muslims expressly for this purpose. Besides learning French, the young bureaucrats studied history, arithmetic, and similar subjects. Their daily routine kept them in contact with developments in Europe and many of them served as diplomats in Western capitals. These men, possessing that very rare skill, a knowledge of European languages, were to become the outstanding reform leaders of the next generation.[76]

The demand for trained bureaucrats, which had become evident in previous decades, accelerated greatly during this period as the number of bureaus and offices proliferated owing to the increasing activities of the state. Not only did new schools have to be created, but the nature of the training itself had to be reformed. Many years of study were required for a person to acquire the level of literary ability necessary to write state documents, and much attention was paid to the style in which documents were written. The traditional training involved a long period of carefully supervised apprenticeship in a bureau of the administration. One reason why so many years were required to become a full-fledged scribe was the complexity of the language used in official transactions, with its very heavy Arabic and Persian accretions. Punctuation was practically ignored; it was possible to write a thirteen-page document using only two sentences. One example should suffice to illustrate the intricacy and involuted character of the official language: An Ottoman scribe would write, "Your slave has been engaged in the exercise of cogitation in respect of the proposals vouchsafed by your exalted person"; a modern bureaucrat, "I have been thinking about your suggestion." [77]

The difficulties created by the use of such language had become increasingly obvious in previous decades. Various unsuccessful efforts had been made from the eighteenth century onward to simplify it, but only in the reign of Mahmud II could significant reform be achieved. Aware of the extent to which this flowery, complex language handicapped his efforts to centralize control of the communications and administrative network of the Empire and limited the output of the administration, Mahmud II sponsored the first effective measures to

---

[76] Davison, *Reform*, p. 29.

[77] Geoffrey Lewis, *Turkey* (New York: Praeger, 1955), p. 99. See also Davison, *Reform*, p. 176.

simplify and clarify the language. A new administrative literary style marked by simplicity and directness evolved under the guidance of the great Grand Vizier Mustafa Reşid Pasha who "opened a new path in stylistic matters. Most of the bureau employees began to imitate him. The Minister of Foreign Affairs Ali Efendi and Fuad Efendi who had stepped into the office of the Imperial Referendar from that of interpreter of the Imperial Divan . . . also followed Reşid Pasha's work in this respect." [78] To train administrators he initiated a program of free lessons in Arabic and Persian for clerks and established two new schools, the Mekteb-i Maarif which was to produce some of the leading reformers, and the Mekteb-i Ulum-u Edebiye, which was not only to train translators and interpreters but also to serve as a center for the translation of many European scientific works.[79]

Thus, beginning in 1838 with the establishment of a law school, one civilian institution after another was opened, and before long a number of higher civilian schools to train experts for the bureaucracy had been built up which paralleled the traditional system and supplemented the military colleges. Though they benefited from the experiences of the latter, the new institutions also suffered from many of the same deficiencies, the most serious being the lack of adequate preparation in the lower schools. Various remedies were again adopted: The school of medicine, for example, where all courses were taught in French, increased its program of studies to nine years in 1843; the first four were wholly preparatory, the students learning mathematics, history, geography, and French literature.[80]

The experiences of the higher civilian institutions spurred reformers' efforts to establish primary and secondary schools. To do so involved a major break with past practice, since education at these levels was traditionally the responsibility of rich and pious persons. Hence a new educational philosophy gradually emerged and led ultimately to the development of an integrated and comprehensive state-controlled educational system. As early as 1824, Mahmud II, recog-

[78] Şerif Mardin, "Some Notes on an Early Phase in the Modernization of Communications in Turkey," *Comparative Studies in Society and History* (April 1961), 262.
[79] Berkes, *op. cit.*, pp. 106–107.
[80] *Ibid.*, p. 177.

nizing the fundamental importance of education to his efforts, had issued an edict concerning primary education and a minister of education was subsequently appointed in 1838. The decree stated:

While, according to Muslims, learning the requisites of religion comes first and above everything else and while these requisites take precedence over all worldly considerations, the majority of people lately avoid sending their children to school and prefer to give them to a trade as novices to artisans when they reach the age of five or six because of their ambition to earn money immediately. This condition is the cause not only of widespread illiteracy but also of ignorance of religion and, hence, has been a primary cause of our misfortune. As it is necessary to deliver the Muslims from these worldly and other-worldly misfortunes, and as it is a religious obligation . . . irrespective of trade or occupation, to learn the affairs of religion and the faith of Islam, no man henceforth shall prevent his children from attending school until they have reached the age of adulthood. . . . As for the school masters they shall instruct their pupils carefully and, following the teaching of the Glorious Kur'an they shall educate them in the faith and obligations of Islam.[81]

This decree, however, merely reaffirmed the traditional view of education, and a modern integrated educational system was not to be created for many years.

Sultan Abdul Mejid shared his predecessor's interest in education and on March 7, 1845, proclaimed: "the will of the Padishah is that ignorance, the source of much evil, should vanish from among the people." To implement this concern a commission was convened shortly thereafter which issued an imaginative though unrealistic report calling for the creation of an integrated system of primary and secondary education culminating in an Ottoman university. Most of these proposals remained on paper, and quantitatively the results of the reform were not particularly impressive. By 1851 six new secondary schools were in operation, attended by 870 students who received free instruction in Arabic, Turkish, Persian, Islamic, Ottoman, and world history and religion.[82]

These schools were called *rüşdiye* (from *rüşd,* "adolescence") and

[81] *Ibid.,* pp. 100–101.
[82] Davison, "Westernized Education," p. 296; Kazamias, *op. cit.,* p. 59; B. Lewis, *op. cit.,* p. 112.

were designed to prepare graduates of the traditional primary schools for the higher military and civil colleges which already existed. As a result, their curriculum was a mixture of modern and traditional subjects. The precise date of the founding of the first of these schools is uncertain. Some scholars place the date as early as 1838; others as late as 1847. To meet the obvious need for teachers in these new schools the Darül-muallim was opened in 1848. Its students were recruited from religious schools, and its curriculum included, besides courses in science and the humanities, many religious subjects as well as Arabic and Persian.[83] Hence, once again traditional methods and values were grafted onto a new institution. Traditional values also affected efforts to establish a university. The first classes—in effect, public lectures—were held in 1863; opposition from conservatives led to its closing soon thereafter. A second attempt in 1870 was also short lived, and only in 1900 was the Ottoman University finally organized.

The opening of these schools, however, must be viewed as a truly innovative breakthrough in the creation of a modern educational system for the Empire. For the first time in Ottoman history, secular public schools had been established, and control of education was no longer the sole responsibility of the ulema but was vested in a Council of Public Instruction, the forerunner of the Ministry of Education.[84] This was an important step toward the creation of an integrated secular educational system.

Expansion and Development

Subsequent steps were closely linked to the general efforts at reform in the Empire, and the next major change in education came after the Crimean War, following the issuance by the sultan of the Hatt-i Humayun (1856), which restated and expanded the Gülhane Rescript of 1839 that had affirmed the equality of all Ottomans, Muslim and non-Muslim. The rights of all Ottomans were reaffirmed and all phases of the administration were to be overhauled. Once again the importance of education as the keystone of all further reform was

[83] Berkes, op. cit., pp. 175–176. On the date of the founding, see Kazamias, op. cit., pp. 53–54.
[84] B. Lewis, op. cit., p. 112.

reiterated. In the decade that followed, significant educational innovation culminated in the publication of the Regulations for General Education in 1869, whose provisions envisaged the complete reorganization and integration of existing schools and their expansion, especially at the secondary level. It provided for compulsory free education in the *subyan* (elementary schools) which were to be opened in every village and every town quarter, and free instruction in *rüşdiye*s and *idadiye*s (secondary preparatory schools), which were to be established throughout the Empire—the former in towns with 500 or more families, the latter in communities with 1,000 families or more. Secondary education was to be provided by *sultaniye*s (*lycées*) in every provincial capital, and higher education by a university in Istanbul. A teacher-training college was also to be established there. Besides this organized and differentiated system, provision was made for the reorganization of educational administration both nationally and locally, and the reform of teaching methods and teacher promotion.[85]

The implementation of these provisions proceeded rapidly, especially at the lower levels, and by 1868 about 2 per cent of the populace was literate and 11,008 primary schools with an enrollment of 242,017 boys and 126,459 girls were to be found throughout the Empire. The number of *rüşdiye*s increased rapidly to 108 with 7,830 students in that year. By 1876, 362 such schools were enrolling 18,750 students and about 5 per cent of the populace was literate.[86]

The degree to which modern education had become a matter of vital importance to all persons concerned with the future of the Empire was further evidenced by the inclusion of several clauses dealing with education in the constitution of 1876. Article 114 reiterated the principle previously stated in the Regulations for General Education that primary education was compulsory for all children in the Empire, and Article 15 decreed that education was to be free. Article 16 reaffirmed the concept of a secular, integrated, and centralized school system by assigning responsibility to the state for supervision, co-

---

[85] Kazamias, *op. cit.*, p. 63; Davison, *Reform*, pp. 248–249.
[86] These figures are taken from Davison, *Reform*, pp. 245, 177, and from Sadrettin Celal Antel, "Tanzimat Maarifi," in *Tanzimat* (Istanbul: Maarif Matbaasǐ, 1940), p. 458.

ordination, and regulation of all educational institutions. Religious education, however, was not to be interfered with and thus remained the province of the ulema.[87]

Of all the schools established in this period, perhaps the best known is the Galatasaray Lycée, which is reputed to have produced many of the personalities who profoundly affected the fate of the Empire. The founders of the school naturally looked once again to France for inspiration; its curriculum almost duplicated that of the nineteenth-century French *lycée;* courses consisted of Latin, history, geography, mathematics, science, drawing, and calligraphy, as well as Ottoman, Persian, and Arabic.[88] The director of the school and most of its teachers were French, and French was the language of instruction for most subjects. Six hundred students, half of whom would be non-Muslims in accordance with the goal of promoting Ottomanism among the various ethnic groups of the Empire, were to be admitted into the preparatory classes and, upon passing an examination, into the regular classes. Generous scholarships were to be provided.

This farsighted plan aroused opposition from two unexpected quarters, foreign powers who either did not wish the *sultaniye* to become the spearhead of a genuine reform movement or who feared the extension of French influence into the area, and the minorities:

The Greeks, naturally, but little inclined to favor anything which might give strength and cohesion to the empire, complained of the little attention given to the study of their language, and were exceedingly dissatisfied. The Jews . . . would not place their children in a Mohammedan institution under Christian teachers. . . . Even the Catholics, to a great extent, refused their sympathy to an establishment where all creeds were to be equally protected. . . . the Pope forbade all Catholic families to place their children in this lyceum under the penalty of being deprived of the sacraments.

Nevertheless, in September 1868, 147 Muslims, 48 Gregorian Armenians, 36 Greek Orthodox, 34 Jews, 34 Bulgarians, 23 Roman Catholics, and 19 Armenian Catholics enrolled. The number of students increased to 430 one month later and to 640 by the end of the

[87] Robert Devereux, *The First Ottoman Constitutional Period* (Baltimore: Johns Hopkins Press, 1963), p. 76.
[88] Kazamias, *op. cit.*, p. 65–66.

second year. This increase reflected the appeal of the new institution, which soon added courses in economics, engineering and law.[89]

This famous school, with its distinguished history, is usually considered to have had a profound impact upon developments in Empire and Republic. Bernard Lewis has said:

The influence of the Galatasaray School on the rise of modern Turkey has been enormous. As the need for administrators, diplomats, and others with a Western education and a capacity to handle Western administrative apparatus became more and more pressing, the graduates of Galatasaray came to play a preponderant role in the politics and administration of the Ottoman Empire and after it, of the Turkish Republic. The Imperial Ottoman Lise had no playing-fields, but not a few of the victories of modern Turkey were won in its classrooms.[90]

Yet if we are to assess impact in terms of the number of graduates who came to occupy high administrative positions then the importance of Galatasaray was negligible. A study of the careers followed by its graduates has shown that, although about two-thirds of the pre-1900 graduates entered the military or civil bureaucracy, only five individuals attained high positions, and in subsequent decades most graduates entered the professions. To assess impact in such a limited sense, however, overlooks the genuine contributions that Galatasaray made as a channel for the introduction of new ideas and the socialization of new attitudes and beliefs. For this reason, Andreas Kazamias has astutely concluded that the role of Galatasaray "lay more in providing a fertile ground and a substratum of bureaucrats, administrators, professionals, and so on, who were ready to accept innovation and the modernization of the institutions of government." [91]

[89] M. de Salve, "Education in Turkey," *Revue des Deux Mondes,* Oct. 15, 1874, pp. 60, 61 (246, 247).

[90] B. Lewis, *op. cit.,* p. 120.

[91] Kazamias, *op. cit.,* pp. 106, 103.
A recent discussion of the personnel of the Foreign Ministry, however, reveals that both in the Ottoman Empire and the Turkish Republic a large percentage of these officials attended Galatasaray and that that school produced, in the last decades of the Empire, eight ministers (including six foreign ministers, only four of whom actually graduated, however) and a high palace official. George S. Harris, "The Ataturk Revolution and the Foreign Office 1919–1931, a Preliminary Study," paper presented at the 6th Annual Meeting of the Middle East Studies Association of North America, November 2–4, 1972, mimeo., p. 11.

The second institution that is often thought to have played a major role during the last decades of the Ottoman Empire and throughout the history of the Turkish Republic is the Mülkiye, founded in 1859 to prepare civil servants. At first training consisted of a one-year course which was lengthened in 1877 to between two and four years depending upon an individual's background. In 1934 it was renamed the School of Political Science, and in 1936 moved to Ankara; in 1950 it became a faculty of Ankara University. A study of the careers achieved by the graduates of this institution suggests that the Mülkiye did, in time, come to play the important role often attributed to it because a significant number of its graduates were represented in the highest administrative ranks.[92]

In its early years the school had little impact upon political and social developments. None of the students who graduated before 1877 achieved a high-level post, and the deficiencies of the school during that period were widely criticized; a memorandum submitted by Cevdet Pasha to the Grand Vizier stated:

It is an urgent necessity to expand the mülkiye school in accordance with the time and situation, to rearrange the programme of studies correspondingly, to employ its graduates progressively in important posts, and thus to train competent administrative officials. Our immediate obligation is to take care to choose and employ those who are already fairly experienced and thus put the state administration on the right path.[93]

In the years following this reorganization, its graduates began to fill important positions in ever increasing numbers. One calculation shows that about 28 per cent of those who graduated before 1908, 55 per cent of the 1908–1919 graduates, and 44 per cent of the 1920–1931 graduates who entered the bureaucracy came to occupy high-level administrative posts.[94]

Thus one can differentiate between the impact of the Galatasaray and that of the Mülkiye upon the modernization of Turkey. Although

[92] Joseph S. Szyliowicz, "Elite Recruitment in Turkey: The Role of the Mülkiye," *World Politics,* 23 (April 1971), 371–398. For a detailed discussion of the development of the Mülkiye, with biographies of its graduates, faculty, and directors, see Ali Çankaya, *Yeni Mülkiye Tarihi ve Mülkiyeliler* (8 vols.; Ankara: Mars Matbaası, 1968–1969).

[93] Cited in B. Lewis, *op. cit.,* p. 368.

[94] Szyliowicz, *op. cit.,* p. 383.

both served as important socializing agencies for modern, and even revolutionary, ideas and values, the role of Galatasaray was limited to the creation of a middle-level group of professionals and intellectuals who were receptive to such ideas. The Mülkiye, on the other hand, also prepared students for the administrative elite and thus played a far more direct role in future developments. Among its graduates were many high-level bureaucrats who were responsible for making and implementing decisions concerning change and innovation in both Empire and Republic. And from their ranks were also recruited many members of the political elite of the Turkish Republic. Hence it may be appropriate to suggest that if many victories of modern Turkey were indeed won in the classroom, those classrooms were located not in Galatasaray but in the Mülkiye.

Sultan Abdul-Hamid II

These institutions and the other modern schools continued to function during the reign of Abdul-Hamid II. Despite his apparent commitment to the principles of the 1876 constitution, he quickly moved to consolidate power into his own hands and the center of power shifted from the reformers to the despotic Sultan and his entourage. Although Abdul-Hamid has often been considered a reactionary, it is a mistake to regard these decades as a period of conservatism. Professor Lewis has pointed out that

Abdulhamid was far from being the blind, uncompromising, complete reactionary of the historical legend; on the contrary, he was a willing and active modernizer. . . . It would not be an exaggeration to say that it was in these early years of the reign of Abdulhamid that the whole movement of the *Tanzimat*—of legal, administrative, and educational reform— reached its fruition and its climax.[95]

Certainly during these decades educational developments, under the guidance of the great reformer Mehmet Said Pasha, accelerated greatly. Between 1879 and 1895 he opened four *idadiye*s, started building twenty-four more and planned to locate one in each urban center, increased the number of *rüşdiye*s from 253 to 389, and sponsored the opening of schools of finance, law, fine arts, languages, commerce,

[95] B. Lewis, *op. cit.*, pp. 174–75.

and engineering. He was responsible for an emphasis upon vocation and technical education and the addition of vocational sections to many of the *idadiyes*.

In 1900, as a part of the twenty-fifth anniversary celebration of Sultan Abdul-Hamid II's reign, a university was opened. Said Pasha also played a prominent role in sponsoring this project and in alleviating the Sultan's fears of potential risks involved.[96] The problems faced by this institution were very different from those confronting the reformers who had attempted unsuccessfully to establish an institution of higher learning in the Ottoman Empire heretofore. By the end of the nineteenth century, their efforts had created a modern educational system capped by the exclusive *lycée* of Galatasaray that was preparing qualified students. Trained faculty could also be recruited from the many intellectuals and scholars who had studied in Europe.

These advantages, however, were more than offset by political considerations. Despite his willingness to establish a modern educational system, Abdul-Hamid II remained greatly worried about the potential threat to his regime that such a system might foster. Concerned with the dangers of a concentration of students in Istanbul and with the ideological content of practically any course in the social sciences and humanities, he took positive measures to ensure that the new institution would not be a hotbed of sedition. No courses in politics, sociology, philosophy, or even history were included in its curriculum. Inspectors of the Ministry of Education attended classes in order to control the teaching of the faculty, and an effective network of secret police kept the university under strict surveillance as it did all educational institutions. As a result, the university was of low quality, intellectually passive, and very small in size. In 1903, for example, twenty-five students were enrolled in literature, thirty in science, and another thirty in religion. Nor did other schools escape his attention. In the Mülkiye, for example, teachers were selected with great care and were forbidden to discuss with their students any topic not directly related to the course.[97]

Despite such controls, and perhaps partly because of them, discon-

---

[96] Ercümend Kuran, "Küçük Said Pasha (1840–1914) as a Turkish Modernist," *International Journal of Middle East Studies*, 1 (April 1970), 127–128.

[97] Ergin, *op. cit.*, III, 1002ff. See also Enver Ziya Karal, *Osmanli Tarihi*, VIII (Ankara: Türk Tarih Kurumu Basimevi, 1962), 395–396.

tent was rife within the civilian and especially the military schools, where "politics illegally and unofficially dominated the curriculum." [98] The first revolutionary group was organized in the military medical school in 1889, and before long the conspirators had gained numerous adherents among students in other educational institutions and enjoyed the support of many members of the new intellectual group that had graduated from the modern schools in previous years. Although Abdul-Hamid's secret police uncovered many of the plots and many persons were exiled, opposition continued to thrive within the Empire. The degree of alienation—and practically overt opposition—that existed even in the civilian schools has been attested to by a graduate of Galatasaray. In 1906 the majority of students, even those from families close to the palace, used on ceremonial occasions to substitute "down with the Emperor" for "long live the Emperor." [99]

We shall later analyze the causes of the 1908 revolution, but it is appropriate to note that the size of the civilian groups involved was still relatively small. Altogether about 2,500 persons had received a higher education by that time: 1,042 in medicine, 1,392 in law, 100 in literature, and 55 in science.[100] This total, the overwhelming majority of whom were doctors and lawyers, does not, of course, represent the entire population within the Empire who were potential political activists. To this figure must be added the graduates of the Mülkiye—which, from its founding until the Young Turk revolution, graduated 1,236 students[101]—and of the other specialized high schools established in the nineteenth century and all the military schools. If we limit ourselves to the civilian schools, however, it appears that about 5,000 persons possessed a higher education and that it was this small group that provided the intellectual leadership for the Empire.

Their impact upon the society, however, was far greater than these numbers would suggest, for new means of communications had become available, and a new public to which they could address themselves had been created by the extension of educational opportunities

[98] Feroz Ahmad, *The Young Turks* (Oxford: Clarendon Press, 1969), p. 48.
[99] B. Lewis, *op. cit.*, p. 191.
[100] Cemil Bilsel, *İstanbul Üniversitenin Tarihi* (Istanbul: Kenan Matbaası, 1943), p. 48.
[101] Calculated from Çankaya, *op. cit.*

during Sultan Abdul-Hamid's reign. The literacy rate tripled in the last quarter of the nineteenth century, and the new literates created a demand for news and opinions that had never existed before. Journalism became an important profession, and the number of newspapers, journals, and books proliferated rapidly, though Abdul-Hamid's censor exercised the utmost caution in attempting to prevent the dissemination of dangerous ideas. Royalty and heads of government proved especially susceptible to disease in the turbulent decades preceding 1908; the King and Queen of Serbia died suddenly and simultaneously of indigestion in 1903, the Empress Elizabeth died of pneumonia, President Carnot of apoplexy, and President McKinley of anthrax.[102]

Finally, one should note that it may also be a mistake to equate revolutionaries and moderns. Many students from the Mülkiye entered a bureaucracy which supported and executed the policies of Abdul-Hamid, but their preparation may well have socialized them into an acceptance of change and innovation. To implement the reforms adopted during his reign was the function of the bureaucracy; that it was able to do so may well have been due at least partly to the fact that many of its members were graduates of the new schools. In any case, an extensive and differentiated administration had been created which could, and did, provide the framework for implementing the radical policies that were to be adopted in the coming decades.

Foreign Schools

As in Egypt, foreign schools were an important channel for the transmission of Western educational principles into the society. On the eve of World War I an estimated 500 French schools with 59,414 students and 675 American and 178 British Protestant schools with 34,317 and 12,800 students respectively were functioning in the Empire. In addition, there was a sprinkling of German, Italian, and Russian schools. Despite these impressive figures, the impact of these institutions upon the Turkish community was slight, since most of them were located in the Arab provinces and catered almost exclusively to Christian minorities. The number of Muslim Turks who at-

---

[102] B. Lewis, *op. cit.,* pp. 184, 455.

tended these schools was negligible. In the forty years following the founding by American missionaries of Robert College (1863), even though it was located in Constantinople, only one out of 435 graduates (194 Bulgarians, 144 Armenians, 76 Greeks, 2 Jews, 17 Europeans, and an American) was a Muslim Turk—and he was a member of the class of 1903. Another seven-year hiatus ensued before the second Turk was graduated in 1910. By 1908 the number of Turks enrolled in Robert College comprised about 3 to 5 per cent of the student body of about 300.[103]

The second type of foreign school operating within the Empire consisted of those operated by the different religious communities. Jews, Armenians, and Greeks all had their own schools in which standards, especially in the better institutions, appear to have been quite high. During the nineteenth century all these schools served as important models for reformers to emulate and, when government schools were established, as standards against which the quality of the official institutions could be judged. One official, for example, bitterly pointed out that although ten-year-old Greeks and Armenians could read newspapers, few fifteen-year-old Turkish boys could do so.[104] Thus the significance of these institutions is, once again, that they served essentially as a powerful stimulus to educational reform by the government. If they had a more direct impact upon the Empire during the nineteenth century it was completely negative; the missionary schools, especially, promoted feelings of nationalism and separatism among the minorities.

For many Muslims the 1908 revolution and its aftermath proved to be a turning point, and the number of Turks attending foreign schools increased sharply thereafter. One official addressing the staff of Harput College expressed a popular view: "Hitherto only Armenians have been able to avail themselves of the privileges of this college. We Turks have been forbidden to send our children here. That is all changed now, and we will share with you in the enjoyment of what this institution offers." Nevertheless, the number was never very large. Overall it was estimated that 7 per cent of the students enrolled in the American schools were Turks. Around World War I the number increased again; of 470 students enrolled at Robert Col-

---

[103] Davison, "Westernized Education," pp. 291, 293.
[104] *Ibid.*, p. 299; see also Kazamias, *op. cit.*, pp. 93–96, 103.

lege in 1913, 67 were Muslim Turks, and 23 non-Turkish Muslims, but most of these appear to have been enrolled in the preparatory school since only one or two Turks were graduated from the college each year. By the mid-1920's the number of Turkish graduates had risen to about five or six per year. Altogether, between 1868 and 1930 a total of 1,083 students graduated from the college. Of these 61 were Turks, as compared to 308 Armenians, 312 Greeks, and 279 Bulgarians.[105]

Education and Ottoman Society

All these educational developments had marked consequences for Ottoman society and culture, and practically every scholar who has written about the nineteenth century has discussed the ways in which a modern education became a prerequisite for elite membership, the ways in which different social groups gained access to the modern schools, and the tensions between the graduates of the modern and the traditional schools. In the view of many, the *leitmotif* of the nineteenth century is a struggle between the ulema and the graduates of the modern schools for power and influence. One scholar has vividly depicted this struggle: "On one side were the 'modernists' influenced by a Western-oriented, secular education. . . . Grimly opposed . . . in mentality and in action, was the other part of the educated elite—the madrasa-trained intellectuals.[106]

This view, however, is at best an oversimplification, for much evidence is available that shows that during the reign of Selim III and Mahmud II many of the leading ulema were not only supporters, but active proponents, of administrative and military reform.

Members of the ulema sanctioned, among other innovations, the decisions to introduce printing, destroy the Janissaries, and abolish the Bektashi Order of Dervishes. Besides willingly legitimizing and supporting proposed reforms, the ulema suggested additional innovations including the employment of foreign experts in various fields, a regular translation program, the reorganization of the administration, meas-

---

[105] Davison, "Westernized Education," p. 294; *Alumni Register, Robert College* (Istanbul: The College, 1931), pp. 38–39.

[106] Frederick Frey, *The Turkish Political Elite* (Cambridge: M.I.T. Press, 1965), pp. 37–38.

ures to spur trade and entrepreneurship, and the opening of the military medical school.[107]

Support by religious leaders for important reforms was not limited to the first decades of the nineteenth century. Though detailed studies of the role of the ulema for the remainder of the century are lacking, it appears that many madrasa graduates sponsored and participated in activities that could only be considered as innovative, especially in the educational sphere. Some studied abroad or learned European languages, others served as faculty and directors in various modern schools including that interesting experiment, the Ottoman School in Paris (1857–1874). Nor did the religious elite oppose the opening of the Galatasaray Lycée even though Muslims would be studying there with the minorities.[108] Paradoxically, the ulema did force the closing of the Ottoman University about a year after its opening in 1870, but even this episode illustrates the conflicting attitudes that existed within the religious institution; the director of the university, Tahsin Efendi, was of ulema background.

One scholar has suggested that the reason why the ulema opposed the university and not the *lycée* was that, "if once established, the university would be the madrasa's real rival—in subject matter, in its human material, in intellectual function—in everything," whereas the *lycée* was viewed as being "of no concern to [the ulema's] realm." [109] Whether this was indeed the case deserves further research, especially since it is hard to explain the lack of foresight and imagination of the religious elite at this late date.

The difficulties inherent in attempting to categorize the entire religious hierarchy, or even its elite, during these revolutionary decades should be apparent. Nevertheless, it does appear that the high ulema were not, by and large, adamant reactionaries. Rather they were characterized by a remarkable degree of flexibility and a willingness, as we have noted, to assist in the transformation of the state. Especially in view of the common identification of madrasa training with con-

---

[107] Uriel Heyd, "The Ottoman Ulema and Westernization in the Time of Selim III and Mahmud II," *Scripta Hierosolymitana,* Studies in Islamic History and Civilization (Jerusalem: Magnes Press, Hebrew University, 1961), I, *passim.*

[108] Richard L. Chambers, "The Mekteb-i Osmani in Paris," in Polk and Chambers, *op. cit.,* p. 329; Kazamias, *op. cit.,* p. 66; Berkes, *op. cit.,* pp. 190–91.

[109] Berkes, *op. cit.,* pp. 191, 188.

servatism, the reasons why so many graduates had a positive attitude toward change and innovation remains unclear. For the late eighteenth and early nineteenth centuries, however, certain factors have been identified.

The flexibility of the ulema elite was motivated by several considerations, including fear: Mahmud II was not the type of ruler who hesitated to use his powers of dismissal to establish control over the religious institution. His efforts were facilitated by the widespread venality and corruption and by the division among the leading families who competed for the highest positions in the religious hierarchy. Both Selim III and Mahmud II followed the strategy—not unknown in the contemporary Middle East—of demonstrating their deep attachment to Islam by performing rituals and ceremonies, building and restoring mosques and other holy buildings, and conceding frequently to the ulema on matters of secondary importance. The ulema's support, however, sprang from positive considerations as well. Hostility between these families and the plebeian Janissaries and their supporters, who were regarded as a potential threat to the stability of the society and hence to the position of the religious hierarchy, was quite intense. The concern of the ulema with the preservation of the Empire was also heightened by their representation in important decision-making and consultative bodies, which made them aware of domestic realities, and by the intimate personal ties that bound many of them to the court and to leading military and administrative personages. Nor can one overlook their faith in the superiority and invincibility of Islam and their limited awareness of the European experience, which combined to blind them to the long-term implications of the reforms.[110]

Equally subtle was the role of the modern schools and the attitudes of their graduates toward reform and change. The relationship between education, social core group patterns, and change has been summarized by one historian who has pointed out that the products of the secular civil schools became the political elite of the Ottoman Empire following the Crimean War:

These "Men of the Tanzimat" formed a new ruling class of relatively well-educated and well-motivated individuals whose main desire was to

[110] Heyd, *op. cit., passim.*

modernize their state . . . many were themselves children of members of the older Ottoman ruling class. . . . It was only when the Tanzimat produced a new generation of 20th century reformers not directly tied to the older ruling class that significant reform was possible. This new generation consisted mainly of men from relatively modest families who rose through the army and the civil schools created by the Tanzimat. . . . It was men such as these who united in the Society of Union and Progress.[111]

Such a summation, however, somewhat oversimplifies a complex phenomenon, as we shall attempt to show.

First, the graduates of the modern schools did not represent a homogeneous group dedicated to reform, for many ideological currents were represented among them. The "Men of the Tanzimat"—the great reformers—were opposed by the Young Ottomans who argued against the centralization of power and the increasing influence of foreigners in all areas. Nor were the latter group ideologically united; their criticisms and prescriptions also ranged widely in scope and content. The Young Ottomans and the Tanzimat reformers, however, had two things in common: Both were deeply influenced by Western ideas and values, and both were largely drawn from the official classes.

On the other hand, the Young Ottomans differed from their opponents in one significant aspect—they were not members of the bureaucratic elite; rather, they represented largely persons of middle or lower official backgrounds whose discontent could be attributed to the fact that they were confronted with a situation wherein a high degree of Western exposure and a modern education no longer sufficed for the achievement of membership in the powerful administrative elite. Moreover, they enjoyed the support of military and religious personages,[112] a fact which further indicates the degree to which the essence of conflict in the nineteenth century did not lie in the struggle between religious conservatives and modern reformers but in the impact of the reforms upon the religious, military, and administrative institutions and in the dynamics of social core groups and elites in particular. We shall attempt to demonstrate this point below.

As was noted earlier, the social structure of the Ottoman Empire closely resembled the feudal society model. The upper class was sepa-

---

[111] Shaw, "Some Aspects," in Polk and Chambers, *op. cit.*, pp. 36–37.

[112] Şerif Mardin, *The Genesis of Young Ottoman Thought* (Princeton: Princeton University Press, 1962), Chap. 4, *passim.*

rate and distinct from the mass in terms of appearance, manners, customs, and even language, and hence minimal social mobility existed between these two strata, although it was possible for able and talented individuals to achieve elite status. The three most important elite groups within the state were the military, the bureaucracy, and the ulema, each of which represented a separate career. Membership in these elites had once been determined by ability, but concurrently with the decline of the Empire channels of mobility became frozen and careers became largely hereditary. Appointment to high office, whether religious, military, or administrative, came to be determined by influence, favoritism, and corruption, and by the end of the eighteenth century a ruling class had emerged. Its members dominated each of the core elites, but their position was based not on holding a particular office, but upon lineage and wealth—a radical departure from the classical pattern in which only the ulema enjoyed the right of inheritance and a "slave's" property, indeed his very life, depended upon the whim of the ruler. Although the right of the sultan to confiscate the riches of his servants was not formally abolished until 1826, various means of avoiding such expropriation had developed. One might place a son in a religious office or make provision for a charitable endowment which, though usually founded for pious reasons, might be used to perpetuate wealth. The founder would specify that his heirs administer the endowment and that, when his male line ceased, the *wakf* would become the property of the religious institution. The weakness of sultans, coupled with the exploitation of such arrangements, enabled many persons to establish their families securely, and by the end of the eighteenth century Ottoman stratification patterns were markedly different from those described earlier. Now a ruling class existed at the center and its members filled elite posts. No longer were training and ability primary requirements for membership in the religious, military, or administrative elites; now questions of blood, kinship, and connections were dominant considerations.[113]

This pattern was disrupted by the reforms, particularly in educa-

[113] Norman Itzkowitz, "Kimsiniz Bey Efendi, or a look at *Tanzimat* through Namier-Colored Glasses," in *Near Eastern Round Table*, R. Bayly Winder, ed., (New York: Near Eastern Center and Center for International Studies, New York University, 1969), pp. 49–50, analyzes the new pattern.

tion, of Selim III and Mahmud II which we have described. Mahmud II was supported by many members of the ruling class, both religious and civil, but his policies created opportunities for mobility that were seized by persons of official background who were not members of that class. They were the ones who possessed the motivation to engage in such un-Ottoman practices as learning foreign languages and acquiring a Western education, and before long a considerable number of reformers of nonelite backgrounds were occupying the highest posts in the administration. This period of mobility, however, lasted only through part of the Tanzimat (1839–1876), for in time it became obvious that a modern education was the key to power, and members of the upper class who had formerly been unwilling to engage in such nontraditional behavior now moved to protect their own position within the society. The result was a second change in mobility patterns into first, the administrative, and later, the military elites, and in the composition of these two elites. From the mid-nineteenth century onward, opportunities for mobility became increasingly restricted and the bureaucratic elite came to consist of an amalgam of persons of upper class backgrounds and of those who had achieved mobility in the first half of the century.[114]

Moreover, during the reign of Mahmud II and his successors, the high bureaucrats achieved unprecedented and unrivaled power until the accession of Sultan Abdul-Hamid II to the throne. On the one hand these sultans took many steps to consolidate control and to increase the effectiveness of the administration by reorganizing it and staffing it with people trained in the new schools. On the other, potential rival centers that might compete with the bureaucracy were crushed or otherwise rendered impotent. Following the destruction of the Janissaries in 1826, Mahmud II took positive measures to ensure that the modern army he wished to create would be a passive tool. He did so by recruiting personnel from social strata without any ties to powerful elements within the Empire. The ulema elite, as we have seen, cooperated with the bureaucrats and the sultan.

---

[114] For a preliminary discussion of these findings, which form part of an ongoing project that seeks to analyze the bureaucratic elite from 1810 onward, see Joseph Szyliowicz, "Pasha, Bey and Efendi: The Nineteenth-century Ottoman Provincial Administrator, A Preliminary Profile," a paper delivered to the International Seminar on the History of Palestine and Its Jewish Settlement under Ottoman Rule, mimeo. (Jerusalem: Hebrew University, 1970).

Increased power was accompanied by the closure of opportunities to achieve such power, and by the mid-nineteenth century the bureaucracy was again marked by a cleavage between the higher and the lower levels, the former occupied by the new ruling class and their offspring, the latter by persons of more humble origins who had also attended the new educational institutions in the hope of achieving elite membership. Their hopes, however, were frustrated by the control over high level positions by the powerful families, and thus many persons with a modern education were disappointed in their attempts to rise within the administration. It was from their ranks that the Young Ottomans who so bitterly attacked the arbitrary rule of the Tanzimat reformers were largely recruited.

Moreover it was precisely because this new ruling class recognized the importance of modern schooling that it was able to maintain and strengthen its position within the society. This point has been well summarized:

[The bureaucracy's] former grip over the life and livelihood of the administrative machinery subordinate to it had to be loosened since administrative codes came to regulate the rights of the occupants of lower rungs of the ladder. But conversely, the upper ranges of this revamped Ruling Institution accumulated wealth that was now legally protected and could be transmitted to heirs. It acquired access to modern education and the study of foreign languages for its progeny. The latter were thus launched into life with an even more crystallized privileged status than had been the case with the ulema.[115]

Even though the ruling class ensured that its offspring would enjoy the advantages of exposure to Western civilization, the proliferation of new roles created insatiable demands for persons equipped to fill them, and many persons who did not come from the upper class also enrolled in the modern schools, which increased rapidly.

Further spurring the diversification of the student body in these schools was Abdul-Hamid II's attempt to create new bases of support for his regime among the landed gentry and various minority groups and the growth of communication, transportation, and educational opportunities throughout the Empire. The number of Arabs who at-

[115] Şerif Mardin, "Historical Determinants of Social Stratification, Social Class, and Social Consciousness in Turkey," *Siyasal Bilgiler Fakültesi Dergisi*, 22, no. 4 (1968), 135.

tended the Mülkiye, for example, is quite large during these decades. Similarly many students of rural background were also enrolled and some were apparently able to achieve high administrative posts.[116] On the other hand there were many who did not possess the necessary prerequisites to rise to high office. Their expectations could not be met, for the ruling class appears to have been able to retain its control over high office, a factor of great importance in explaining the causes of the 1908 revolution. These developments have been summarized as follows:

Toward the end of the 19th century the further modernization of Turkey brought with it a further change in the structure of the bureaucracy: a pyramid with a somewhat narrow base was transformed into one with an increasingly wider base. To staff the lower and middle echelons of the bureacracy, new Western-oriented schools were created. Since tuition was free and room and board were provided in addition, a number of provincials flowed to these schools. These provincials came mainly from the stratum of the lesser âyân and eşraf and a few prosperous peasants. . . . It is these new recruits who in the 1890's revolted against the upper reaches of the bureaucracy which had turned into a semi-aristocracy.[117]

Similar factors also provoked the high degree of discontent that was evident within the military establishment during the reign of Abdul-Hamid II. There the pattern of mobility and blockage was even more evident than in the case of the administration. Prominent persons had originally been very reluctant to enroll their children in the new military colleges, even those that provided technical training such as the medical school, and the government turned to orphans and children of the very poor for its officer corps. One Englishman, for example, described the students in the military medical school as "all . . . taken from the very poor classes: I was told that the Turks were one and all of the lowest grade . . . and that no Turk of the high or even middle class ever sent his son to the College." [118]

Such an attitude was welcomed, and perhaps even encouraged, by Malmud II, who was above all concerned with ensuring the dependency of the army and therefore recruited persons of unquestioned loyalty or without ties to established power groups for his new military

---

[116] See Szyliowicz, "Elite Recruitment," pp. 377–378.
[117] Mardin, "Historical Determinants," p. 139.
[118] Cited in Mardin, "Genesis," pp. 130–131.

organization. Thus the military represented an effective channel for social mobility, and many important officers were of lower-class background as evidenced by the report of the famous German officer Von Moltke, who served as an advisor to the Ottoman army. He reported: "The weakest side of the Army . . . were the officers. Two Generals in the Army stem from Muhammad Hasai's Harem, a third one was only a porter ten years ago, and the fourth had been a galley-slave. . . . Often very young men were made majors." [119]

Although most of the officer corps came from such humble origins, they quickly began to develop hereditary privileges for their children. The extent to which they were able to do so is indicated by the fact that sons of high-ranking military officers received preferential treatment in military schools. Following the 1908 revolution all officers who had received their commissions in this way were downgraded. Thus persons of middle- and lower-class origin could, at first, use the army as a means of improving their social status, but mobility soon became dependent, not upon achievement criteria, but increasingly upon ascriptive ones. Favoritism came to be rampant and promotions were often secured by personal influence or informing on one's fellow officers. Furthermore, the financial position of the officer corps was poor. The salary scale was relatively low and pay was usually in arrears; most officers were forced to discount their income to speculators to maintain themselves and their families. [120]

Students in the military schools were, of course, aware of these conditions, and this awareness led to revolutionary activity. The group that actually staged the revolution, however, was organized in Salonika in 1906 by junior officers, who quickly gained widespread support among the graduates of the secular schools, especially intellectuals, professionals, and low-level bureaucrats. These were the groups that formed the backbone of the revolutionary movement but they also enjoyed the support of many middle and lower-level ulema. One contemporary European journalist analyzing the movement in class

[119] Cited in Amos Perlmutter, "The Arab Military Elite," *World Politics,* 22 (January 1970), 282. See also Dankwart A. Rustow, "The Military: Turkey," in *Political Modernization in Japan and Turkey,* Robert E. Ward and Dankwart A. Rustow, eds. (Princeton: Princeton University Press, 1964), p. 360.

[120] Mardin, "Historical Determinants," p. 139; Ernest Edmondson Ramsaur, Jr., *The Young Turks: Prelude to the Revolution of 1908* (Princeton: Princeton University Press, 1957), pp. 116–117.

terms viewed it as basically middle-class: "The high officials, generally speaking, were hostile to the movement. . . . The lower classes . . . were, as a rule, indifferent. It was among the junior officers of the army and navy, the middle and lower grades of the civil service, the professional classes, and the *ulema,* that the movement for reform carried all before it." [121]

The role of the ulema in the Young Turk movement deserves careful analysis, for it is not clear to what extent religious personages were, in fact, either actively or passively involved, especially when the counterrevolution of 1909 (which took a reactionary religious form) is considered. Nevertheless, it does appear that discontent was rife among the middle and lower levels of the religious institution and among madrasa students, as well as among several religious brotherhoods.[122]

These attitudes can also be attributed to conditions within the religious institution and to the impact of Abdul-Hamid II's policies upon them. In contrast to the military and the administration, stratification patterns remained relatively unchanged, and the traditional division separated the powerful and prosperous ulema elite from the rank and file. A few families enjoyed a monopoly of the high positions; their members received important appointments without regard to merit or ability, often at a ridiculously young age (six was not uncommon), while the ordinary student had to struggle for up to twenty years before qualifying as a professor.

Even more humble positions, however, became increasingly difficult to obtain as the number and type of offices for which a madrasa education qualified a graduate shrank steadily in number and type owing to the steady secularization of the bureaucracy, the judiciary, and the educational system during the nineteenth century. Those most able to protect their position in this situation were, of course, the leading ulema families who enrolled their children in another career or whose members would themselves combine careers in secular and religious law in order to preserve their position in the face of the declining power and prestige of the religious institution.[123]

[121] Ahmad, *op. cit.,* pp. 16–17, the quote is from p. 18.

[122] Edwin Pears, *Forty Years In Constantinople* (New York: D. Appleton and Co., 1916), pp. 236ff., cited in Kazamias, *op. cit.,* p. 99.

[123] Şerif Mardin, "Historical Determinants," p. 135.

Naturally, ulema in the lower ranks were especially concerned with any threat to whatever channels of mobility remained available to them and were therefore bound to oppose reform programs that would inevitably restrict the opportunities open to persons with a madrasa education. Their feelings were strongly shared by the theological students, whose position was even worse. Their numbers had increased sharply to several thousands at the same time that one sultan after another expropriated the revenues of the pious foundations that had heretofore provided for their support. Thus their conditions deteriorated at the same time that the competition for the decreasing number of posts available to them was increasing.

At the same time, the modern schools continued to benefit from ever increasing inputs of financial and human resources. As a result, the disparity between the two types of institutions grew wider and wider, the quality of the religious schools dropping steadily, that of the modern schools improving greatly. Under these conditions, it is not surprising that from the madrasa students, who became ever more frustrated and alienated as their environment deteriorated and their career prospects became gloomier, were drawn the student activists of the nineteenth century.[124]

Somewhat surprisingly, in view of Abdul-Hamid II's reliance upon Islam as a basis for his rule, this trend continued during his reign. As part of his Pan-Islamist policy, he favored the mystic and orthodox religious orders, especially those in the Arab countries. Contributing to his policy was his concern with the possible danger of an alliance between the ulema and the bureaucrats directed against him. Thus, though he used Islam to maintain a strong base of support among the mass of the people, he generally bypassed the existing Ottoman religious hierarchy and allowed the quality of the religious schools to deteriorate to even lower levels than before.[125] The result, of course, was alienation, and it is probably for this reason that many ulema supported the Young Turk movement.

Hence, in our view, the *leitmotif* of the nineteenth century was not one of reform versus obscurantism, but rather a conflict between the ruling class and other elements within the society, most of whom also possessed a modern education, for power and status. The fundamental

[124] Şerif Mardin, "Genesis," pp. 127–130.
[125] Berkes, *op. cit.*, pp. 258–259.

cleavage, therefore, did not lie between those with a traditional education and those with a modern education, as has so often been suggested, but between those of upper-class background and those from nonelite backgrounds who attempted, unsuccessfully, to ride the reform movement and a modern education into positions of leadership and power. This is especially true of the bureaucracy and the military; the lower bureaucrats and the junior officers had graduated from modern schools, and many of them did know a foreign language, but their hopes of using these new skills as a means of advancement were frustrated by the existing stratification pattern and by the policies of Abdul-Hamid II.

Finally, it should be noted that the easy correlation between the social and economic background of the Young Turks and their subsequent radical policies may also not be completely valid. It does not appear that the persons who made the Young Turk revolution were driven to assume power in order to bring about reform and change; on the contrary, they were truly the intellectual heirs of the Young Ottomans and possessed a fundamentally conservative outlook. One student of the movement has pointed out that the Young Turks seized power to preserve the existing structure, not to transform it:

They were by and large conservative in outlook with little or no interest in promoting social change. The importance of the 1908 *coup d'état* is not that it was revolutionary in profession; it was not. Its aim was to restore a constitution which had been granted 32 years earlier and thereby save the State. The revolutionary nature of the movement emerged later partly as a result of the failure of its pragmatic policies, and partly as an outcome of incidental reform and the social change this brought about.[126]

Moreover, this scholar cites the nonelite background of the Young Turks as a fundamental reason why they did not assume direct control of the state after the revolution of 1908. Thus the social background of the Young Turks can be used to explain both their early conservative attitudes and their later radical behavior.

The Young Turks

In a very real sense the 1908 revolution represents a watershed with the past in terms of the structure and character of politics. Power

---

[126] Ahmad, *op. cit.*, pp. 15–16.

now resided not with a sultan and his entourage or with a group of administrators striving to maintain their power positions vis-à-vis the ruler but with a political elite which relied upon control of military and administrative institutions. To strengthen their position the Young Turks also developed a hitherto unknown base of power, the political party. The Committee of Union and Progress (CUP) became a nationwide organization with branches in all urban areas, and its activities led to marked changes in patterns of participation and recruitment. Political rallies and demonstrations became commonplace as the CUP sought to mobilize support, and the growth in literary and journalistic activities further spurred urban politicization.

Moreover, the composition of the political elite differed markedly from previous patterns. As we have emphasized, the revolutionists were not of upper-class backgrounds but were recruited essentially from nonelite elements within the Empire. Now the circle of recruitment expanded even more and groups that were formerly passive developed a new awareness of and concern with national affairs.[127]

Despite these changes, however, the existing social order was not transformed totally. The position of the rural elite remained essentially unchanged and many important families in the center retained their membership in administrative and other elites. Scions of the ruling class continued to attend modern schools during these decades, and these individuals appear to have possessed the necessary prerequisites for career success. Though detailed studies are lacking, the rate of career success for children of upper-class families who studied at the Mülkiye was higher, despite a lower academic performance, than that of students from more modest backgrounds, thus suggesting that in the early years of the twentieth century many members of the bureaucratic elite were of ruling-class background.[128] Even today, many of the leading figures within Turkish society are descended from such families. For this reason it does not appear likely that the former ruling class was totally displaced by the 1908 revolution. Rather the monopoly they formerly exercised upon entry into key elites was broken. As a result of later developments, these elites also expanded greatly in size. From then on, membership was no longer

[127] Dankwart Rustow, "The Army and the Founding of the Turkish Republic," *World Politics*, 11 (July 1959), 541.
[128] See Szyliowicz, "Elite Recruitment," p. 396.

restricted to persons of upper-class backgrounds but came to include large numbers of individuals who were able to achieve mobility via the modern schools. Thus the 1908 revolution can best be considered as having made possible transition from a ruling-class social core group to a political-elite group whose ranks included scions of entrenched families.

Concomitantly, new, more ruthless rules of the game were established and new lines of cleavage emerged. During the nineteenth century, the politically salient conflict at the center of Ottoman society had been between elite and nonelite (though official) elements. Now cleavages within elite groupings became apparent as ideological issues emerged as a major cutting point, for the Young Turk period was an era of ferment and experimentation almost without parallel in the history of the Ottoman Empire. Political, social, religious, and economic topics were discussed by the intelligentsia with passion and vigor, and many important measures were adopted to reconstruct Ottoman society, especially during the war years.

Nor was education neglected; in fact, the liberals of the period regarded education as a panacea for the evils of society, and a new group of educators vigorously debated the principles and goals of education. In this they were joined by such intellectual leaders as Prince Sabahattin and the famous Ziya Gökalp. Some of them emphasized the need to break with past tradition as far as physical activity was concerned—they extolled oratory, which hitherto had been reserved for the ulema; athletics, which had been regarded as fit only for the lower class; and standing erect, which had been regarded as a mark of disrespect, if not of outright rebellion: "Talk, move, work, play—these were the first formulae of these empirical pedagogues, their fundamentals for the new education." [129]

Although such activity may indeed have caused people to question useless traditions and customs, it did not represent an educational philosophy, and the discussion over education reflected the debate between Islamists, Westernists, and reformists, the three major ideological currents of the time, each with a different perspective on reform and change. The Islamists rejected the necessity for drastic change. They argued that the problems of the Empire were due to

[129] Berkes, *op. cit.*, pp. 402–403.

the continuing erosion of Islamic values and practices and that the modern schools were one of the main agencies for the dissemination of a secular ideology. They insisted that while students should be prepared to learn Western sciences, the school had to serve as a socializing agency for traditional values and education had to be based upon Islamic principles.

The reformists were headed by Ziya Gökalp, the founder of modern Turkish nationalism and one of the great Turkish intellectuals of modern times. A prominent member of the Young Turk movement, he was elected to the Central Committee of the ruling party (CUP) in 1909. Philosophically he sought to synthesize what he felt to be conflicting value systems held by three groups within the Empire: the uneducated mass, the madrasa graduates, and the graduates of the modern schools. Education, though responsible for creating the cleavage in society, could also resolve it. In his words, "one portion of our nation is living in an ancient, another in a medieval, and a third in a modern age. . . . How can we be a real nation without unifying this three-fold education?" [130] Thus, in Gökalp's eyes, education had to forge a new unity within the Empire, a unity based on a combination of Islamic, Turkish, and modernist principles. He felt that "culture" could and should be separated from "civilization"; that the former, which had been corrupted over centuries, had to be based on a new definition of its Turkish and Islamic principles, while the latter consisted of science and technology. Hence Gökalp, emphasizing the importance of the national tradition (including a reformed Islam), urged the Turkification of all aspects of the culture which had to be preserved and maintained above all; only the material and technological aspects of Europe should be adopted—and these only after the country had sufficiently developed its own culture based upon the Turkish heritage so that its Turkish character would not be affected by innovations. He favored a secular state, but since he considered Islam to be an integral part of the national culture, he felt it should play an important role in every person's life. The nation was the highest moral authority and the intelligentsia were its natural leaders. From an educational viewpoint, this meant that the curriculum

[130] Ziya Gökalp, *Turkish Nationalism and Western Civilization,* ed. and trans. by Niyazi Berkes (New York: Columbia University Press, 1959), p. 278.

should emphasize Turkish language, history, and literature, Islamic history and religious sciences, and European languages.

This résumé is an oversimplification since Gökalp was not a consistent ideologue and changed his views rather sharply throughout his life in the light of political, social, and personal developments. Nevertheless, the most influential and consequential aspect of his thought—his attempt to reconcile modernization, nationalism, and Islam as evidenced in his famous slogan, "We belong to the Turkish nation, the Muslim religious community, and the European civilization"—placed him and the other reformists in direct opposition to the view of the Westernists.

They argued that it was impossible to divide European civilization into institutional and value components, that the various parts comprised an interrelated whole that had to be adopted in its entirety. Furthermore, they felt that any emphasis upon traditional values in the schools was inimical to development. Sabrettin Celal made an eloquent statement of this position:

Traditions and institutions which are foundations for value judgements are not logical and untouchable. These institutions were created out of necessity and came to be conservative and dominating. Times changed but they did not. The pedagogue's duty is not to help harmful traditions to survive, but to destroy them.[131]

Out of this debate came the intellectual underpinnings for the Ataturk revolution, but, as we shall see, Ataturk lay far more in the Westernist than in the reformist tradition, and his views on secularism and the adoption of Western culture conflicted very sharply with Gökalp's views. His acceptance of some of Gölkap's philosophy and his rejection of the rest was to influence future educational development in a very unexpected way as we shall demonstrate later.

In addition to this vigorous ideological debate, the Young Turk era witnessed many concrete accomplishments in education. One of their first steps was the reorganization in 1908 of the university that had been established by Abdul-Hamid II eight years earlier. It

---

[131] Cited in İlhan Başgöz and Howard E. Wilson, *Educational Problems in Turkey, 1920–1940*, Uralic and Altaic Series, no. 86 (Bloomington: Indiana University Press, 1968), p. 27. See also Berkes, *op. cit.*, pp. 407ff.

was moved to more adequate quarters and the curriculum was restructured to include the many subjects proscribed by that sultan for
political reasons such as history, philosophy, and sociology. The student body was greatly expanded and the former fee system abolished.
In 1914, 2,119 students were enrolled in the faculty of law, 348 in
religion and literary sciences, and 200 in mathematical sciences.[132]

The institution prospered greatly during these years, especially
from 1913 on, when many professors from Germany were recruited
and new libraries and scientific equipment of all sorts obtained. The
use of foreign professors proved to have both functional and dysfunctional aspects. Although their standards were higher and they engaged
in genuine research activities, their ignorance of Turkish limited their
effectiveness.

The university's relative vitality served to mask many serious deficiencies which were revealed by a study carried out in 1919. One of
the major problems cited was the lack of cooperation between various
faculties. Not only were all branches of learning separate, but the
spirit of each was very different and even conflicted directly, as, for
example, between the highly traditional school of religion and the
modern faculty of philosophy. Contributing to this cleavage was the
heterogeneous character of the faculty. Some were administrators
who had graduated from the Mülkiye, some were graduates from
European schools, others were former madrasa students. Furthermore, most of them maintained positions outside the university, so
their primary concern was not with the institution and its future. In
this atmosphere no collegiality could develop among the faculty, no
administration could provide unity of goals and purpose, and the university remained a mixture of old and new, East and West, with but
a limited impact upon the society.[133]

The other educational reforms of the Young Turks proved far
more significant. In 1913 a compulsory primary education law was
passed and there was a marked increase in school construction.
Equally important, the first step toward secularization of the religious
schools was taken in these years; the elementary schools, which had
previously been administered by the Ministry of Pious Foundations,

[132] Berkes, *ibid.,* p. 378.
[133] Ergin, *op. cit.,* III, 1017ff.

were placed under the direction of the secular Ministry of Education in 1916.[134]

The position of women also underwent a most significant change. Heretofore education for women had been limited to the few girls' schools, but the number of girl students at all levels of the system now increased sharply. This process, spurred by the manpower demands created by the strains of wartime, led to pressures for the admission of girls to the university. In 1915 they were permitted to attend a series of lectures and about 600 to 700 women did so in that year. This step was soon followed by the decision to open a women's section of the university, a decision provoked by the need to train women teachers for the growing number of secondary schools or teacher-training institutes for girls. This branch, which was separate from the male portion of the university owing to the strength of traditional attitudes concerning the position and the role of women in society, consisted of three sections: literature and humanities, natural sciences, and mathematics.

Despite the manpower shortages created by World War I, which forced a steady increase in the ultilization of women in administrative and clerical positions, women were still viewed in highly traditional terms by the mass of the populace. They were denied entry into parks until 1913, and they were assigned separate places in public facilities such as theatres and cinemas and even in the conferences organized by the nationalist Turkish Hearths organization. In this environment it should not be surprising that violent arguments arose when women workers began to dress without a veil, or over the fact that male and female university students, though attending lectures in separate classrooms, were sharing the same building and therefore were using the same doors, stairs, and corridors. As a result, the girls' college was moved to a separate building in another part of the city.[135]

The debate over women's rights continued to agitate the intellectuals during World War I but no steps were taken in the direction of coeducation at this time. The controversy, however, and the steady flow of women into the professions (except for medicine; Turkish women were unable to enroll in the medical school until 1917, and

[134] Başgöz and Wilson, *op. cit.*, p. 76.
[135] Ergin, *op. cit.*, IV, 1285ff.

even foreign women doctors were not permitted to practice until that date) commerce, industry, and administration continued.

Though their numbers were relatively few, these women formed the core of the feminist movement in Turkey, and with the support of many intellectuals they made great strides toward the emancipation of women. Their biggest victory was the family law of 1917 which gave women new rights in such matters as divorce and monogamy, and placed the religious courts that dealt with these matters under the control of the secular Ministry of Justice.[136]

Thus the Young Turk era proved to be, despite its conservative beginnings, a revolutionary decade. In many ways the Young Turks can be considered modernizers, for they were willing to remake the entire structure of the Empire in order to preserve it. Indeed, their dedication to change may well have caused the collapse of the Empire; the attempt to replace the existing social fragmentation with a new Ottoman national identity for Turks, Arabs, and Albanians alike proved disastrous as the Arab provinces broke away from the Empire. Thus the failures provided the geographic framework for the Turkish Republic, the successes the ideological and institutional foundations for the new nation. In about a century the Empire had been governed successively by adapters, reformers, and modernizers. But the greatest modernizer was yet to come.

Iran

Like the Ottoman Empire, Iran was compelled to attempt the painful task of transforming itself from a traditional society into a more powerful and modern country because of the pressures exerted by foreign powers who wished to extend their territories at its expense. As in the Ottoman Empire, a cataclysmic event was required to shake the strong Iranian feeling of superiority and to persuade the ruling shah to undertake reforms within the society. This took the shape of a series of successively more disastrous wars with Russia, culminating in the Treaty of Turkomanchai (1828). Once the weakness of Iran had become obvious, Russia expanded her effort to extend her influence within the country and was soon joined by Britain who, regarding Iran as an important buffer zone, viewed the

---

[136] Lewis, *op. cit.*, pp. 224–225

increased Russian encroachment as a direct threat to her position in the East. For Iran to preserve her independence in the face of this strong challenge, it was vital that reforms be undertaken in many areas, but in practice, relatively few changes took place within the country; her rulers, concerned primarily with preserving and strengthening their own position, quickly realized that Iran's sovereignty was safeguarded by the conflicting interests of Britain and Russia, who, in any case, were prejudiced against programs designed to strengthen the country. As a result, despite superficial similarities with the situation in the other contemporary Middle Eastern states, Iran remained essentially a feudal society and could best be classified as an adaptive political system.

The beginnings of adaptation to European power did take place in the nineteenth century, which witnessed the first attempts at establishing a modern military and bureaucratic establishment. As in the Ottoman Empire, the former was the primary focus; many Iranians still felt that although Iran could be defeated by Western armies, her inferiority was limited to military spheres and that the adoption of a new military technology would be adequate to ensure the survival of the state.[137] Accordingly, Fath Ali Shah and his successors sought to create an effective military establishment based on European patterns and armed with modern weapons. The first prerequisite was the integration of the tribal levies, which were traditionally relied upon to supplement the small standing armies, into a disciplined, effective body. To achieve this, various measures designed to institutionalize recruitment, conditions of service, and promotions were adopted. These efforts culminated in the successful creation of a standing army of 20,000 men by Amir Kabir, the able grand vizier of Nasr-ed-Din Shah who had acceded to the throne in 1848.[138]

Realizing that a new army needed new officers, Amir Kabir founded the first modern school in Iran, the Darolfunun, in 1852. He personally supervised the entire project, and because of British-Russian rivalry, turned to France and Austria for teachers. Some were recruited from the twenty-nine Persians who had been sent

---

[137] See F. Kazemzadeh, "Ideological Crisis in Iran," in Walter Laqueur, ed., *The Middle East in Transition* (New York: Praeger, 1958), pp. 196ff.

[138] Ann Lambton, "Persian Society under the Qajars," *Royal Central Asian Journal,* 48 (1961), 161ff.

abroad for training since 1811.[139] The spirit of the institution was from the outset French, as was the language of instruction. Fields of study included such military subjects as artillery, infantry, cavalry, and military engineering, as well as medicine, science, and mathematics.

The school was an elitist institution, and the students were recruited from the sons of the aristocracy, a not surprising practice since military officers were usually selected from this group. Although the school expected to admit a class of 30, the demand was so great that 105 students, 61 of whom studied military subjects, were enrolled, and within a few years, 270 students were admitted annually. Students entered at ten or eleven years of age for six or seven years of study.[140] Tuition was free and pupils were also subsidized with "two uniforms, or suits of clothes annually, summer and winter, daily breakfast, a small premium as the reward of passing certain examinations, a medal on learning. . . ." Since the students apparently tended to be lazy, punishments ranged from guard duty to flogging with a cat-o'-nine-tails and the bastinado, "the only punishment that is really feared." [141]

An Englishman who visited the school in the late nineteenth century described it as follows:

The first room we entered was the French class-room, where, under a Persian teacher, a large class was reciting and taking good hold of the language. The walls of the room were covered with very fair pencil-sketches and oil-paintings, the work of the pupils. In the English room Professor Tyler showed us a class of bright boys translating our mother-tongue. . . . These, with Russian, Arabic, and Turkish are the foreign languages taught. Had we come in the morning the sciences would have been on the programme. There was scientific apparatus and a small library representing many languages.

[139] Marvin Zonis, "Higher Education and Social Change in Iran: Problems and Prospects," paper delivered at the conference "Iran in the 1960's: A Consideration of Problems and Prospects," Columbia University, Nov. 7–9, 1968, mimeo., pp. 14–15. The paper was subsequently published in *Iran Faces the Seventies,* Ehsan Yar-Shater, ed. (New York: Praeger, 1971), pp. 217–259.

[140] Reza Arasteh, *Education and Social Awakening in Iran* (Leiden: E. J. Brill, 1962), p. 21; Ali Mohammed Kardan, *L'Organisation scolaire en Iran* (Geneva: Imprimerie Reggiam et Jaccoud, 1957), p. 47. According to Zonis, *op. cit.,* p. 8, students were admitted between the ages of fourteen and sixteen.

[141] Lord George Curzon, *Persia and the Persian Question* (2 vols.; New York: Barnes and Noble, 1966), I, 495.

The extent of the curriculum, the drill, and the evident success of the instruction in the shah's college were a great surprise to us. The number in attendance was two hundred and fifty composed of Persians and Armenians, with a few Hindus. All the native races and religions are admitted . . . all are in some degree supported. Some are given only a few tomans, while others have full support, the morning and evening meals being provided at the college. . . . His Majesty's object in maintaining the college is to prepare educated officers for the army and the civil service.[142]

The Darolfunun flourished until the end of the century when it was changed into a high school by the shah because he feared student unrest would be imported into his country from the Ottoman Empire, and it had a tremendous influence upon Iran. The school represented the first attempt to introduce modern education into the country, and in its classrooms Iranians were exposed to modern subjects taught by Europeans in Western languages. European works were translated to serve as textbooks and the school constituted the first translation bureau in the country. Most of its 1,100 graduates became important army officers or government employees, and many were also active in the intellectual and political movements which developed in Iran at this time.

The relatively slow pace of reform and change in Iran as compared with either the Ottoman Empire or Egypt is reflected in the almost total neglect of education after the establishment of the Darolfunun. Altogether only five more specialized institutions—two military colleges (1883, 1886) and schools of languages (1873), agriculture (1900), and political science (1901)—were opened in the next half century. The School of Political Science was designed to train students for the foreign service and its graduates were expected to serve without pay for several years—a device that ensured that the school would recruit its students only from the upper class, which was thus assured a practical monopoly of important bureaucratic positions.[143]

The turn of the century witnessed a resurgence of interest in education. Two more specialized colleges, a teacher-training institute and a medical school, were opened, and in 1898 the Council for National

[142] S. G. Wilson, *Persian Life and Customs* (New York: Fleming H. Revell, 1895), pp. 151–52.
[143] Zonis, *op. cit.*, p. 9.

Schools was established, the first attempt to initiate a modern, comprehensive network of schools. The impetus for these activities can, to some extent, be attributed to the influence of the missionary schools which had been in operation for about fifty years. The first were opened by the French Lazareths in 1837 in Azerbaijan, and before long other orders had established numerous French schools in the country. American missionaries were also active during this period and organized an American boys' school in Urmia in 1837; other schools were subsequently founded in 1872, 1873, 1881, and 1883. British missionaries opened several schools in the south of Iran in these decades. In addition, primary and secondary schools were sponsored by the Alliance Israélite Universelle and the Alliance Française. By 1926 there were forty-five foreign-sponsored schools in Iran.[144]

Before 1837, no modern primary or secondary schools had existed, and the influence of these educational establishments, despite their religious orientation, was apparently considerable. Because of their European character they were greatly admired by the ruling class, and before long pressures were generated to open similar institutions to be run by Iranians. The ensuing agitation led to the establishment of the Council for National Schools, which sponsored a number of modern primary schools; the first were opened in 1898, and by 1901 twenty-one such schools had been established, seventeen of which were located in Teheran.[145]

These very halting educational reforms were paralleled by equally limited changes in other spheres of Iranian life, and throughout the nineteenth century, popular unrest increased steadily since the limited Western impact that did occur created serious dislocations within the social order and made possible further exploitation by an upper class notorious for its rapacity.[146] The Qajar shahs were widely, and justly, regarded as inept rulers concerned only with exploiting the country for their personal benefit, a state of affairs that was facilitated by the

[144] Kardan, *op. cit.*, p. 45.

[145] *Ibid.*, pp. 46, 51. Another scholar states that twelve elementary and secondary schools were opened in Teheran in this period and that twenty-four more were opened by 1906. Hafiz Farman Farmayan, "The Forces of Modernization in Nineteenth-Century Iran: A Historical Survey," in Polk and Chambers, *op. cit.*, p. 148.

[146] Nikki R. Keddie, "The Iranian Power Structure and Social Change," *International Journal of Middle East Studies*, 2 (Jan. 1971), 5.

structure of Iranian society, which until the middle of the nineteenth century remained stratified along medieval lines.

The shah was the head of the government, and all administrators were his deputies. Bureaucrats, even those at the highest level, possessed limited prestige and ranked lower than large landowners and great tribal leaders. In other words, the bureaucrats were not members of the ruling class nor were they very numerous—the administration consisted essentially of a Bureau of Financial Affairs. As the century progressed, however, the need to expand and differentiate the administrative functions became obvious, particularly during the reign of Fath Ali Shah, and in 1858 Ministries of the Interior, Foreign Affairs, War, Finance, Justice, Stipends, and Waqfs were established.

This expansion and diversification of the civil service led to the rise to prominence of the high-level bureaucrats, many of whom were graduates of the Darolfunun. Their status and prestige increased greatly and many administrators of nonaristocratic background were co-opted into the ruling class. Various elites within the country also became more closely intertwined during this period. Persons of wealth, whether merchants (who performed the banking function for the country and whose financial resources were often relied upon by the upper class), ulema, or landowners often acquired government posts, most of which were available to the highest bidder. On the other hand, land remained a favored form of investment, and many persons who had amassed wealth, whether as bureaucrats, merchants, or ulema, often acquired large holdings. Thus tribal chiefs and landowners often filled government posts, bureaucrats and others became landowners.[147]

In effect, a new ruling class emerged which controlled all the important positions within the state and which, as we have seen, limited entry into the new educational institutions so as to retain a monopoly of the new skills required for these positions. Hence, as in the Ottoman Empire, the existing ruling class proved flexible and innovative enough to ensure the preservation of its position within the society. Unlike the situation in the Empire, however, so little economic, social, educational, cultural, and technological change took place that the social core group remained practically unchanged.

Ascriptive criteria for recruitment were accompanied by attitudes of

---

[147] Lambton, *op. cit.*, pp. 162ff.

social irresponsibility. Administrative positions were viewed solely as opportunities to increase one's wealth and power, and nepotism, intrigue, and corruption were rampant. Even the army was not a military machine but an institution for the enrichment of the upper class; sizable allocations for salaries and equipment seldom reached the bulk of the officers and enlisted men, many of whom supported themselves through trade.[148]

Mediating between this venal and corrupt upper class (which did number some reformers among its members) and the mass was the function of the ulema, whose members played the same roles as in earlier centuries. Their monopoly of educational institutions had continued virtually unchallenged, and despite obscurantism and nepotism the representatives of the religious institution continued to enjoy the respect of the populace who looked to them for guidance and protection from the government. In addition, the ulema in Iran were far stronger than in either the Ottoman Empire or Egypt, where their power had declined markedly as a result of the many reforms enacted during the nineteenth century; in Iran the process was reversed and their power actually increased because of the very ineffectiveness of the Qajar Shahs in achieving reform.[149]

No member of this dynasty was especially concerned with change, and Nasr-ed-Din Shah devoted his long reign (1848–1896) to safeguarding the status quo and preserving his own position. The country's backwardness was maintained, and the kinds of administrative and educational reforms that would have limited the bases of the ulema's power were not undertaken. The Shah's seeming passivity in the face of the strong external forces that impinged upon Iran can be understood in the light of the way these forces affected his own position. Not only did both Russia and Great Britain oppose fundamental change within Iranian society, but the rivalry between these two countries ensured his position. The balance between the two contending forces eliminated any need to develop a strong army to preserve the state and so the opening wedge of military reform was never driven deeply

---

[148] Keddie, *op. cit.*, p. 10.

[149] Nikki Keddie, "The Roots of the Ulama's Power in Modern Iran," a paper presented to the Middle East Studies Association meeting Chicago, December 8–9, 1967, multilithed, p. 2. See also Hamid Algar, *Religion and State in Iran* (Berkeley: University of California Press, 1969).

into Iranian society. Equally strong opposition to change was manifested by vested interests within the country, especially the ulema, whose strength, though ultimately derived from Shiite theological doctrine, was sufficient to prevent the adoption of any project that would threaten their position.[150]

In this situation reform was possible only with the support of the ulema. Not only was the religious elite a veto group within the state, but it alone possessed the ability to mobilize the lower classes and thus create the necessary pressures for change. At times it made strange alliances (as in the Tobacco Revolt of 1891) when it joined the struggle against foreign imperialism, and the ulema even went so far as to support the reformers' demands for a constitution. The result was the revolution of 1906, and ironically it was the West that provided the cement for this curious coalition since its influence was feared by both reformers and conservatives.

How these two factions could unite is exemplified by their attitude toward education. Both were opposed to the activities of the foreign schools; the ulema feared the religious influences of the missionary institutions; the nationalists appreciated the importance of modern education but feared that the nation's youth was being indoctrinated into an acceptance of foreign allegiances and loyalties that would destroy the state. As a result, the ulema and the reformers agreed that education had to be the responsibility of the state and that it had to be utilized to inculcate patriotic feelings and values.

This agreement was embodied in Articles 18 and 19 of the Constitutional Law of 1907, which provided for compulsory modern education for all Iranians and for the establishment of a Ministry of Science and Arts to control all schools (including the religious ones) within the country. This law was a truly revolutionary one; for the first time in the country's history the government accepted responsibility for education and entrusted the regulation of all schools to a Ministry. These principles were elaborated in 1910 when further legislation reorganized the Ministry of Education, stressed the need for compulsory elementary education, and advocated the collection of educational statistics, adequate teacher training, adult education, the publication of textbooks, the sending of students to Europe, and the

---

[150] *Ibid., passim.*

establishment of libraries, museums, and institutes. These principles were reaffirmed in the Fundamental Law of the Ministry of Education (1911), which gave this department control over all schools (religious and secular, public and private), emphasized compulsory primary education (though parents could choose to educate their children at home), established a comprehensive system of schools to be financed by the government, and called for free education for those who could not afford tuition. At the same time, the power of the religious conservatives was reflected in various provisions that called for the inclusion of the Shiite catechism in the elementary and secondary curriculum (Article 17) and the exclusion of any books that might endanger the students' religious belief (Article 14).[151]

All this legislative activity was not translated into significant educational achievements—nine elementary schools were opened and thirty students were sent to Europe—owing to the serious obstacles that lay in the path of creating an entirely new educational system. These were the problems previously faced by Egypt and the Ottoman Empire: the almost total lack of teachers and administrators, the entrenched opposition of religious conservatives, and the economic and political instability within the country.[152]

As a result, the nineteenth century did not witness the development, on any significant scale, of a modern educational system. Yet the efforts that had been made were evidently leading toward the emergence of the same sort of educational enterprise as in the other Middle Eastern states. Here, too, education was regarded in purely functional terms and schools were designed from the outset to provide trained manpower for the army and the bureaucracy. No consideration was given to the lower level of education, which remained largely the prerogative of the religious schools (except for foreign missionary activity). In time, however, it became obvious that the few colleges could not function in a vacuum and that if standards were to be raised, better prepared students would have to be recruited; as a result, modern educational institutions were opened at lower levels. This embryonic system encountered the same difficulties. Finding qualified teachers and students was a major problem throughout the period. As elsewhere, many

---

[151] For the text of these laws see Arasteh, *op. cit.,* pp. 135–142.

[152] Amin Banani, *The Modernization of Iran, 1921–1941* (Stanford: Stanford University Press, 1961), p. 91.

of the students who attended the modern schools were graduates of the traditional religious institutions; when primary schools were founded, most of the teachers were supplied by the madrasas. Once again it was to France that the government turned for advice and inspiration. For Iran, this country was a natural choice in view of the antipathy toward England and Russia, and most students who were sent abroad studied there. Thus French became the most common foreign language in the country, and French influence spread until it permeated the entire educational system.

All these developments, however, were on a very small scale. Iran entered the first decades of the twentieth century essentially a feudal society, and many educational and other reforms that had already so deeply affected Ottoman and Egyptian life had often not been initiated here. Iran still lacked an adequate infrastructure of human and physical resources, and any reformer determined to build a modern educational system would essentially have to begin anew.

IV

The Creation of
National Educational Systems

In the aftermath of World War I the political configuration of the Middle East changed drastically. The Ottoman Empire disappeared and from its provinces emerged the new states of the region. The former Arab portions of the Empire were largely under British occupation and the map of the Middle East was redrawn to suit the desires of the victorious allies. Such new countries as Syria and Lebanon became mandates of France; Iraq, Palestine, and Trans-Jordan mandates of Great Britain. Great Britain also maintained its control over the Persian Gulf states.

The war ended all ties between Egypt and the Ottoman Empire. At the same time an intense nationalist fervor continued to grow and an Egyptian delegation headed by Saad Zaglul sought unsuccessfully to obtain a formal hearing at the Paris Peace Conference. Nationalist agitation was far more influential within Egypt itself, and the turbulent postwar years revealed graphically the limited control which Great Britain could, in fact, exercise over events within the country. In 1920 an investigating commission headed by Lord Milner, concluding that nationalism had gained the support of practically all Egyptians, recommended that the protectorate be replaced by an alliance between an independent Egypt and Great Britain. Two years later this proposal was implemented; Egypt became nominally independent, Great Britain retaining control over defense and communications within the country. Not until 1936 did Egypt become truly independent.

Turkey, on the other hand, emerged from World War I as an independent and sovereign state though the Allies had intended to carve up most of the Anatolian heartland for themselves. Greece was to administer the area around Izmir, southeast Anatolia was to be autonomous, Armenia was to become an independent state. Though the Treaty of Sèvres which provided for this partition was reluctantly approved by the Ottoman government in Constantinople, the Turkish nationalists under Mustafa Kemal drove all foreign troops from the area and established the new state.

Iran, too, retained its independence, though events immediately following the end of the war seemed to presage extensive British control and the treaty of 1919 practically established a British protectorate. But in Iran, as in Turkey, nationalist sentiment proved sufficiently strong to withstand the challenge of colonial powers, and in the next few years Reza Khan emerged as a strong nationalist ruler.

As we shall see, however, each of the three countries with which we are primarily concerned was to develop along unique lines and each was characterized by a different type of political system: Turkey under Ataturk, the radical; Iran under Reza Shah, the reformist; and Egypt, the adaptive. It is to an examination of the educational developments that took place within these contexts that we now turn.

Egypt

Educational Expansion

The victory of the Nationalists and the proclamation of the constitution in 1922 did not mean the end of British influence in Egypt, an influence that was enhanced by the fragmentation, as in so many other countries, of the groups which had united in the drive for independence. A triad of forces—the King, the British High Commissioner, and the Wafd—dominated the political arena for many years so that Egypt suffered from an unstable polity characterized by a power struggle among the three main actors and dominated by personality politics. The British supported both the King and the Wafd at various times, but their importance declined after the conclusion of the Anglo-Egyptian treaty in 1936 which provided for the termination of the Capitulations, restricted their troops to the Canal Zone, and abolished the office of High Commissioner.

The King was the most powerful domestic political actor for, although the constitution provided for parliamentary government, he was accorded extensive powers which Fuad, concerned with self-aggrandizement, expertly utilized to prevent the consolidation of power by any strong personality. Upon his death in 1936, his son Farouk, who shared his father's concern with power, ascended the throne and degenerated into a corrupt playboy.

Because of the manipulations of the King and the High Commissioner, the Wafd—which enjoyed widespread support within the country—held power for only ninety months between 1922 and 1952. This party has been vividly described:

It contained all the generosity, intellectual muddle, good nature, contradictions and mythomania of its millions of supporters. It united the unlimited poverty of some and the insultingly bloated fortunes of others, the demand for change and the demand for conservatism, reaction and movement.[1]

From such a party functioning in such an environment, no coordinated program of social and economic change was to be expected, and in time it fragmented and deteriorated into a repressive nepotistic organization. Hence, the country's serious social and economic problems were never tackled and Egypt in this period can best be considered an adaptive polity. Its social core group consisted of a ruling class whose members were drawn from the royal family, the large landowners, the few entrepreneurs, the high-level administrators, and some important professional men.[2]

The politics of adaptation profoundly influenced education, which had assumed an almost mystical quality as a result of the heritage of Lord Cromer, and was widely regarded as a panacea for the country's problems. Only education of all social and economic issues was accorded its own clause in the new constitution; Article 19 provided for compulsory, free elementary education. Although this clause indicated the deep popular faith in education as a prerequisite for development and, indeed, for a viable democratic order,[3] it also reflected the existing dualism of the educational system and served to further reinforce it. Elementary schools, which provided a terminal education for the masses, were to be free. Primary schools, which led to an academic,

---

[1] Jean and Simone Lacouture, *Egypt in Transition* (New York: Criterion Books, 1958), p. 91.

[2] See P. J. Vatikiotis, "Some Political Consequences of the 1952 Revolution in Egypt," in *Political and Social Change in Modern Egypt*, P. M. Holt, ed. (London: Oxford University Press, 1968), p. 370.

[3] Nadav Safran, *Egypt in Search of Political Community* (Cambridge: Harvard University Press, 1961), pp. 147–148.

secondary, and higher education, were to remain on a fee basis and hence further strengthen the position of the ruling class.

A determined effort was made to universalize elementary education. Free compulsory schools were established in 1925, offering a six-year course (later reduced to five years) on a half day basis to provide for the largest possible number of students at minimum expense, and to gain parental support by allowing rural children to continue to assist their parents in the fields.[4] Elementary education also continued to be offered in the traditional kuttabs which were upgraded to some degree by the addition of modern subjects to the curriculum. A third type of school—the rural elementary school—was founded in 1943 in an attempt to provide children in rural areas with an education directly relevant to their needs. Thus the elementary system consisted of three different kinds of schools which were free and more or less traditional in subject matter. None of them, however, provided the great majority of the graduates any opportunity to advance further up the academic ladder, though a few students did transfer to primary schools after two years. Some students continued in the religious system and a few more went on to acquire a vocational or technical education.[5]

Total enrollments expanded rapidly from 324,000 in 1913 to 942,000 in 1933 to 1,600,000 in 1951,[6] but this growth appears far more impressive than it actually was. A rapidly increasing birth rate resulted in more and more children of elementary school age, and higher enrollments often served merely to accommodate the newcomers and not to increase the percentage of the population enrolled in schools. As late as 1944 only one-third of school age children actually attended school. A second reason why these apparently impressive growth rates were largely illusory is to be found in the nature and the quality of the education provided. Although this period was characterized by frequent curricular revisions, the reforms did not affect the basic concepts and methods of teaching or the general organization of the system. Most changes were minor, including attempts

[4] Russell Galt, *The Effects of Centralization on Education in Modern Egypt* (Cairo: Dept. of Education, American University at Cairo, 1936), p. 15.

[5] Roderick Matthews and Matta Akrawi, *Education in Arab Countries of the Near East* (Washington: American Council on Education, 1949), Chap. 2.

[6] Charles Issawi, *Egypt at Mid-Century* (London: Oxford University Press, 1954), p. 167.

to simplify an overcrowded syllabus and to introduce more practical subjects in the elite schools and more cultural subjects in technical schools, the de-emphasis of European languages, the classification of subjects into groups, the introduction of some degree of flexibility into the curriculum, and an increased concern with extracurricular activities.[7] Particularly in elementary schools, the traditional approach with its emphasis upon memorization of the Koran, religious instruction, and the teaching of Arabic remained consistently strong. A new syllabus drawn up in 1933, for example, provided for twenty-four periods of forty minutes each, half to two-thirds of which were devoted to these subjects.[8]

The benefits that a child might have received from exposure to such subject matter for a few years were further limited by the quality and methods of instruction, which remained highly traditional. Students were expected to memorize a large body of facts, discipline remained important, and examinations continued to dominate the thoughts of students and teachers alike. Although some measures were taken in 1935 and 1951 to reduce the importance of examinations, these had but limited effect. Rigidity and formalism dominated the educational system to such an extent that the schools of the 1930's were practically identical to those established by Mohammed Ali a century earlier. A report of the situation in the schools spoke of the "military rigidity of the daily life of the pupil," the "sad countenances of the greater part of the pupils . . . rigid behind their desks without any possibility of moving or stirring," and described conditions in one rural elementary school as follows:

We were present at a dictation exercise, given to small children from 6 to 7 years old, sons of peasants. The Egyptian professor who accompanied us told us that the text of this dictation exercise was so difficult that even he himself hardly understood it, and that certainly not one of the children to whom it was dictated could understand a word of it. Furthermore, the expressions of this exercise would never be used by these children, nor by peasants.[9]

[7] Mohammad Ahmad El-Ghannam, "Egyptian Public School Administration: An Historical Analysis and Appraisal" (Ph.D. diss., Columbia University, 1958), pp. 283, 352ff.

[8] Galt, *op. cit.*, p. 16.

[9] Dr. Claparède, *Rapport général présenté au Ministère de l'Instruction Publique* (Cairo: Ministry of Education, 1929), cited in Galt, *op. cit.*, p. 17.

Under these circumstances, few graduates remained functionally literate for any extended period. Nor did many children who entered an elementary school of one sort or another ever complete the course. Almost half of the total number of students enrolled in the compulsory elementary schools were in the first-year class and 77 per cent attended the first two classes—a clear indication that the great majority of the students attended school for only one or two years.[10]

One reason for the high dropout rate was the deterioration of standards resulting from the fact that the rapid increase in enrollments was not matched by a concomitant increase in physical and human facilities. Though the percentage of the budget devoted to education rose from 3.9 per cent in 1920 to 11.7 per cent in 1946, this increase could not be translated into enough schools or teachers, and before long all available resources were greatly strained. The situation was worsened by the fact that many school buildings were now taken over for the secondary schools so that primary education had to be conducted in inadequate structures that had not been designed for this purpose. Similar difficuties were encountered in the recruitment and training of teachers. Enrollments in teacher-training institutes as well as the number of these institutes and the length of their programs fluctuated widely. Whenever educational opportunities expanded, any available manpower, regardless of qualifications, had to be utilized; as a result: "Institutions for the training of teachers have, for the most part, developed as a particular type of school experienced a shortage of teachers or as a new type of school was established. Courses in such institutions have been shortened at need and lengthened when an emergency was less acute." A haphazard system of teacher training institutes developed: schools for elementary male teachers; schools for elementary female teachers; schools for teachers of primary schools for boys; a higher institute for women teachers of domestic sciences, the venerable Dar al-Ulum, founded in 1873, which had developed into a school specializing in the training of teachers of Arabic at all levels; the Institute of Education for Men and the Institute of Education for Women, which offered professional training to holders of B.A.'s.[11]

Morale in the teaching profession was already extremely low owing

[10] Matthews and Akrawi, *op. cit.*, p. 33.
[11] *Ibid.*, pp. 168, 95; Chap. 5.

to inadequate salaries and a lack of opportunities for advancement; these varied with the level at which the teacher taught—the higher the level the higher his prestige and the greater his remuneration. Thus everyone's goal was to enter the highly selective and elitist secondary level. If this were not possible then the teacher would strive to be assigned to a primary school; only the most unfortunate taught in the elementary schools where requirements tended to be lower than anywhere else.

The fragmentation of the teacher corps also led to the creation of further divisions within the Ministry of Education. This organization had expanded greatly in size and complexity, also in a haphazard manner, without any coherent consideration of the principles of effective administration. One result was that a large part of the educational budget was absorbed by the Ministry itself, another that what coordination and communication did exist was further weakened by the intense factionalism within all departments. This situation was described by Taha Hussein, a former minister of education, as follows:

I can testify without fear of contradiction that no other ministry in Egypt is so ridden by fierce rivalries, hatreds, suspicions and intrigues as the Ministry of Education. Not only individuals, but groups and classes, are pitted against each other. . . . graduates of the College of Dar al-Ulum are critical of the graduates of the highest school of teachers. These, in turn, form a hostile combination against a few graduates of the University and the Institute of Education who have begun slowly to move into the Ministry of Education.[12]

Under these circumstances, rational planning was impossible and the growth of the educational system took place without any systematic attempt at rationalization, although numerous commissions held countless meetings and published many plans for reform which were largely ignored. All plans were drawn up by high officials in the Ministry of Education, most of whom had little if any practical experience or contact with the schools. Thus most recommendations were not noted for their attention to practical considerations and, despite the proliferation of committees and groups concerned with education, each problem was dealt with separately. No attempt was made until 1943 to produce a coherent comprehensive national plan for education.

[12] El-Ghannam, *op. cit.*, pp. 297ff. Taha Hussein, cited in *ibid.*, p. 329.

The many weaknesses of the Ministry of Education adversely affected the quality of education in every school in the country, since the organizational structure provided for the total centralization of all activities in Cairo. Every aspect of education ranging from syllabi to curricula and from staffing and examinations to equipment and maintenance in every elementary, primary, and secondary school was controlled by the Ministry, which permitted no deviations of any sort from its detailed regulations, thus effectively stifling any possible initiative or flexibility within particular schools. To improve the administration of education, various attempts were made at decentralization, especially in 1938 when the country was divided into educational zones with a director possessing rather limited powers in charge of each, but few changes actually took place in the functioning of the system since the Ministry tended to retain ultimate control.[13]

To ensure that each school did conform to the established pattern was the responsibility of ministerial inspectors. These individuals were primarily interested in demonstrating their power and authority, and were viewed by the teachers with fear, hatred, and suspicion. Nor were many inspectors concerned with meaningful educational practice. On the contrary, their emphasis was upon strict adherence to central rules and regulations. As a result of such factors, the inspection system was highly authoritarian in character and tended to be worse than useless since it was positively damaging for teachers and students alike. In 1948 an attempt was made to reform the inspection system so as to render the visits a more meaningful educational experience.[14]

All these reforms had but limited consequences for the educational process, which remained highly scholastic, authoritarian, and rigid. These characteristics were most marked in the elementary schools; the primary and secondary schools, though sharing many of these deficiencies, operated at a somewhat higher level. Not only did they attract abler teachers, at least those with more influence in the ministry, but the elitist part of the system was allocated the greatest part of the educational budget and thus enjoyed better facilities of all sorts. In the 1942–1943 school year, for example, about 57 per cent of all teachers were assigned to elementary schools enrolling 80 per cent of all students; in the modern schools 43 per cent of the teachers taught

---

[13] *Ibid.,* pp. 352ff.
[14] *Idem.*

20 per cent of the students. The student-teacher ratio was one teacher per forty-two students in the elementary schools, and one teacher per fourteen students in the other institutions.[15] Yet here, too, the emphasis remained upon rote learning and the memorization of as large a body of data as possible within the time that the student spent in school.

Secondary and Higher Education

The most attention was devoted to the secondary and higher levels of the system where the percentage of enrolled students increased at a faster rate than in the elementary and primary schools; the number of secondary students increased from 2,500 in 1913 to 15,000 in 1933 to 122,000 in 1951.[16] Here, too, numerous efforts were made to reform the schools. In 1925 secondary education was reorganized on a five-year basis, the first three years being devoted to general subjects, the remaining two providing for specialization in either science and mathematics or social studies and literature. In 1935 the curriculum was revised to provide more balance between general and specialized subjects by instituting an examination after four years of general education. If he were successful, the student spent a year specializing in mathematics, science, or literature, after which he would take a second examination in his field. This program continued until 1949 when the curriculum was reorganized to permit the student to begin specializing in one field at an earlier age. For the first two years the pupil would study general subjects and then at about age fifteen was permitted to begin concentrating on his basic field. This reform was never fully implemented, though it was incorporated into a 1953 proposal which created a preparatory stage covering the last two years of primary and the first two of secondary education.[17] Despite all these revisions, secondary education remained largely medieval in orientation with an emphasis upon preparation for the dreaded examination by rote memorization of a large quantity of unrelated factual data.

A similar approach pervaded the colleges and universities. Despite great popular demand, an official Egyptian University was not formally

[15] Matthews and Akrawi, *op. cit.,* p. 37.
[16] Issawi, *op. cit.,* p. 67.
[17] Mohammed Khairy Harby and Mohammed Al-Hadi Afifi, "Education in Modern Egypt," *International Review of Education,* 4 (1958), 430.

established until 1925. It incorporated the private institution of 1909 as the college of arts, and the other existing higher institutions—law, medicine, engineering, agriculture, and commerce—became its other colleges. The name was changed to Fuad University in 1936 and to the University of Cairo in 1953. A second university was begun in Alexandria in 1942, a third in Ain Shams in 1950. University enrollments had reached 41,000 in 1951.[18]

The rapid expansion of facilities at the secondary and university levels bore no relation to the needs of the country in terms of either numbers or specializations and created serious political problems. Higher education remained a passport to government employment, but the number of positions open to graduates shrank steadily in relation to the number of applicants during the period. At the same time, given the nature of the political system, attempts to control admissions were bound to be unsuccessful. Hence the expansion in university enrollments was accompanied by a drop in standards and by a growing problem of absorption. As early as 1920, the Milner Commission, which investigated conditions in Egypt and made recommendations for a new constitution, noted that "the supply of such candidates has long exceeded the demand, both of the Government service and the professional colleges. . . . the number of certificate holders largely exceeds the number that can actually be employed by the State." In future years this situation worsened appreciably, especially for persons of non-ruling-class background who sought a higher education in increasing numbers, and as early as 1937, 11,000 university graduates could not obtain any employment at all. An even greater number were unable to find positions commensurate with their expectations.[19]

Although the bureaucracy continually overexpanded to provide such persons with positions (one former minister of finance estimated that about half of all government employees were superfluous),[20] this policy did not resolve the fundamental problem, for many who were hired in this manner found themselves occupying positions of low prestige and remuneration. The discrepancy between their self-image

---

[18] Issawi, *op. cit.*, p. 67.

[19] Malcolm Kerr, "Egypt" in *Education and Political Development,* James S. Coleman, ed. (Princeton: Princeton University Press, 1965), pp. 185–186; Safran, *op. cit.*, p. 207.

[20] Abu Al-Futouh Ahmad Radwan, *Old and New Forces in Egyptian Education* (New York: Teachers College, Columbia University, 1951), p. 117.

and the actual positions they filled was frustrating, and frustrations quickly translated into political action. As the university students' perceptions of the future that awaited them became increasingly dismal, they turned to political activism, a phenomenon that, as we shall see later, was to be repeated in other Middle Eastern countries. Strengthening such feelings were the many physical, psychological, social, and economic problems which students, particularly those from more traditional backgrounds, encountered in attempting to adjust to the demands of university life. Egyptian students and recent graduates were also deeply affected by ideological considerations. The growing tide of nationalism that swept across the country following World War I had a tremendous impact upon them, as we have seen, and they formed an important component of the nationalist movement led by Saad Zaglul in 1919. Subsequent decades, especially the thirties, witnessed a great burst of intellectual vitality in which students actively participated. Between 1937 and 1947, for example, the number of writers and journalists in the country increased from 1,200 to 8,200.[21]

One result of this intellectual ferment was the ever increasing politicization and polarization of the students. Radical and extreme ideologies of various kinds gained rapidly in popularity within the country and in the universities as the moderates, represented by the Wafd, proved unable to resolve the country's serious social, economic, political, and cultural problems. The internal weaknesses of the Wafd were compounded by the pressures from extremists and by the maneuvering of the king, which further undermined its legitimacy and spurred its fragmentation. The growing disillusionment with liberal doctrines deeply affected the students, most of whom had originally been highly sympathetic of the Wafd. By the end of the massive anti-British and pro-democratic demonstrations of 1935–1936 this support had been deeply eroded, and more extreme parties such as the religious, revolutionary Muslim Brotherhood and the neo-fascist Young Egypt gained in popularity among all sectors of society, including college and secondary students who were soon organized as extensions of the major political groupings, the Wafdists as "Blue Shirts," and the supporters of Young Egypt as "Green Shirts." The political climate degenerated rapidly and frequent bloody clashes between paramilitary

---

[21] Raoul Markarius, *La Jeunesse intellectuelle d'Egypte au lendemain de la deuxième guerre mondiale* (The Hague: Mouton, 1960).

student factions espousing different ideologies and supporting rival factions took place in the streets of Cairo, notably in 1936–1937 and in the period after World War II. Such demonstrations, in which thousands of other persons participated, had a profound impact upon the political scene and were responsible for many of the numerous cabinet crises that occurred during these years.[22]

The students at Al-Azhar were also affected by these developments. Demonstrations were no new phenomenon for them, though usually these were provoked by academic questions. In the thirties, however, student agitation here as in the secular institutions became more politically motivated, fragmented, and extremist, for, as we shall see, employment prospects and job security also played an important role in driving these students toward activism. All parties were represented at Al-Azhar, though the degree and type of student involvement is unclear. However, it does not appear that the Muslim Brotherhood enjoyed as great a following here as in the secular universities. It has been estimated that nearly one-third of the students at the universities of Cairo and Alexandria were active members or supporters of the Brotherhood.[23]

Despite the many common problems and the often common reactions that characterized the Azharites and students in the other institutions of higher learning, the gap between the two continued to grow steadily as Al-Azhar remained a stronghold of traditionalism where students received age-old training in Islamic subjects. Ancient teaching methods continued to be used, as did many of the historic textbooks that had been used for centuries. Practically the only change that took place was the reorganization of the system of religious schools to correspond to the primary, secondary, and higher levels of the modern schools. The primary religious stage lasted for four years, the second-

[22] P. J. Vatikiotis, *The Modern History of Egypt* (New York: Praeger, 1969), pp. 315ff; see also James P. Jankowski, "The Egyptian Blue Shirts and the Egyptian Wafd, 1935–1938)," *Middle Eastern Studies*, 6 (Jan. 1970), 78. Makarius, *op. cit., passim.*

[23] See Sylvia G. Haim, "State and University in Egypt," in *Universität und Moderne Gesellschaft,* Chauncy D. Harris and Max Horkheimer, eds. (Frankfurt, 1959), pp. 103ff; Christina Phelps Harris, Nationalism and Revolution in Egypt (The Hague: Mouton, for The Hoover Institution on War, Revolution, and Peace, 1964), pp. 158ff; Jankowski, *op. cit.,* pp. 78ff; Markarius, *op. cit.,* pp. 55ff.

ary course for five years; Al-Azhar provided undergraduate and graduate training in its three faculties on Muslim law, theology, and Arabic.[24]

The degree to which Al-Azhar remained unaffected by the modern educational currents that swept through the country in these decades cannot be exaggerated. A director of that institution observed in 1929:

> For the last few centuries the leaders of the Azhar have taken a rest. . . . They have remained unconscious of the new ideas and new schools of learning that have come into the world. . . . there are leaders of the Azhar who think it is a sin to study geography, arithmetic or history. They write articles in the daily press against these subjects. . . . With the greatest sorrow I can declare that the endeavors made with regard to the improvement of the Azhar and other religious institutes during the last twenty years have proved fruitless.[25]

His judgment was equally valid twenty years later.

Al-Azhar remained a medieval institution in the face of significant efforts at reform from both within and without because the question of its future became a vital dimension of the power struggle between the king and the Wafd. The monarch regarded the religious institution in general and Al-Azhar in particular as important sources of legitimacy and power in his struggle with the Nationalists over royal prerogatives. All attempts at reform were viewed in political terms: Would the position of Al-Azhar and its graduates vis-à-vis the secular institutions be affected? Would the traditional position and role of the institution within Egyptian society be altered? With the strong support of the king, the conservatives who controlled the institution were able to maintain the status quo. Ironically, this policy proved self-defeating, and their success in preventing change was to produce the very results that they fought so vigorously against—the ultimate extinction of the power and influence of Al-Azhar and its graduates within Egypt.

Although many of the ulema showed reformist tendencies, attempts at reform were inevitably beaten back by the leadership, and the insurgents, including such noted figures as Taha Hussein, were dis-

---

[24] See Jorg Kraemer, "Tradition and Reform at al-Azhar University," *Middle East Journal*, 7 (March 1956), 89–94. See also Matthews and Akrawi, *op. cit.*, Chap. 6.

[25] Cited in Galt, *op. cit.*, p. 31.

ciplined or coerced. One illustration will suffice to demonstrate the extent to which Al-Azhar was able to withstand challenges to its scholasticism: Although English was listed in the curriculum in 1901, and King Farouk subsequently commanded that it be taught, the first course was not offered until 1958.[26]

The success of the Azharites in staving off attempts at change by outside forces—essentially the Nationalists, whose stronghold was the Parliament and who represented the major challenge to conservative domination of Al-Azhar—was achieved only at a heavy cost to both the institution and the country. In 1927, Parliament, as a part of the struggle to reform and secularize different aspects of Egyptian life, attempted to extend its authority over Al-Azhar by appropriating its budget and abrogating the right to make important appointments within it. This attempt was foiled by the alertness of the Azharites who enlisted the support of the monarch and conservative elements within Parliament. The consequences of this victory were disastrous for Al-Azhar: Parliament reacted by discriminating against its graduates seeking official positions and by refusing to provide funds for the school, forcing it to become more than ever dependent upon the king and implacably opposed to the nationalists. Under these circumstances, reform was impossible and the liberals bypassed the institution completely, a policy which hastened its stagnation and isolation. Thus, though religious purity was maintained within Al-Azhar, its influence diminished, the position of students and teachers deteriorated, and most importantly, the cleavage within the society widened.[27]

The differences between the modern universities and the religious institutions also extended to the background of the students who were attracted to these schools. Persons enrolled at Al-Azhar tended to be the children of religious leaders or of farmers and peasants. For them this institution provided practically the only opportunity for occupational mobility and further schooling. Many of the students at the University of Cairo, on the other hand, were of upper-class background and considered themselves members of the ruling class, not only because of their training, but also because of their membership in wealthy and powerful families. The vocational aspirations of the

[26] Daniel Crecelius, "Al-Azhar in the Revolution," *Middle East Journal,* 20 (Winter 1966), 34.
[27] *Ibid.,* p. 33.

two groups also differed greatly. Those from the University of Cairo wished to enter the professions and the administration; those from Al-Azhar preferred to remain in the religious hierarchy or to teach traditional subjects.[28] Some of them came to teach such subjects as Arabic and theology in the modern schools, so that the medieval methods and attitudes which continued to be the norm at Al-Azhar were transplanted into the modern parts of the system. For this reason, much of the formalism and traditional emphases that marked the modern schools can be attributed to the influence of the religious institution.

The most important consequence of Al-Azhar's stagnation, however, was to promote the emergence of conflicting outlooks and aggravate the cultural gap within the country. As Taha Hussein noted:

In any issue that arises or event that occurs, the graduate of the Azhar conceives it in one sense, while the graduate of the modern schools conceives it in another sense. . . . Thus, the two different graduates agree neither in their thinking nor in their evaluations; nor do they agree in judgment and decisions; nor in procedure and action.[29]

Reform and Stagnation

This division between religious and secular was but one of the cleavages within the society that was reflected and reinforced by the educational system. Another was the elite-mass gap, reinforced by the distinction between primary and elementary education until 1943, when the fee system for the former was formally abolished and the number of free positions in the secondary schools increased.[30] But, despite a considerable amount of discussion, elementary education was not unified so as to allow the graduates of the elementary schools to advance up the academic ladder until well after World War II. A new program adopted in 1951 provided for a common six-year course culminating in an examination and a certificate, but the reform could not be implemented since the elementary schools did not possess the resources to teach all the prescribed courses. The biggest bottle-

[28] See Mahmoud A. R. Shafshak, "The Role of the University in Egyptian Elite Recruitment: A Comparative Study of Al-Azhar and Cairo University" (Ph.D. diss., University of Chicago, 1964).
[29] Taha Hussein, cited in Radwan, *op. cit.*, p. 112.
[30] Matthews and Akrawi, *op. cit.*, p. 17.

neck was foreign language instruction (knowledge of a foreign language was a requirement for admission to the secondary level), which very few of the former elementary schools could provide. As a result, the intent of the reform was largely negated, the great majority of the elementary students were still effectively barred from continuing their education, and education remained practically as elitist as ever.

The other changes during this period proved even less realistic. In 1950 the Wafd government, in an attempt to gain popular support, amended a year-old law which provided free tuition to qualified students in the first two years of secondary schooling so as to provide free secondary education to all. No thought was given to the explosion of demands for admission to the secondary schools or to other disastrous consequences of this change. The resulting flood of applicants strained existing facilities to the utmost, placed new strains upon educational budgets, diverted students away from the technical and vocational schools, and would shortly have placed intolerable pressures upon the universities and the absorptive capacity of the bureaucracy had not the postrevolutionary government, in 1953, limited admission to the secondary schools.[31]

The damage done vocational and technical education by this measure was considerable, and the quality of this largely neglected field declined dramatically. Several different vocational and technical schools were in operation during this period, but though they apparently provided training in a wide variety of subjects, they were very inadequate in terms of quality, quantity, and relevance to industrial requirements. Boys could attend schools of trade where they studied such subjects as carpentry, automobile repairing, sheet-metal work, or tailoring; schools of commerce where they could study business practices in preparation for careers as clerks; schools of agriculture where they learned to be competent farmers; a school of applied engineering designed to train them as foremen, supervisors, and junior officials; or a school of applied arts where they could specialize in weaving, wood and ivory carving, enamel work, or photography. Girls could enroll in schools of home economics, embroidery, and dressmaking.[32]

Even in terms of numbers these schools left much to be desired;

[31] Kerr, *op. cit.*, pp. 175–176.
[32] Matthews and Akrawi, *op. cit.*, pp. 66–70.

only 30,132 students were attending institutions of this type, including teacher-training ones, in 1944–1945. By and large, only students who could not qualify for admission into academic institutions were enrolled; they were considered low-prestige schools and were unappealing to most students, owing to their weaknesses as well as to cultural factors within the society. These schools made only a small contribution to meeting the country's needs for middle-level manpower. They prepared students in fields that were not particularly relevant to industry's needs and did so badly. The schools were poorly administered, inefficient, and inadequately equipped. The quality of the teaching staff was also poor; most instructors were teaching subjects in which they had not had any practical experience. Most graduates sought not a position in industry but a clerkship in the bureaucracy and even those who wished to follow a vocational career had great difficulty in finding jobs, since employers were unwilling to pay a premium to hire such personnel, and regarded them as unqualified and irresponsible troublemakers.[33]

The elitism of the educational system in this period is also evidenced by the role of private and foreign-supported schools. These schools enjoyed much prestige and constituted an important segment of the educational system. In the 1942–1943 school year, for example, 25 per cent of all pupils enrolled below the secondary level were in these schools (mainly private Muslim schools) and about 50 per cent of all secondary level students were also enrolled in such institutions. Their program closely paralleled that of the public schools and prepared students for the official examinations, though the foreign schools also provided their students with the opportunity to prepare for study abroad.[34]

The number of persons who had the opportunity to receive such an education was very limited. The educational system during these years produced thousands of graduates who have been described by an Egyptian scholar who has analyzed the school system as lacking in initiative and adventure, social intelligence and vision, the ability to think independently, and an appreciation of knowledge and culture.

[33] Frederick H. Harbison and Ibrahim A. Ibrahim, *Human Resources for Egyptian Enterprise* (New York: McGraw-Hill, 1958), pp. 120–228. The figures are from Matthews and Akrawi, *op. cit.,* Table 3, p. 34.
[34] Matthews and Akrawi, *op. cit.,* pp. 111–113.

He pointed out that all students sought to obtain an administrative position, regardless of its routine nature or low salary, that they were incapable of understanding or participating in the national life, let alone directing it, that they lacked the ability for creative, innovative thought, and that since they had forgotten the information with which they had been stuffed they were practically illiterate.[35] The political consequences of such education were disastrous for:

The only lessons related to social and political life which the students learned well was an intransigent, negative nationalism and an understanding of patriotism as a readiness to commit and suffer violence in the name of the nationalist slogans. . . . Hence the failure of education to instill any guiding principles of personal behavior left the growing generations from the middle classes in a moral and spiritual vacuum which they filled by opportunism, reckless pursuit of pleasure, and destructive political adventures or agitation.[36]

Thus by 1952 Egypt was rift by numerous social, political, and cultural cleavages, a state of affairs to which the educational system had contributed greatly. Its elitist, fragmented structure ensured that divisions between elite and mass, town and country, graduates of the religious system and of the secular schools, would become ever deeper; its ethos ensured that even the graduates of the modern schools would be ignorant automatons possessing the negative attributes described above.

The cost to Egypt of such an educational enterprise was, of course, immense, but the essential reason for this state of affairs was to be found not in the schools but in the character of the society itself. As long as Egypt remained an adaptive polity marked by political instability and an absence of dynamic leadership the schools would naturally continue to be agencies dysfunctional to national aspirations. Only if the polity were transformed could the kinds of basic reforms required to revitalize such an educational system be undertaken.

The Arab World

The status of education in the other Arab countries of the Middle East in the interwar period more or less resembled the situation in

---

[35] Radwan, *op. cit.,* pp. 116ff.
[36] Safran, *op. cit.,* p. 208.

Egypt. School attendance expanded greatly everywhere as governments in all Arab countries (except Lebanon) assumed primary responsibility for education. Despite these great advances in school enrollments, however, significant numbers were still not attending school everywhere—the proportion of children enrolled in 1942–1945 ranged from 72.7 per cent in Lebanon to 47.4 per cent in Egypt, 39.4 per cent in Syria, 28 per cent in Jordan, and 20 per cent in Iraq.[37]

Even those students attending school often benefited little from their experience. Western models, especially French and British, were widely imitated though in many cases they contained administrative, curricular, or other structural features that were inapplicable to conditions in the country adopting them. One important reason for this uncritical transplantation was the lack of trained educational personnel in these countries, though Ministries of Education were established everywhere. Few specialists in education were available to staff the various departments, so that school administration in practically every country was "carried on in an amateurish fashion."[38] This difficulty was aggravated by the high degree of centralization whereby all educational policies, including financing, determination of syllabi, curricula, textbooks, examinations, and staffing, were all carried out in the metropolis. This characteristic dampened local interest and initiative and denied local schools much-needed flexibility. Thus, whether the child was an Egyptian, an Iraqi, or a Jordanian, he usually had to memorize a mass of data with limited applicability to his environment or to the national situation in order to pass the appropriate examinations. Seldom was the curriculum geared to local needs. Syllabi were decreed by the central ministry and did not permit any gradation or variation in the choice of courses. The natural result was a very high dropout rate; often the student averaged only two years of school or so. In Iraq, Syria, Jordan, and Egypt, usually less than 10 per cent of the total student body was enrolled in the upper grades.

Those students who successfully completed the elementary schools found the same conditions at the higher levels. The dominant type of secondary school was academic, designed to prepare students for the university and largely limited to students who could afford to pay the fees charged. The fee system was common to all the Arab coun-

[37] See Matthews and Akrawi, *op. cit.*, Table 92, p. 544.
[38] *Ibid.*, p. 542.

tries, though the amount of tuition varied greatly; Iraq and Syria were noted for low fees. Some countries, especially Iraq, also provided general scholarships and other exemptions to enable qualified students of lower-class origin to attend these schools. The availability of secondary places also varied considerably, the most limited system being found in Jordan which in 1945–1946 possessed but one secondary school.

Vocational education was sadly neglected everywhere and the many unfilled places served as mute testimony to the low esteem enjoyed by this type of education. Low prestige, poor quality, and limited opportunities after graduation inhibited the expansion of vocational schools, whose general condition throughout the Arab world can perhaps best be appreciated when one realizes that the Egyptian system was the best in the region.

Another common feature was the examination system which everywhere served as a means of eliminating students at each stage. From 20 to 50 per cent of the applicants normally failed, thus creating intense pressures for an education geared to passing the dreaded tests. Any subject not included in the examinations was always neglected, and any tendency to experimentation was effectively stifled by the need to prepare for the examination. This system was usually defended on the grounds that it raised standards in all schools, especially the private ones, and that it served to promote national unity by ensuring that such subjects as history, geography, and Arabic were taught in the same way in all schools. However, high scholarly standards were maintained in many countries "without the necessity of rigid examinations which create mistrust in all the teaching body, hinder experimentation, and are a constant source of neurotic worry besides being detrimental to character in the incentive they give to cheating." [39]

One of the basic weaknesses in all countries was a shortage of teachers, although significant differences existed within the area. Only Egypt and Iraq were training adequate numbers of primary school teachers; Lebanon, Jordan, and Syria were graduating far too few to meet existing needs. Even where adequate numbers had been produced, however, quality remained a fundamental problem. The length of training varied considerably from country to country, ranging from

[39] *Ibid.*, p. 555.

less than the secondary level to two years of graduate study. Most teachers received less rather than more preparation, but even those teachers who possessed a high level of formal training were not usually effective teachers, since the highly formal and academic preparation bore little relationship to classroom realities in town or village. To a large degree this was due to the poor quality of the faculty responsible for teacher training. Institutes were staffed and administered by persons without adequate professional training or practical experiences; low standards tended to be the norm. Furthermore, in all countries, the worst teachers were to be found in villages, compounding the many problems confronting rural education.

Finally, it should be noted that the place of foreign schools in the national system of education became increasingly controversial throughout the Arab world as nationalist feelings spread. Missionary schools were criticized for religious proselytizing and some foreign schools, especially the French and Italian, for serving as centers of propaganda for their countries of origin and for neglecting the teaching of the national culture. All foreign schools were accused of contributing to the perpetuation of divisions within the state. Such feelings led to legislation in every country regulating the activities of these schools in various ways and bringing them more or less completely under state control, and, more importantly, to the fundamental political changes that were to take place in the Arab countries after World War II.

Turkey

The Modernization of Society and Education

Unlike Egypt, Turkey in this period enjoyed the leadership of a man of vision, courage, and ability who forged a new nation out of the remnants of a defeated empire and launched it effectively on the path to modernization. That man was Mustafa Kemal (Ataturk) who, following the establishment of the Turkish Republic, promptly forced through fundamental changes in social and political institutions, changes that he rightly considered essential to modernization. In our terms, therefore, the Turkey of Ataturk represents a radical political system.

Education was an important component of his program, for Ataturk realized that the essence of modernity lay in the minds of people. His concern with education is attested to by the fact that the nationalists established their own Ministry of Education as early as May 2, 1920, while still fighting against the Allied-supported Ottoman government in Istanbul.[40] A national congress to discuss educational problems was convened a year later, but a major Greek assault in the direction of Ankara forced its postponement. The Greeks were finally expelled from Turkey in 1922, and the Treaty of Lausanne (1923), which recognized the sovereignty of the Ankara government, marked the end of a decade of fighting. Mustafa Kemal immediately turned his attention to problems of nation-building; one month later the sultan was deposed and the Turkish Republic proclaimed, with Mustafa Kemal as the first president.

The problems confronting the new government were immense; most of the country was almost totally underdeveloped, its people exhausted by years of fighting, most of its meager resources destroyed. Only the larger towns had been affected to any extent by Western values and technology, and even the majority of the urban dwellers could, at best, be classified as transitionals. More importantly, only a minority of the political elite was convinced of the necessity or desirability of the radical transformation envisaged by Mustafa Kemal. From the majority often came strong opposition to many specific reforms, an opposition usually supported by religious and other traditional elements within the country. If the political elite was divided, the masses were apathetic and ignorant. Feelings of loyalty to the new nation and an acceptance of modernity had to be inculcated in the great majority of the inhabitants of the new state. Accordingly, Mustafa Kemal embarked upon a radical policy of transforming the very nature of the polity and of adopting reforms that would change not only the outward appearance but ideally the mentality and behavior of the people as well.

In this effort education was to play a vital role, but the existing educational system was in a pathetic state; physical facilities and human resources were totally inadequate, the overwhelming majority of the populace was illiterate, and the structure inherited from the Ottoman Empire was of limited utility for nation-building and de-

---

[40] İlhan Başgöz and Howard E. Wilson, *Educational Problems in Turkey, 1920–1940,* Uralic and Altaic Series, no. 86 (Bloomington: Indiana University Press, 1968), pp. 37–38.

velopment. Accordingly, from the beginning Mustafa Kemal adopted a conscious policy of reorganizing the entire educational system, expanding it in a systematic way and harnessing it to national goals. He moved almost at once to create a unified integrated system of education which could serve as the mainspring for the drive to modernity.

The Great Reforms

The first step was to create a coherent, integrated, and secular system out of the many modern schools that had developed rather haphazardly in the past decades. In 1924 the Law for the Unification of Instruction placed all educational institutions under the control of the Ministry of Education. This reform, like so many others, had been discussed for many years, and during the Young Turk period the religious primary schools had been transferred to the Ministry of Education. Nevertheless, it was not until Mustafa Kemal assumed power that any steps were taken to abolish religious schools or to eliminate religious teaching from public schools.

Secularization was one of the basic principles of Ataturk's ideology and he quickly moved to destroy the form, substance, and institutional bases of Islam. In rapid succession he forced the removal of the caliphate, abolished the religious courts, introduced Western law codes, abolished the powerful religious orders and the madrasas, and assigned the religious endowments and their revenues to the Ministry of Education. Altogether 479 madrasas with a total enrollment of 18,000 (of whom perhaps 6,000 were genuine students) were closed.[41] This step marked the end of the dual system of religious and secular schools. At one stroke Mustafa Kemal eliminated the cause of the cultural separatism which had afflicted Ottoman society—and which continued to affect other Middle Eastern countries, especially Egypt, so deeply—namely, the gap between those trained in modern schools and those trained in the madrasas. From then on Turkish schools were to produce only persons prepared to function in the modern world. In 1928 the principle of secularism was formally incorporated into the constitution.

[41] *Ibid.*, pp. 77–78. According to Robert J. Kerner, *Social Sciences in the Balkans and Turkey* (Berkeley: University of California Press, 1930), p. 117, the Republic abolished 490 madrasas with 12,000 students.

Secularization also entailed the elimination of religious instruction from the curriculum of the modern schools, and before long, no religious subjects were taught in urban schools. What is often overlooked, however, is that Mustafa Kemal moved cautiously in dealing with the rural populace on this and, as we shall show, other matters as well. Religious instruction was not forbidden in rural schools. There it remained a part of the curriculum though it was placed within the framework of a liberal philosophy emphasizing respect for different beliefs, avoidance of fanaticism and fatalism, and the importance of good citizenship.

Secularism applied to foreign and missionary schools as well as to Turkish schools, and no religious instruction was permitted in these institutions. All religious pictures and symbols had to be removed from textbooks, buildings, and classrooms, and when missionaries did not comply with these provisions, their schools were closed—nor could intervention by a foreign government modify the edict.[42]

Foreign and private schools remained in as delicate a position in Turkey as in the rest of the Middle East despite the official policy of the Turkish government that foreign schools would be permitted to function within the country as long as they did not infringe in any way upon secularist and nationalist principles. In 1927 a *cause célèbre* involving the alleged conversion of several Muslim girls in an American school led to vociferous demands within the country for the closure of all foreign schools. The government reacted strongly, closing the school involved and enacting strict controls over these institutions. Religious propaganda of any sort was absolutely forbidden, and new regulations covered the teaching of politically significant subjects; Turkish history, geography, and literature were to be taught only by Turkish nationals and in accordance with the specifications of the Ministry of Education concerning the time allocated and their content. That the Turkish government was not inherently hostile to foreign schools was evidenced in 1930 when the American schools were exempted from a tax which would have bankrupted them. The official attitude could perhaps best be described as cool tolerance, and all foreign schools suffered harassments of

---

[42] Başgöz and Wilson, *op. cit.,* pp. 79–80.

various sorts. As a result of this climate and of internal weaknesses, the contributions of these institutions to the development of Turkey were not especially significant as is evident from an examination of the role of the two most important American institutions, Robert College and the Girls' College.

Their activities were restricted by the world depression and by the reluctance of the Turkish government to permit expansion or development of new programs in such fields as medicine and engineering. This policy produced a reaction within the colleges. Administrators and faculty were somewhat hostile toward the many new regulations imposed upon the schools by the Ministry of Education; this attitude can, to some extent, be attributed to the inadequacies of the faculty, most of whom, being unsure of their role, tended to isolate themselves from Turkish society. Thus the colleges made only very limited contributions to Turkish development, though some professors did serve as consultants on various projects for the government. In such a climate few Muslim Turks enrolled in these institutions, and from its inception until 1931, Robert College produced only fifty-five Turkish alumni. Of these, twenty were graduates of the Engineering Faculty established in 1912; of the remainder, one became an ambassador, one a high-ranking civil servant, one a prominent politician, and two commercial attachés. More significant was the example set by the Girls' College, which contributed enormously to the emancipation movement in Turkey. Not only was it the best women's school, but its graduates (including the novelist and political figure Halide Edib) were leaders in the fight for emancipation.[43]

Secularism and nationalism also applied to the very core of Turkish culture, its language, and perhaps the most dramatic and psychologically most shattering change enacted by Mustafa Kemal was the language reform, with its revolutionary political, religious, social, and educational implications. Until Mustafa Kemal decreed the adoption of the Latin alphabet in 1928, the Arabic script, which did not really suit the character and subtlety of the Turkish language, had been used.

---

[43] Robert L. Daniel, "The United States and the Turkish Republic before World War II: The Cultural Dimension," *Middle East Journal,* 21 (Winter 1967), 56–60. The figures for Robert College are based on data kindly supplied to the author by the college administration.

Besides its limited applicability, the Arabic letters rendered more difficult the task of overcoming illiteracy and achieving Mustafa Kemal's educational goals. These points have been well summarized by one scholar who has argued that:

Adult education was practically an impossibility as long as the Arabic alphabet remained the instrument of literacy. . . . Not only was this (borrowed) literation ill adapted to the expression of Turkish sounds, but also so difficult that children who had studied it for three years were just beginning to master the six hundred and twelve letter forms used in printing, plus a number of variations peculiar to longhand script.[44]

Despite its many drawbacks, however, Arabic was the language of the sacred Koran, and its use symbolized the unity of the Turks with the millions of other Muslims throughout the world. If the script were changed, how could the faithful learn to read the holy books? Because the Arabic script was regarded as a pillar of Islam the question of alphabet reform which had, like many of the other reforms, been discussed in some circles since the Tanzimat period, was inevitably tied to questions of secularization and social change. Only a strong, modernizing regime could enact such a reform, and without Mustafa Kemal's determination the Arabic script would have been retained in Turkey as it was in Iran. Despite the many years of debate on the subject and the example set by the adoption of a Latin alphabet by Turks living in the Soviet Union, resistance to the change was widespread. Opposition was not limited to traditional elements; it also included many intellectuals and high administrative officials. Most members of the cabinet, led by Prime Minister İsmet İnönü, university professors (who announced "they would break their pencils" and publish no more if the script were changed), and the bulk of the civil service and army officers opposed Latinization.[45] Even such strong opposition could not sway Mustafa Kemal from his belief that language reform was an essential step if modernization were to be achieved, that Turkey had to become a new nation freed from the shackles of the traditionalism of Ottoman culture.

[44] Donald Webster, *The Turkey of Atatürk* (Philadelphia: American Academy of Political and Social Science, 1939), pp. 221–223.
[45] Başgöz and Wilson, *op. cit.*, p. 85.

This far-reaching change—which meant that all the literates had to return to school—was accomplished in a very short span of time. As one commentator noted:

In retrospect it staggers the imagination that every school child, newspaper reader, or office clerk, seeing the only writing most of them knew disappear in a matter of weeks, carried on in the new writing with hardly a pause. How long did it take? The new alphabet was decreed on May 24. Schools assigned it to pupils for summer homework. Reopening of schools was delayed that fall until October, when all textbooks were issued in the new letters. Then it was nothing but woe for pupils who had not thoroughly minded their ABC's during the summer. On Dec. 15 every newspaper appeared in new type. Officially the change was declared complete in one year. Subsequently, in 1929, Arabic and Persian were eliminated from the secondary school curriculum.[46]

In this reform Mustafa Kemal had been, to some extent, influenced by the reports of the Western educators to whom he had turned for counsel on the creation of an educational system suitable for development. The first and most famous of these was John Dewey, who was invited to Ankara in 1924, almost as soon as the Republic had been established. He was followed by the German Professor Kühne in 1925, and the Belgian Homer Buyse in 1927.

In his report Dewey suggested that the government should spend a year or two in carefully delineating a long-term plan for the development of education. Special commissions focusing upon such subjects as physical facilities, teacher training and supervision, and administration should be set up to make recommendations for programs in these areas. He was specifically concerned with improving the quality of the teaching staff. Higher salaries and allowances should be provided for teachers. In the field of rural education he stressed that educational programs should be integrated with the environment so that both primary and secondary schools would serve as centers for community development, and he urged the establishment of a mobile library system to make books available to rural children. He emphasized the importance of a unified educational system in the country but warned of the dangers of excessive centralization.

[46] Eleanor Bisbee, *The New Turks: Pioneers of the Republic, 1929–1950* (Philadelphia: University of Pennsylvania Press, 1951), p. 28.

Few of these recommendations were of any practical value in view of the realities confronting the Turkish government, and it is unlikely that many changes in Turkish education can be attributed to Dewey's influence. The report contained two basic flaws; it urged the maintenance of the existing system with its strong religious components for at least one year, a proposal totally unacceptable to Mustafa Kemal; and it ignored the serious fiscal problems of the country so that many of Dewey's recommendations, especially those concerned with the status of teachers, were unrealistic.[47]

The Kühne report was somewhat more influential, especially because it contained a recommendation urging the adoption of the Latin alphabet. Other provisions called for emphasizing technical and vocational education, more opportunities for women, higher salaries for teachers, dual shifts to maximize limited facilities, expansion of the number of secondary schools, and close reliance upon German practice and experience.

Buyse was invited to study the technical and vocational aspects of Turkish education and his report emphasized the need for a new appreciation of the values of technical and vocational work by intellectuals and others. He urged the establishment of a comprehensive network of vocational schools, culminating in a technical university, and suggested various means of funding and staffing these institutions. He also urged that the military establishment be utilized as an educational institution.

All in all, the reports of these foreign advisors proved of little value to the Turkish government. Not one contained a specific plan based on articulated criteria to resolve the country's educational problem. This may have been due to the fact that none of the experts had any previous knowledge of Turkey and its problems or spent a sufficient amount of time within the country to familiarize themselves with local conditions. As a result, each man suggested reforms which had little applicability to Turkish needs, goals, and capabilities. Although some of the proposals were highly reasonable and may, in fact, have had some influence upon the thinking of Turkish educators and govern-

[47] Başgöz and Wilson, *op. cit.,* pp. 63ff. See also Fay Kirby Berkes, "The Village Institute Movement of Turkey: An Educational Mobilization for Social Change" (Ph.D. diss., Teachers College, Columbia University, 1960), pp. 110ff.

ment officials, the overall results of this early use of foreign advisers in educational affairs was not especially encouraging.[48]

After the reports had been consigned to the appropriate files, the Turkish government was still confronted with the immense task of restructuring the educational system and providing it with a new philosophical orientation. For this purpose curriculum reform was an urgent need, and in short order regulations dealing with all aspects of this area were published. In 1924 the curriculum was amended to bring it into line with the new ideological orientation by eliminating such subjects as Ottoman history and the Islamic religion. Textbooks were rewritten to include discussions of the establishment of the Republic, its principles and goals. Together with the nationalization of the subject matter went the effort to modify the heavily theoretically oriented program inherited from the past. Heretofore courses in psychology, law, and the history of science had been offered at the middle-school level. These were now replaced by more practical subjects such as shopwork and home economics. In 1926 these reforms were extended to the primary-school curriculum and the influence of Dewey's philosophy is perhaps reflected in an emphasis upon the integration of hitherto isolated subjects. The officially announced goal of education was to stimulate the interests of the students and to allow them to learn by doing. In 1927 similar principles were applied to the middle and secondary levels and new regulations issued which stressed student participation and emphasized the need to develop critical, responsible, and creative citizens in the schools.

To implement these new programs was no easy task. Steeped in tradition, the majority of teachers were totally unprepared and lacked the necessary background to apply these new principles. The few whose imaginations were kindled by these reforms usually lacked the necessary facilities to put them into practice. Although some special courses were held for teachers and a number of publications were issued, these efforts were far too limited in scope to affect traditional

---

[48] Berkes, op. cit., pp. 110ff. See also Başgöz and Wilson, op. cit., pp. 67ff. The Turkish texts of these reports, as well as of those submitted by the Kemmerer Commission in 1933–1934, by Dr. Beryl Parker on Primary Education in 1934, and by Professor Albert Malche on University Reform in 1932, were published, together with various statements pertaining to education, by Ataturk and İnönü, in Maarif Şurası Neşriyatı (Ankara: Maarif Vekaleti, 1939).

approaches and philosophies. The problem of implementation was aggravated by the failure to restructure the teacher-training institutes whose graduates were to apply the new curriculum so that the students continued to be trained along traditional lines.[49]

Educational Expansion and the Polity

Besides restructuring and reorganizing the existing educational system, the new government also moved to expand educational opportunities for all citizens. The 1924 constitution declared that primary education was compulsory for all, and all fees were abolished in 1926. Universal education, however, could not be achieved, principally because of the insufficient funds available for education in this period and the inadequate physical and human facilities that existed, and partly because of the opposition of traditional elements to the very concept of the modern schools. Although the percentage of the national budget devoted to education rose from 3.17 per cent in 1927–1928 to 5.4 per cent ten years later,[50] total allocations remained relatively small in view of the demand for investment in other sectors of the society. Thus education was never accorded—and perhaps never could have been, in view of the country's limited income and competing demands—the kinds of financial inputs that would have been needed to achieve a major educational breakthrough. Nor could the problem be resolved through local financing in view of the prevalent social and economic conditions. Attempts to enforce the relevant provisions were met with apathy and opposition, which strengthened the position of those—and there were many—who did not support the new educational philosophy. Many persons with such views were represented on local administrative boards, and the violent struggles between local conservatives and educational administrators promoted the tendency toward centralization. Increasingly, all power over educational affairs was removed from these boards and placed in the hands of the Ministry of Education.[51]

Partly as a result of the financial difficulties, which made it absolutely impossible to create a separate school system for girls, but mainly owing to the philosophy of Mustafa Kemal, the place of

[49] Başgöz and Wilson, *op. cit.*, pp. 111ff.
[50] Webster, *op. cit.*, Table 21, p. 219.
[51] Başgöz and Wilson, *op. cit.*, pp. 92ff.

women in education changed drastically. In 1923–1924 women were admitted to the same classes as men in all university faculties. In 1927 coeducation was inaugurated at all levels of the system—a far cry from the days when women's schools were surrounded by high walls and staffed by women instructors or occasionally by carefully selected old or unattractive men.[52]

In the late 1920's a compulsory program of adult education was launched. Every Turkish citizen between the ages of fifteen and forty-five was required to attend courses in civics, literacy, mathematics, and health, which were conducted in any suitable place. In the first year almost 600,000 persons were enrolled, but the initial enthusiasm could not be sustained and the experiment declined rapidly to a low of about 41,000 students in 1933–1934. Altogether almost two million persons participated in the program.[53]

Perhaps the most important institution for adult education was the military, which proved valuable in exposing recruits to modern weapons and ideas. In addition to this socializing function, the military provided training in a wide variety of technical and vocational skills in order to meet its own needs. Besides its direct role as an educational institution, the army also spurred the development of education in a more subtle way. Throughout this period the military was of prime importance and its needs were often given priority; these needs extended to the field of education, for many military leaders were concerned with the quality of their recruits. From their point of view, the higher the recruit's level of education, the easier their task of molding him into an effective member of an efficient army. For this reason, many military leaders strongly supported educational expansion during these decades.

Yet, despite all efforts at reform and expansion, the gains, even in quantitative terms, during the first decade of the republic were rather small. Between 1923 and 1931–1932, the primary school population increased from 341,941 to 489,299 (the percentage of girls enrolled, however, increased from 18.4 to 35 per cent). At the secondary level (first and second cycle) the number of students increased from 7,146 to 32,792, and at the higher level from 2,914 to 4,186 (here the percentage of women increased from 10.8 to 19.5 per cent). In voca-

[52] *Ibid.*, pp. 109–110.
[53] *Ibid.*, pp. 119–120.

tional and technical schools enrollments rose from 6,547 to 9,296, the percentage of girls rising from 21 to 34.5 per cent.[54]

Nor do these statistics reveal the many qualitative problems. Educational standards remained extremely low, as was noted by the Kemmerer Commission, a group of American experts that studied economic development. Using official information, the report revealed a very high level of wastage, especially in rural areas where less than half of all students who attended the first grade entered the second, and only about 30 per cent graduated from the three-year elementary schools. The urban situation was equally serious; less than 30 per cent of those entering the five-year elementary schools graduated. Serious imbalances between the rural and the urban sectors of society were also evident. Opportunities for higher education were restricted to urban areas; almost none of the rural students continued their education beyond the elementary level, whereas most of the urban graduates did so.[55]

Several factors were responsible for this limited educational progress. Among these, environmental constraints, notably the lack of financial resources and the high degree of traditionalism that pervaded the society, especially in rural areas, must be considered. Reluctance to change and to promote innovation, however, was not limited to rural areas; persons with conservative ideas were entrenched at all levels even within the Ministry of Education. Its orientation is most vividly evidenced by its strong opposition to such reforms as coeducation, the adoption of the Latin alphabet, and the reorganization of rural education.[56] If significant educational advancements were to be achieved in this environment, strong leadership was essential, but Mustafa Kemal never provided it himself and was apparently unable to find the appropriate person to fill this role. None of the first five ministers remained in office for any extended period of time, and only when Necati Bey served (1925–1928) was any progress achieved. The Ministry of Education was reorganized and most of the reforms discussed above were inaugurated in these years.

The vacuum existing at the ministerial level was fatal to educational

---

[54] Richard E. Maynard, "The Lise and Its Curriculum in the Turkish Educational System" (Ph.D. diss., University of Chicago, 1961), Table III, p. 58.

[55] Başgöz and Wilson, op. cit., p. 129.

[56] Ibid., pp. 91–92.

reform. Although Ataturk was convinced of the crucial importance of education, his knowledge of this field was limited and unsophisticated. Moreover, his primary concern was with more immediate and pressing problems, especially the consolidation of his position and the enactment of his program of reform designed to create the institutional framework of a modern state. That this is indeed the case is suggested by the fact that after 1924 he no longer emphasized education in his speeches. In these circumstances, if significant educational progress was to be made, strong leadership had to be provided by the minister of education, and specific policies to achieve the goals of Ataturk designed by the educational leadership of the country. Unfortunately only Necati Bey possessed the ability and determination to meet this challenge; after his untimely death three years after assuming office, despite the structural changes, the Ministry quickly returned to its old ways. It "degenerated into a bureaucracy within which the successive ministers never managed to take more than fragmentary day to day measures which often conflicted with one another." Under these conditions it is not surprising that so little educational progress was achieved in these years.[57]

In 1933, when Reşid Galip became minister, a sense of purpose and dynamism once again characterized education. Though remaining in office for only a year, he revitalized the Ministry in that brief period, launching many plans and experiments. His efforts were not in vain. He was followed by equally able men so that education in the mid-thirties evidenced a new vitality marked by the inauguration of many significant innovations, including projects designed to expand education to rural areas and to strengthen the quality of the training provided to the emerging elite.

This resurgence is attributable only partly to the energy and ability of the men who served as ministers of education. Ultimately, one must look at the political system in general and at Ataturk in particular in order to understand the structure of policy and the shape of development. In an attempt to explain the lack of concern with rural education and development some scholars have pointed to the character of Ataturk's party, the Cumhuriyet Halk Partisi (CHP) and the pattern of interests represented therein. Essentially, the party

---

[57] *Ibid.,* pp. 203, 135.

consisted of two separate groupings, one at the center, the other in the provinces. The national elite was comprised largely of intellectuals, bureaucrats, and former military officers. In sharp contrast stood the party's local organs staffed by the rural elite (landowners, town notables, important rural personages, and the like) which had strongly supported the nationalist movement during the struggle for independence. This alliance between Kemalist elite and local gentry was born out of a common interest—the preservation of the state against the direct threat of dismemberment posed by the Greeks and the allies—and was forged by the needs of Ataturk for support in his struggle for supremacy and by the advantages which accrued to the rural elite from the tacit alliance. Ataturk's reforms did not threaten their social and economic position and, in fact, support of the Kemalist revolution provided them with substantial benefits including the legitimization of their position, marked economic advantages, and opportunities for further advancement.[58]

It is probably an oversimplification, however, to attribute the lack of rural development and the absence of land reform to an "implicit tradeoff" between the political elite and the rural elite, and it is necessary to consider the role of other factors especially in view of the limited influence that the rural elite is acknowledged to have wielded on national policy making.[59] Similar considerations apply to the judgment that the shape of development stemmed from the fact that Ataturk deliberately "*exploited* the educational bifurcation in the society." [60] One of the earliest formulations of this thesis states that

the attempt to evoke and raise up enough truly new styled Turks, enough thoroughly westernized Turks, to make a truly new Turkey viable had to begin with the ruling group itself rather than with the peasants. It is

---

[58] Ergun Özbudun, "Established Revolution Versus Unfinished Revolution: Contrasting Patterns of Democratization in Mexico and Turkey," in *Authoritarian Politics in Modern Society,* Samuel P. Huntington and Clement H. Moore, eds. (New York: Basic Books, 1970), pp. 387ff; Michael P. Hyland, "Doctrinal and Tactical Problems of Turkey's Republican People's Party (RPP)," paper delivered at the Middle East Studies Association meeting, Toronto, Canada, November 14–15, 1969, pp. 14ff.

[59] The phrase "implicit tradeoff" is from Özbudun, *op. cit.,* p. 389; on the limited power of the rural elite, see p. 388.

[60] Frederick W. Frey, *The Turkish Political Elite* (Cambridge, Mass.: M.I.T. Press, 1965), p. 41,

not only that large-scale and deep-seated changes in the peasants were practically impossible. Quite beyond that there was the consideration that only an upper class itself united in effective westernization and determined eventually to bridge the gap with the peasantry could hope for success in what would be a nationwide Operation Bootstraps.[61]

It is true that Ataturk sought to create an elite committed to his vision of modernization and that he was always concerned with the political power, actual and potential, of particular groups, including the peasantry, but neither in the steps that he took to create such an elite nor in his policy toward rural areas can one find the kind of coherent and developed strategy suggested by the above thesis. Thus, one can point to Ataturk's genuine concern for the peasantry and to the fact that one of the earliest major laws passed by the Assembly, the Village Law of 1924, was designed to promote rural well-being, though by self-help, a naive expectation. Moreover, Ataturk apparently believed that ample land was available, a fact which may well explain why he did not promote land reform legislation until the late thirties. It is, however, true that, except in rhetoric, little attention was paid to rural affairs until the late thirties, and that by and large no substantial changes occurred in peasant life, for Ataturk's famous reforms did not penetrate village life very deeply. Most peasants remained largely unaware of the significance of the new law codes, and even when their content was known, they were simply ignored since, for example, the new position granted to women conflicted sharply with existing social customs and values.[62]

Similar inconsistencies characterize his educational policies. It is clear that in the twenties elementary education did not expand greatly; in fact, between 1927 and 1935 the percentage of school-age children enrolled in elementary schools actually dropped from 58 to 41 per cent.[63] Nevertheless, higher education expanded only slightly during these years, and the Ottoman University, a major elite institu-

---

[61] Lewis V. Thomas and Richard N. Frye, *The United States and Turkey and Iran* (Cambridge: Harvard University Press, 1952), p. 72.

[62] On Ataturk's feeling for the peasantry and his attitude toward land reform, see Özbudun, *op. cit.,* p. 397; on the 1924 Village Law and the impact of the reforms in general, see Joseph S. Szyliowicz, *Political Change in Rural Turkey: Erdemli* (The Hague: Mouton, 1966), pp. 36ff.

[63] Nuri Kodamanoğlu, *Education in Turkey, 1923–1960* (Istanbul: Ministry of Education, 1965), p. 38,

tion which was noted for its conservatism and intellectual sterility (as we shall see below), was essentially ignored until 1933.

In view of Mustafa Kemal's concern with the creation of a modern,
reformist elite, one may wonder why university reform was not undertaken many years earlier. His dissatisfaction with the university
was not a new phenomenon, yet he certainly exhibited remarkable
patience with its reactionary tendencies. Two possible answers suggest themselves. Firstly, Ataturk, with his unique ability to weigh
various strategies and to establish priorities, may have felt that other
changes were more basic. Secondly, he may have waited because he
did not think it possible to transform the Darülfünun into a modern
university without a dramatic input of new faculty, and no such personnel were available until Hitler assumed power in Germany.

Such possibilities reflect once again the degree to which one must
take into account Ataturk's goals, values, and experiences. Many of
his reforms represented the logical culmination of ideas whose roots
can be traced back to the nineteenth century, particularly those
enacted in the twenties when, possessing only limited human and
financial resources, he assigned priority to structural change. Not
only was such a priority dictated by existing conditions, but Ataturk
possessed only a vague appreciation of the problems of social and
economic transformation. We have already noted how his deep faith
in education was not matched with an understanding of this topic
and how he apparently lacked a realistic understanding of rural conditions. Similar conclusions can be drawn concerning his economic
policies. Thus, only when confronted with unforeseen crises did he
recognize the need to deal with social and economic issues, and one
mark of Ataturk's greatness is precisely this flexibility and prag-
matism. In contrast to the twenties, therefore, the thirties witnessed
an emphasis upon educational expansion at all levels and among all
sectors of the populace, the establishment of innovative institutions
to promote rural change and to disseminate the Kemalist ideology
and a new economic policy.

Two cataclysmic events midway through his rule forced the intense
reappraisal of policy that led to the adoption of these bold and innovative programs of social and economic change. The great depression had a powerful impact upon the country and economic problems
received a new priority. Subsequently, the principle of etatism was

adopted and the state began to play a dominant role in promoting economic growth. The second event which deeply affected Ataturk were the consequences that flowed from his decision to permit the establishment of an opposition party in 1930 by some of his close and trusted associates, an experiment which brought into sharp relief the degree to which traditionalism remained a major force within the country and thus may well have served as the catalyst for new educational and cultural policies. At this time widespread unrest existed within Turkey. Poor economic conditions aggravated by bad harvest added to the discontent which many persons, including members of the administrative and intellectual elites, felt with the pace and content of the reforms. Accordingly, Ataturk may have seized the opportunity to achieve his goal of a democratic society while at the same time creating a safety valve for discontent. The new party, the Liberal Republican party, proved to be a rallying point for all dissatisfied persons and quickly acquired a large and fanatical following. Riots broke out in various towns; debates in the Assembly assumed a new and bitter tone. Confronted with such an obvious threat to the achievement of Ataturk's goals, the party leadership itself asked for dissolution. Despite its short existence, however, the Liberal party had a profound impact upon developments in Turkey, for it vividly demonstrated that many politicized elements remained uncommitted to Ataturk's program, that the mass of the people had not been affected by the reforms, and that a significant elite-mass gap existed.[64]

This disastrous attempt to increase popular participation obviously brought into focus the need for additional reforms if the kind of modern state that Ataturk envisaged was to become a permanent creation. In an effort to discover the economic and social realities that had caused the debacle and to obtain the necessary information on which to base forthcoming changes, Ataturk undertook a three-month tour of the country. Accompanied by a large staff, he visited all regions and talked with people of all sorts—officials, townsmen, students, peasants.[65] After analyzing his impressions, it is likely that

[64] On the Free Party, see Walter F. Weiker, "The Free Party of 1930 in Turkey" (Ph.D. dissertation submitted to the Department of Politics, Princeton University, 1962).

[65] Lord Kinross, Ataturk: The Rebirth of A Nation (London: Weidenfeld and Nicolson, 1964), pp. 454–455.

Ataturk decided that specific reforms in three major areas were vital: first, to change the orientation of many intellectuals; second, to bridge the elite-mass gap; and third, to raise the cultural, social, and economic level of the mass of the populace. The great educational reforms which were promulgated in coming years—the closing of the Darülfünun and its reopening as a modern university, the establishment of the People's Houses throughout the country, and the new efforts at expanding education in rural areas—were designed to achieve these goals.

Educational Transformation

Ataturk moved first against the institutions molding elite opinion, and in 1931 the Turkish Hearths were abolished and replaced with a national network of People's Houses. The first of the Turkish Hearths had opened in 1912 with the aim of disseminating Turkish principles. The impetus came from 190 students at the military medical school who published a letter in 1911 in which they stressed the need to revitalize and develop the Turkish nation and suggested the creation of a nonpolitical organization to achieve these goals. This suggestion was readily accepted by a group of Turkish intellectuals who had been active for some years (they had established the Turkish Society shortly after the revolution of 1908 and they joined with the students to organize the Turkish Hearths). Prominent in the movement was Ziya Gökalp, whose philosophy we have already discussed. Essentially he believed that nationalism, Islam, and modernization were complementary dimensions of an integrated and harmonious whole, and that Westernization should and could be limited so as to prevent any encroachment upon the national culture with its religious component. This philosophy was to bring him and his disciples into direct conflict with Ataturk, who believed in the total transformation of all aspects of Turkish society along modern lines. The closing of the Turkish Hearths in which Gökalp was so active, and their replacement with the People's Houses, can be seen as reflecting Ataturk's disappointment with the intellectual elite in general and with Gökalp's philosophy in particular.

The People's Houses were designed to serve as agencies for political socialization. They were organized and run by the CHP, and their program stressed Turkish nationalism and Westernization. The first People's Houses were opened in 1931 in fourteen provinces. Their activities were organized into various branches, including languages, literature and history, fine arts, dramatics, sports, social assistance, adult education, libraries and publications, rural welfare, and museums and exhibitions. Thus they served as centers for educational and cultural activities and for social welfare. By 1940 there were more than 300 in operation and they proved so successful that the idea was extended to the rural areas through the People's Room program. By 1945 there were over 400 People's Houses and 2,338 People's Rooms.[66] Through their constant emphasis upon modernization, laicism, and nationalism, they served as important agencies for political communication and socialization. In this way new patterns, symbols, and loyalties were disseminated throughout the society and helped to socialize the mass in the values of the Republic.

A second major blow at conservative institutions came in 1933 when Istanbul University replaced the Darülfünun. The change was far more than merely one of nomenclature. For years, discontent with the poor academic reputation of the institution, its notorious in-fighting, and its conservative orientation had been widespread. Not only did the Darülfünun continue to suffer from all the weaknesses elaborated in the 1919 report discussed earlier but, as we have noted, many professors opposed various aspects of Ataturk's reforms, condemning students who had their pictures taken and fighting against Latinization of the alphabet.[67] This opposition was rooted in an ideology that accepted change and innovation in only some aspects of social life—a philosophy closely related to that of Ziya Gökalp, who had been appointed professor of sociology in 1915. It is highly probable that the teaching body was composed in large part of men who had been influenced by his views.

To corroborate the need for change, Ataturk turned once again to a foreign advisor, Albert Malche, who was invited to examine the structure and functioning of the university. He prepared a devastating report which criticized every aspect of the institution. The faculty

[66] Webster, op. cit., pp. 186–187; Bernard Lewis, The Emergence of Modern Turkey (London: Oxford University Press, 1961), p. 376; and Kemal H. Karpat, "The People's Houses in Turkey: Establishment and Growth," Middle East Journal, 17 (Winter–Spring 1963), 55–67.
[67] Başgöz and Wilson, op. cit., pp. 61, 85.

was especially singled out for condemnation. Most members were concerned primarily with teaching and engaged in little or no research; faculty publications were practically nonexistent. Despite the apparent concern with teaching, a very low standard prevailed; most faculty pursued careers outside the university and spent little time preparing lectures, which they would read and expect the student to memorize. Even in the natural sciences, the usual technique was for the teacher to give a demonstration which students would be permitted to observe. Few teachers devoted any time to students outside the classroom and student-faculty contacts were rare. Nor was the spirit of the institution consonant with academic discipline or intellectual endeavors because faculty divisions were so great that instead of collegiality, mutual distrust and aversion prevailed, with appointments and promotions determined by personal intrigues and subjective criteria of all sorts. Above all, the work of the university was in no way related to the needs of the society. Curricular and course content remained highly theoretical and even religious in orientation; the Darülfünun had apparently ignored the great changes that had swept through Turkish society since the establishment of the Republic.[68]

Mustafa Kemal moved quickly to restructure the university, and the Law of Reorganization, passed on June 6, 1933, provided for the abolition of the Darülfünun on July 31 and the opening of Istanbul University on August 1. The entire faculty was dismissed and only selected members who knew foreign languages and who had demonstrated scholarly aptitude were rehired, 59 out of 151 persons. Vacancies were filled with foreign professors, especially refugees from Germany, who were expected to learn sufficient Turkish within three or four years to eliminate the need for a translator in the classroom. As always, the use of foreign faculty possessed many advantages but also created many difficulties. First, the language problem remained important—few achieved the ability to lecture in Turkish. Second, the salary differential between foreign and Turkish faculty was considerable, a factor which promoted jealousies within the institution. Nevertheless, there is no doubt that far higher stand-

---

[68] For a discussion of the Malche Report and its implementation, see *ibid.*, pp. 159–169. See also Cemil Bilsel, *İstanbul Üniversitenin Tarihi* (Istanbul: Kenan Matbaası, 1943), pp. 35ff.

ards were achieved in the university than had ever been the case, and that many of the eminent Turkish faculty who staff the universities today were ably trained by these men.

To ensure that the university would function in the expected way, vastly expanded resources were allocated to it, and the previous policy of autonomy was replaced by one of strict government control. Several new units such as the Institute of the National Economy and the Society were created to encourage research on important questions in various specific problem areas. From the viewpoint of overt political socialization, the most important was the Institute on the History of the Turkish Revolution, whose courses had to be taken by every university student. A few years later the University of Ankara was established (1937) by merging existing faculties (law, agriculture, language, history, and geography) and opening new ones.

Language and history were a focal point in Ataturk's attempts to create and disseminate a new heritage to fill the vacuum created by his wholesale destruction of Ottoman institutions and culture, and to arouse and strengthen a national consciousness within the country. He turned to Turkish pre-Ottoman history and sponsored the Sun Language Theory to demonstrate that practically all civilizations are descended from the Turks of Central Asia who developed speech and writing.

This theory was quickly introduced into the schools. The 1938 *lycée* curriculum, for example, emphasized nationalist ideals and principles and stated that the aim of the history courses was to "teach the student the thesis that our race has been the leader in civilization. It will show how Central Asia was the cradle of civilization and the importance of this fact." Similarly, the sociology course was designed to familiarize the student with the failings of the Ottoman Empire and the philosophy and principles of the Turkish Republic.[69]

Closely related was the attempt to Turkify the language by purging all foreign words and replacing them with "Turkish" ones. This activity was entrusted to the new Türk Dil Kurumu (Turkish Language Association). Simplification of the language was a useful goal: Ottoman Turkish remained so convoluted and elaborate that the language of the ruling class had become almost unintelligible to the mass, even

[69] Maynard, *op. cit.,* p. 227.

though, as we have noted, various steps were taken in the nineteenth century to simplify it. From a political viewpoint, changes in language would serve not only to promote nationalistic feelings, but also to narrow the gap between elite and mass by creating a common means of communication; no longer would writing and speaking be carried on in two different languages. At first, however, owing to the excessive and exaggerated way in which the reform was carried out, precisely the opposite result was achieved, and an artificial language very different from that used by either elite or mass was created. Beginning with the elimination of Arabic and Persian grammatical constructions, the movement spread to the elimination of Arabic and Persian words and their replacement by new words that were discovered in various Turkish dialects or, when no suitable words were available, by Turkified foreign words. The atmosphere in which this reform took place and Ataturk's role in it has been vividly recreated:

From now onwards Kemal spent much of his time surrounded by piles of dictionaries, old and new, searching for "pure Turkish words" or trying to trace some philological link between Turkish and foreign words. In pursuit of purification the whole public was invited to co-operate in the suggestion of Turkish equivalents for them, through lists of words published daily in the press. The Gazi would try out in his speeches new and incomprehensible words, to the bewilderment of his audience, while Falih Rifki, hero-worshipper though he was, would "writhe with fury" at the sound of them and "helplessly ask myself how he could possibly bring himself to perpetuate so heinous a crime." Those anxious to gain favour found themselves avoiding in his presence the use of essential everyday terms simply because their origin was Arabic or Persian, while others tried to please him by learning up new words and dragging them into their conversation.[70]

The result was overwhelming confusion, and though the extremist approach was replaced in 1935 by a more moderate policy, problems remained for many years. As late as 1952, for example, glossaries containing the meanings of the new words which had been introduced into textbooks on psychology, philosophy, sociology, pedagogy, and other subjects had to be published for *lycée* students. Another unintended consequence of the language reform was its contribution to

[70] Kinross, *op. cit.*, p. 466.

the further removal of classroom subjects from everyday reality, as many students found it difficult to link the terms they learned in school to concrete institutions or concepts they encountered daily.[71] The reform also cut off the student from anything written before 1928 and the extent to which the new generation is isolated from its heritage— even its nationalist one—is starkly revealed by the "new Turkish" into which Ataturk's famous Seven-Day Speech has been translated so as to make it comprehensible to the new generation. Nevertheless, despite the many absurdities, the language reform was, on the whole, highly useful:

It has aroused general interest in the development of the Turkish language, prompted scholarly research into its history and structure, sharpened the linguistic feeling, done away with much outmoded conventionalism, induced writers to use simpler, clearer and more exact language, and introduced a considerable number of good and necessary words and technical terms.[72]

Complementing the attention paid to the education of the elite was Ataturk's new emphasis upon rural development. Convinced that the mass had not yet been sufficiently affected by his reforms, he launched a major drive to extend educational opportunities into hitherto largely neglected rural Turkey. Under the leadership of Reşid Galip, the minister of education, a Village Affairs Commission was convened in 1933 which emphasized the need for a new type of schoolteacher for rural areas—a person who was trained not only in traditional pedagogy, but who was also prepared to serve as an agent of change for the community. The ideal person would, in addition to educating children, replace traditional ideas and practices with the new ideology and modern ways and act to raise the community's standard of living. This idea was carried to fruition through the efforts of İsmail Hakkı Tonguç, who devised an innovative solution to the problems of teacher training. Upon being appointed minister of education in 1935, he prepared a report for Prime Minister İnönü which emphasized the extent to which rural education had been neglected. At this time only about 5,000 village schools—80 per cent of which had only one teacher—were

[71] Maynard, *op. cit.*, pp. 222–223.
[72] Uriel Heyd, *Language Reform in Modern Turkey* (Jerusalem: The Israel Oriental Society, 1954), p. 110.

available for a total of 32,000 villages. Furthermore, the drastic shortage of primary teachers could not possibly be met by the existing institutions: only 800 teachers would be graduated within the next three years, and at that rate the need would not be met for seventy years. Hence Tonguç suggested that young persons who had served as noncommissioned officers be trained as rural teachers and that their curriculum include practical as well as traditional academic subjects. Following a short period of experimentation, the Village Educator's Law was passed in 1937, and by 1942–1943 almost 6,000 eğitmen were teaching 172,800 students. This program was complemented by the Village Institute Program into which it was later merged.[73]

The first two institutes were opened in 1937, and in 1940 the Village Institute Law was passed. The philosophy of these institutes was similar to that of the eğitmen program, but instead of recruiting young veterans, primary school graduates underwent a five-year training program which stressed agricultural and mechanical subjects and their application to common rural problems. Nor was practical work limited to the shop. Students and staff were responsible for building their own institute, which was normally located in a remote rural area to preserve the rural ethos of the program and to avoid the risk of exposing young villagers to urban life and thus arousing expectations and desires that could not be fulfilled in a rural community. To visit one of the former village institutes and to look at the pictures depicting its construction is a moving experience. Dedicated teachers and administrators with very little, if any, technical assistance successfully aroused the enthusiasm of the village children and together created an educational institution that was unique. Often they had to do so in the face of official apathy and inefficiency, but their courage and determination overcame many such obstacles.

After graduating, the new teacher was expected to undertake the following duties: administer and teach in the village school; develop the economic and cultural level of the village by organizing ceremonies on national holidays; establish and operate fields, gardens, and lots as models for the villagers; teach villagers the proper use of tools and machines; help establish cooperatives; promote athletics among the

[73] Maynard, op. cit., Table 15, p. 111. The text of Tonguç's report is in Berkes, op. cit., pp. 919–938. This thorough dissertation represents the most detailed analysis of the Village Institute Movement available in English

young; and be responsible for the management and protection of forests and antiquities.[74]

Sometimes the graduate would find upon arriving in his assigned community that he also had to build the school. Although the villagers were expected to erect the school themselves, they often did so only when compelled by the administration. The absence of physical facilities was usually one of the minor problems confronting the new rural teacher, as is evidenced by the experience of one graduate who was assigned to a village in his own region:

Nürgüz is a village of seven hundred people. This year, for the first time, it has a school. . . . It was rather difficult to have ourselves housed in the Mosque. . . . The Hatib [religious leader] was adamant: "I'm not going to open the Mosque for you to run a school on infidel lines," he said. And whatever an Imam says, the congregation says too. The people of the village nearly had an uproar. As luck would have it, however, the district supervisor was very popular and his good words won them over. "He's not after women or girls—he's a decent fellow," people decided, and from that point on there was no further trouble. . . . "Anyway you'd enough equipment?" you will ask. Nothing of the kind. Each child brought a sheep-skin and spread it on the mud floor. As for benches, blackboard, and that sort of thing, they might never have been heard of. Nor should you assume that all our difficulties were at an end once the school was opened. The next problem was to persuade the children's fathers to send them to school.[75]

Despite such difficulties and the inferior status of institute graduates as compared to urban teachers—they had to work in the place to which they were appointed for twenty years as opposed to a five-year term for urban teachers, and they were paid a salary of 100 TL a month instead of 175 TL which the beginning city teacher received —the idealism and vision of the program proved contagious and by 1940–41, 5,371 students were enrolled in village institutes as compared to 2,805 in other primary teacher training schools. By 1950–1951, the number had increased to 13,972. Furthermore, the institutes engendered a fundamental shift in educational practices away from an elitist toward a mass-oriented system. For the first time, large

[74] *Ibid.*, pp. 145–146.
[75] Mahmut Makal, *A Village in Anatolia*, Sir Wyndham Deedes, trans. (London: Valentine, Mitchell, 1954), pp. 1–2.

numbers of rural children had the opportunity to pursue an education —"there were approximately *three times* as many rural children for *secondary education* in 1950 as there had been urban *primary* school graduates in 1935." [76]

The movement also had important political consequences. It has been suggested, perhaps somewhat optimistically, that it played a major role in narrowing the urban-rural gap, in awakening the rural population, and in transforming a traditional rural mass into a more sophisticated citizenry, aware of its political power in a multi-party system. In other words:

The free-holding peasantry was aware, from 1946 onwards, that the era when it could be ignored had come to an end. Not only were there village institute students and their graduates in a position to tell their co-villagers of their constitutional rights, but also the spotlight cast upon rural Turkey by the Movement endowed the majority electorate with a sense of its power.[77]

At best, however, only a minority of the peasantry had been so mobilized—an estimated one-third of all Turkish villages were affected in one way or another by the institutes—and in many of these life changed but little. The gap which continued to exist between town and village can perhaps best be highlighted by the comment of a student from Istanbul who visited an institute graduate in his village several years after the death of Ataturk: " 'Mahmut—my dear fellow,' " he said, " 'the squalor, the primitive conditions in this village —they're indescribable! What do people mean by having houses and stables in these conditions? It might be the Stone Age, which one only reads about in history books!' " [78]

Whether the village institutes could in time have transformed rural Turkey remains a matter of conjecture. After World War II, the changes that took place within the political system were to have important consequences for the institutes. Following a violent debate with cries of Communism and immorality on the one hand and charges of reaction and betrayal of Ataturk's principles on the other, the institutes were combined with the regular normal schools. Although

[76] Maynard, *op. cit.,* Table 24, p. 148; Berkes, *op. cit.,* pp. 671–674.
[77] Berkes, *ibid.,* pp. 671–672.
[78] Makal, *op. cit.,* p. 162.

the issue was a highly emotional one, it is possible to look at the institutes from a purely educational perspective and to note significant weaknesses. Some of these have been attributed to a lack of understanding by key people of the movement's significance, of its radical and innovative approach, and to a lack of coordination with other national projects.[79] More fundamental, however, is the fact that a totally different type of training and education was being provided to different societal groups. Now the former distinction between traditional and modern was replaced by one between rural and urban, with possibly equally divisive consequences in the long run. On a more practical level, many persons criticized the requirement that forced parents to pledge the future of an eleven- or twelve-year-old child for twenty years, the inadequacy of the five-year training period, and the impossibility of ever achieving the tasks assigned the eighteen- or nineteen-year-old teacher. Even if these duties had not been so unrealistic, it was very unlikely that tradition-oriented villagers who respected age so highly would accept a youth with innovative ideas as a community leader. In other words, the task of transforming traditional communities could not possibly be carried out successfully by poorly prepared though highly motivated young men alone, and no thought was given to programs for reinforcement and support.

That the goals of the movement were highly unrealistic is unquestionable, but the total impact was undoubtedly great and the institutes represented an innovative and significant attempt to resolve one of the country's basic problems, that of rural development. Since every developing country faces similar problems, the history and functioning of the movement deserves to be studied to determine the extent to which its principles and structures can be adapted to the needs of Asian, African, and Latin American countries. As we shall see later, the literacy corps project in Iran is quite similar to the Village Institute Program.

Rather surprisingly, vocational education progressed but little during most of the Ataturk era, despite the early attempts to restructure this field with the aid of foreign advisers. Various steps were taken to upgrade and expand the existing schools, including sending teachers and students abroad, the use of foreign teachers, and curricular and

[79] Berkes, *op. cit.,* pp. 706ff.

administrative reorganization, but relatively little quantitative or qualitative change resulted.

The expansion of vocational education was retarded by the same factors as hindered development in the other educational sectors, a lack of resources and a lack of leadership. Many of the trade schools were, until 1929, dependent upon local financing, a weak source of support even under the most favorable conditions, which made it difficult to obtain adequate equipment. After the great depression, these funds were almost totally shut off, and many of the technical and vocational schools were saved from bankruptcy only by a legal device.[80] Nor was strong leadership forthcoming to spur the development of this field, which suffered from Ataturk's lack of concern for problems of economic growth. Not until 1932, when a national development plan was finally drawn up, were additional resources allocated to this field. Despite this new emphasis, its development from then on was hampered by the fact that the government never coordinated official salary scales with type of educational preparation. In other words, no steps were taken to encourage students to select vocational schools instead of academic *lycées*. If income differentials favoring graduates of the former had been introduced, it is likely that the development of technical skills throughout the society would have been far more widespread than was actually the case.[81]

The most powerful impetus to vocational training was provided by the outbreak of World War II, for the astute and able Minister of Education, Hassan Ali Yucel, persuasively argued that vocational training should be considered part of the defense effort and that the necessary appropriations be considered part of the military and not the educational budget. He pointed out that an expanded system of vocational training could help meet the shortages and difficulties caused by the war and that technical and vocational training represented an important part of the infrastructure necessary to maintain a strong military establishment. Obtaining a favorable decision was only the first step. Next came the problem of acquiring necessary equipment for the new schools. Since none could be imported owing to war-

[80] Başgöz and Wilson, *op. cit.*, p. 178.

[81] M. T. Özelli, "The Estimates of Private Internal Rates of Return on Educational Investment in the First Turkish Republic, 1923–1960," *International Journal of Middle East Studies,* 1 (April 1970), 162.

time conditions, the existing schools were ordered to manufacture what was needed. They apparently did so effectively and a rapid increase in the numbers of schools and students ensued. There were 60 schools with about 9,000 students in 1930–1931, 87 with 19,000 students in 1940–1941, and 230 with 55,000 students in 1950–1951.[82]

Despite such achievements, social and cultural factors continued to handicap the development of this field. Manual labor was still looked down upon generally, an attitude that was fostered by the history of vocational education. Early attempts, dating back to the 1860's, to establish technical schools in the Ottoman Empire had been designed to provide training for the indigent; the first vocational schools, known as reformatories, housed waifs and orphans and taught them a trade. Vocational schools became ever more identified with poverty in succeeding years, so that even during Republican times, their prestige and attractiveness remained low and only students from the lowest classes would apply for admission. Even those who did enroll regarded these institutions not as a place to learn a skill, but as a means of achieving social mobility, since a graduate could often obtain a white-collar position in the bureaucracy. So many persons were able to do so that figures on enrollments and graduations do not reflect accurately the degree to which vocational and technical skills were, in fact, disseminated within the society.[83]

The Legacy of Ataturk

Despite many such weaknesses in various fields, Ataturk had, by the time of his death, created the structures of a modern state, and his educational reforms established a modern educational system within the country. The system was unified, coherent, secular, and closely tied to the goals of the regime in terms of socialization and political values. As we have suggested, Ataturk's reforms can be divided into two parts; in the first, the era of the twenties, the emphasis was upon the creation of the structures of a modern state, including those pertaining to education. In the thirties, on the other hand, the

---

[82] Lester I. Bruckner, "History of Accounting Education in Turkey, 1923–1960" (Ph.D. diss., New York University, 1965), pp. 201ff. Other data indicate that the number of schools expanded even more rapidly, though there is agreement on student enrollments. See appendix 4.

[83] Ibid., pp. 224, 226; see also Başgöz and Wilson, op. cit., pp. 175ff.

goal was economic development and social and cultural transformation. In fact, it is no exaggeration to suggest that the dissemination of modernity in the first part of his rule occurred outside the formal educational system. Ataturk understood fully the relationship between law and modernization, and the Grand National Assembly became the principal schoolroom of the country as one important piece of legislation after another, most of which had important educational ramifications, was passed.

A brief glance at educational statistics reveals both the degree of progress that was achieved in education and the extent to which these developments occurred in the thirties. Educational expenditures climbed from 3 per cent of the budget in 1927 to 5 per cent in 1935 to 7 per cent in 1940, while the actual expenditures rose from 7 million TL in 1927 to 10 million in 1935 to 21 million in 1940.[84] These investments resulted in a doubled literacy rate from 10.7 per cent in 1927 to 22.4 per cent in 1940 (male literacy rose from 17.6 to 35.3 per cent; female from 4.8 to 9.9 per cent). The number of students in elementary education increased from 331,941 in 1923 to 905,000 by 1940, of whom 534,000 were in villages; the number of students enrolled in middle schools from almost 6,000 to about 25,000 in 1929 to over 92,000 in 1939. The *lycée* level showed the sharpest percentage increase, the number of students rising from 1,231 in 1923–1924 to about 5,700 in 1930–1931 and to almost 25,000 in 1940. At the university level the number of students increased from 2,914 in 1923 to 4,331 in 1930 to 12,844 in 1940–1941.

The momentum created by the great educational effort in the thirties continued during the arid years of World War II and even after. By 1950 the literacy rate had reached 33.6 per cent (47.5 per cent male, 19.4 per cent female) and the number of primary school students had almost doubled to 1,591,000. At the same time, the continuing emphasis upon vocational and technical education resulted in a sharp decrease in academic enrollments at the secondary level (first and second cycle), from about 117,000 to 88,000. As large numbers of students were diverted to trade and vocational schools, the percentage of elementary graduates pursuing academic careers also

[84] Slight differences can be found among the data cited by different sources, but I am using here, for the sake of consistency, figures from the tables in *ibid.*, pp. 233ff.

dropped from 55 per cent in 1939 to 19 per cent in 1949–1950. And, though the percentage enrolling in technical schools, which had increased sharply during World War II, dropped sharply afterward (12 per cent in 1939–1940, 21 per cent in 1945–1946, 7 per cent in 1949–1950), the total number of students in these schools increased from about 11,000 to more than 59,000 in the same period. University enrollments continued to rise sharply, almost doubling to 24,-815 between 1940 and 1950–1951.

A modern educational system had indeed been established, and although many serious problems of quality and educational opportunities for different segments of the populace remained, Turkey now possessed the kind of educational establishment that could serve as the basis for continued rapid development. Whether it would do so would depend upon the decisions that would be made within a political system which had been profoundly affected by the expansion of educational opportunities and the many other changes that had occurred during the Ataturk era.

The most important of these was the emergence of new elites and resulting strains within the pattern of social-core-group and elite configurations within the society. Originally the nationalist elite encompassed the same groups that had been the source of Young Turk support, the bureaucracy, the military, and the intelligentsia, though as we have seen, the basis of recruitment had been greatly diversified. With the increase in educational opportunities, patterns of recruitment to the professions, the bureaucracy, and the intelligentsia continued to broaden and became ever more heterogeneous. At the same time that the social background of the traditional elites was becoming more diversified, new specialized elites were emerging, especially businessmen and entrepreneurs. This process was facilitated by the results of the exchange of populations following the Greek-Turkish war, which largely eliminated the commercial elements of the Empire. Their roles had to be filled, and these opportunities, coupled with the redistribution of the minorities' property, resulted in the emergence of a Turkish business and commercial elite.

This new elite soon articulated its interests with confidence and came into conflict with members of the traditional elites. It represented, however, a powerful political force, with political knowledge, skills, and influence. Many businessmen and entrepreneurs possessed close ties with the political elite, having taken advantage of administrative or military connections and offices to achieve economic success. Thus for the first time in Ottoman-Turkish history businessmen emerged as a major factor in the country's political life.[85] To the former triad of intellectual, bureaucrat, and administrator was added this new elite grouping, and the existing political balance within the country was seriously challenged. Thus the very success of the Ataturk reforms laid the basis for inter- and intra-elite conflict and the major issue of the postwar years was whether the existing political structure could be maintained under these conditions.

Iran

During the decades that Ataturk was transforming Turkey, Iran, too, enjoyed strong leadership. In the turbulent unrest that followed World War I, Colonel Reza Khan, a self-educated officer of humble origins, emerged as the strong man of the country; he became Shah in 1925 and established the Pahlevi dynasty. During his reign he sought to transform what was still essentially a feudal society into a strong and respected member of the international community, and, despite many superficial similarities with Ataturk, Reza Shah can best be compared not to his Turkish contemporary whom he so often emulated, but asynchronously with reformist dynasts of the nineteenth century such as Mahmud II. In many ways, Reza Shah confronted the same difficulties, possessed the same resources, and adopted the same policies; very few areas of life had been affected by the West, the central government exercised only limited powers in many areas; ancient divisions—ethnic, religious, tribal—dominated the Iranian scene, and powerful traditional groups, especially the tribal, religious, and landowning elites, still retained much power.

Like the nineteenth-century reformers, Reza Shah had as his first concern to consolidate power, and he accorded priority to building a strong military. He reorganized and strengthened the army so as to make it an efficient force capable of controlling the unruly and rebellious tribes that were virtually independent entities, and of suppressing dissent and opposition within the state. The military was his power base, and throughout his reign Reza Shah accorded army offi-

[85] Hyland, op. cit., p. 15; Kemal Karpat, Turkey's Politics: The Transition to a Multi-Party System (Princeton: Princeton University Press, 1959), p. 477.

cers privileges of all sorts. To create a strong and reliable army, however, Reza Shah faced the same problem as Mahmud II had—training officers in modern methods of warfare. Accordingly, he developed a network of military schools consisting of army high schools in the provinces and a war college in Teheran. This training was supplemented by further study in Europe.

The suppression of centripetal forces and divisive elements and the consolidation of power in the center represented a necessary prerequisite for further change. The second prerequisite was, as in the nineteenth century, the creation of a modern administrative structure staffed by officials trained in modern schools, for control and development is contingent upon an efficient civil administration. Accordingly, the Shah took steps to create a functional centralized bureaucracy with the help of advisers from various European countries. Especially noteworthy was the work of the American Mission headed by Arthur Millspaugh, which overhauled financial and budgetary procedures to make them conform to modern practice.[86]

Structural reorganization is always the simplest of the many difficulties confronting any ruler seeking to create a modern bureaucracy. Most pressing is the task of finding qualified cadres to staff the new structures, and Reza Shah sought to meet this need by emphasizing the higher levels of the educational system at the expense of elementary education. As we shall see, most of the available limited resources were diverted to secondary and college-level institutions whose enrollments expanded at a far more rapid pace than did elementary schools. Thus from the outset the traditional elitism of the Iranian educational system and its previous role as a supplier of manpower for the bureaucracy were reinforced.

The retention of traditionalistic orientations was not limited to this aspect of education but was inevitably stamped on all educational processes, for Reza Shah's regime can best be classified as a reformist polity. It is for this reason that such a sharp distinction can be drawn between developments in Iran and Turkey in this period. This difference, however, does not stem from differences in levels of development and integration—even though Iran had not yet undergone the kinds of changes that had occurred in Egypt or in the Ottoman Em-

[86] A detailed description of this project is to be found in Arthur C. Millspaugh, *The American Task in Persia* (New York: Century, 1925).

pire during the nineteenth century—but from the kinds of leadership that each state possessed and the goals, strategies, and personalities of the leaders. Unlike Ataturk, Reza Shah was never committed to the goal of democratization and modernization, nor did he always place country above self-aggrandizement. His fundamental purpose was not to transform the society but to secure his own position within a stronger, more advanced country and to lay the foundations for a new dynasty—his own. Particularly after the mid-thirties, he became a tyrannical despot who used fear and terror to safeguard his power and to acquire vast wealth. Thus, whereas Ataturk deliberately created a new Turkey with a new capital, a new culture, a new political system, and a new ideology, Reza Shah retained the monarchy and never sought systematically to transform the way of life of his countrymen. As one Iranian scholar has stated: "One could borrow from abroad technical innovations, or even political institutions such as a parliament. These belonged to the material sphere, but one must not pollute the national spirit by an excessive admiration for foreign ways, or by the use of Latin letters in algebra and geometry." [87] This outlook is highly reminiscent of the philosophy of the early reformist sultans and of Ziya Gökalp, but the sharp contrast with Ataturk's orientation is evident.

Such a philosophy coupled with a lust for power inevitably led Reza Shah to attempt to concentrate all decisions in his own hands, to prohibit attempts to organize political parties, and to use the legislature solely to approve his decrees. Hence none of the institutions and organizations that are critical for political development developed within the country. Moreover, Reza Shah lacked a coherent program or ideology of modernization and was willing only to adopt reform programs that would modify traditional structure, seldom to implement changes that might endanger his position. He operated largely on an ad hoc personalist basis within the traditional framework; the army buttressed his rule, traditionalism legitimized it.

Some important changes, of course, did occur, particularly in such fields as communications, industry, transportation, and social relations. The country was integrated more than before as the tribes were

[87] Firuz Kazemzadeh, "Ideological Crisis in Iran," in *The Middle East in Transition,* Walter Z. Laqueur, ed. (New York: Praeger, 1958), p. 198.

brought under government control, and a degree of secularization occurred as Reza Shah adopted various measures to limit the influence of the religious institution. Secular legal codes were adopted, the Shiite pilgrimage discouraged, passion plays abolished, and pious foundations expropriated. The nucleus of a modern educational system was built, the position of women changed somewhat, and an economic base laid.

Yet these reforms never penetrated Iranian life very deeply, and the country never generated a sense of dynamism and development. Traditionalism continued to dominate many areas of the society and Reza Shah gave little consideration to bringing about change in such fundamental areas as rural life and social structure. In fact, the deep cleavages between the rural and urban sectors and between social classes were not only retained but strengthened. The gap between rich and poor remained very great—no income tax was ever adopted during these years and the country's development efforts were financed largely through inflation and regressive taxation. Little consideration was given to rural development, although the peasantry comprised an overwhelming percentage of the country's population and change in this sector was vital if Iran were to become a modern society. At the end of Reza Shah's reign the peasantry remained as oppressed and isolated from national developments as it had been two decades earlier. As a result the gap between town and village actually widened, since the various reform programs did affect urban life to some degree.

In sharp contrast to the peasantry's lot, the landowning elite which made up a large proportion of the ruling class—investment in land being highly favored—prospered greatly during these years. It was heavily represented in parliament, accounting for between 52 per cent and 59 per cent of all deputies in this period, and took advantage of such opportunities as the sale of state lands in the thirties to enhance its wealth and strengthen its position. Nor were landowners oppressed by a heavy tax burden; in 1939 land taxes accounted for only four million rials out of a total revenue of 1,528,000,000 rials.[88]

[88] James A. Bill, *The Politics of Iran* (Columbus, O.: Charles E. Merrill, 1972), Table 11, p. 124; Peter Avery, *Modern Iran* (New York: Praeger, 1965), pp. 308–309; Richard H. Pfaff, "Disengagement from Traditionalism in Turkey and Iran," in *The Contemporary Middle East: Tradition and Innovation,* Benjamin Rivlin and Joseph S. Szyliowicz, eds. (New York: Random House, 1965), pp. 425–426.

Similar opportunities in other areas enabled many other persons to make fortunes, for Reza Shah's development programs opened up new ways of acquiring wealth in such new fields as construction and the import trade. Many individuals of humble origins, especially those who enjoyed royal favor, including high-ranking military officers, became very rich and were coopted into the ruling class. Counterbalancing the rise of such persons was the fall of others; many members of the upper class who incurred the Shah's displeasure lost their lands and fortunes and sometimes their lives as well. Thus upward and downward mobility were both possible, but the core group pattern and the composition of particular elites remained essentially unchanged. Unfortunately only limited data are available on this subject, but it appears that former patterns were usually retained and that wealth, power, and position continued to go hand in hand. Even many members of the ulema, especially those with aristocratic connections who did not oppose the Shah, successfully retained their positions.[89]

The result of such policies for Iran was not happy; Reza Shah succeeded in weakening traditional forces in many areas and in laying the foundation for a modern nation-state, but he never created structures and institutions to facilitate succession and development or set the society so firmly on a path of modernization that it could not easily regress. In fact, the opposite was true, and upon his abdication in 1941 "the imposing façade of Reza Shah's regime collapsed . . . revealing the jerry-built structure behind." [90]

Expansion and Change

Reza Shah's accomplishment in building any structure at all in the face of formidable obstacles should not be underestimated. In the field of education, like the nineteenth-century reformers, he had to overcome an almost total absence of human and physical resources. Few trained administrators and teachers were available, and teaching materials, textbooks, and school buildings were either inadequate or unavailable. To solve these problems he resorted to the same approaches;

[89] Avery, op. cit., pp. 273–275; Leonard Binder, Iran: Political Development in a Changing Society (Berkeley: University of California Press, 1962), pp. 67–68.

[90] Kazemzadeh, op. cit., p. 199.

sending students abroad, opening new institutions, hiring foreign experts, and publishing curricular materials.

The first step was to integrate and centralize the existing schools into a hierarchical system and to make education, which until now had varied from school to school, uniform in all elementary and secondary schools. To achieve this, detailed programs were published in Teheran by the Ministry of Education. The curriculum of the elementary school (six years) included religious instruction, Persian (Arabic until 1930), history and geography, writing, arithmetic, and physical education; art and music were added in 1936. Secondary education consisted of two cycles; the first a three-year cycle, the second a three-year academic program for boys and girls or a two-year terminal program for girls. The curriculum of the first cycle consisted of Persian, Arabic, foreign languages, mathematics, sciences, history and geography, art, religion, and physical education. Girls also took courses in home economics. In the second cycle boys could take the academic program and specialize in either literature or science, girls the general course or the normal one.[91]

This revised program was not particularly successful. Since the educational philosophy underlying the new curriculum had as its core the concept that the students should be crammed full of theoretical information on a wide variety of isolated topics, the students studied a very large number of subjects—as many as fifteen in a given year. This philosophy also led inevitably to the further entrenchment of traditional Islamic emphasis on rote learning and memorization. The standard teaching method was the lecture, the best student the one who could memorize the most. Scholasticism was carried to ridiculous extremes; in botany, for example, the good student was expected to be able to recite the names of all the vegetables but was not expected to differentiate between poisonous and edible mushrooms. Nor was there any attempt to relate the curriculum to the needs and conditions of the country. The constitution was taught only in the law school, and history consisted of memorizing biographies of important personages, especially the dates of their reigns and of the wars they en-

[91] Reza Arasteh, *Education and Social Awakening in Iran* (Leiden: E. J. Brill, 1962), pp. 56, 66.

gaged in. One commentator has summarized these problems as follows:

The job of revising the school program was entrusted, for the most part, to individuals who had been trained in France. Their blind imitation of the French system of education, and even more, their limited understanding of the purpose of education, severely damaged Iranian education. They valued knowledge *per se* more than its applicability, theory more than practice, and the lecture method in preference to the laboratory approach. . . . The result was a secondary school curriculum extremely broad in subject matter but unrelated to the life experiences of the student.[92]

One reason why these changes did not affect the functioning of the schools was the lack of qualified teachers, the most severe bottleneck hindering Reza Shah's attempts to create a new educational system. The first teacher-training institution, also patterned along French lines, had been opened in 1918, and by 1927 there were two secondary level schools turning out male teachers, one producing female teachers. Their few graduates, however, could not meet existing needs, let alone the demands created by a reorganized national system of education. Attempts to expand output foundered upon the unattractiveness of the profession. Because of the low remuneration and status that teachers enjoyed, few persons were willing to become educators, and evening classes that were begun in several locations in an effort to produce more teachers generally were discontinued within a few years owing to a lack of applicants. Under these circumstances it is not surprising that the majority of teachers were poorly prepared or that many were graduates of the religious schools. In this manner traditional educational methods and philosophies were once again grafted onto potentially modern institutions. The sad state of the profession at this time can perhaps be appreciated by realizing that in 1929 there were 2,428 teachers in the whole country, 93 per cent of whom were ineligible for salary increases or promotion owing to their lack of qualifications.[93]

[92] Ali Mohammed Kardan, *L'Organisation scolaire en Iran* (Geneva: Imprimerie Reggiam et Jacond, 1957), pp. 99–100. The quotation is from Arasteh, *op. cit.*, pp. 65–66.

[93] Kardan, *op. cit.*, p. 89; see also Manuchehr Afzal, "The Cultural Setting of the Problems of Teacher Training in Iran" (Ph.D. diss., Columbia University, Teachers College, 1956), p. 209.

To deal with this problem, especially at the higher levels, a large number of students were sent abroad for training. Beginning in 1928, 100 students, of whom 35 per cent were to become teachers, were sent abroad annually over a five-year period. Altogether, by 1934, 640 students had participated in this program, studying mainly in France, and about 200 had become secondary and college teachers.[94]

It was not until 1934 that Reza Khan turned his attention to problems of elementary education and adopted the necessary measures to resolve the acute teacher shortage there. Legislation enacted in that year provided for the founding of twenty-five teacher-training colleges to produce teachers for primary and secondary schools within five years and for the professionalization of this career with preference in terms of salary and promotion being accorded to the graduates of the new colleges. In fact, the goals of the act were exceeded; thirty-six colleges were founded and many new teachers entered the profession.[95] Nevertheless, it is doubtful whether the optimistic assessment that "A new, relatively secure, and respectable professional class, admirably placed for furthering the national goals of the regime, was created, and a corresponding change in social attitudes came about" is completely valid. Despite the vast improvement in the position of teachers, their economic and social position was still relatively poor, and although a large number of persons were now attracted to the profession, standards remained low and traditional patterns remained the norm.[96]

The primary reason for the lack of improvement was the low standard of most of these institutions. Curricula were theoretical and rigid, and the quality of the faculty, many of whom possessed only a religious education, was not high. The oldest and most prestigious teacher-training institution, the Daniş-i Saray, which provided college-level instruction, neglected practical aspects and emphasized theoretical and abstract subjects, thus producing graduates who were ill-prepared to serve as secondary school teachers. They tended to be authoritarian, formalistic, and apathetic and would "stick to the text and

---

[94] Arasteh, *op. cit.*, p. 87.

[95] Amin Banani, *The Modernization of Iran, 1921–1941* (Stanford: Stanford University Press, 1961), p. 94; according to Arasteh, *op. cit.*, p. 91, there were thirty in 1941 and forty-three in 1943.

[96] The quote is from Banani, *op. cit.*, p. 94; cf. Kardan, *op. cit.*, p. 93.

repeat what they had learned themselves as students." At least one scholar has argued, therefore, that much of the blame for the low level of secondary education during this period must be laid to the inadequacies of the Daniş-i Saray. Such an assessment, however, ignores the importance of the societal context, and it is difficult to see how one modern institution could function effectively in this setting. Moreover, even if a teacher were trained along modern lines, the lack of resources available to him and the nature of his environment would effectively stifle any attempt at originality and meaningful teaching, and his relationship with students would probably become as formal and routinized as those of his more rigidly and formally prepared colleagues.[97]

The worst situation was to be found in the neglected rural areas. Not only were few educational opportunities available for young peasants but the quality of the few schools that were located in rural areas was very poor. Since no attempt was made to provide special training for teachers serving in these localities, teachers were totally unprepared to teach village youths. In fact, they considered appointment to a rural school as exile and made every effort to obtain a transfer, preferably to Teheran. Such attitudes did not make for effective education. As one observer familiar with rural conditions observed:

as a result of their unsound education and of living in town [the teachers] are not able to work independently in the villages. . . . One of the main difficulties confronting them is their failure to bridge the gap between themselves and the peasants . . . they consider themselves superior . . . their whole attitude circles around the sole aim of finishing the period of work in the villages as soon as possible . . . they have little interest in the village and village work.[98]

Of course, given the nature of the political system and the priorities established by Reza Shah, the neglect of rural education is not surprising. The attempt to introduce educational reforms there would

[97] Kardan, *ibid.*, p. 116. The quotation is from *Report on Seven-Year Development Plan for the Plan Organization of the Imperial Government of Iran* (New York: Overseas Consultants, 1949), II (Public Health, Education), 113; hereafter referred to as *Seven-Year Plan.*

[98] Comments by an Iranian working for the Near East Foundation cited in Afzal, *op. cit.*, pp. 281–282.

have roused opposition from landowners and others who had an interest in maintaining the status quo in rural Iran.

Although the educational process was of lower quality and more irrelevant to student needs in rural than in urban areas, primary education was neglected everywhere owing to Reza Shah's emphasis of the higher levels to supply administrative personnel. Thus, though elementary enrollments increased markedly, especially after 1930 when more attention was paid to this level (the number of students rose from 100,600 in 1928–1929 to 262,200 ten years later), secondary education expanded far more rapidly, the number of students rising from 3,300 in 1924 to 14,500 in 1934 and 28,200 in 1940.[99] Even these new totals, however, were not very significant in terms of the country's needs, for only a very small percentage of school-age children were actually enrolled in any school.

The strong elitist orientation of the system also discouraged educational expansion. To gain admission to a college or a university was the goal of every student, but the number of openings each year was far smaller than the number of applicants, which increased steadily while the number of places available to them grew at a slower rate. Many students therefore, especially those without the proper social background, dropped out of school upon becoming aware of their future prospects. This was especially true for girls, whose education lagged far behind that of the males; the percentage of girls enrolled at the secondary level was small, the dropout rate was extremely high: though 128,000 were enrolled in the first year of elementary school in 1949, for example, only 30,000 attended the sixth-year course. Similarly, whereas 20,000 students attended first-year classes at the secondary level, only 2,000 were enrolled in the sixth year.[100]

Ideology, Education, and Politics

Since Reza Shah accorded priority to establishing and maintaining his own position within the country, he, like Mohammed Ali, cen-

---

[99] Enrollment data are from Marvin Zonis, "Higher Education and Social Change in Iran: Problems and Prospects," paper prepared for delivery at the conference "Iran in the 1960's: A Consideration of Problems and Prospects," Columbia University, Nov. 7–9, 1968, mimeo. p. 12. The paper was subsequently published in *Iran Faces the Seventies,* Ehsan Yar-Shater, ed. (New York: Praeger, 1971), pp. 217–259.

[100] *Seven-Year Plan,* p. 103. See also Kardan, *op. cit.,* p. 99.

tralized all power into his own hands and attempted to supervise personally every administrative detail. The results were disastrous for, as a contemporary high-level official of this period observed:

During the Pahlevi reign no one had a will to do things. Every matter had to be presented to the Shah, and whatsoever he commanded was carried out. . . . I pointed out [that] it was not always possible to predict the outcome of a situation and responsible government officials should be given the authority to act. He agreed with me but did nothing about it.[101]

This extreme centralization extended to the educational system. The Ministry of Education exercised absolute control over every phase of the educational process ranging from examinations to library practices. The result was great inefficiency and wastage of both resources and personnel, as no attention was paid to greatly varied local needs and problems. Instead of flexibility and originality, refuge was sought in "highly detailed regulations and ever-stricter supervision." One obvious example of the way in which the imposition of the national curriculum was dysfunctional lay in the problems of the large nomadic populations which customarily migrated in spring and fall and whose children could thus not attend school. Meticulous adherence to rules and regulations was enforced by inspectors whose visits struck fear into teachers and administrators alike. To meet this threat teachers resorted to various stratagems, including surreptitious attempts to "turn back to a lesson which had long since been thoroughly prepared, . . . call upon the brightest students or . . . shift to some teacher-directed activity." In the rare school that had a laboratory, the teacher, being personally responsible to the director for every single item, took great care to avoid breakage. The usual way was to prohibit students from using the equipment. Similarly, since the librarian was legally accountable for each book, they were all kept under lock and key, and students were seldom permitted access to them. The result of the application of this educational philosophy was that the graduates of any school were prepared, at best, to continue their studies. No attempt was ever made to produce creative thinkers

[101] Cited in Reza Arasteh, "The Role of Intellectuals in Administrative Development and Social Change in Modern Iran," International Review of Education, 9 (1963/64), 331.

or persons with analytical minds, or to relate education to the needs and realities of the society. The criterion of good teaching was the number of students who successfully passed the dreaded national examinations designed to eliminate those considered unfit for further study. And since success depended upon the ability to parrot the contents of a text, the tradition of blind memorization was grafted onto modern materials and it was common practice to expect the student to memorize the textbook of a particular course and to repeat endless series of virtually meaningless and unrelated facts.[102]

All parts of the system were characterized by rigidity, formalism, and scholasticism but, reflecting the elitist orientation, the higher levels were favored with larger allocations of human and physical resources and enjoyed facilities that were better than those of the lower, though still inadequate. Various inducements were also utilized to strengthen the already strong attraction of these schools. Graduates could look forward to good positions and deferments from military service. When they did serve they were sent to military school in Teheran and they remained in service for a shorter period than the rest of the populace.[103]

Reza Shah's emphasis upon higher education dates back to 1921, when a school of law staffed by French and Iranian teachers was founded to train personnel for the Ministry of Justice. Night courses for Ministry employees were also offered. By 1927 seven colleges existed—law, medicine, arts and sciences, theology, war, agriculture, and veterinary medicine. Most of these were integrated into the University of Teheran when it was formally established in 1934.[104]

The concern with higher education, as well as the extremely limited nature of its development when Reza Shah assumed power, is reflected in the sharp increase in the number of students attending institutions of higher learning—91 in 1922, 1,645 in 1935, 3,395 in 1944. Unfortunately the French model was once again followed blindly without any attention to the delicate relationship that exists between an institution and its environment, so that the new University of Teheran possessed all the deficiencies of a French university and none of its strengths—"intellectual short-sightedness, coupled

---

[102] The quotations are from the *Seven-Year Plan*, pp. 83, 116.
[103] Arasteh, *Education*, p. 67; Kardan, *op. cit.*, p. 94.
[104] Arasteh, *Education*, p. 25.

with the attendant vices of exclusiveness, jealousy, social and personal rivalries, and political ambitions, prevented the University from attaining a high academic standing." [105]

Besides expanding—or creating—the structure of a modern system at all levels, Reza Shah also sought to unify and integrate the many different components. Not only did the government specify the curricula to be followed in all schools, but Reza Shah moved directly against the foreign and missionary schools as well. His first step was to bring the foreign schools under the control and supervision of the Ministry of Education by a series of more and more stringent regulations. Beginning in 1928 various decrees specified that official curricula had to be followed in both primary and secondary schools, that the language of instruction had to be Persian, that textbooks and instruction had to be identical with those of the public schools, and that teachers had to be approved by the Ministry of Education. In time the foreign elementary schools were forbidden to enroll Persian students (which cost them 75 per cent of their pupils) and in 1939 and 1940 the ultimate steps were taken. All these schools were nationalized, and all foreign missionary teachers were expelled from Iran on the grounds that the Russians would be entitled to open their own schools if the other nationalities retained theirs. One unexpected result of the law was that more and more upper-class parents sent their children abroad for even an elementary education.[106]

Reza Shah's concern with the creation of a sense of national identity also deeply affected the school system, for he emphasized their political socialization function. As part of his overall ambition to build an Iranian nation out of the many diverse ethnic, religious, and linguistic groups within the country, he developed an official ideology based on the ancient glories of Iran. Archaeological and historical research into the Safavid dynasty was encouraged, and the favorite architectural style for public structures was neo-Persepolis. At the

---

[105] The figures are from the *Seven-Year Plan*, Exhibit B-7. According to Zonis, *op. cit.*, Table II, p. 13, 1,550 students, including 120 girls, were enrolled in institutions of higher learning in 1935. Of these, 1,311, 45 of whom were girls, were studying at the University of Teheran. The quotation is from Banani, *op. cit.*, p. 100.

[106] Banani, *ibid.* pp. 95ff; Peter Avery, *Modern Iran* (New York: Praeger, 1965), p. 278.

same time, he attempted to purify the Persian language of foreign accretions and created, in 1935, the Iranian Academy, which was charged with language reform and the preparation of a pure Persian dictionary. Many words were invented to replace widely accepted administrative, geographic, and scientific terms of Arabic or European origin. The result was to hinder educational progress, since textbooks had to be emended to incorporate the new vocabulary that teachers and students also had to learn to use.

Reza Shah's actions in this field typify his approach to reform, especially the extent to which he was influenced by Ataturk's policies and his reluctance to proceed as rapidly or as thoroughly as Ataturk. Partly because of the strength of traditionalist sentiment in the country, but mainly because of his concern with the preservation of Iranian culture, he never adopted the Western alphabet even though such a change had been discussed for several years and indeed awaited by many Iranian intellectuals, especially after the example of Turkey. As a result, the struggle against illiteracy was handicapped and educational progress rendered more difficult.

The new ideology which stressed love of Shah and country and emphasized that public service was the highest duty and reward of any citizen was actively disseminated through all the communications media and educational institutions. Great emphasis was placed upon the indoctrination of future generations, and all students were expected to memorize patriotic verses and songs. In 1934 a national scouting program was established which was soon made compulsory for all secondary school students. The movement, in effect a paramilitary organization, was another channel of political indoctrination, the emphasis being upon allegiance to the Shah and to the state. In 1939 boys from the tenth to the twelfth grades were required to take four hours of military drill and indoctrination per week.[107] Such indoctrination of feelings of nationalism and loyalty pervaded the entire educational system, with damaging consequences. It reinforced the ancient tradition of servility as the goal of the educational process and transformed the schools into quasi-military institutions; the atmosphere in the elementary schools was "almost invariably rigid, authoritarian, and severe," and in the secondary schools:

[107] Banani, *op. cit.*, p. 104.

The students normally stand at rigid attention while reciting. The class is considered "disciplined and good" when it springs to its feet at a quasi-military command from the student chosen "leader"; . . . sits in mobile silence except when an individual is called to recite; and rattles off the required memorized answer to any question which is put to it. . . . An especially well-disciplined class is one which to the foreign observer appears to cringe at authority.[108]

Partly because of his concern with creating an integrated national system of education, partly because of his concern with the power of the ulema and the need to secularize various aspects of Iranian life, Reza Shah also moved against the traditional religious schools, which still comprised the only available educational opportunity for the majority of the populace. Throughout his reign he took many steps to regulate Islam to a subsidiary place in the society. Although Shiism was never formally disestablished, he stripped the ulema of much of their influence, often treating them with contempt, and moved to restrict the bases of their power by legal reforms and by diverting *waqf* funds away from purely religious purposes. As part of his campaign he imposed a new curriculum upon the madrasas and adopted regulations governing the opening of new religious schools. Before long, however, more positive measures were taken, and the Ministry of Education began to utilize the revenues and endowments of the pious foundations for nonreligious instruction. In 1941 the Ministry of Education was authorized to sell lands belonging to pious foundations and to use the proceeds for general educational purposes, but the fall of Reza Shah prevented the application of this decree. As a result of such measures, the number of madrasas and of students enrolled therein declined steadily from 1932 onward, though primary religious schools were not affected until relatively late in his reign.[109]

Complementing this aspect of his anti-Islamic policy was Reza Shah's emphasis upon secularism in the modern schools. Though in the first years of his reign the curriculum included Islamic subjects and the students observed various Islamic practices such as fasting during the month of Ramadan, the revised curriculum for the primary

---

[108] *Seven-Year Plan,* pp. 91–105.
[109] Zonis, *op. cit.,* p. 12.

schools published in 1937 omitted religious instruction for the first three grades, and another revision in 1941 abolished religious instruction for all students.[110]

Closely connected to his policy of secularization were Reza Shah's efforts to improve the position of women. Beginning in the early 1930's he attempted to destroy the traditions which kept women secluded and instituted a series of legal changes which made marriage and divorce civil instead of religious matters, strengthened women's property rights, and made polygamy more difficult. In 1929 the change to Western dress was promulgated and in 1936 the veil was abolished. The schools were an important instrument in the drive to emancipate Iranian women. In 1935 the first coeducational primary schools were opened, and the following year women were admitted for the first time to higher educational institutions. In all schools, female students and teachers had to wear Western clothes. Physical education was stressed, and a national Girl Scout movement organized.[111] Nevertheless, social and cultural conditions were such that the position of women remained largely unchanged at the end of Reza Shah's reign.

In order to disseminate his ideology more widely and to further strengthen his position as well as to supplement the other educational efforts, Reza Shah inaugurated a program of adult education in 1936. Its goal was to diminish the widespread illiteracy and " 'to provide adults with the useful individual and social training conducive to good citizenship.' " Fifteen hundred evening classes were opened throughout the country to the accompaniment of a massive propaganda campaign. Books, pamphlets, and articles were widely distributed and numerous lectures given by university students and others on civic responsibility, patriotism, and similar subjects; in 1937, 700 such lectures attended by 181,250 persons were organized. One reason for their popularity was that many persons feared to decline invitations to attend. The same year evening classes were established in twenty-two secondary schools whereby adults and young people who could not attend during the day could receive a secondary education. Altogether, 137,703 persons had enrolled in these courses

[110] Afzal, *op. cit.,* p. 185.

[111] Reza Arasteh, "The Struggle for Equality in Iran," *Middle East Journal,* 18 (Spring 1964), 197.

by 1939, but the overall results were limited. Relatively few people, mainly those living in urban areas, were affected by the campaign.[112]

In addition to neutralizing and weakening power groupings such as the ulema elite and seeking to build feelings of loyalty to his dynasty and the new Iran, Reza Shah also needed technically trained personnel for the new economic enterprises, government monopolies, and transportation and communications networks which were established as part of his program of economic development. The Trans-Iranian railroad was built, linking the Caspian Sea to the Persian Gulf and plants for sugar refining, food processing, textiles, and chemicals opened. As in other areas, however, no systematic planning was undertaken, so that after the first step of sending students abroad for study was taken—almost one-third of all students whose education abroad was sponsored by the government were studying technical subjects—no effort was made to produce persons with technical and vocational skills domestically until very late in Reza Shah's reign. The number of students who could be trained abroad was very small, and except for one polytechnic institute opened with German assistance in 1922 no technical school existed in Iran until 1935, so that the country suffered from a serious shortage of skilled manpower during these years. From 1935 onward, however, several technical schools, mainly at the secondary level, were finally opened. The course of study in the Honarestan lasted six or seven years. During the first five years, students studied general academic courses, including Persian and German as well as industrial arts; in the last two or three years the curriculum emphasized practical training in such subjects as electricity, engineering, and carpentry.

To some degree the critical need for skilled personnel was met through the special institutes in such fields as railroading, law enforcement, and finance which were established by various agencies to meet their obvious needs for qualified personnel. The Institute of Post, Telegraph, and Telephone, for example, provided in-service training for ministry employees at various levels. For two years they studied both theoretical subjects including Persian, a foreign language, mathematics, and sciences, and applied subjects such as machine maintenance, telephone equipment, servicing of radio transmission

---

[112] Banani, *op. cit.*, pp. 103–106; the quote is cited on page 104.

equipment, and so on. Some graduates or those persons with a degree in engineering or its equivalent were eligible for a postgraduate one-year course which prepared them for supervisory and specialized positions. Another source of technical personnel was the courses offered by foreign companies which, from 1923 onward, were required to provide technical training for Iranian nationals. The most important of these was the oil industry which established a vocational secondary school and a Higher Institute of Petroleum Industry in 1940.[113]

Even the new technical schools, however, proved unable to meet the critical need for skilled manpower adequately. They left much to be desired in orientation, quality, and relevance. Few possessed the necessary equipment and all stressed theory at the expense of practical application. Furthermore, their numbers, their geographical distribution, and their relationship to the actual skill requirement of the country were inadequate and inappropriate. As a result, Iran's development continued to be greatly hampered by a shortage of trained personnel, and, as one Iranian educator observed:

The result of this negligence is that at present we lack cadres and specialists, both for our modern economic life and for the new services of the state. Our railroad operates under the direction of hundreds of workers and Swedish, Danish, Czech, Belgian, French, and other engineers. Almost all the architects who build new houses, new factories and new schools are foreigners. In the secondary and higher schools courses are given by teachers and French, German, and American professors! . . . there are still no competent Iranians to replace them.[114]

Throughout these years, study abroad was the principal technique used by Reza Shah to resolve shortages of educated personnel in various fields. It has been estimated that between 1922 and 1928, 396 students completed their studies (mainly in France) and that another 452 were still studying overseas. In addition, about 1,500 persons were sent abroad by the other ministries and by wealthy families. Many more Iranians also attended the American University in Beirut.

The overall impact of foreign education upon these Iranians and

[113] Kardan, *op. cit.*, pp. 104ff; Arasteh, *Education*, p. 44.
[114] I. Sadigh, cited in Kardan, *op. cit.*, p. 98 (translation by the author).

upon the country is not easy to evaluate, and conflicting viewpoints have been expressed by different authors. One scholar, for example, has written:

It is impossible to overemphasize the role of the returning student in spreading Western influence in Iran. He brought about a revolution, not only in the fields of intellectual activity and scientific, technical, administrative, and professional enterprise, but also in the less tangible but perhaps more significant areas of cultural traditions, social relations, and personal habits.[115]

Whether this assessment is not somewhat optimistic, however, deserves further consideration, for it is hard to believe that the impact of this relatively small group was so great or, indeed, that, in view of our earlier discussion of the role of psychological, social, cultural, and institutional variables, persons with these skills could be utilized so effectively in what was still in so many respects a traditional environment not oriented toward change. This point has been made by another scholar who has reached very different conclusions covering study abroad, namely that the common result of study abroad was frustration because of cultural shock both in Europe, where many Iranians found it difficult to adjust to a Western environment, and at home, where many returnees experienced problems of readjustment to their own culture. In fact, the more successfully they adapted to European values and technology, the more likely they were to experience difficulty in reintegrating themselves in a society that had changed but little since their departure. Often they found themselves more or less rejected and ignored, sometimes they encountered overt opposition from various groups, especially from those who held administrative office and who regarded the highly trained returnees as a direct threat. In the resulting bitter struggles entrenched bureaucrats often proved able to maintain the status quo; the returnees were almost always assigned to a position far removed from their specialty or to a post without any duties. Some students, of course, adapted easily and performed useful work, but one can easily believe that in far too many cases frustration, despair, and alienation characterized those who had studied abroad.[116]

---

[115] Banani, *op. cit.*, p. 102.
[116] Avery, *op. cit.*, pp. 281–282.

It is also unlikely that all young Iranians who returned from Europe encountered such opposition, and it may be possible to reconcile the opposing viewpoints concerning the contribution of the returnees by considering the role of social background. As we have already noted, social core group and elite recruitment patterns continued essentially unchanged in this period. Traditional ascriptive considerations remained important in determining recruitment into the administrative elite, and perhaps students of upper class background with appropriate connections were absorbed easily and, in social relations, were regarded as models to emulate. Students without these advantages, on the other hand, may have found it difficult to achieve positions of prestige and status even though they possessed more modern skills than most persons within the bureaucracy.

To verify this hypothesis, specific information on the background of those who studied abroad as well as on their career patterns would be necessary, but only fragmentary data are available. In 1960 a sample survey was undertaken in Teheran of Iranians who had studied abroad. Of the 388 who responded, 25 per cent had done so prior to 1940, the remainder between 1940 and 1959. Thirty per cent were sons of merchants, 20 per cent of "office employees," 15 per cent of landowners. The remainder were offspring of fathers with a wide range of occupations, including peasants. Though the data were not stratified by time, it does appear that some persons from middle- and even lower-class backgrounds studied abroad during this period. Since no tabulations by father's position and the occupational level of the respondent are reported, it is impossible to test our hypothesis further, but it is known that foreign training rendered persons of upper-class background eligible, if politically reliable, for the highest positions in the land.[117] Those without the requisite personal contacts, on the other hand, probably found it far more difficult to adjust to their new environment. Some did achieve high administrative posts, acquire wealth, and even upper-class membership, but the expectations of the majority could probably not be realized in a system where proper connections and other traditional factors still carried far more weight than professional ability.

Their frustrations were shared, albeit to a lesser extent, by the

[117] George B. Baldwin, "The Foreign-Educated Iranian: A Profile," *Middle East Journal,* 17 (1963), 268–269; Arasteh, *Education,* pp. 31–32.

graduates of the local institutions who entered the bureaucracy and whose expectations could also not be realized. They too regarded education and bureaucratic position as a means of social mobility, and for the few who managed to climb into the higher ranks of the bureaucracy, this was indeed the case. This seldom happened, however. The vast majority of the University of Teheran graduates, being the sons of merchants, tradesmen, and craftsmen, filled the lower levels.[118] For them a government job was unrewarding, both in terms of the duties involved, which were routine and boring, and of prestige, which dropped steadily as increasing numbers of graduates entered an administration that could no longer utilize them productively.

The flow of graduates from the colleges was absorbed easily throughout the 1930's, but the saturation point was reached by the early 1940's, the number of administrators having tripled from 18,500 in 1926 to 56,800 in 1941.[119] Nevertheless, thousands of students continued to complete their secondary education with the aim of either entering the university or of obtaining an official post immediately. To accommodate them and thus prevent a possible threat to political stability, the usual policy of overstaffing the bureaucracy was initiated. At first such a policy could be implemented easily, but before long severe problems of absorption were encountered as ever-increasing numbers of graduates continued to seek positions in the government.

The Legacy of Reza Shah

Such problems and their political implications were to be evident in subsequent decades, for Reza Shah's reign was one of stability maintained by force. Nevertheless during his term in power Reza Shah laid the foundations for further change in many areas of the society and culture as he painfully but inexorably moved Iran into the twentieth century and exposed the country to modernity. Particularly important in this regard were educational developments which closely reflected the character and orientation of Reza Shah's reformist polity. Only a small elitist, modern educational system had been created, and educational opportunities remained very restricted, for Reza Shah never accorded priority to promoting public education and he allocated quite small financial resources to the modern schools. During

[118] Arasteh, "Intellectuals," pp. 328–329.
[119] Kardan, *op. cit.,* p. 69, n. 19; see also Arasteh, "Intellectuals," p. 330.

his reign educational expenditures averaged only 4 per cent of the total budget and much of this small sum went to the higher levels. The limited character of this elitist system and the degree to which access to modern schools was restricted can be seen from the fact that, as late as World War II, only about 1 per cent of the populace attended public elementary schools. Only 10 per cent of those who graduated from any elementary school (public or private, religious or secular)—about 2 per cent of the population—enrolled in secondary schools. Thus, despite all efforts, 80 per cent of all Iranians still had no access to any schooling and the literacy rate was less than 10 per cent.[120]

The new schools, few in number and poor in quality, did not contribute greatly to Iranian development. One analysis of Iran's educational system shortly after World War II concluded:

It is evident that illiteracy is critically and unnecessarily high; that educational expenditures are lower than required as well as wastefully applied and that good teachers are few and difficult to secure under present salary and teaching conditions. Likewise it is clear that present curriculae are overcrowded and usually too theoretical, that training for leadership or for the humblest skills required for national development is grossly inadequate, that public health and agricultural education are far below national needs and that school facilities, equipment, libraries, books, and teaching materials are generally lacking both as to quantity and quality.[121]

Whatever the shortcomings of his educational and other reforms, however, Reza Shah had at least taken the first steps toward the creation of a modern system. Much had been accomplished since the early twenties; the few disparate components were integrated and unified into a coherent and, in comparison with the situation that had existed, greatly expanded educational system. How this system functioned was determined by the character of the regime. The new schools were essentially designed to provide Reza Shah with the skills that he needed in such a way as not to threaten his position. Hence education was heavily centralized and elitist, and its very ethos was geared to maintaining the cultural, social, and political status quo as defined by the ruler. The stress throughout was upon the inculcation

[120] Banani, *op. cit.,* p. 108; Kardan, *op. cit.,* pp. 125–126.
[121] *Seven-Year Plan,* p. 124.

of traditional values supplemented by loyalty to the shah. The system was designed to produce not independent, innovative graduates, but obedient servants who would carry out orders unquestioningly and who would never constitute a danger to his rule.

With such an orientation one might have expected Reza Shah to meet his manpower needs by promoting the advancement of new elements without ties to established power groupings within the state. This may have occurred to some degree, but unlike the situation in Egypt or the Ottoman Empire the overall patterns of social stratification inherited from the past were reinforced. The ruling class proved flexible enough to engage, from the start, in the kinds of innovative behavior that would safeguard its position by ensuring that its offspring would acquire an appropriate educational experience, often abroad. Thus the schools functioned as a channel for social mobility only to a limited extent, and served primarily to reinforce existing class differences within the society.

Though integrative and supportive of the status quo, the new schools also held the promise of change. In the Ottoman Empire and Egypt in the nineteenth century, the creation of such a system led to the emergence of new groups of professionals, officials, and intellectuals, who supported reform and revolution. Now Iran, too, possessed the nucleus of such groups and the institutions to produce more. Though they did not yet represent a significant social force, problems of absorption and frustrated aspirations were becoming evident, and it was possible that if their numbers continued to grow, the existing structure of political power would be challenged.

V

The Arab Republic of Egypt:
Toward a Modern Educational System
in a Revolutionary Society

The Political Background

The 1952 revolution marked a watershed in Egypt's long history. A new regime, dedicated to the goal of modernization, came to power and adopted policies designed to metamorphose an ancient society into a powerful modern state. That state was the vision of President Gamal Abdul Nasser who evolved into one of the greatest and most charismatic leaders the Middle East has ever known. In the eighteen years of his rule he not only transformed Egyptian society but was a dominant force in the Arab world and came to play an important role in the international arena as well.

His early years were devoted to securing his position. Although the mastermind behind the 1952 revolution, Nasser found himself threatened by the aspirations of General Mohammed Naguib, the official chairman of the junta, and did not succeed in gaining complete control until 1954. After winning the power struggle, President Nasser moved quickly to consolidate his authority and systematically eliminated all possible competitors. The monarchy and all political organizations were abolished and all associations—religious, communal, or social—proscribed so that power in Egypt became far more centralized than ever before. To mobilize popular support, legitimize his authority, and further the goals of national development Nasser established a single party. Originally known as the Liberation Rally, the party was subsequently reorganized as the National Union and later as the Arab Socialist Union. These changes reflected both the evolution of the government's orientation and the difficulties that President Nasser encountered in attempting to institutionalize and legitimize his rule and to achieve modernization. Egypt since 1952, therefore, may best be characterized as a radical system though, as will become evident, important discrepancies exist between actual conditions and the ideal type.

The life of each party corresponds closely to a particular period of recent Egyptian history.[1] The first, which lasted until 1956, witnessed the consolidation of power by the revolutionists, the emergence of President Nasser, and the creation of the Liberation Rally to mobilize support against potential and active opposition forces within the society, notably the powerful and well organized Muslim Brotherhood. During these years President Nasser used traditional appeals, including religion, to legitimize his position and did not inaugurate any comprehensive program of social and economic development. Apart from land reform, few basic changes are evident in this period for at this juncture President Nasser had not yet evolved a coherent program of political, social, or economic action, and, indeed, Egypt lacked the organizational and ideological infrastructure that is necessary for the successful transformation of any society. Essentially the policies that were adopted consisted of pragmatic improvisations designed to deal with specific immediate problems, notably the serious economic situation that the government inherited.

The second stage began in 1956 and lasted until 1961. This period was marked by a growing concern for economic and social reorganization, and various nationalization measures were implemented. Accompanying the extension of state control was the establishment of various agencies to plan and direct the growth of the economy. The new constitution adopted in 1956 emphasized the government's dedication to the achievement of social justice and provided for a mixed economy. It also called for the creation of a new political organization, the National Union, to replace the Liberation Rally, which had become so large and amorphous as to be ineffective. During this period foreign policy issues came to the fore and, following the Suez crisis of 1956, President Nasser emerged as a leading actor on the

---

[1] These stages are based on the discussion by Anouar Abdel Malek, *Egypt: Military Society* (New York: Random House, 1968), translated by Charles L. Markmann, pp. xiff. For the changes in party structure, see Samuel P. Huntington, *Political Order in Changing Societies* (New Haven: Yale University Press, 1968), pp. 246–248. See also R. Hrair Dekmejian, *Egypt under Nasir* (Albany: State University of New York Press, 1971), *passim*.

world scene. Now a shift could be discerned in his ideological orientation; he became a leading exponent of Arab nationalism, which became an important legitimizing factor as foreign policy successes enhanced his charismatic appeal.

The third stage, which began in 1961, was marked by the final emergence and implementation of the new ideology as Nasser moved decisively to transform the social and economic basis of Egyptian society. All leading industrial and major economic enterprises were nationalized, and more emphasis was placed on economic planning and industrialization. A new organization, the Arab Socialist Union, was organized after the breakup of the union with Syria, though along elitist instead of mass lines, since the National Union had proven as ineffective as its predecessor.

In this period too, President Nasser played a very active role in international and regional politics. But whereas formerly he had successfully followed a policy of nonalignment, accepting support from both the United States and the U.S.S.R. and avoiding complete dependence upon one side or the other, he now found himself unable to sustain this policy because of conflicting national, regional, and international pressures. Besides wishing to create a strong modern state and give his people a new sense of dignity and achievement, Nasser was deeply moved by the ideal of Arab unity and was actively concerned with his leadership role in the Arab world. The attempt to extend his influence engulfed him in regional quarrels, not only the Arab-Israeli conflict, but the many inter-Arab quarrels as well, and ideological and prestige factors sometimes proved more decisive than questions of Egyptian national interest in dictating policy on various issues, notably the Yemeni Civil War and the events preceding the 1967 Arab-Israeli War. As a result the President lost his former flexibility, alienated the Western powers, and thus denied himself of an important source of support. Since the country was already confronting serious economic problems stemming from lack of capital, inadequate planning, and an ineffective bureaucracy, the domestic consequences were disastrous. The U.A.R. approached bankruptcy and the rate of domestic change declined rapidly. Subsequent support from the U.S.S.R. greatly ameliorated this situation but defense requirements have continued to represent a heavy drain upon the country's developmental resources.

Despite his failures, President Nasser was undoubtedly the most successful Arab leader of modern times. One reason for his enormous stature was his great political ability. An extremely clever, pragmatic, and flexible leader, he possessed a highly developed capacity to perceive and exploit opportunities to achieve his goals. At no time was this skill more evident than in the aftermath of the 1967 war, which had a traumatic impact upon Egyptian society and forced a fundamental reappraisal of many policies and institutions. The army, the police, and the Arab Socialist Union were all attacked by various groups, including, as we shall see, university students, who raised demands for greater efficiency and less repression.

That President Nasser was able to contain the intense frustration and unrest can be attributed to his charisma, ability, and flexibility, qualities that he exhibited in his decision to reorganize political life in Egypt. On March 30, 1968, he announced ten guidelines to serve as the basis for a new constitution. Emphasizing the basic ideological tenets of Arab nationalism and socialism, they also provided for the liberalization and democratization of Egyptian society. This program of reform was approved in a referendum in May 1968 by practically every Egyptian voter. Subsequently the ASU was reconstructed and a new National Assembly elected. What consequences President Nasser's death will have for the implementation of this program is as yet unclear, but his successor, Anwar Sadat, has indicated that questions of internal reform have high priority. Whether his rhetoric will actually be translated into specific programs aimed at resolving the country's many serious domestic problems and whether President Sadat will be able to implement them effectively cannot be foreseen, but such action is clearly required if Egypt is to modernize.

Twenty years have elapsed since the revolution, and many aspects of Egyptian life have still not undergone the transformation that was anticipated by most observers. Nevertheless, although Nasser's vision of a powerful modern Egypt remains elusive, one fundamental area that has been transformed is the social core group. What had essentially consisted of a ruling class was metamorphosed into a political elite, with the military, many of whose members have acquired permanent bureaucratic functions, as its core. Because the military now controls decision-making in most state administrative services, the present Egyptian social core group has been titled a "stratiocracy," "a regime which, in contrast to a 'military oligarchy' involves the total military institution as a new political elite." Within the political elite a second group can be distinguished, a technocratic, civilian element. It emerged into prominence following the exodus of foreigners after 1956 and the passage of the socialist legislation in 1961–1962 which expanded the public sector greatly, thereby creating a need for qualified Egyptians to fill a wide variety of technical positions.[2]

By developing a mixed military and technocratic administration, President Nasser skillfully strengthened his position and acquired the skills necessary for the implementation of his developmental goals without diluting his own power or permitting possible opposition groupings to emerge because:

Theoretically, the new limitors of public power are the technocrat-bureaucrats, alongside the military, since the modernizing leader as a *civilian chief* depends on them for the attainment of his economic and technological goals, and must delegate some authority to them for the fulfilment of their tasks. In these circumstances, again theoretically, the technocrats acquire interests they must defend. But the *civilian chief* is also a *military chief* who so far depends for his coercive power upon his soldiers. Consequently, he is well-placed between these two heterogeneous groups in the *elite* to maintain the continued personal authority of his . . . popular leadership *vis-á-vis* the masses.[3]

To what degree Nasser's death will lead to change in the composition of this social core group remains to be seen. It is obvious that the political elite pattern will continue to characterize Egyptian society, but it is likely that tensions in evidence within the social core during the fifties and sixties will become ever more acute and may well lead to changes in composition as well as to a redefinition of relations with elites and mass.

If the composition of the political elite is analyzed over time it is evident that important changes have taken place during the past twenty years, though, unfortunately, little social background data are available. Because of clashes over policy and ideology, as well

[2] P. J. Vatikiotis, "Some Political Consequences of the 1952 Revolution in Egypt," in *Political and Social Change in Modern Egypt*, P. M. Holt, ed. (London: Oxford University Press, 1962), pp. 370, 372–373.

[3] *Ibid.*, pp. 374–375.

as personal considerations, only seven of the eleven original core of Free Officers who made the revolution and who largely came from lower and middle-class backgrounds still enjoyed leadership positions in 1964, and by 1968 this number had shrunk to four, including Nasser. At the same time those more junior officers who had also been heavily involved in the plot and who subsequently supported Nasser continued to be heavily represented in important administrative positions. They, too, however, did not constitute a cohesive grouping but were divided along various lines including ideology.[4]

Throughout this period civilians accounted for about two-thirds of all leadership positions, but their actual power was limited by several factors, particularly Nasser's creation of a "stratiocracy" and the policy of having officers serve as ministers of all strategic departments and as second-level administrators in technical ministries headed by civilians. Also noteworthy is the emergence of officers with technical expertise. Beginning in the late fifties a growing number of such "officer-technocrats" came to prominence, thus enabling the military to maintain a greater scope and range of control than had heretofore been possible.

Nevertheless, a clear trend toward increased civilian representation is evident over time; in the fifties the military was dominant but in the sixties the trend was toward greater and greater civilian participation, a trend that was accelerated by the events of 1968. This pattern is likely to continue but it remains to be seen for how long and to what extent the civilian technocratic elite, whose importance is bound to increase as the country continues to develop, will accept the direction of military officers, most of whom possess markedly inferior training and education. To view the divisions within the social core group only in this manner, however, probably simplifies a complex pattern, for it is not clear to what extent the technocrats possess similar ideological and policy orientations. It is also possible that latent or existing differences will be exacerbated by the consequences of Nasser's death and by the ambitions of other elements including the thousands of university graduates who aspire to elite membership but whose aspirations remain largely unfulfilled.

From this perspective questions of educational policy carry impor-

---

[4] This discussion is based on Dekmejian, *op. cit.*, Chap. 11.

tant political implications, and, indeed, it appears as though the course of educational development has been profoundly affected by the efforts of a technocratic "lobby." In 1967 an article in *Al-Ahram,* the semiofficial newspaper stated: "all arguments to limit the educational framework in any stage or field must be viewed with concern since it points to the formation of a new class in Egyptian society, and especially among the technocrats who have seized the key positions and are, of course, uninterested in moving from these positions or in making some room for troublesome competitors." [5] Despite such opposition the policy favored by the technocrats was adopted and the expansion of educational opportunities slowed appreciably during the late sixties. Nevertheless, conflict over educational policy remains apparent. In 1971 Louis Awad, the cultural editor of *Al-Ahram,* denounced the "reactionary forces" who, in order to preserve their own position, had been responsible for limiting enrollments first in higher education and subsequently at the secondary and primary levels as well. [6]

Educational Transformation

This struggle not only reflects the degree to which education is a political issue in any society but also the complexities involved in transforming a dysfunctional educational system into one that is consonant with the requirements of modernization. Since 1952 the revolutionary government has attempted to restructure the educational system in order to bring it into harmony with its political, social, and economic goals. Various reforms were implemented, including structural reorganization to eliminate existing blockages and to open up linkages between hitherto isolated components and a stress upon vocational, technical, and scientific training. Also noteworthy are the explosive expansion of educational opportunities, the emphasis upon political socialization, and an Arab nationalist orientation that has unified the structure and curriculum of the Egyptian schools with those of other Arab countries. Nevertheless, as we shall

[5] Cited in Moshe Efrat, "Educational Progress in the United Arab Republic," *New Outlook,* 2 (Oct. 1968), 30.

[6] Louis Awad, "The Counter-Revolution and Egyptian Education," *Al-Ahram,* Feb. 26, 1971 (in Arabic).

see, these efforts have not proven particularly successful, and it is no exaggeration to state that education today requires as profound a transformation as occurred in the last two decades if it is to reinforce and facilitate the country's development. Egypt possesses more or less similar educational structures and goals as other Arab states, and confronts many of the same problems.

Accordingly we shall first analyze the changes in Egyptian education since 1952 and then consider these educational patterns and problems within the context of the Arab world as a whole. How political variables affect education is also evidenced by the course of educational reform since 1952, for the kinds of changes that were adopted in each of the three stages of recent Egyptian history that we have delineated reflect the character of the policy at that time. During the first stage the concern with the consolidation of power, the pragmatic and nonideological style, and the focus upon other domestic problems ensured that educational policy would not be geared toward fundamental change and would not be the object of detailed and systematic planning. In fact the changes that were made in this period essentially represented a continuation and elaboration of reforms that had been initiated by various governments after World War II. To lessen the cleavage between the elementary and primary schools, for example, fees had previously been abolished and elementary school graduates permitted to take the primary school examinations. Now the remaining vestiges of dualism were eliminated. In 1953 Law 210 providing for unified primary schools was promulgated. Law 213 of 1956 extended the duration of the elementary cycle from four to six years, provided for automatic promotion (if the student attended 75 per cent of his classes) instead of promotion by examination, as had hitherto been the case, and reformed the curriculum to include economic, social, and hygiene courses. In many cases, however, children graduate to the next cycle after completing the fourth form if they pass a promotion examination. Grades 5 and 6 are reserved for students who either failed or did not sit for the examination, and the emphasis appears to be upon reviewing and preparing for the examination.[7]

[7] Amir Boktor, *The Development and Expansion of Education in the United Arab Republic* (Cairo: The American University in Cairo Press, 1963), pp.

The first stage did, however, witness the first attempts at planning and a national plan consisting of priority projects for the 1955–1960 period was drawn up. In the field of education its general targets included universal primary enrollments within ten years, diversification and upgrading of postprimary education with an emphasis upon technical and vocational education, and qualitative improvements in such areas as curricula, teacher training, and educational administration.[8] Serious planning, however, did not begin until the second stage, when the emergence of ideology and evolution of a socialist program were accompanied by an emphasis upon rationalization, the politicization of schools, and attempts to relate educational policy to developmental requirements. Various administrative and coordinating agencies including the Supreme Council for National Planning and the National Planning Commission were established, and in 1960 the Institute of National Planning with research and training functions was set up. In that year the first integrated, comprehensive plan was published. It spanned a ten-year period but stressed the first five-year cycle; only vague projections were included for the 1965–1970 period.

The third stage, the "socialist phase," witnessed the first systematic and integrated efforts at radical change but many of the problem areas which had slowed the pace of development in the fifties— notably the failure to create an effective and integrated political party, to revitalize an inert bureaucracy, and to develop and implement a dynamic program to mobilize meager resources and harness the energies of the populace—continued to affect the rate and direction of change. Furthermore, internal conflicts within and without the social core group and external considerations which led to the accordance of high priorities to the military establishment created additional parameters for internal reform and ensured that the at-

---

27–28; Efrat, *op. cit.,* p. 25; "Report on the Development, of Education in the United Arab Republic in the School Year 1967/1968" multilithed (Cairo: United Arab Republic Ministry of Education, Documentation and Research Centre for Education, May 1968), p. 22; hereafter referred to as "Report, 1967/68."

[8] "Educational Planning in the United Arab Republic," multilithed (Cairo: U.A.R. Ministry of Education, Documentation and Research Center for Education, 1962), p. 7; hereafter referred to as "Educational Planning, UAR."

tention of decision-makers would not be focused upon education. Subsequent developments, including the 1967 war and its aftermath, have not altered these fundamental aspects but rather have rendered even more complex the challenge of modernization that confronts President Sadat.

Further complicating efforts at educational development were the weaknesses of planning in the fifties and sixties. Despite greater sophistication and expertise in its formulation and implementation, the preparation of the ten-year plan created serious problems for educational planners and administrators. The most obvious difficulty was the lack of an adequate statistical base. The results of the 1960 census, with vital demographic information on such elementary though crucial variables as the age structure of the population and its occupational and regional distributions, for example, were not published until two years later. Nor were reliable data on a wide range of socioeconomic topics available until the early sixties, when standing committees began to examine various fundamental areas, such as manpower needs, in detail. Other problems included a shortage of planning experts, a lack of trained personnel, inadequate coordination between the planners and administrators at various levels, and difficulties of implementation. Such deficiencies are even more fundamental than lack of data, for to correct them involves basic change in the orientation of administrators at all levels. One study concluded that the inadequacy of planning efforts

arises not from the planning machinery itself, but from the administration habits of the total government, and from the lack of administrative force and orderliness which characterizes government managements as such.

The present habits of management are not geared to planning. The men who run the agencies, and their top civil servants, never lived in a world of comprehensive social and economic planning before. The whole psychology of the thing is new to them. Such planning was never part of their work habits.[9]

[9] Luther Gulick and James K. Pollock, *Government Reorganization in the UAR, Report Submitted to the Central Committee for the Reorganization of the Machinery of Government* (Cairo, 1962), pp. 30–32, cited in Nimrod Raphaeli, "Development Planning in Iraq, Israel, Lebanon, and the U.A.R." (Ph.D. diss., University of Michigan, 1965), p. 296. On the shortcomings of

To remedy such deficiencies is no simple matter, and though various measures were adopted no new comprehensive plans were issued despite the need to change targets and projections on the basis of the results that were in fact achieved. As one scholar commented in 1967, "the plain fact is that the country has now been running for two years of the second five year plan period without one." Nevertheless, over the past decade Egyptian experts have generated a number of impressive studies on various economic and related issues such as manpower supply and demand, the impact of population growth, and the functioning of the educational system. Thus there is little doubt that planning today is on a far higher plane than ever before, and, as we shall see, a considerable amount of attention is being accorded to the many shortcomings of the existing educational system.[10]

Despite the widespread belief that education requires a complete transformation, however, the goals of the third five-year educational plan (1970–1975), which is presently being implemented are essentially similar to those of earlier plans. These include the universalization of primary education, the extension of compulsory schooling from six to nine years for all primary school graduates wishing to attend preparatory school, the development of scientific, technical, and vocational education, the reorganization of private education, and the upgrading of standards by providing more ade-

---

planning in the U.A.R. see also "Educational Planning in the Arab States and Possibilities for its Development," paper prepared for the Conference of Ministers of Education and Ministers Responsible for Economic Planning in the Arab States, Tripoli, Libya, March 5–10, 1966, mimeo. (Paris: UNESCO/MINED/ARAB STATES/12, 1966), *passim;* hereafter referred to as "Educational Planning," pp. 9–10; also M. K. Barakat, "Planning of Primary School Education," mimeo. (Cairo: Institute of National Planning, March 1964), p. 4. For details on how the plan was prepared, see M. Hamza, "Educational Statistics and the Educational Plan in the UAR," mimeo. (Cairo: Institute of National Planning, March 1964), *passim.*

[10] Bent Hansen, "Planning and Economic Growth in the UAR, 1960–65," in *Egypt since the Revolution,* P. J. Vatikiotis, ed. (New York: Praeger, 1968), p. 19. For a list of studies published by the Institute of National Planning, see Mahmoud A. Hashad and Mahmoud M. Eid. "Subject-Guide to Memos of the Institute of National Planning," mimeo. (Cairo: Institute of National Planning, January 1967).

quate facilities and enhancing and expanding pre- and in-service teacher-training programs.[11]

The universalization of primary education, like the other targets that were established without adequate consideration of the variables involved, was not reached in 1965 and had to be postponed, first to 1970, now until 1975. Nevertheless, strenuous efforts were made to provide every child with a primary education and the number of students grew at an extremely rapid pace during the first decade and has continued to expand rapidly since then, rising from 1,310,169 in 1953 to 2,663,247 in 1960 and 3,618,751 in 1969–1970. These aggregate figures, however, disguise several important points. First, there are marked urban-rural differences. It was estimated that, in 1963–1964, 90 per cent of all urban children were attending primary school but that only 65 to 75 per cent of rural children were enrolled. More important, the growth rate slowed appreciably with each suc- ceeding year in the sixties. Thus, although the overall rate of increase was 3 per cent per annum between 1960 and 1968, the rate declined from about 5 per cent per year at the beginning of the decade to about 2 per cent in the later years. A final disturbing factor is that the rate of increase in the number of girls enrolled in this period slowed even more appreciably. In 1960–1961, 997,266 girls were attending primary school. By 1964–1965 the total had climbed to 1,285,008 but in the next five years only another 101,423 girls were enrolled.[12]

During these years primary education received sizable resources. How much money has been spent on this stage, as well as the great

---

[11] "Report on the Development of Education in the United Arab Republic in the School Year 1969/1970," multilithed (Cairo: United Arab Republic Minis- try of Education, Documentation Centre for Education, May 1970), p. 11; hereafter referred to as "Report, 1969/70."

[12] *UNESCO Statistical Yearbook, 1969* (Paris: UNESCO, 1970); "Report, 1969/70," p. 7. Report of the Ministerial Committee for Manpower (1965) published as *Takrir al-Lajmah al-Vizaiyah lil-Quwa al-Amilah an Siyasat at-Talim* (Cairo, n.d.) (in Arabic), pp. 21–22; hereafter referred to as *Manpower Report*, Awad, *op. cit.* "Survey of Educational Progress Achieved in Arab States since Ministers and Directors of Education Met in Beirut in February 1960," paper prepared for the Conference of Ministers of Education and Ministers Responsible for Economic Planning in the Arab States, Tripoli, Libya, March 5–10, 1966, mimeo. (Paris: UNESCO/MINED/ARAB STATES/ 8/1966), p. 69; hereafter cited as "Survey"; "Report, 1969/70," p. 7.

problems involved in analyzing educational finance, is readily illustrated by the available data. According to UNESCO estimates, primary education accounted for 15.4 per cent of the total educational budget in 1920, 38.7 per cent in 1945, and more than 60 per cent in 1964–1965. The 1960–1965 educational plan, on the other hand, allocated 31.5 per cent of total expenditures for primary education, and a detailed study published in the mid-sixties indicated that expenditures for primary education amounted to 43 per cent of total outlays.[13]

Regardless of which figures are correct it is obvious that extremely large resources have been devoted to primary education and that these outlays have not led to the creation of a dynamic system of elementary education for even a majority of Egyptian children. On the contrary, the emphasis upon democratization has resulted in an aggravation of the many qualitative problems that have characterized elementary education for decades.

Physical facilities remain inadequate, and various measures including split shifts, the utilization of temporary quarters, and the elimination of separate schools for boys and girls are still resorted to. Problems of teacher quality are also widespread, and the primary stage is marked by high dropout rates. Although it is claimed that over 80 per cent of primary school age children enter the first grade as compared to 45 per cent before the revolution, it was estimated in the mid-sixties that, because many do not continue for very long, only about 55 per cent of all children between the ages of six and twelve are actually enrolled in school.[14]

Various measures have been adopted to remedy the deficiencies, including programs to upgrade teacher quality, the introduction of new curricula, and the preparation, for some subjects, of teachers' handbooks for in-service training that explain the purpose of a course, how it should be taught, and how the interest of the students can be aroused and maintained.[15] Despite these efforts, however, quality remains a major problem, one important reason being that the number of pupils to every teacher increased from thirty in 1953

[13] "Survey," p. 31; "Educational Planning, UAR," p. 16; *Manpower Report,* p. 21.
[14] Efrat, *op. cit.,* p. 25.
[15] Report, 1967/68," p. 29.

to thirty-nine in 1967. Such a ratio has deleterious effects upon standards, a fact recognized by Egyptian experts who have pointed out that since increases "in the number of pupils to each teacher affect the pupils' educational standard, exhaust the teachers and consequently reflect on the extent of the pupil's comprehension of what they are given, it is necessary to make an all-out effort to find the suitable solutions in order to reduce these rates." [16]

Furthermore, it is generally accepted that in the absence of reinforcement through the mass media and the provision of reading matter to rural areas, most of those who do graduate from rural schools lapse back into illiteracy within a few years. Thus primary education does not produce the kinds of orientations that are so vital for modernization, and the emphasis upon universalizing this level can be criticized as being nonfunctional and wasteful of limited resources. As one Egyptian scholar has asked: "Is it not time to question the expenditure of so much money, time, and energy on a primary school system which is producing such meager results?" [17]

To proceed from the primary to the next level, the preparatory stage, is no simple matter. The first five-year plan (1960–1965) allowed for only 20 per cent of the graduates to continue their education; a competitive examination screened out the other 80 per cent. This examination represents a formidable hurdle limiting access to the higher levels at a time when the demand for education is extremely great. In the mid-sixties about 70 per cent of all pupils in the sixth grade took this examination. The passing rate was 58 per cent, so that only 38 per cent of those registered in the sixth grade were able to continue their education. Overall the percentage of the 12–15 age group attending school has risen from 16 per cent in 1953–1954 to almost 20 per cent in 1965–1966. The total number of students enrolled in 1969–1970 amounted to 793,891, of whom 253,779 were girls.[18]

[16] *The Increase of Population in the United Arab Republic and Its Impact on Development* (Cairo: Central Agency for Public Mobilisation and Statistics, Sept. 1969), pp. 229–230; hereafter referred to as *Population;* the figures are from Table 3.2.19, p. 257.

[17] Boktor, *op. cit.,* p. 164.

[18] "Educational Planning, UAR," p. 16; *Manpower Report,* p. 25; Efrat, *op. cit.,* p. 26; "Report, 1969/70," p. 7.

A significant difference, however, distinguishes the growth of this stage in the fifties from that in the sixties. As part of its emphasis upon scientific and practical training the government originally attempted to stress technical and vocational training as early as possible in order to involve the largest possible number of students. Hence, when the preparatory stage was created in 1953 to cover what had been the last two years of the primary school and the first years of the secondary school, it consisted of academic and vocational programs. In 1956 it was reorganized as an independent three-year stage that did not overlap with or duplicate the other levels and was coordinated with them, but the emphasis remained upon technical and vocational training. By 1962, however, as a result of the attempts to train and place these students, it became obvious that the graduates' educational background was not sufficient to enable them to acquire vocational skills, and this policy was abandoned in favor of secondary-level vocational training.[19]

The failure of this experiment has affected thousands of youths. The number of students enrolled in vocational schools at this level rose dramatically from 3,000 in 1953–1954 to 50,000 in 1962–1963 before it began to decline sharply to 4,272 in 1969–1970. Thus many graduates (there were 17,033 in 1964–1965 as compared to 500 in 1953–1954) have neither learned a trade nor received appropriate training to enable them to continue their education. Since the general preparatory stage will become compulsory for all students at a future date, all technical preparatory schools are presently being converted into secondary-level institutions.[20]

While the number of students enrolled in vocational schools at this level rose sharply during the fifties and early sixties, the number of students attending general preparatory schools was also declining markedly: from 328,470 in 1955–1956 to 249,129 in 1959–1960. In the sixties, on the other hand, enrollments at this level exploded, climbing to 300,853 in 1961–1962, 472,568 in 1964–1965, and

[19] M. S. Fahmy, "A Tentative Plan for the Future Development of the Educational System in the U.A.R." mimeo. (Cairo: The Institute of National Planning, February 1964), pp. 22–23; "Survey," p. 23.

[20] *Population*, Table 3.2.21, p. 260; "Report, 1969/70," p. 7; Efrat, *op. cit.*, p. 26; "Report, 1967/68," pp. 16–17.

793,891 in 1969–1970. On a year-to-year basis, however, this stage has also been marked by a steady decrease in the rate of growth, which dropped from 17 per cent between 1960–1961 and 1961–1962 to 15 per cent, 13 per cent, and 9 per cent in succeeding years, and reached 2.4 per cent at the end of the decade.[21]

Nevertheless demands for admission to these schools are great, as indicated by one official comment that enrollments at this level increased owing to "the parents' keenness to enroll in the preparatory schools their sons and daughters who have passed the entrance competitive examination . . . so that they may not miss the opportunity of completing their education." [22] Partly to meet these pressures, partly for ideological reasons, the government has moved to a policy of gradually expanding this stage until it becomes compulsory in the future. The rise in absolute numbers, however, has already affected standards and has increased the pressures upon the higher levels. Unless careful preparations are made, the implementation of the decision to universalize this level will further aggravate these problems.

To proceed beyond the preparatory stage and gain admission to an academic secondary school is also no easy matter. The first integrated five-year plan (1960–1965) provided that only 43 per cent of those who pass the preparatory school certificate examination would be admitted to secondary schools, and the examination represents a difficult challenge; a significant percentage of all students fail it. Overall, however, the number of students continuing their education has risen markedly from about 6 per cent in 1953–1954 to 10 per cent in 1965–1966, but this increase is attributable largely to the growth in vocational and technical training at the secondary level. Thus, between 1953 and 1961, the total number of students enrolled in secondary schools rose by about a third from 92,062 to 124,607, whereas the number of students attending secondary-level industrial, commercial, and agricultural schools quintupled from 14,356 to 67,895. By 1969–1970 the number of students enrolled in academic institutions had more than doubled, rising to 293,144, but

[21] "Educational Planning, UAR," Table 3, p. 23; "Survey," p. 70; "Report, 1969/70," p. 7; Awad, *op. cit.*
[22] "Report 1967/68," p. 16.

the number of students receiving technical training quadrupled to 241,590.[23]

Despite the apparent success of the government in channeling students into those fields which provide the skilled manpower necessary to achieve developmental goals, marked shortages of skilled and technical workers continued to hinder Egypt's development throughout the sixties. The gap between supply and demand grew ever greater with each succeeding year, and in mid-decade it was estimated that the demand for semiskilled manpower would amount to 434,000 by 1970 but only 150,000 persons could in fact be trained in existing facilities, thus leaving a shortage of 284,000. By 1975 the demand was expected to rise to 500,000, by 1980 to 656,000. A similar pattern was evident in the demand for skilled workers and assistant technicians. Whereas the demand would amount to 139,000 by 1970 the lack of facilities and the continuing preference of students for academic training would limit the supply to a mere 19,000, leaving a deficit of 120,000. By 1975 the demand would grow to 267,000, by 1980 to 759,000. Equally acute problems were evident in the demand for technicians, of whom 213,000 would be required by 1970, 263,000 by 1975, 373,000 by 1980. However no institutions to meet these demands now existed because the system of higher institutes, which we shall discuss below, were subverted from their original purpose of preparing this category of skilled manpower to academic training.[24]

A major factor making for goal displacement by higher institutes and for the failure of all other efforts to meet the demand for middle-level manpower is the continuing distaste for technical occupations that still characterizes Egyptian society. A detailed study of secondary and college graduates, for example, concluded:

The UAR is rapidly becoming an industrial country. . . . This led to a great demand of specialized personnel. . . . The government finds great difficulty in preparing these numbers. On the other hand a big surplus of

[23] "Educational Planning, UAR," p. 17. According to Boktor, *op. cit.*, pp. 41–42, about 60 per cent fail; in 1965–1966, 31 per cent failed (Efrat, *op. cit.*, p. 27). *Education in the United Arab Republic*, 12 (New York: Arab Information Center, 1966) (Jan. 1966), 277–279; "Report, 1969/70," p. 7.

[24] *Manpower Report*, p. 16.

unemployed graduates of theoretical faculties are with no work at all. Another notable phenomenon is that the occupations that we called the "white collar type" are always preferred to the "blue collar type." . . . All the second type of occupations are better paid and enjoy much better chance of promotion, yet it has always been noticed that secondary school graduates who fail to join higher education prefer the white collar job.[25]

This report noted that various "strict" measures were being applied in order to resolve these problems but, as we have discussed, serious manpower shortages continued to hinder the country's development during the remainder of the 1960's.

Another important factor contributing to the manpower bottleneck is the inadequacy of existing vocational and technical education. The explosion in enrollments that has taken place since 1952 occurred with limited planning and attention to available resources so that existing human and physical facilities have been badly strained, and serious imbalances between training and needs have been common. The shortage of teachers, who enjoy less prestige and lower incomes than their colleagues in other fields, is particularly acute, and often schools are forced to hire almost totally unqualified personnel with obvious consequences for the quality of the training received by the students.[26]

These deficiencies have been widely recognized and many specific reforms have been undertaken to upgrade the quality of the vocational and technical schools and make them more relevant to the country's actual needs. Various measures to train qualified instructors have been adopted in recent years and several committees established to deal with this problem. The content of the curriculum has also been revised and specializations in new fields introduced to meet national needs, including forging and heat treatment, readymade clothes, and general decoration. Other changes that are presently under consideration would introduce a system of optional subjects, limit the number

[25] Research Project on Employment and Unemployment among the Educated (Cairo: Institute of National Planning, 1963), pp. 133–134; hereafter called Research Project.

[26] Fahim I. Qubain, Education and Science in the Arab World (Baltimore: Johns Hopkins Press, 1966), pp. 29–30.

of students to meet plan requirements and available spaces in higher technical institutes, and establish linkages with industrial and agricultural enterprises. A new law designed to reorganize various aspects of technical training along these lines was adopted in 1970 and new curricula for the industrial secondary schools were to be inaugurated in 1970–1971. It is also expected that standards will rise following the conversion of all technical preparatory schools into academic institutions since students will be admitted to secondary-level vocational training with a far stronger background than was the case heretofore.[27]

The government's emphasis upon science and technology is also reflected in the academic institutions, whose curriculum has been revised to permit more attention to these subjects. Furthermore, though all students study general courses for the first year and then specialize in either literature or science, the number of students enrolling in the former is being limited while the number of those specializing in science continues to increase. The first five-year plan (1960–1965) envisaged a ratio of three students enrolled in this branch for every student studying literature.[28]

As in the vocational schools, standards in the academic institutions have remained at a very low level and in most cases have fallen further as enrollments increased without adequate inputs of physical and human resources. Various attempts have been made here also to achieve qualitative improvements in recent years by producing new textbooks and teaching materials, rewriting curricula to conform with modern practices for courses in the physical sciences, social studies, Arabic, and foreign languages in both the preparatory and secondary stages, and developing more adequate methods of teacher training. But, again, appreciable results have not yet been obtained and quality remains very poor: In 1966 more than 60 per cent of the students failed the English matriculation examination that they take after three years of secondary schools; 54 per cent failed mathematics, and 45 per cent failed chemistry.[29]

[27] "Report, 1967/68," pp. 31, 23–24; "Report, 1969/70," pp. 10, 13; Efrat, op. cit., p. 27.

[28] "Educational Planning, UAR," p. 17.

[29] "Report, 1967/68," pp. 27ff; Efrat, op. cit., p. 27.

One result of the low standards that characterize secondary education is that students are poorly prepared for college, and standards there are adversely affected as well. In the words of one scholar:

These schools . . . do not give an education as we understand it; they even establish bad habits such as memorization, the cramming of notes, etc. . . . Even today one can apply the words of the Egyptian Minister of Public Instruction (1935) concerning most graduates: "most of them lack the personality and the spirit of decision; they hesitate to think for themselves and do not dare to express their opinions; if they arrive by chance to make one, they are careful to enunciate verbally or in writing in concise and correct phrases whether in Arabic or in a foreign language." Since independence and the Arabization of education the knowledge of foreign languages at the secondary level has dropped. The majority of students entering a university are not capable of reading a publication in a foreign language. Many of them are not even capable of taking individual notes, so that the professors are led to dictate the résumés of their courses.[30]

Inadequate preparation is at least equally harmful for the thousands of students who find that they cannot gain admittance to an institution of higher learning and must find some sort of employment, often a difficult task. This group evidences a marked level of dissatisfaction with their educational experience. One study showed that whereas 94 per cent of persons with a higher education were content with their training, similar feelings were expressed by only 56 per cent of those with a secondary education. Such feelings are closely linked to questions of job satisfaction, and it is not surprising that whereas 44 per cent of university graduates preferred the position they occupied, only 18 per cent of those with a secondary education fell into this category.[31] The implications of such a situation for modernization and political stability are obvious and we shall discuss this problem in more detail later.

One of the major causes of the low standards obtaining at the secondary and lower levels of the system is the poor quality of instruction. Egypt, like many other countries in the region, had to face

[30] Jean-Jacques Waardenburg, *Les Universités dans le monde arabe actuel* (Paris: Mouton, 1966), I, 45–46.

[31] *Research Project,* Tables 24, 29, pp. 92, 101.

serious problems of teacher recruitment and training, and it too relaxed formal requirements in order to accommodate the great inflow
of students at all levels after the 1952 revolution; as a result, the
quality of the average teacher, which was never particularly high,
dropped even further. This deficiency can be largely attributed to the
low standards obtaining in the teacher-training institutes—a large
number of separate institutions on different levels. This fragmented
network can be divided into several categories. The first enrolls
graduates of the preparatory schools whom it prepares as primary
teachers. Above these are various colleges which combine professional
and technical education with teacher training. These enroll secondary
school graduates who are trained as preparatory school teachers.
Graduates of university faculties who plan to teach at the secondary
level are required to take one year of graduate work at the college
of education of Ain Shams University, the only institution of its kind
in Egypt. Regardless of their differences, all the institutes suffer from
severe limitations. Curricula stress the theoretical rather than the
practical, courses overlap, and there is no conscious attempt to integrate the variety of courses offered. The neglect of practical preparation also extends to practice teaching, which is of too short duration
and inadequately supervised, and to the widespread neglect of general
and specialized teaching methods.[32]

The result of such training is that most teachers possess no enthusiasm for their occupation but accept it as a way to survive in a harsh
environment. They carry out their tasks mechanically and routinely
and show little if any interest in their students. Projects to upgrade
the qualifications of experienced teachers or to enrich them culturally
or professionally have affected but a small minority. Few teachers can
afford to buy books, and in those rare cases where schools possess
libraries, the normal pattern is for teachers and students alike to be
granted limited access to the materials, which are considered too
precious to be used. Not surprisingly, as one observer has noted:
"Teachers on the whole do not grow. They teach the same thing in
the same way and entertain the same ideas and methods to such an
extent that they become stagnant, plodding along in the same groove
from the time they start teaching until the time they retire." [33]

[32] Boktor, *op. cit.,* pp. 10, 90–91.
[33] *Ibid.,* p. 166.

For most teachers the only pedagogical technique is memorization, and at all levels little attention is paid to stimulating students to think for themselves. The normal pattern is for the teacher to condense textual materials into notes that they either dictate or hand out and for the student to further abridge and memorize them as thoroughly as possible in order to pass the final examination. Various efforts to mitigate the traditional emphasis upon the memorization of facts so as to produce independent, flexible thinkers have been largely unsuccessful, one reason being the importance to the student of passing the examinations at the end of each cycle.

Many of these problems were foreseen by the first educational plan (1960–1965), which stressed the desirability of raising standards. It called for upgrading the large number of unqualified personnel who had been hired to meet the rapid expansion in enrollments through in-service training programs and proposed establishing higher qualifications for appointment. Instructors at the middle level were henceforth to be recruited from higher institutes and teachers' colleges and not from intermediate-level institutions. Teachers with such backgrounds were to be transferred to primary schools or appointed to administrative tasks. Teachers at the secondary level were henceforth to be graduates of colleges and universities. Technical school teachers, most of whom were graduates of middle-level schools, were also to be upgraded through in-service classes; new teachers were to be graduates of the higher institutes. Subsequent plans also include measures to achieve these objectives, and a program to enable unqualified primary teachers and principals to improve their qualifications by enrolling as external students (we shall discuss this approach below) in teacher-training institutions was inaugurated in 1968. Numerous other measures are also being implemented in order to raise the quality of the teachers' colleges that train preparatory and secondary teachers. Some of these institutions were amalgamated and all are now affiliated with a university. Efforts are also being made to increase the attractiveness of the profession by appointing persons to schools in their own localities, facilitating transfers between various regions, and providing housing for teachers serving in remote areas.[34] How effective these programs have been and to what extent qualitative improve-

---

[34] *Ibid.*, pp. 92ff; "Report, 1967/68," p. 25; "Report, 1969/70," pp. 15–16.

ments can be achieved remains uncertain, particularly in view of the magnitude of the task.

One encouraging factor is the degree to which the present educational system is regarded by Egyptian experts, administrators, and intellectuals as inadequate for the achievement of the country's goals. Such criticism became particularly evident in the sixties when, as we have seen, systematic and sophisticated analyses of the educational system were undertaken. A study published in 1964, for example, analyzed each stage and type of schooling and found that at the primary level the emphasis upon expansion had so lowered quality that

parents are often complaining that the primary school is not good in doing its job. Many pupils leave the school without being able to read correctly, to write a simple letter or to solve a simple arithmetical problem. . . . Primary education has not contributed to community development especially in rural areas.

Of the preparatory and secondary academic institutions the study reported:

Our system . . . has failed to adapt itself to the socio-economic forces of this time. . . . [It] is still the privilege of our strong middle class. . . . The majority of their pupils are the sons of government officials, people of the professions, industry and commerce. . . . Secondary schools still follow a pre-university preparatory model.

The assessments of technical and vocational training were equally harsh:

Our system of technical education has gravely neglected the special requirements for the training of higher grade technicians. . . . The secondary technical school has failed to adapt itself to the changes in the structure of occupation. . . . The structure is . . . rigid, its curricula neither diversified nor flexible, and the school itself is not aware of the actual requirements of the labour market.

Not surprisingly the author concluded: "It is . . . clear that our educational system at all its levels is not meeting the requirements of this society. Our educational system needs a radical overhauling both in structure and content." [35]

[35] Fahmy, *op. cit.,* pp. 20–22, 24–25, 26.

Another official study severely criticized the educational policy that was adopted in the fifties and sixties on the following grounds: (1) The overriding concern of the planners was with quantity not quality. (2) Many scientific fields were not expanded adequately. (3) No coherent, integrated strategy for educational development was ever adopted; rather each sector was examined independently and various measures adopted without regard for linkages with other fields. (4) Despite the emphasis upon vocational training too many children received an academic education. (5) Investments were misallocated, being made in theoretical rather than technical and vocational fields. (6) Teachers in technical and vocational schools never enjoyed the same prestige or income as teachers in other branches. (7) Teacher preparation was not based on sound criteria, and many incompetent persons entered the profession. (8) No relationships were established between curricula and the problems of Egyptian society. At every level curricula were crowded with unnecessary subjects; in primary school the child was expected to read ninety books or 1,500 pages a year for six years, in preparatory school seventy-one books or 2,838 pages a year for three years, in the scientific stream at the secondary level, seventy-nine books or 3,950 pages a year for three years, and in the literary stream at this level, sixty-six books or 3,300 pages a year. (9) Because of dropouts and repeaters the educational system is characterized by a considerable amount of wastage.[36]

Such analyses have received widespread publicity in recent years and various measures have been adopted to remedy some of the worst features of the existing system. Nevertheless these assessments remain valid and no new educational policy has yet evolved though there are many indications that change may be forthcoming. The degree to which what was previously a matter for experts has now become a topic of concern to the highest policy-makers in the state is reflected in the fact that in late 1970, on at least two separate occasions, the prime minister noted that a profound transformation was necessary because only minor technical difficulties had been resolved so far and serious weaknesses remained. Further indications of the new concern with educational problems are provided by the amount of publicity accorded to prevailing educational shortcomings. In early

[36] *Manpower Report*, pp. 15–16. The study recommended that textbook authors no longer be paid by the page (p. 33).

1971, for example, Dr. Louis Awad, the cultural editor of *Al-Ahram,* the influential, semiofficial paper, published the first of a series of scathing analyses of the contemporary educational scene. He emphasized the need to further democratize the educational system and pointed to the dismal fact that even with all the efforts and investments since 1952 not only had the illiteracy rate, which had stood at 75 per cent when the revolutionaries came to power, not declined but if present enrollment trends continued the same proportion of the population, 75 per cent, would be illiterate in 1990.[37]

That the government is paying serious attention to the development of a new educational policy is also evidenced by the fact that, timed to coincide with the first article of this series, a well-publicized Conference on Education in the Modern State was convened. Its purpose was to define major problem areas and recommend appropriate solutions. In his opening speech the prime minister referred to his earlier remarks on the importance of educational reform and stressed the need for change by stating, "Beginning with the new academic year we must go from remnants of the 19th century to the horizons of the nuclear age." How much was actually accomplished, however, is unclear. Committees were established to discuss curricula and textbooks, administration, teacher training, student services, and educational economics, but one Egyptian who participated reported that the discussants lost themselves in details and generalization and that the resolutions which were adopted "even failed in pointing to a start on the way of educational reform and development." [38] Thus, whether the decade of the seventies will, in fact, witness the transformation of educational structures and processes remains to be seen, but the new mood of public awareness and the concern exhibited by influential decision-makers with the many dysfunctional aspects of the present system augur well for the future.

One area in which change will be forthcoming in the next few years is private schooling, which has continued to play an important role in the country's educational efforts. Significant changes reflecting the

[37] *Al-Ahram,* Nov. 26, 1970; Dec. 18, 1970; Awad, *op. cit.*
[38] The prime minister's speech was reported in *Al-Ahram,* Feb. 21, 1971; the conference is discussed by Nissim Rejwan, "Sadat's Exposed Second Front: Increasing Illiteracy despite Special Measures," *New Middle East,* 3 (November 1971), 9.

regime's ideological orientation have already taken place in the position of minority and foreign schools. The latter, which had traditionally maintained relatively high standards, were deeply affected by the educational policies adopted after 1952, notably the emphasis upon nationalization and integration. They were widely regarded as having failed to emphasize nationalist ideals and values, to have ignored the teaching of Arabic, and to have given preference to the culture and history of their country of origin. As early as 1948 these schools became subject to government supervision and their students were required to attain the same standard of proficiency in Arabic as students in the government schools. The teaching of history, geography, and civics was also regulated; each of these courses must be taught by an Egyptian in accordance with the decrees of the Ministry of Education. In 1956, following the Suez crisis, the British and French schools were nationalized, and in 1958 this policy was extended to all foreign schools. Since that time, with the exception of foreign language teachers, administrators and staff have to be Arab, the national curriculum has to be followed, and the state examinations must be administered to all students. Similar controls were placed over minority schools in 1958 when they were brought fully under the control of the Ministry of Education. Nevertheless, private schools have continued to enroll a large percentage of students, particularly at the preparatory and secondary level. In the mid-sixties, 5 per cent of all primary students, 29 per cent of all preparatory students, and 32 per cent of all secondary students were attending these institutions.[39]

Concern with nationalization also extended to the public schools and is reflected in the stress upon political socialization at all levels. At the lower stages, the emphasis is upon building support for the regime and upon Arab nationalism and anti-Zionism. Texts and lectures stress the glories of ancient Egyptian and Muslim heroes, frequent discussions concerning such political events as the evacuation of the British and French troops from Egypt in 1956 are held, and specific holidays such as Palestine Refugee Day are celebrated appropriately. Underlying all efforts at political socialization is a common theme, the development of martial feelings. Especially at the

---

[39] Boktor, op. cit., pp. 74ff; Manpower Report, p. 34.

higher levels great stress is placed upon military subjects. In the secondary schools two courses per week are devoted to such training: in their first three years at the university all students are required to take military drill for two hours weekly. All students must also attend, in their last year, a course called Arab Society which, though aimed at providing a better awareness and understanding of Egyptian social and economic problems, does not, in fact, contain any objective discussions of the country's problems but is devoted largely to the propagation of official propaganda and myths.[40] The purported object of such courses is "not to propagandize but to train people for positions where such information will be needed," but there is little doubt that a systematic attempt at ideological indoctrination of all students has been underway in the Egyptian schools since the revolution and is continuing. This effort is supplemented by extracurricular activities such as scouting, athletic clubs, and the like. At the university level student groups are carefully supervised and, together with the student sections of the Arab Socialist Union, are expected to propagate the ideals and goals of the regime among their colleagues.[41]

Only very limited evidence is available to indicate the degree of success of this massive propaganda effort. One research project has indicated that at least one aspect of the official ideology, that pertaining to women's rights, is not accepted by all students. Although intensive study of the 1962 charter, which emphasized equality for women, is required in secondary schools, the investigator found that many boys did not feel that women should receive equal pay even though several teachers had pointed out that the question was unnecessary since the charter gave the correct answer.[42] The finding that traditional cultural attitudes retain a powerful hold is supported by the abortive plot of the Muslim Brotherhood in 1964. Playing a central role in the conspiracy were highly educated men such as engineers, pilots, chemists, scientists, and students, a fact which has led one scholar to conclude that the regime's efforts to change existing

[40] Waardenburg, op. cit., I, p. 36. Leonard Binder, "Egypt: The Integrative Revolution" in Political Culture and Political Development, Lucien W. Pye and Sidney Verba, eds. (Princeton: Princeton University Press, 1965), pp. 413ff.

[41] Binder, op. cit., pp. 414, 413.

[42] Peter Dodd, "Youth and Women's Emancipation in the United Arab Republic," Middle East Journal, 22 (Spring 1968), 165.

values had proven ineffective. Subsequently the propaganda agencies were reorganized and even greater emphasis placed upon the dissemination and inculcation of the official ideology. In 1967 new courses on the principles and philosophy of socialism and the philosophy of revolutions were introduced in some institutions of higher learning" so that they may become closely connected with the requirements of the Arab socialist community." [43]

From another perspective one scholar who possesses an intimate knowledge of the country has suggested that the very intensity of the political socialization program will in the long run prove most damaging to the country's development.[44] That this may well be the case is also indicated by the recent attack leveled at the quality of primary-school education by Louis Awad in his series of articles in *Al-Ahram*. He argued that President Nasser's stress on political socialization, particularly the emphasis on Arab nationalism, has led to a decline in standards. Comparing the education that French and Egyptian children receive in elementary school he pointed out that while the French child is studying the poems of Victor Hugo and the fables of La Fontaine the Egyptian youngster is learning the following poem:

> I am an Arab, I love the Arabs.
> My father is an Arab, he loves the Arabs.
> My brother is an Arab, he loves the Arabs.
> Long live the Arabs, long live the Arabs.

Upon reaching the fifth grade the Egyptian child begins to study politics and reads about "The Arab World," "The New Army," "The Games of Workers," "The Dam," and the "Arab Hero," whereas the French youth is reading the poetry and literature of many lands.

In other articles he ridiculed the degree to which history and geography textbooks are politicized. Geography books do not refer to the course of the Blue Nile through Ethiopia or of the White Nile through Uganda, "as if the mention of the names of foreign countries were a nakedness that should be hidden because it detracts from the Arabism" of the river. Omissions in history are so prevalent that the poor Egyptian student is exposed to "textbooks that are like fairy

---

[43] "Report, 1967/68," p. 28; see also Dekmejian, *op. cit.*, p. 233.

[44] Charles Issawi, *Egypt in Revolution: An Economic Analysis* (London: Oxford University Press, 1963), p. 100.

tales." Not only do they contain many mistakes but such rulers as Abbas, Tewfik, and Fuad are ignored, and except for the 1952 revolution the child would never learn of the existence of King Farouk. In short: "The French child does not learn the opinion of the Minister of Education on Louis Phillipe or Napoleon III but the poor Egyptian child does not learn anything that is not accompanied by either insults or praise, as if he were reading a paper or listening to the radio." [45]

Higher Education, Students, and Politics

The emphasis upon political socialization at the university level is but one indication of the attention paid higher education by the new government, which on many occasions declared that science and technology were indispensable for the achievement of national goals. In these as in other fields enrollments increased rapidly; the four universities (Cairo, Alexandria, Ain Shams, and Assiut) enrolled 34,842 students in 1951; 77,087 in 1958; 122,492 in 1967; and 139,552 in 1969. In the 1969–1970 academic year, 32,159 students were also attending higher institutes of various types, and another 21,100 students were studying at Al-Azhar, for a grand total of 192,811 students.[46]

Of all the changes that have taken place in higher education since 1952 few have been as successful as the reform that transformed Al-Azhar into what is essentially the counterpart of a Catholic University in the United States. From the outset the military officers were aware of the need to integrate that medieval institution into the mainstream of education, but at first they moved slowly and cautiously in religious affairs and even made concessions to the leaders of Al-Azhar in order to gain their support against the only threat to the revolution that existed within Egypt—the powerful and well-organized Muslim Brotherhood. Following the attempted assassination of Colonel Nasser in 1954, the government moved decisively to eliminate the Muslim Brotherhood as a political force and inaugurated a number of important reforms, including the abolition of religious courts and the creation of a unified, secular legal system. This move had serious implications for Al-Azhar since the already restricted employment

[45] *Al-Ahram,* March 12, 19, 26, 1971; see also Joseph Kraft, "Letter from Cairo," *New Yorker,* Sept. 18, 1971, pp. 94–95.
[46] Boktor, *op. cit.,* p. 99; "Report, 1969–70," p. 7

opportunities available to graduates—one study revealed an unemployment rate of 25 per cent, more than twice that of the second most serious situation, 11 per cent for graduates in commerce—would now be limited even further.[47]

Accordingly the government changed its policy of cautiously enacting reforms within the institution by working with cooperative staff members and gradually replacing highly placed ulema who sought to preserve traditional patterns with reformers to a more radical one of direct confrontation. In 1961 it sponsored a law calling for the elimination of the gap between Al-Azhar and the other institutions of higher learning so that its graduates would enjoy parity of educational and employment opportunities with the products of the other universities. Debate in the National Assembly lasted for seven hours as conservative religious leaders sought to prevent the law from being passed, but their efforts were futile. The government was determined to resolve the problem of a separate religious university once and for all; as one of the military leaders stated: "we *gave* reform to al-Azhar because the shaykhs never want it." [48]

Al-Azhar was thus metamorphosed into a modern institution with new administrators and faculty. Power was transferred from conservatives to government appointees whose position was further strengthened by the addition of new faculties, including engineering and medicine, where instruction is in English. In 1968, Al-Azhar contained the following faculties; Jurisprudence and Islamic Law, Theology, Arabic Studies, Business and Administration, Engineering, Agriculture, Medicine, Institute of Languages and Translation, and the Higher Institute of Islamic Studies.[49]

Despite its transformation Al-Azhar continues to play an important role both domestically and internationally. Within Egypt the ulema are regarded as important leaders who can serve as useful channels for political communication. Although few of the older religious leaders can fulfill such a task adequately, the graduates of the new

---

[47] For a discussion of these reforms see Daniel Crecelius, "Al-Azhar in the Revolution," *Middle East Journal* (Winter 1966), 31–50. *Research Project,* p. 65.

[48] Cited in Crecelius, *op. cit.,* pp. 38–39.

[49] "Report, 1967/68," p. 25.

institution will receive specific preparation, including systematic exposure to the ideology of the regime, to enable them to function in this manner. On the world scene Al-Azhar represents an important asset in attempts to develop and strengthen religious, cultural, and ideological ties with many of the new states of Africa and Asia.

While Al-Azhar was undergoing qualitative change, the secular universities were undergoing quantitative change. Their growth predates 1952, but the philosophy of the new regime and its policies, particularly the marked expansion of educational opportunities at the lower levels, accelerated the trend tremendously. Thousands of additional students began to graduate from secondary schools with only one concern: to gain admission to a university. This powerful drive, deeply rooted in traditional status and prestige considerations, has been analyzed in one official study as follows:

People want to go to academic secondary schools in order to be able to go later to the universities. . . . They go to the universities because they lead to the professions and to some of the highest posts in society, or because one is interested to follow a certain line of study. But this is not all, for many . . . go . . . for the sake of bearing a university degree. . . . Why all this? There is social imitation by which families look to each other and young men (and women) want to be not less than their somewhat better neighbours or relatives. There is the social prestige and status . . . which can influence one's life and social relationships—even to the extent that a young man may find it difficult to marry a middle-class girl because he is not a university graduate.[50]

Motivated by political, ideological, and developmental considerations, the government proved highly receptive to such demands. It democratized higher education and took steps, by eliminating financial constraints, to enable any Egyptian to obtain a university degree. In July 1962 all public education was made absolutely free, and a significant number of fellowships and grants were provided to poor students wishing to attend a university. Manpower requirements also dictated an increase in the output of skilled personnel in certain fields, especially science, engineering, medicine, and agriculture if developmental goals were to be achieved. At the same time the other faculties were

[50] *Research Project,* pp. 110–111.

also permitted to expand to accommodate students' and parents' demands for higher education so as to reduce the possibility of discontent and political instability. Thus between 1957 and 1968 the proportion of secondary school graduates who continued their education rose from a third to two-thirds of the total, a total which itself was increasing markedly.[51]

Pressures for admission were so great that they simply could not be accommodated by the expansion of the regular institutions, and the government resorted to two stratagems. In 1953 the system of external students was created: Any secondary school graduate unable to qualify for admission to an institution of higher learning may take the same examinations as regularly enrolled students and receive the same degrees. External students are barred from attending classes and since the colleges of arts, commerce, and law have no attendance requirements, they attach themselves only to these three faculties, which in 1962–1963 enrolled 30,000 regular and 20,000 external students.[52]

This procedure has been defended on the grounds that thousands of young men who could not otherwise, because of financial or other reasons, receive a university education are given the opportunity to do so. On the other hand, it represents an extreme form of the "do-it-yourself" approach to higher education, the external students being expected to study for the examinations without any guidance whatsoever. They naturally do so by attempting to memorize the appropriate textbooks with the obvious result that even those who graduate acquire only a most elementary type of education and attain only a minimal cultural level. At the same time they present an added burden to the already overworked faculty who, forced to read several thousand additional examinations each year, find themselves able to pay even less attention to their regular students. A further consequence of this program is that the aspirations of thousands of poorly trained individuals are further heightened. Possessing all the privileges of regular university students, they come to share the latter's expectations concerning future employment opportunities but they are, in effect, being poorly prepared for fields which are already saturated and in which there is no demand for their services. The frustration

[51] Efrat, *op. cit.*, p. 27.
[52] Qubain, *op. cit.*, p. 76.

and alienation that result is one of the most serious problems confronting government planners and administrators in Egypt.[53]

The system of external students also handicaps the attempts of the government to emphasize vocational and technical training. Not only are students encouraged to continue in an academic course so as to prepare themselves for university training on either a regular or an informal basis, but those who are compelled to enter the vocational schools now possess a means of obtaining a university degree also. Upon graduating from technical schools they accept positions as elementary teachers which entitle them to enroll as external students, supposedly to upgrade their skills. In practice they do so to gain the necessary qualifications for entry into the bureaucracy.[54]

The second expedient developed by the government to handle the pressure for university education was, from 1957 onward, to establish a number of higher institutes providing training in various professional fields including fine arts, music, agriculture, commerce, and industry. By 1963–1964 over 25,000 students were enrolled in thirty-eight institutes, and by 1968–1969 enrollments had risen to 36,425. Originally these institutions were designed to provide specialized, practical training in areas that were not covered by the universities. All students were to take a year of field work, and through this program 4,189 students were sent abroad between 1956 and 1964, mainly to West Germany. Before long, however, a classic instance of goal displacement occurred and the distinction between these institutes and the regular universities disappeared. Today their curricula are basically the same, the length of training is identical, and graduates receive the same degrees. The only distinction is one of quality: Their resources are more limited, they do not provide any graduate training, and they prepare students even more poorly. As a result, although these institutes have served to diminish the pressures for further expansion of the university faculties to some extent, no facilities now exist to provide highly skilled technical experts that are so vitally needed; further, a dual system of higher education was once again created within Egypt. The gravity of this situation led to the establishment of a ministerial committee which recommended that duplication be reduced, various unproductive or unnecessary institutes closed, the

[53] *Ibid.*, pp. 76–77, 150–151.
[54] Kerr, *op. cit.*, p. 191.

quality of the training upgraded, and graduates permitted to enter graduate schools. These policies are being implemented, and the goal, as stated in the current educational plan, is to achieve complete equality between these institutions and the regular university faculties.[55]

While the quality of the universities may be higher, they too face serious difficulties as evidenced by the fact that the number of students enrolled is roughly two to four times more than the existing facilities were designed for. All faculties suffer from severe shortages of physical and human resources; as the student population grew, the number of faculty did not keep pace and teaching loads increased. In 1962–1963 it varied from 1:15 in medicine to 1:22 in science, 1:32 for agriculture, 1:43 for engineering, 1:45 for economics and dentistry, 1:54 for art, 1:95 for law, and 1:92 for commerce. To indicate the extent of these changes over time, suffice it to point out that in 1930 the ratio for the Faculty of Letters was 1:7.4; in 1962, 1:107.[56]

From these figures it is obvious that the colleges of arts, law, and commerce which "have become the dumping grounds of the university system in Egypt," were processing about ten times more students than their capacity. The quality of instruction in these institutions can readily be imagined, and one must not forget the system of external students which has driven what academic standards remained to even lower depths. How sad the situation has become is evidenced by the very high failure rate and a dismissal rate of about 10 per cent. It has been estimated that only 30 per cent of the students graduate from the faculty of letters in three years; 57 per cent have to repeat one or more subjects. The degree of bankruptcy of higher education is perhaps best indicated by the conclusion of a recent official study which, after surveying the functioning of the educational system and analyzing the factors that have led to a decline in quality at all levels, stated "These reasons led to a degradation of the level of education *especially among* university graduates" (my emphasis).[57]

[55] Qubain, *op. cit.,* pp. 67–68, 71; Efrat, *op. cit.,* p. 29; Fahmy, *op. cit.,* pp. 19–20; "Report, 1967/68," p. 26; "Report, 1969/70," p. 9, 11.

[56] Qubain, *op. cit.,* p. 76, Table 15. According to A. B. Zahlan, "Science in the Arab Middle East," *Minerva,* 8 (January 1970), 16, the teacher-student ratio stood at 1:40 in the sciences in 1962–1963. The faculty of letters ratios are from Dr. Louis Awad, cited in Waardenburg, *op. cit.,* p. 64.

[57] Qubain, *op. cit.,* p. 76; *Manpower Report,* p. 16.

Admission to the universities is determined officially by the results of the secondary school certificate examinations and by a quota system established by each faculty. Those with the highest scores enroll in the faculty of their choice, those with lower scores in their second choice, and so on. Admission standards vary widely; medicine, engineering, and science have the most stringent requirements; arts, law, and commerce admit students with lower scores and it is they, as noted above, that have witnessed the greatest expansion and the most rapid decline in educational standards.

In practice, however, the system is far more flexible than it appears, and political considerations have, at least once, determined how it would actually function. In 1965–1966 it was decided to give a 10 per cent bonus to all candidates who had a relative who was a veteran of the war in Yemen or who was affiliated with a university. Some students who were known to be politically reliable and others who excelled in sports also benefited from this arrangement. It has been estimated that over two-thirds of the freshmen in that year consisted of such students.[58]

The quota system has also been criticized on the same grounds as similar devices in other Middle Eastern countries. It heightens the importance of formal examination and filters out many who might be late bloomers. Furthermore there is often little relationship between a student's field of interest and the faculty he is assigned; someone wishing to study engineering may end up in the law school. Since specialization begins in the first year, it is difficult for a student to transfer to another field unless he is willing to start all over again in the new discipline.

The lack of cooperation and coordination that characterizes the component parts of an institution also applies to the separate colleges and universities, which, administratively and organizationally, are practically identical and have been subject since 1961 to the control of the Minister of Higher Education. In 1959 a determined attempt was made to coordinate the activities of the universities so as to avoid duplication by colleges and departments dealing with similar and related subjects. In 1961 the unwieldy Ministry of Education was divided into two separate ministries; the existing Ministry retained

[58] Efrat, *op. cit.*, p. 27n.

responsibility for elementary and secondary education, the new Ministry of Higher Education was assigned responsibilities for all aspects of college- and university-level training in Egypt and abroad. Nevertheless, the goal of coordination and integration remains as elusive as ever and "even after these reforms, a great deal of improvement is to be desired." [59]

Obsolete administrative concepts and practices greatly aggravate one of the major weaknesses in Egyptian higher education, the shortage of faculty. All universities suffer from serious staffing problems, particularly in practical subjects, but recruitment and promotion processes that are still characterized by a traditional concern with formal qualifications and requirements make it difficult to fill vacancies with able teachers. The faculty is judged, not on the basis of teaching ability and interest or quality of research, but on the number of degrees its members hold. Similarly, promotions are determined primarily by tenure and age rather than achievement, so that the older and senior members of the department are favored at the expense of junior faculty. One must spend five years as a lecturer before being promoted to assistant professor and another five years before being eligible for promotion to full professor. This policy tends to restrict initiative, discriminates against ability, and discourages prospective staff members.

Another reason for the shortage of faculty is that although by and large the salary scale is adequate, salaries in both private and state economic enterprises tend to be much higher, thus facilitating "raiding" by these organizations who often turn to the universities as sources of skilled personnel. The government also engages in this practice and often recruits able faculty for administrative positions of various sorts. A third factor is that faculty members are allowed to accept outside employment. Such positions are not supposed to infringe upon university obligations, but many lawyers, doctors, and engineers retain a university affiliation because of the prestige it confers and neglect their academic responsibilities to a greater or lesser degree. Abuses of this privilege are not limited to Egypt and have created serious problems for universities in Turkey and Iran, especially for the quality of instruction and student-teacher relations in

---

[59] Qubain, *op. cit.*, pp. 67–68.

general. In Egypt the emphasis remains upon formal lecture, and students are accorded little opportunity for discussion, questioning, or meeting with the professor. Moreover, the student is graded only upon his success in the annual examination, so that once again the aim of the student is not to learn creatively or to exercise his mental faculties in a disciplined manner but to prepare for examinations by cramming and memorizing the factual information contained in the lecture notes or the textbook. From the teacher's viewpoint, too, these examinations are intellectually stultifying, about two months being spent on grading hundreds of similar papers. It has been estimated that in the Faculty of Letters of Cairo University, 180,000 test sheets have to be graded by 100 persons.[60]

Besides strengthening such characteristics, the rule permitting faculty to occupy nonuniversity posts contributes directly to staffing problems; departments whose members do not enjoy extensive opportunities for outside employment (professors of anatomy as compared to professors of surgery, for example) find it very difficult to recruit staff and to fill positions. To remedy this situation it has been suggested that the special allowance received by faculty members who devote all their time to the university be increased significantly so as to correspond more closely to the income that can be earned from private practice.[61]

Similar problems also plague the scientific and technological fields that form such an important component of the country's developmental effort. A rapid expansion in student enrollments, spurred by the generous financial support offered to students in these areas and by the growing prestige and power considerations, has taken place, and between 1953–1954 and 1965–1966 the proportion of registered students studying medicine, engineering, agriculture, and science rose from 38 to 55 per cent. In this period the number of graduates quintupled in engineering and science, tripled in medicine, and sextupled in agriculture. What this has meant for the country is that, whereas in the first half of this century 6,210 doctors, 434 dentists, and 1,359 pharmacists graduated, from 1956 to 1965 8,777 doctors, 998 dentists, and 2,467 pharmacists were trained. In 1966–1967 en-

---

[60] Awad, cited in Waardenburg, *op. cit.,* p. 65; see also Qubain, *op. cit.,* p. 77.

[61] Qubain, *ibid.,* p. 79.

gineering faculties graduated 3,206 students, medicine 1,753, and the sciences 1,709.[62]

The government's emphasis upon science and technology did not, however, extend to the provision of adequate buildings, lecture halls, laboratories, or faculty. As a result, though quality here is higher than is the case in the theoretical faculties, standards are not particularly high and have deteriorated steadily. Teaching is still carried on in a more less traditional manner with little laboratory or experimental work.[63]

Contributing greatly to this state of affairs is the serious problem of finding qualified staff for the practical faculties. Such persons are in especially short supply, and competition for their services by state enterprises and government institutes is very keen. Many faculty members are also engaged in postdoctoral research abroad or teach in other Arab countries or have joined the brain drain, thus further limiting the number. To remedy this shortage the government, in 1960, embarked upon an extensive study-abroad program that emphasizes science and technology, especially at the graduate level, and in 1964 and 1965 about 1,800 students were sent abroad for graduate training as compared to 321 in 1960. In subsequent years however, the number declined steadily to 1,575 in 1966, 1,250 in 1967, 1,046 in 1968. Overall it has been estimated that about 500 new faculty members will be available each year until 1975. Simultaneously the Egyptian universities have increased the production of persons with doctorates so that many of the vacancies in the lower ranks will be filled, although the level of quality will be uneven because of inadequate selection procedures, and those with doctorates from these institutions will be of relatively inferior quality. It is not expected that the acute shortage at the professorial level will be alleviated, especially in such fields as engineering, where thirty or forty senior positions have remained vacant for several years.[64]

All scientific fields also suffer from the same critical deficiencies in physical facilities of all sorts as the other disciplines. Few institutions

[62] Efrat, *op. cit.*, p. 28; Malcolm S. Adisheshiah, "Brain Drain from the Arab World," address to the eighth Arab Cultural Conference on the Training of Scientific Workers in the Arab World, Arab League, Cairo, Dec. 22, 1969, mimeo. (Paris: UNESCO, DDG/69/13), Table 2, p. 4.

[63] Zahlan, *op. cit., passim.*

[64] *Population,* Table 3.3.22, p. 262; Qubain, *op. cit.,* p. 95.

possess needed books, periodicals, and abstracts. Laboratory equipment of all sorts is inadequate, and even when it is available, problems of maintenance arise because of the grave shortage of spare parts and skilled technicians. The result is that expensive and elaborate pieces of imported equipment often lie idle for extended periods.[65]

Furthermore, sophisticated equipment is often not utilized because the faculty do not possess appropriate training, and necessary research often cannot be undertaken owing to inadequate financial and administrative support and obsolete concepts of science. Such institutional barriers are common to a greater or lesser degree to all Middle Eastern countries and further hinder the development of a productive scientific program of research and training. Confronted with inadequate facilities, a lack of recognition and support, heavy teaching loads, misemployment of skills, mediocre colleagues, uninterested superiors, and intellectual isolation, the able young scientist finds it extremely difficult to engage in productive research. As a result the scientific effort in the U.A.R. is not making the contribution to national development that might be expected from the emphasis placed upon science since the revolution. Cairo, where three of the country's major universities, the small American University in Cairo, and two important research centers including the atomic facility at En Shass are located, does possess the potential to become an important scientific center. Nevertheless much remains to be done and one expert has concluded that "though the United Arab Republic has the best record of all Arab governments it still falls short of what is necessary and possible." [66]

One result of these conditions is that many of Egypt's most highly trained and able scientists, particularly those who have received their graduate education in Europe or the United States choose to join the brain drain. Between 1962 and 1967, 2,400 professionals, 249 engineers, 138 scientists, and 191 physicians left Egypt, a significant proportion of the country's human resources. The results of this

[65] Qubain, *ibid.*, pp. 105–106; see also the discussion of Adel A. Sabet's paper, UAR Commitments to Science and Technology," *Science and Technology in Developing Countries* in Claire Nader and R. B. Zahlan, eds. (Cambridge: Cambridge University Press, 1969).

[66] Zahlan, *op. cit.*, p. 28.

migration need no elaboration. The financial loss amounts to tens of millions of dollars, and one study showed that the departure of these men, 70 per cent of whom had Ph.D.'s, seriously damaged the quality of teaching and research in Egypt. Most importantly, the brain drain has been growing steadily and rapidly in recent years. Even though emigration involves losing practically all one's property, 764 Egyptians entered the United States in 1970, and it has been estimated that at least as many migrated to other countries.[67]

A fundamental problem in science teaching, with significant implications for the future development of these subjects, is whether instruction should be provided in Arabic or in English. By and large, the first-year science courses are taught in Arabic, and from the second year on instruction is given in English. The problem of language, as we noted in Chapter I, confronts all Arab countries, but from the viewpoint of science teaching certain nonideological considerations are especially important. Advocates of Arabic argue that most students have not received a thorough enough training at the secondary level to enable them to follow lectures or to read scientific books in English, that the use of Arabic would make Egypt self-reliant and eliminate the dependency upon foreign materials, and that the use of Arabic would enrich the Arabic language by the incorporation of scientific terms, a development that would in time help to produce a modern mentality among the populace since language cannot be separated from thought patterns.

Opponents point to the serious drawbacks that would result from the change to Arabic. Above all, scientific research involves an awareness of what is being done by other scholars in a particular field, and this knowledge can only be obtained by following the abstracts, which are published only in major Western languages, and by becoming familiar with the related literature, practically none of which is available in Arabic. Furthermore, if the higher-level science courses were to be taught in Arabic a major effort would have to be undertaken to provide new textbooks and reference works, a task that would require highly trained manpower that cannot be spared for such an activity. And even if skilled translators were available, the time lag would be considerable since a scientific text is written in

---

[67] Adisheshiah, *op. cit.*, pp. 8, 9, 10, Table 1, p. 3; see also Sabet, *op. cit.*, p. 210. *New York Times,* Aug. 24, 1971.

about two or three years and its translation would consume a similar period; thus by the time an Arabic version could be published the text would be five to ten years old, practically obsolete. Finally, many faculty members, having been trained abroad, are familiar with foreign terminology and find difficulty in teaching scientific subjects in Arabic.[68]

Despite the changes in emphasis and the greatly increased number of graduates in practical fields, serious imbalances continue to characterize the manpower situation in Egypt. Engineers are especially in short supply; presently about 4,000 are needed. Projections of the second five-year plan (1965–1970) called for the production of 21,502 engineers, but it was estimated that only about half that number would graduate, thus creating a shortage of approximately 11,000. Because this figure takes into account only developmental needs, it has been suggested that a more accurate projection would be a shortage of about 16,000 engineers by the early 1970's. No disagreement exists, however, concerning the shortage of skilled technicians of all sorts; manpower of this type, it is agreed, is desperately needed if maximal results are to be obtained from more skilled and highly trained personnel. If enough technicians were available, for example, it has been estimated that only about half as many engineers would actually be needed. Industry alone will have 38,000 such positions by 1970, and if vacancies in research institutes and educational institutions are included, the total rises to at least 50,000. As a result a 1969 study concluded: "In spite of the increase in the number of students in the practical faculties in general and the faculties of engineering in particular, we still do not have the sufficient number of specialized technicians who can carry out the programmes and projects of the Plan. But the number of graduates from the other faculties exceeds the needs of the Plan. This makes it necessary to undergo some changes in the policy of education in order to realize the required balance in the labour market particularly with reference to the category of professionals on a university level." [69]

As a result of such demand it would seem that students in the favored scientific faculties, who view themselves as an elite within the university because they have succeeded in gaining admission to a

[68] Qubain, *op. cit.*, pp. 87–89.
[69] *Ibid.*, pp. 217, 219; *Population,* p. 234.

high-prestige faculty and tend to have higher aspirations than the majority, could look forward to satisfactory positions in Egyptian society. But this is seldom the case; after graduation they, like students in other fields, find themselves confronting a shortage of suitable jobs. In 1964–1965, for example, only one opening was available for every ten graduates from science faculties. Equally dismal prospects are faced by their brethren in other disciplines. The large numbers of university graduates in law, commerce, and art (including the extension system) simply cannot be absorbed readily by Egyptian society. As early as 1920 the legal profession was already overcrowded, but the number of lawyers tripled between 1948 and 1958 and has since continued to expand. In 1964–1965 it was estimated that 691 positions were available for 1,584 law graduates. Law students are traditionally reputed, as freshmen, to look forward to becoming prime ministers, as sophomores, cabinet members, as juniors, judges, and as seniors, to any position whatsoever.[70] Graduates of other faculties are also in overabundance and find it difficult to obtain employment; often they have to wait for at least two years for a position. In 1964–1965 there were 14 openings for 139 graduates of the School of Languages, 30 for 189 students of economics and political science, and 197 for 2,049 graduates in arts.

Although the development plans of the country will, if implemented successfully, create additional opportunities in industry and other sectors, the results to date have not been encouraging, and the administration remains the hope of thousands of university graduates. Sanctified for decades as the most desired goal, the bureaucracy has already expanded far beyond appropriate limits. The wave of nationalization decrees created a demand for additional personnel but, as always, the supply far exceeded available positions. Nevertheless graduates have had to be accommodated and in 1961 from 7,000 to 10,000 were absorbed when an emergency decree forced the ministries to find places for them.[71]

One important outlet for surplus graduates has been Egypt's educational assistance projects abroad. About thirty African countries have received Egyptian teachers but the majority are sent to Arab

---

[70] Data on the number of graduates and openings for all faculties cited here are derived from *Manpower Report,* Table I, p. 62; Kerr, *op. cit.,* p. 184.

[71] Binder, *op. cit.,* p. 413.

states, especially Saudi Arabia, Sudan, Libya, Kuwait, Morocco, and Lebanon. Large numbers of students from these countries also study in Egypt, about 13,000 in 1963 as compared to 3,500 a decade earlier. Furthermore there are twenty-three Egyptian schools in the Sudan, one in Morocco, and one in Somalia. Branches of Egyptian universities also exist in Khartoum and Beirut.[72] Such programs, of course, represented important channels for the dissemination of President Nasser's ideology and for the enhancing of his influence regionally and internationally.

Thus, in one way or another, most graduates are ultimately provided with some sort of employment but the consequences are not particularly conducive to individual or national growth. The first result, as one unnecessary job after another is created, is an increase in inefficiency in a bureaucracy long noted for dysfunctional administrative processes. A second is personal dissatisfaction as most graduates are assigned to low-paying positions within nontechnical ministries for which they are not really prepared and where they perform no useful function; one study, conducted in the early sixties, indicated that only 60 per cent of respondents with a higher education were satisfied with their positions and that less than half would voluntarily choose that particular job. The two primary reasons for this discontent were low salaries and an imbalance between their education and their duties.[73] The plight of the thousands of young Egyptians who fit this category has been vividly described:

The arts, law, and commerce graduates, therefore, constitute a large and rapidly growing group whose skills are largely sub-standard and unwanted, and whose native talents are mediocre, but whose sights have been trained since childhood on the attainment of a dignified job carrying economic rewards and social prestige. The disappointments are naturally sharp as these thousands of not-so-bright young men in their soiled collars and cheap suits eke out a shabby and insecure but desperately respectable existence on ten pounds a month as minor clerks, bookkeepers, school teachers, and journalists. They are assured from time to time in the press and in the president's speeches that as educated men they are the "van-

[72] Qubain, *op. cit.*, pp. 200–201.
[73] *Research Project*, pp. 99–101; see also Morroe Berger, *Bureaucracy and Society in Modern Egypt* (Princeton: Princeton University Press, 1957), *passim*.

guard" of the nation's progress, but they are impotent to fashion even their own progress, and they can only listen anxiously to the officially propagated theme of equal and widening opportunities under the new socialist economic development plan which ambitiously pledges to double the national income in ten years.[74]

How serious are the implications of such a situation for political stability and development need not be elaborated.

The most obvious indicator of the degree of frustration and alienation among students is the resurgence of activism in recent years. No new phenomenon in Egypt, frequent, violent student unrest was, as discussed earlier, a major component of the country's political life prior to the revolution. Upon gaining control however, President Nasser moved swiftly and decisively to depoliticize the universities; in 1954 forty faculty members were fired and a large number of students expelled.[75] Subsequently Nasser was able to gain and retain student support, and the kinds of demonstrations and incidents that were so characteristic of the previous regime became but historical memories. The 1967 war, however, shattered the remaining sense of dynamism and momentum among the youth and created a climate wherein their frustrations concerning the university environment, the kinds of positions to which they could aspire, and the repressive political context became as explosive as in the past. The first indication of unrest came in February 1968 when, following a violent strike by workers in a suburb of Cairo, students in Cairo and Alexandria staged a massive demonstration sympathizing with the workers' denunciations of the mild sentences handed out to four Air Force officers for their conduct in the 1967 war. Clashes between students and police ensued and continued for several days, in the course of which more than seventy-five persons were reported injured and the universities had to be closed. The intensity of student dissatisfaction and the character of their specific grievances was readily evident in the slogans calling for more freedom, "an end to one-man government," and more jobs. When a delegation was received by Anwar Sadat, then President of the National Assembly, the students reiterated these themes, demanding that clemency be denied to the military officers who were incompetent and corrupt, that the regime be liberalized and democratized

---

[74] Kerr, *op. cit.*, p. 187.
[75] Dekmejian, *op. cit.*, p. 32.

through the holding of free elections and the granting of greater freedom to the press, that a student association free from state control be established, and that informants and police agents be expelled from the faculties.[76]

Confronted with such a major challenge to the character of the regime, President Nasser moved swiftly to re-establish legitimacy. He granted some of the student demands and inaugurated a far-reaching program of reform. As one of his first steps he reshuffled the cabinet, greatly reducing its proportion of military officers. The number of civilian ministers doubled and, of the newcomers, half consisted of respected and popular academicians who were sympathetic to student concerns.[77] Soon after, Nasser announced the 30 March Program, to which we have already referred, which called for the drafting of a new constitution and the liberalization and democratization of Egyptian life. Subsequently he turned his attention to the Arab Socialist Union, which had been as severely criticized as the military. Many persons had condemned its ineffectiveness, and in the violent National Assembly debates that followed the demonstrations many deputies had identified the causes of the riots as "the emptiness of the political organization in the country, the sterility of the . . . party, the weakness of the youth organization, the lack of coordination between the popular organizations and the authorities." As a result, the ASU was transformed in terms of both structure and personnel.[78]

Despite these significant developments a second eruption occurred in November when, incensed by a change in administrative regulations that would have ended automatic promotion, several thousand high school students in Mansura, a delta town, attacked a police station. Rioting quickly spread to include university students, first in Alexandria and then in Cairo. Several pitched battles were fought in Alexandria, mostly on university grounds. In view of our earlier discussion of the unrest among students in technical fields, it is noteworthy that the fiercest conflict centered around the faculty of engineering, which

[76] "United Arab Republic," *Deadline Data on World Affairs* (New York: McGraw-Hill, 1969), pp. 210–211; hereafter cited as "UAR"; *Arab Report and Record*, Feb. 16, 1968ff; Mahmoud Hussein, *La Lutte de classes en Egypte, 1945–70* (Paris: François Maspero, 1971), pp. 289ff.

[77] Dekmejian, *op. cit.*, pp. 258ff.

[78] *Le Monde* Feb. 3, 1968, cited in "UAR," p. 211; Dekmejian, *op. cit.*, pp. 269ff.

was stormed by police after a three-day siege. Sixteen persons were reported killed and scores wounded. All the universities and other higher educational institutes were closed. In the course of these incidents students demanded educational reforms, freedom of the press, and an end to repression, the same themes that were articulated in February.[79]

Once again President Nasser reacted quickly and moved to absorb and accommodate this latest evidence of continuing popular dissatisfaction. He convened an extraordinary Congress of the Arab Socialist Union at which he reported on the implementation of the 30 March Program, blamed Israel for having stirred up student dissent, and warned against future outbreaks. He also stated that all the student demands had been granted, and, soon after, forty-six teachers and students who had been indicted for their participation in these demonstrations were pardoned, the student section of the ASU was reorganized, and students were granted a greater voice in university and national affairs.[80]

That President Nasser was able to re-establish the legitimacy of his regime in the face of such internal discontent is a tribute to his political acumen and to the strength of the system he had developed. That the unrest reached such proportions, on the other hand, is an indication of the problems that remain to be tackled, and it did not take long for the students to voice their discontent with national developments once again. On January 15, 1971, only a few short months after Nasser's sudden death in September of the previous year, several thousand students took part in another series of demonstrations. The unrest began in protest against conditions at Assiut University and quickly spread to the universities of Alexandria and Cairo. The timing of the outburst is significant, for only two days earlier President Sadat had made a major policy speech in which he sought to explain why 1971, the "year of decision" for the Arab-Israeli conflict, had, in fact, not produced either a peaceful or a military solution.

The rebellious students called upon the government to repudiate all

[79] *Time,* Dec. 6, 1968; *Arab Report and Record,* March 16–31, 1968.

[80] *Arab Report and Record,* Dec. 1–15, 1968; Jan. 1–15, 1969; *Time,* Dec. 6, 1968; *Newsweek,* Dec. 9, 1968; "UAR," pp. 217–218; Dekmejian, *op. cit.,* p. 265.

proposals for a peaceful settlement and the mobilization of national resources in preparation for a military confrontation with Israel. They also demanded such domestic political changes as free elections and an end to censorship. These issues reflect their frustration at the continuing impasse with Israel and may well be the harbinger of a national mood of desperation that could lead to renewed fighting. Above all, however, they can be interpreted as a direct attack upon President Sadat, and one commentator has suggested that, in contrast with the situation in 1968, the students actively sought to bring down the regime. Raising the issue of war with Israel clearly embarrassed Sadat, whose policy had obviously failed; their stand for political freedom posed a challenge to Sadat's position, for such democratization would enhance the status and power of his opponents.

If that was their purpose, however, the students did not succeed. Sadat reacted swiftly with a mixture of force and concession. He refused to permit their resolutions to be published and used the police to restore order; he reorganized the cabinet to include more technocrats, a step which may have been long planned but was hastily implemented; he relaxed censorship, restored political rights to an estimated 12,000 persons, and publicly declared that Egypt was committed to war at the appropriate time.[81] These measures enabled President Sadat to stabilize the situation, but the very fact that such a challenge occurred is an indication of perceived weakness. Despite his success, therefore, further challenges to the new regime by students acting either alone or allied with other political actors can be foreseen. Their outcome will depend upon President Sadat's qualities as a leader, including his ability to develop programs that will satisfy the aspirations of students and other important groups within the country, particularly the military.

To do so will be no simple matter, in view of the existing situation. On the other hand the national mood is one of realism as far as the country's capabilities and problems are concerned. The 1967 war was a watershed; many Egyptians have learned the lesson that military strength is dependent upon the achievement of modernity, and the wave of self-criticism and evaluation that followed the war left few

---

[81] Amnon Kapeliuk, "Student Unrest in Egypt," *New Outlook*, 15 (February 1972), 28–32; see also William H. Dorsey, "1968 Re-visited: Student Power in Cairo," *New Middle East*, 4 (February 1972).

institutions or aspects of Egyptian life untouched. There is today no tendency to underestimate Israel's military prowess or Egypt's many weaknesses, and if President Sadat can provide his countrymen with a renewed sense of dynamism, then many dysfunctional aspects of Egyptian life that hinder the achievement of modernity can receive the continuing and systematic attention that is necessary. Such areas as population growth, the bureaucracy, and the educational system all require immediate action, but to promote the necessary basic changes is no easy matter under the most favorable circumstances. So far President Sadat has successfully maintained his credibility with the majority of his countrymen and with such politically salient elements as the military and technocratic elites, but given the character of the domestic political scene and of regional and international political configurations it is no great exaggeration to state that the achievement of President Nasser's vision of a powerful modern Egypt represents the greatest challenge that that ancient country has ever faced.

Education in the Arab World Today

Educational cooperation between Egypt and the Arab countries is facilitated not only by common language and culture but also by similar structural and functional aspects in the educational enterprises in the Arab world. As we have already noted, the Arab countries have systematically sought to coordinate their efforts at educational development through a continuing series of conferences, workshops, and seminars at all levels.

Administratively the structure of education in all these states is practically identical. Apart from some variations of detail the common pattern is one of extreme centralization, the ministries of education exercising almost dictatorial control over all aspects of education. Their size and organization differ markedly in various countries, but they generally have primary responsibility for administration and supervision of the construction and maintenance of physical facilities; training, appointment, and promotion of teachers, supervisors, and administrators; construction and preparation of curricula; writing and publication of textbooks and teaching materials; and the administration of examinations. If these ministries were staffed by able and competent administrators then the high degree of centralization might be beneficial. Unfortunately this is not the case. Overall the quality of personnel is not very high, and the administrative process in all fields is characterized by obsolete concepts and procedures that lead to a marked degree of inefficiency and substantial wastage.[82]

Similar problems exist at all administrative levels. Although different regions are theoretically accorded a certain amount of autonomy, little actual decentralization has yet taken place even in Egypt, Morocco, and Algeria, which are actively seeking to grant local agencies greater autonomy in such fields as education. Nor has the limited decentralization produced the anticipated results. The usual pattern is for the new regional agency to become a replica of the national one and to function in the same way. Thus in practice local bodies exhibit similar behavioral characteristics; they tend to concentrate authority in their hands and to blindly carry out orders and directives issued by the minister of education. They seldom display any initiative in meeting local needs, in adapting national policy to local exigencies, or in involving the local populace in the educational process.[83]

Primary Education

The most obvious consequence of ignoring local requirements is to be found in the many weaknesses of rural education, especially the high dropout rates which represent much of the wastage that characterizes the educational enterprise throughout the region. In every country of the Middle East a serious imbalance is evident in both quality and quantity between urban and rural schools. In some countries more schools are located in the few urban areas than in all their villages. Furthermore, rural schools are nearly always of lower quality than the urban institutions and often offer only from one to four grades of instruction. Very few schools provide the six grades that comprise the primary cycle so that if a student wishes to graduate he must change schools. To do so represents additional costs and difficulties for rural families who tend to be traditionally oriented and thus reluctant to send their children, especially girls, to any school at all.

---

[82] Qubain, *op. cit.*, pp. 1–2; Mohammed A. El-Ghannam, *Education in the Arab Region Viewed from the 1970 Marrakesh Conference*, Educational Studies and Documents, 1 (Paris: UNESCO, 1971), p. 19.

[83] "Survey," p. 13.

The natural consequence is a high dropout rate, and, although precise data are lacking, it is certain that the rural dropout rate is far higher than the urban one. The severity of this problem cannot be exaggerated; overall only about half of those who enter primary school ever reach the sixth grade, and in the Sudan, Saudi Arabia, and Yemen less than a third do so. Hence the conclusion by one scholar that "there has been some improvement in recent years, but in most countries [the dropout rate] continues to be uncomfortably high, while in others it is appalling" [84] is unfortunately only too valid.

Repeaters are another important element of educational wastage, and in some countries less than 25 per cent of primary school students graduate without repeating a grade. In Algeria, for example, recent calculations showed that at the first level an investment of 13.7 pupil-years (more than twice the normal six years) was required for each graduate. Thus the input-output ratio, optimally 1:1, stood at 2.29:1. At the middle and secondary levels the ratio was 1.35:1 and 1.78:1 respectively. These figures indicate the degree of overinvestment that takes place within the Algerian educational system, particularly at the primary levels. Because of such forms of wastage it was estimated in the mid-sixties that, in the Arab world as a whole, about one-third of all expenditures on education, well over $150 million annually, was nonproductive.[85]

High dropout rates also perpetuate illiteracy. Although most governments have proclaimed the goal of universal literacy and many countries possess constitutions guaranteeing every citizen a certain level of education as well as laws that make some education free and compulsory, the achievement of this goal remains elusive. One reason is the inadequacy of facilities in rural areas and their inefficiency. It is generally accepted that at least six years of formal education are necessary for a child to achieve a standard of literacy that will remain

[84] El Ghannam, op. cit., p. 20; Qubain, op. cit., p. 12.

[85] "Literacy and Development in the Arab Countries," paper prepared for the Conference of Ministers of Education, op. cit., 13, 1966, mimeo., p. 31. The figures on repeaters are from "Trends in General, Technical, and Vocational Education in the Arab States," prepared for the Third Regional Conference of Ministers of Education and Ministers Responsible for Economic Planning in the Arab States, Marrakesh, 12–20 January 1970, mimeo. (Paris: UNESCO/MINED/ARAB/4, 1970), p. 36; hereafter referred to as "Trends," p. 14.

with him for the rest of his life but, as we have noted, very few children in the rural areas attend school for this period.

A second fundamental difficulty in the struggle against illiteracy is the question of women's education, which, as we have seen, remains a major problem despite the growing awareness by all governments of the important relationship between the education of women and modernization. Some governments, notably Egypt, Iraq, Jordan, and Syria, have in recent years made significant attempts to deal with this problem. They have ignored the traditional idea of separate schools for boys and girls and have emphasized coeducational education at least through the lower grades. Although this policy violates the Islamic tradition dealing with the separation of the sexes and has therefore encountered opposition from religious conservatives, it has resulted in greatly expanded educational facilities for girls. Another consequence has been a significant saving per unit cost, since duplicate facilities are no longer necessary and capital and operating expenditures can be consolidated. Furthermore, it is economically feasible to construct coeducational schools in smaller communities where the number of children of each sex is too small to warrant the building of separate institutions.[86]

Nevertheless traditional beliefs are still extremely strong and the opportunities for girls to acquire any education at all are very restricted; on the average there is one girls' school for every three or four boys' schools, and in the entire Arabian peninsula female education is practically nonexistent. What facilities do exist tend to be concentrated in urban areas; the further the distance from a town or city the more limited are the educational opportunities available to girls. Not surprisingly dropout rates are also universally higher for girls than for boys.[87]

Overall the rate of female enrollments is growing at all levels faster than male enrollments, thus indicating a rapid increase, but serious inequalities between the sexes remain apparent. In 1967–1968 more than 80 per cent of the male age group were enrolled in primary school as compared to only 44 per cent of the girls, and it has been estimated that whereas universal primary enrollments could be achieved for boys by 1977, this prospect could not be realized for

[86] Qubain, *op. cit.,* pp. 11–12.
[87] *Ibid.,* p. 11; "Survey," p. 16.

girls until 2004. Since the proportion of girls is highest at the primary level, this problem is even more serious at the higher stages. In grades seven to twelve enrollment ratios (of the relevant age groups) are 25.2 per cent and 9.8 per cent for males and females respectively; at the college and university level they are 6.1 per cent and 1.7 per cent.[88]

Similarly, illiteracy rates remain much higher for women than for men, although the level of female literacy has been rising, and for rural inhabitants than for urban dwellers. In the region as a whole the percentage of male literates over fifteen years of age rose from 48.3 per cent in 1960–1961 to 63 per cent in 1967–1968, whereas the percentage of female literacy rose only from 20 to 31.3 per cent. In every country the percentage of female illiterates is much higher than the male percentage; in Algeria 91 per cent and 70 per cent, in Iraq 86 per cent and 71 per cent, in Jordan 85 per cent and 50 per cent, in Lebanon 20 per cent and 13 per cent, in Egypt 80 per cent and 60 per cent. In the Arabian peninsula, Libya, Morocco, and Tunisia female illiteracy rates are over 95 per cent. These rates will continue to drop in the coming decade since most Arab governments are emphasizing primary education, but the prospects for universal literacy in the foreseeable future are not bright owing to the unfavorable pattern of female enrollment growth and the high dropout rate for girls. One UNESCO report summarized this problem as follows: "if the battle against illiteracy is to be won the enrollment and retention of females in primary school must increase at a rate even higher than that achieved thus far." [89]

To a lesser degree the same conclusion applies to the possibility of realizing the goal of enrolling every school-age child in primary school by 1980. At first glance significant advances were achieved in the sixties, the percentage of children in the 7–11 age group attending school rising from 50 per cent in 1960 to 62 per cent in 1967, the total number of students climbing from 7,117,300 to 10,708,100. These figures disguise marked differences among various Arab countries; the percentage of students of primary school age not enrolled range from 90 per cent in Yemen to 71 per cent in Saudi Arabia, 67 per cent in the Sudan, and 45 per cent in Morocco, and between 19 per cent and 32

[88] "Trends," p. 114; Table 20, p. 116.
[89] *Ibid.,* p. 132; Table 32, p. 131; El Ghannam, *op. cit.,* p. 57.

per cent in Algeria, Iraq, Syria, and Egypt. In Bahrain, Kuwait, Lebanon, and Tunisia universal primary education has been achieved.[90]

These increases, however, were accompanied by two major trends that do not augur well for the future. First, the growth rate of primary schooling began to slow in the mid-sixties; between 1960 and 1965 the average annual rate of increase in primary education amounted to 5.8 per cent, in 1966 it dropped to 2.6 per cent, in 1967 it amounted to 4 per cent. The second disturbing fact is that much of the expansion that did occur in the sixties was due to repeaters and that the first-time first-grade enrollment figure grew very slowly in the region as a whole. These trends have been attributed to such factors as inadequate planning and financing, the neglect of rural education, rapid population growth, low living standards, and high dependency burdens, and if they continue, universal enrollments in the first grade would not be achieved for eighty-six years.[91]

From a qualitative viewpoint primary education did not fare particularly well in the sixties as the expansion in primary enrollments was seldom accompanied by qualitative improvements. In fact, in many cases quality was sacrificed for quantity and serious problems of teacher quality, curriculum development, and the like characterize the educational systems. Particularly acute is the question of physical facilities because while the number of primary school students rose by 11 per cent annually between 1955 and 1965 the number of classrooms increased by only 3 per cent a year. As a result all countries suffer from serious shortages of school buildings and all have been forced to adopt various expedients to meet the demand, including renting facilities and using split shifts, but overcrowding remains common.[92]

Most school buildings, whether rented or not, are more or less inadequate as educational facilities; they are usually old, in need of repairs, and without adequate hygienic or playground facilities. Despite the desperate need for new and improved physical facilities the share of expenditures devoted to buildings and equipment is falling; thus the problem will become ever more critical. Compounding the difficulties created by the fact that few Arab countries possess the

[90] El Ghannam, *ibid.*, pp. 16, 17.
[91] *Ibid.*, p. 18; "Trends," pp. 93ff.
[92] "Survey," pp. 17, 31–32.

necessary financial resources to undertake a comprehensive program of school construction is the prevailing disdain for the possibilities of utilizing modern technology to mass-produce prefabricated school buildings relatively inexpensively. Since most educators share the view that education can be carried on only in expensive, imposing, and permanent structures this possibility is eliminated.[93]

The concern with façade and structure instead of content and function is of course not limited to the architectural aspects of education. One of the most damaging instances of this concern is the insistence by most Arab countries that the primary student must pass an examination to earn promotion to the next grade. Those who fail are forced to repeat the grade with the obvious result that they tend to become discouraged and often drop out. Furthermore they occupy places that could be assigned to other children. Thus, from the viewpoint of efficiency the practice cannot be justified. Repetition is equally harmful from a qualitative perspective since the importance of the examination reinforces the strong tendencies toward cramming and memorization. Nevertheless this practice, condemned by many educators for years, remains so widespread that the 1966 Tripoli conference and the 1969 Beirut workshop "considered the present incidence excessive" and suggested that the practice be reduced through various means.[94]

Equally harmful is the common practice of making students pass a terminal examination at the end of their primary education in order to receive the certificate enabling them to continue in the higher levels of the system. These tests are defended on grounds identical to those for the promotion examinations, that standards must be maintained and that it is necessary to insure that the student has acquired the knowledge required at a particular level. The deleterious aspects of such national examinations are also similar to those of the promotion examinations, especially the pressures that are created for students and teachers alike to prepare by cramming and memorizing a certain amount of factual data. To these are added tremendous psychological strains. Once again it would appear that the educational objective could be achieved in a less damaging way.[95]

The problem of form versus content is also reflected in the cur-

[93] "Trends," p. 13. Qubain, *op. cit.,* p. 12.
[94] "Trends," pp. 18, 103.
[95] Qubain, *op. cit.,* p. 11.

ricula, which are more or less identical throughout the Arab world. Standardization resulted from the 1957 Agreement on Cultural Unity signed by Syria, Jordan, and Egypt and the Cultural Charter signed by Iraq and Egypt in 1958. These two documents sought to strengthen feelings of Arab unity by eliminating the many variations in education within and between the Arab states and to adapt the educational systems to the needs of development by emphasizing vocational and technical training at all levels. The agreements called for a 6-3-3 educational ladder; six years of primary education followed by three years of general secondary education and three more years of either academic or technical training at the secondary level. This pattern, the most common in the region today, was also endorsed by the ministers of education at conferences sponsored by the Arab League in Baghdad (1964), and Kuwait (1968), as was the concept of similar admission and examination requirements. Nevertheless because of the conflict between national interest and the ideal of unity, discussed earlier, significant differences still exist in the structure of education, and some countries use such variants as the 4-4-4, 5-4-3, 6-4-3, and 6-3-2 patterns. Similar problems have been encountered in attempts to standardize curricula. These agreements also provided for the application of a model curriculum in terms of content and the time allocated to various subjects, but here, too, great differences remain. Seven Arab countries do not include any foreign language instruction while Algeria devotes 30 per cent, Lebanon 19 per cent, and Egypt 11 per cent of the primary curricula to this subject. Algeria devotes 2 per cent to religion while Egypt allocates 11 per cent and Saudi Arabia 36 per cent to its study. The attention accorded to science varies from 2 per cent in Libya to 8 per cent in Egypt to 19 per cent in Jordan; that accorded to the social sciences from 2 per cent in Tunisia to 7 per cent in Egypt to 10 per cent in Lebanon.[96]

Every country has made important changes in its curriculum to reflect advances in educational theory and practice elsewhere, but curricula are still not adapted, as the 1966 Tripoli conference noted, to developmental needs. This conclusion was reiterated by a UNESCO workshop held in Beirut three years later. It emphasized that curricula still tend to allot less time to mathematics, science, and prac-

---

[96] "Trends," p. 7; "Survey," pp. 9, 19.

tical activities than is the world trend, that the orientation of the curriculum continues to be toward success in examinations with traditional methods such as memorization and rote learning emphasized, and that few teachers seek to adapt the curriculum to local conditions. Hence despite attempts to rationalize and strengthen primary education through curricular changes the spirit in thousands of classrooms remains highly scholastic and almost no attempts are made to excite the imagination and curiosity of the students or to develop their creativity, resourcefulness, and independence.[97]

Furthermore, curricula are geared to the preparation of pupils for a secondary education, but only a small percentage ever succeed in gaining admission to the higher levels—whereas 62 per cent of the relevant age group attend primary school only 17.5 per cent are enrolled in secondary education. Thus the needs of the majority are simply not met in any meaningful fashion. They are unable to continue their education, often cannot find employment of any sort, and frequently lapse back into illiteracy. The urgency and gravity of this problem needs no emphasis, but to date little attention has been given to such fundamental questions as the kinds and duration of schooling that should be provided for children who will not continue their education and the kinds of nonformal training that can be provided to upgrade and maintain their skills, particularly literacy. In short, the question of how to assimilate thousands of youngsters with only a primary education into society in a productive way remains an urgent problem everywhere.[98]

If curriculum reform is to be effective and primary education is no longer to be characterized as essentially dysfunctional to the needs of a developing society, a new type of teacher will have to be produced. The teacher represents the vital link between the intentions of planners and reformers and the educational experience of students, and, unfortunately, the quality of teachers in the Arab countries represents a major bottleneck in any attempt to implement educational reforms. Few qualified or dedicated teachers are to be found in the classrooms

---

[97] "Regional Workshop on Pre-Service and In-Service Primary Teacher Training in the Arabic-Speaking Member States," report presented to the Third Regional Conference of Ministers of Education, *op. cit.*, Ref. 1, 1969, Appendix II, p. 13; hereafter referred to as "Regional Workshop"; Qubain, *op. cit.*, pp. 18–19.

[98] "Trends," pp. 19, 24.

of the Middle East, particularly those located in rural areas, because problems of recruitment and training remain grave at all levels despite the adoption of various measures designed to enhance the attractiveness of the profession. In every Arab country teachers are civil servants, and like their colleagues in the administration they are underpaid and often overworked. Unlike other civil servants, however, their prospects for promotion and self-advancement are limited so that even after many years of service a teacher who manages to reach the top of his profession receives a salary that is often inadequate to meet his family's needs. High prestige could possibly compensate for inadequate remuneration, but in all countries the teacher enjoys a very limited respect. With such gloomy prospects it is not surprising that the most promising students never enter this career or that the ablest abandon it as soon as possible.

Problems of quality are particularly acute at the primary level. The number of teachers grew at a rate of 7.3 per cent between 1960–1961 and 1967–1968, while enrollments grew by only 6.1 per cent annually, thus making possible a decline in the number of students per teacher from 38.4 to 35.4; and the percentage of qualified teachers also increased from 75 to 80 per cent of the total number of teachers. But these figures disguise several important factors that make the apparent improvement highly questionable. First, the percentage of untrained teachers varies considerably from country to country ranging from 15 per cent or less in Egypt, Iraq, and the Sudan to between 16 per cent and 50 per cent in Algeria, Kuwait, Saudi Arabia, and Tunisia to over 51 per cent in Lebanon, Libya, Morocco, the People's Democratic Republic of Yemen, and the Yemen Arab Republic. Second, these figures gravely understate the magnitude of the problem, for the category "trained teachers" includes large numbers of persons who have received poor or inadequate training in special programs designed to meet immediate needs on a short-term basis. Hence experts still talk of the "serious shortage of trained teachers and of qualified candidates for the profession." [99]

Compounding this problem is the fact that even qualified candidates do not receive particularly good preservice training and almost no in-service training programs are available for later upgrading.

[99] *Ibid.,* Tables I, II, III, pp. 91, 92, 94; "Regional Workshop," p. 3; Appendix II, p. 7.

Most teacher-training institutions are still highly traditional in orientation. The approach remains quite authoritarian with an emphasis upon rote learning, memorization, and preparing for examinations rather than professional preparations; hence the average graduate is clearly not the kind of teacher who can inspire and stimulate students, a fact which has important consequences for development and whose significance has been summarized in a UNESCO report as follows:

If pupils should be trained to develop initiative, resourcefulness and a sense of social responsibility, the teachers must be trained with methods which will make them capable of educating the pupils that way. Otherwise they will not be able to impart or communicate the qualities so highly needed in a developing society. Most training schools and colleges seem to be conducted on the lecture method, on "listening, recording and reproducing," on "receiving instructions and obeying" and "memorizing," but if a positively active and creative generation is required, then teachers will have to be trained differently.[100]

Secondary Education

Although elementary education is terminal for about 75 per cent of all primary school graduates, the expansion of primary education has caused great strains upon the higher levels of the system as ever growing numbers of graduates have sought to gain admittance to secondary schools. At this level the bias in favor of urban centers is even more pronounced, and the rural areas have almost no secondary schools. Any student wishing to continue his schooling must therefore usually move to a town or city, a requirement that eliminates most rural children from the higher levels.

Even with this limitation the demand for access to education has been so great that all governments have erected a system of examinations and certificates that eliminates many who would like to continue their education. Nevertheless secondary education has witnessed rapid growth, more than doubling between 1960 and 1967, when the number of students climbed from 1,248,100 to 2,733,700. The proportion of the 11–17 age group attending school rose from 9.3 to 17.5 per cent in the same period. These figures also vary widely from country to country. In Kuwait the proportion is 60 per cent, in Bahrain, 46 per cent, Jordan 39 per cent, Syria and Egypt 30 per cent, Lebanon

---

[100] "Regional workshop," Appendix II, p. 21; "Survey," p. 36.

28 per cent, Iraq 24 per cent, Tunisia and Libya 19 per cent, Morocco 12 per cent, Sudan and Saudi Arabia 6 per cent, and Yemen 0.6 per cent. Once again, however, quality was often sacrificed for quantity, and serious deficiencies characterize this educational level. That quality actually declined in the sixties is indicated by the pupil-teacher ratio which changed from 1:16.6 in 1960 to 1:20.0 in 1967.[101]

The structure of secondary education in most Arab countries consists of two three-year cycles; a preparatory one which includes grades 7, 8, and 9 and a secondary one covering grades 10, 11, and 12. Despite some variations the secondary curriculum is also essentially the same particularly in Egypt, Syria, Jordan, Libya, Saudi Arabia, and Iraq, although the latter has a two-year secondary cycle. The normal load is about thirty periods per week. In most countries the students follow the same curriculum through the first cycle and through the first year of the second (grades 6–10) and are then allowed to choose between scientific or literary programs for the last two years. Between 1960–1961 and 1967–1968 the number of students studying scientific subjects more than doubled, rising from 52,700 to 121,900, but enrollments in the literary track increased from 104,500 to 201,000. Thus if enrollments are analyzed in terms of the proportion of students in each specialization one finds that only a slight shift took place, that the percentage of students studying science climbed but slightly during these years (33.5 per cent to 37.8 per cent), and that most of this increase was due to developments in Egypt.[102]

Qualitatively the field of science teaching remained characterized by low standards. It is especially difficult to find qualified teachers (who are supposed to have at least a B.A. or B.S.) because not only is there a shortage of persons with these qualifications, but those who have them tend not to enter secondary teaching. Many attractive opportunities exist in other sectors while teachers suffer, though somewhat less so than at the lower levels, from such disadvantages as low salaries and limited prestige.

Available textbooks are also of poor quality; most are merely unadapted translations of Western texts or works produced by authors

---

[101] El-Ghannam, op. cit., Table 3, p. 53; the pupil-teacher ratio data is from "Trends," Table 3, p. 94.

[102] "Trends," Tables 16, 17, p. 112.

without any practical experience. Laboratory facilities are seldom adequate, and although simple homemade devices can be used very effectively as teaching aids, most science teachers suffer from the concern with façade that we have noted and are convinced that they need the most modern and complicated equipment. Even when such equipment is available, the tendency is for the teacher to monopolize the laboratory. Instead of allowing students to engage in practical work, the teacher demonstrates the experiment to them. The emphasis upon this pedagogical technique is due partly to the cost and scarcity of laboratory equipment, which is usually regarded as too valuable for students to handle. A similar philosophy prevents the utilization of whatever library resources may be available. Such traditional attitudes and techniques affect all fields equally. The emphasis remains upon lectures, memorization, and rote learning, and little or no attempt to discuss or understand the material is ever made. The goal continues to be to pass the examination by memorizing the text—and few students look at any book except that one.

Another important area that is severely handicapped by low quality is foreign language instruction. In most countries every student is required to study at least one. English is the most popular choice. French is second, with German, which was largely neglected until recent years, gaining in acceptance. Despite the importance of this subject and the attention paid to it, the quality of instruction is very inadequate and standards are poor. Few students acquire any meaningful proficiency, and at best (which applies to a small minority) the graduate is able to read a little and to carry on an elementary conversation. Hence the problem of increasing competency in foreign language instruction remains important everywhere.[103]

The degree to which traditional attitudes and values continue to affect the functioning of education in the Arab world is also evidenced by the fact that everywhere higher education is regarded as a criterion for elite membership, and for this reason preparation for college and university continues to be emphasized. But although college and university enrollments have increased sharply to meet the growing demand, only a fraction of aspirants can be accommodated. The remainder, the secondary school graduates who are unable to continue

[103] Qubain, *op. cit.*, pp. 16–19.

their education, represent a major problem for all countries of the Middle East. Employment opportunities are very limited and what openings are available seldom correspond to the graduate's expectations and aspirations. Having completed secondary school he considers himself a member of the elite and will accept only some sort of white-collar job in government or business, a minor proportion of possible openings. Every government has resorted to the same strategy in an obvious attempt to defuse a potentially explosive situation; bureaucratic positions have been created to accommodate these graduates. How much longer such a course can be maintained when administrations are already overstaffed with "urban gentlemen" remains a fundamental question confronting all the governments of the region.[104] The consequences for economic development and political stability of a large number of underemployed or unemployed secondary graduates have already been emphasized.

Of all the various policies that have been adopted in an attempt to deal with this problem, the most difficult to implement, though in the long run the most meaningful, has been the expansion of vocational education. Practically all countries have, since World War II, attempted to channel increasing numbers of students away from academic training into a vocational career. The attempt to develop vocational training, however, has been hampered by the ancient and deep-rooted prejudices against manual labor that still pervade Middle Eastern culture. As we have seen, vocational schools were originally established as charitable institutions to train orphans and destitute children. Their graduates possessed little prestige and were seldom able to find financially rewarding employment, whereas persons with bureaucratic positions, regardless of rank, were highly regarded and enjoyed economic security. The impact of the West served to reinforce this traditional preference by creating demands for large numbers of new skills that could be performed only by graduates of the modern academic schools who therefore came to hold positions of power and prestige.

In recent years the strength of these factors has been somewhat lessened by increasing demands for vocationally trained persons in the industrial sector, especially in the oil industry which has provided

[104] *Ibid.,* p. 23.

ever growing opportunities for large numbers of skilled workers. Economic forces of supply and demand have also affected the marketplace; the demand for skilled workers grew while the supply was limited with the result that wages and status increased. At the same time governments everywhere became conscious of the degree to which the lack of skilled manpower constituted a major bottleneck to the achievement of economic growth. The constant domestic and international crises in the area have also served to strengthen the trend toward vocational and technical education by spurring attempts to build strong armies which today more than ever before are dependent upon highly trained technical cadres and a sophisticated infrastructure.[105]

For these reasons the past decade has witnessed a growing awareness of the need to emphasize vocational and technical education. But despite repeated recommendations of ministers of education and by national and international bodies such as the regional seminar in Tripoli in 1966, few concrete results are yet apparent. One UNESCO report recently noted that despite the "elementary" nature of the resolutions "we may wonder whether these recommendations are not still fully justified in 1970, so far are they from having produced the reactions that might have been expected." In statistical terms the gravity of the problem is evidenced by the fact that between 1960–1961 and 1967–1968 the increase in the number of students enrolled in general education at the secondary level in the Arab world rose by 1.3 million (90 per cent), whereas the increase in the number of students attending vocational and technical schools increased by a mere 111,000 (8 per cent). Thus, despite various attempts to strengthen this field the percentage of enrollments in technical and vocational schools as compared to total enrollments in secondary schools declined steadily, from 12.5 per cent in 1960–1961 to 11.1 per cent in 1967–1968.[106] In short, few changes in traditional patterns are yet evident in the Arab world as a whole, though some countries, notably Egypt, Tunisia, and Algeria, do constitute exceptions to this pattern. In Iraq, Jordan, Lebanon, Libya, and Syria, on the other hand, vocational

---

[105] *Ibid.*, pp. 24–25.
[106] "Trends," Table 13, p. 108, Table 14, p. 109; Table 15, p. 111; p. 34; the quote is from p. 33.

training is not nearly as developed and in the Arabian peninsula it remains even more limited.

The problems of vocational education extend beyond the limited growth in enrollments, for the increase which has taken place occurred largely without coherent planning and coordination. Many institutions were opened without adequate preparations either in terms of needed facilities and resources or of analyses of manpower demand, so that serious imbalances have resulted between vocational training and the needs of the economy. In many cases male and female students have been trained in areas already saturated rather than in specialties where shortages of trained manpower existed. Furthermore, the neglect of planning resulted in efforts at rapid expansion without adequate consideration of the physical and human resources that would be needed, and already serious qualitative problems have been aggravated everywhere.

One of the most serious weaknesses, as in other fields, remains the lack of qualified teachers. The problem is even more acute in this area since no thought was given to the establishment of teacher-training institutes when the network of vocational and technical schools was expanded in most countries. Not only are few qualified teachers available, but industry competes successfully for their services by offering better wages and fringe benefits. As a result teachers in these schools tend to be even less qualified than those in other fields.[107]

Thus vocational education at the secondary level continues to form one of the most serious bottlenecks in the region's development. Not only is this sector actually regressing instead of expanding, but only a small percentage of those who do graduate enter industry. The majority attempt to enroll in a university; failing that, they become primary teachers. The result is a critical shortage of middle-level manpower in many Arab countries with significant consequences for their programs of industrialization and rural development. As we have already emphasized, the importance of these skills cannot be over-

[107] Qubain, *op. cit.*, pp. 25ff; "Expert Meeting on the Access of Girls and Women to Technical and Vocational Education in the Arab States," paper prepared for Third Regional Conference of Ministers of Education, *op. cit.*, Ref. 3, Jan. 8, 1970, p. 2.

stressed since in their absence highly trained professionals such as teachers and engineers are forced to spend time carrying out the kinds of duties that could be performed by nurses and technicians. The converse, the use of unskilled workers to fill technical posts in industry, has also resulted in waste and inefficiency everywhere.[108]

Higher Education and Manpower

The very factors that have served to inhibit the growth of technical education have spurred the pressures for high-level academic training. As one scholar has observed:

The realization of personal ambitions and aspirations . . . is only possible—besides the army—through university studies. That is why there is in each Arab country . . . a veritable flood towards the universities, and an almost infinite prestige attached to the University itself. . . . If the quota in the preferred faculty . . . prevents the admission of the majority of the candidates, one enrolls in any faculty whatsoever; the important thing is to be enrolled in the University.[109]

Because of such pressures higher education has developed extremely rapidly in the past decade; of the thirty-seven colleges, universities, and higher institutes of various sorts in the region, nineteen have been established since 1950. The total student population rose from 145,-000 in 1951 to 241,000 in 1963–1964; the number of girls enrolled in universities rose from 4,000 to 22,000 between 1950 and 1961 and doubled again to 45,000 in 1963. Overall the number of students tripled in the decade between 1956–1957 and 1966–1967, reaching 300,000; another 25,000 students were studying outside the region so that about 5 per cent of the age group was receiving a college education.[110]

Approximately 8,000 of the 300,000 students attending institutions of higher learning in the Arab world are enrolled in foreign institutions, including St. Joseph University, the American University of Beirut, and Beirut College for Women in Lebanon, Al-Hikma University of Baghdad, and the American University in Cairo. The American

---

[108] "Survey," p. 42.

[109] Waardenburg, *op. cit.*, p. 5.

[110] "Survey," Table 22, p. 26; Qubain, *op. cit.*, p. 48; Zahlan, *op. cit.*, pp. 8, 31, 34.

University of Beirut and the American University in Cairo account for only about 1 per cent of total enrollments in higher education in the area but their role in the development of higher education has been, and continues to be, most significant. Essentially they are able to provide higher quality training and to promote more research than is the case in practically any national institution. They enjoy greater financial resources, have closer contacts with scholars in other countries, are more selective in admissions, and are able to recruit more able faculty. In an era of great nationalist fervor these institutions have been, and will inevitably continue to be, subject to pressures of all sorts, but to date these have not resulted in very serious damage to their intellectual standards. Spurring the expansion of higher education have been the pressures generated by increased educational opportunities at the lower levels. Most governments have preferred not to resist these demands very strongly because of ideological and practical considerations; higher education is universally viewed as a source of needed high-level manpower and as a right of all citizens. In at least one case the head of a physics program was informed that a certain number of students had to pass in order to meet the country's needs for teachers—even though less than 1 per cent of the students in this department were qualified for graduate training.[111]

The concern with democratization has led to attempts to make higher education opportunities available to ever more diversified segments of the population. Higher education is free in many Arab countries including Egypt, Iraq, Jordan, Lebanon, Libya, Syria, and Saudi Arabia, and there has been an increase in the fellowships available to students from poor families. Although it is difficult to appraise the efficacy of these steps since relatively little data are available concerning the socioeconomic backgrounds of students, it is reasonable to assume that most students are still drawn from the middle and upper classes and are basically urban in origin. It is unlikely that many students from rural areas or from the urban lower classes are yet enrolled, though it is likely that this pattern is changing and that increasingly student bodies will become more and more diversified.[112]

The dramatic increase in enrollments has been particularly noticeable in the social sciences and the humanities. Except for Egypt,

---

[111] Zahlan, *ibid.,* pp. 9–10.
[112] Boktor, *op. cit.,* pp. 27–28.

the large majority of students are registered in these faculties; in the mid-sixties the figures were as follows: Syria, 85 per cent, Libya, 81 per cent; Saudi Arabia, 86 per cent; Lebanon, 73 per cent; Sudan, 67 per cent; Iraq, 62 per cent.[113] This imbalance is due, as elsewhere, chiefly to the ease with which enrollments in these fields can be expanded and the relatively low costs involved in doing so. To increase the number of students in scientific courses entails large expenditures for the construction of new facilities, the acquisition of expensive equipment, and the employment of large numbers of scarce specialists. In the humanities and the social sciences, on the other hand, such expenditures can be neglected and the same professor can as easily lecture to two or three times as many students. Though of little concern to politicians and administrators seeking to meet the great demand for expansion or even to many faculty members who often regarded the new enrollments as opportunities to sell more copies of their published notes, the result has been that almost every college is overextended, facilities are stretched to their utmost, student-teacher ratios are far too high, mass lectures are common, and many physical facilities are simply incapable of handling all the students enrolled in specific courses.[114]

Despite its slower expansion scientific training shares similar problems. In most cases little attention was paid to the requirements of expansion and all institutions suffer from more or less severe shortages of human and physical resources. Partly because of a lack of even the most elementary equipment and facilities, most teaching remains historical and descriptive and few students are expected to solve any problems in the course of their training. The most important factor making for poor standards is the critical shortage of qualified personnel, a situation that is aggravated by such factors as intellectual isolation, poor training, inadequate support, heavy teaching loads, and a salary scale that virtually compels teachers to seek outside positions to supplement their income. Existing conditions are such that one expert has concluded: "The present shortage of staff members in all academic disciplines in Middle Eastern universities cannot be met without radical changes in the present pattern of selection of candi-

[113] "Survey," p. 27.
[114] See Waardenburg, *op. cit.,* pp. 53ff; Qubain, *op. cit.,* pp. 85ff.

dates, conditions of work at the national universities and the size of the fellowship programmes." [115]

Aggravating these difficulties are the cleavages that characterize institutions of higher learning everywhere. The common pattern is for colleges or faculties modeled after the French tradition to coexist with institutions in the British tradition. Often a staff consists of persons trained in Germany, Britain, France, and the United States. The outstanding example of this diversity is to be found in Iraq, where the colleges of art, science, and medicine at the University of Baghdad are modeled after the British pattern, the college of law, the French, the college of agriculture, the American, and the colleges of engineering and education are mixed. This diversity even extends in some cases to different departments within the same college. In the University of Cairo, for example, the department of Arabic language and literature is basically French inspired, whereas the department of geography follows the British pattern.

The result of such diversity has not been to develop a unique model genuinely applicable to conditions in the region. First, curricula and texts remain based almost entirely on European or American models and seldom include any attempt to relate the material to contemporary national problems. Second, little agreement exists even within the same institution on such matters as degree requirements, curricula organization, or broader questions involving the goals of university training. As a result faculties which follow the American model tend to emphasize general education and those based on European models a much greater degree of specialization and concentration. This leads naturally to the third problem area, the isolation of one discipline from another. By and large requirements are fixed and inflexible so that a student in one faculty finds it practically impossible to take courses in another.[116]

Nor has this foreign heritage spurred the development of graduate training, which has been almost totally neglected. This is partly because of the traditional feeling that the responsibility of a professor, many of whom are employed part-time, is to undergraduate teaching, but also responsible is the fact that few faculty members ever carried

[115] Zahlan, *op. cit.*, p. 13.
[116] Qubain, *op. cit.*, pp. 51–52; Waardenburg, *op. cit.*, pp. 46–47.

on any research and the few that did so were often derided by their colleagues. Attempts are being made to reverse this attitude through financial grants, but the rapid expansion of enrollments has forced even those faculty members interested in research to devote more time to teaching and student affairs. As a result little attention is paid to graduate training or to research except at the American University of Beirut and various institutions in Egypt, and these faculty members, often the best trained and the most able, who are concerned with research and research training tend to join the brain drain, which represents a considerable loss to all Arab countries.[117]

The amount of this loss has been estimated at $100 million a year but the damage to the countries involved far exceeds this huge sum. As one expert has noted:

The scientists, engineers and physicians who are migrating to the developed world are the agents of development, they are the multipliers, the change purveyors, whose worth is above computation in dinars or dollars. It is the educated elite, the most highly skilled professionals, who are the teachers and leaders of our youth, who are the planners and innovators of our society, who are the political, cultural and moral leaders of our world who are leaving us.[118]

Since structural, economic, intellectual, and administrative factors within the Arab colleges and universities are the major determinants of the brain drain, it will be necessary to correct the many dysfunctional aspects of these institutions if this damaging exodus is to be halted. How great a task is involved is indicated by the fact that, with but one or two exceptions, the Egyptian universities are the best in the region.

The major characteristics of higher education in the Arab world have been summarized by one scholar, after extensive study, as follows: (1) The explosive growth in enrollments since 1950 has resulted in "a penury and overloading of all teaching personnel and at the same time, unfortunate consequences for the quality of education and research." (2) Higher education remains highly scholastic and of very low quality: "the Arab universities scarcely offer university

---

[117] Zahlan, *op. cit., passim.*

[118] Adisheshiah, *op. cit.,* pp. 8, 11; for a cross-regional perspective on this problem see: The Committee on the International Migration of Talent, *The International Migration of High-Level Manpower* (New York: Praeger, 1970).

training during the first years. It is only . . . in graduate study that certain quality personnel and intellectuals . . . will be developed." (3) Professors are overworked, often having to teach 20 to 30 hours a week. They are also poorly paid and have therefore to engage in supplementary activities of all sorts. Complementing them are the part-time faculty who teach a few hours but who have little time to devote to research. (4) The administrative structure is "grotesque," precluding coherent planning, efficient decision-making, and/or individual initiative. Essentially the university administration suffers from all the administrative deficiencies of the government bureaucracy. (5) Universities interact closely with the society of which they are a part; events within the society immediately and deeply affect them. (6) Student organizations have great powers. The government is always attempting to maintain the support of the majority and is willing to take whatever steps are necessary, such as admitting all secondary school graduates, to prevent the students from making hostile demands upon it. (7) The Arab university is above all a teaching institution; research is possible only at the higher levels. (8) The prestige of the university is high among all students but is dropping among the faculty, many of whom would prefer to engage in another occupation. Part of the reason is the great gap between the ideal of a university and its reality, of which they are aware but which they are incapable of changing. (9) The university has been deeply affected by the West and remains today in an ambivalent position toward it. The idea of an Arab university is being born but a clear definition of what such an institution should be remains to be elaborated. (10) A balance between the manpower needs of the country and their production by the university remains difficult to achieve; universities and colleges in the Arab world do not constitute the kinds of centers of research and training that are required for national development.[119]

Generally, the inability to match output to manpower needs and the consequences of the brain drain are reflected in acute shortages of personnel in physics, engineering, chemistry, agriculture, medicine, and other scientific and technological fields. The two exceptions are Jordan and Lebanon which, in fact, export teachers, engineers, tech-

[119] Waardenburg, *op. cit.,* pp. 119–123.

nicians, and physicians to the other countries of the Middle East. All other countries suffer from serious shortages of high- and middle-level manpower. At present it is estimated that 5,000 Ph.D.'s are required (1,500 in Egypt, 1,000 in Syria, 1,000 in Iraq, and 500 in the other Arab countries), and other persons with less specialized skills are vitally needed if these countries are to develop. As one observer has commented," Arab countries to date do not have enough lower and intermediate levels of technicians and qualified scientists to make rapid progress possible in any field." [120]

One reason for these shortages is the fact that, despite its popularity, planning in all Arab countries has not attained very high standards. Since the early 1960's practically every Arab country has established a planning office and drawn up some sort of educational plan. These can be divided into three basic types: detailed plans that are integrated into the general national development plan (Egypt), partial programs covering various parts of the educational system within the framework of an overall plan (Morocco, South Yemen), and sectoral programs consisting of priority projects (Iraq, Kuwait, Saudi Arabia, Algeria) or investment programs (Jordan, Sudan, Libya). To date all these efforts have not proven particularly productive and practically no plan has been of much value. The first plans, those published in the early 1960's by Syria, Jordan, and Egypt, were drawn up without such elementary data as accurate census figures, and even though census data are now more widely available, they represent only the most primitive data required by the educational planner—all Arab states lack accurate, comprehensive statistics on most social and economic subjects. Most important is the absence of precise information concerning manpower, mainly its structure and distribution by occupation and sector of economic activity. Although some countries, notably Egypt, have made significant attempts to remedy this deficiency, vital data of this kind remain unavailable. Furthermore most educational plans have emphasized the expansion of the existing system and the calculation of the costs involved rather than ways of relating education to economic or social goals. Even where these goals have been clearly articulated little integration or

[120] Qubain, *op. cit.*, p. 513; Margaretha Bruin, "Some Remarks Concerning Science and Technology Planning in Arabic Speaking Countries," in Nader and Zahlan, *op. cit.*, p. 242.

coordination of educational plans into national plans has taken place and the educational system has seldom been systematically related to their achievement.[121]

Nor has any country, with perhaps one or two exceptions, yet paid sufficient systematic attention to the establishment of a coherent system of priorities for the educational enterprise, though without such priorities it is unlikely that the many dysfunctional aspects can ever be reduced, particularly the wastage, in the content and method of teaching and in inadequate administrative practices. In the mid-sixties it was estimated that about 150 to 200 million dollars of the total 500 to 600 million dollars that was spent on education by the Arab states in 1964–1965 was actually wasted. More recent estimates indicate that expenditures by ministries of education alone were considerably higher, amounting to $994 million in 1964–1965 and $1,171 million in 1967–1968, an increase of 67 per cent. If the earlier estimate of the degree of wastage was at all accurate it is only reasonable to assume that the total wastage is proportionally higher and may amount to well over $300 million per year.[122]

The urgency of this situation is further increased by the fact that resources allocated to education will have to increase to match the rapid population growth and rising social demand for schooling. But one scholar has noted that "many countries . . . have either reached or are fast reaching the saturation point in the amount they can spend on education. They can increase such expenditures only at the expense of other vital services of the state and the development of other sectors of the economy." [123] The result will be, unless radical measures are taken, to deny a large portion of the peoples of the Middle East access to modern schools and the perpetuation of educational practices that are already not conducive to either personal or societal development.

Only with the aid of educational planning is it possible to meet this crisis and to increase efficiency and utilize resources in such a way as to create institutions of learning that serve both the individual and his society. To structure an educational system along modern, functional lines, however, involves more than planning, a fact that explains

[121] "Educational Planning in the Arab States," *passim.*
[122] "Survey," p. 31; "Trends," p. 5.
[123] Qubain, *op. cit.,* p. 4.

the limited degree of success yet achieved. Above all, political will and political decisions are required, and many regimes have proven unwilling or unable to make the kinds of commitment to social, economic, and political development that are basic prerequisites for the transformation of education. Furthermore, even if the appropriate decisions are made, societal and cultural constraints may well prevent their implementation, and a considerable degree of political power and skill will be required to overcome latent and overt opposition to change and to deal with the popular demand for higher education.

The importance of such considerations cannot be exaggerated: the weaker the political system the more likely will educational systems continue to evolve in their own directions, directions which bear little relationship to stated politico-economic objectives. That this has in fact happened in the Arab world is indicated by the following analysis:

Although it is often emphasized that higher education in underdeveloped countries is at the mercy of political pressures, the amazing fact is that institutionally the universities have been totally oblivious to these pressures. Nor is the situation much different in the various fields of applied research which are generally supposed to be directed towards problems connected with economic and social needs.[124]

The result, as we have stressed, is that higher education throughout the region remains characterized by significant deficiencies and does not contribute to the achievement of national development goals.

In this regard the experiences of Turkey and Iran, the former with a competitive, the latter with a reformist political system, are most instructive. Both countries have had to deal with similar problems and have sought to implement sophisticated planning efforts in their attempts to modernize. Accordingly it is to a discussion of recent educational developments in those countries that we now turn.

---

[124] Zahlan, *op. cit.*, p. 24.

VI

Turkey: Toward a
Modern Educational System
in a Democratic Society

The Multiparty Environment

With the end of World War II the strains that had been created by the transformation of Turkey under Ataturk erupted into the open. The political elite splintered into various factions and new elements that had risen to the fore in the twenties and thirties—businessmen, traders, and entrepreneurs—began to articulate insistent demands for a greater voice in decision-making. In their drive for more power the new groups quickly gained the support of many elements within the society who, dissatisfied with the rigidity of the CHP and the bureaucracy in general, and with the wartime economic problems in particular, wished to see a greater degree of freedom within the country. In this atmosphere ideological attitudes ranging from racialism to communism were openly expressed and fundamental political issues became topics of popular debate. This debate culminated in a dramatic change in the political system that could now be characterized as competitive, a change that in turn engendered marked repercussions in every aspect of Turkish life.

For many reasons—including İnönü's dedication to Ataturk's ideal of establishing a multiparty system, internal opposition within the CHP, and demands to end one-party rule—opposition politics were legalized in 1946. In 1950 the DP (Democrat Party), formed by four former CHP leaders, was swept into power by an overwhelming majority. This election marked a turning point in the country's history. Not only had a remarkable transition from dictatorship to democracy taken place, but the new government promptly embarked upon an ambitious program of economic development that would have significant consequences for Turkish society in general and the educational system in particular. What had happened was that the first free elections in Turkish history allowed all segments of society to voice their dissatisfaction with the CHP which had been in power for twenty-seven long years; intellectuals wanted democracy, businessmen resented the etatist economic policy, landowners were disturbed by the attempts—however unsuccessful—to induce change in rural areas, and the peasantry, whose way of life (as we have noted) had changed but little, felt neglected and abused by a tyrannical administration.[1]

Secure in its mandate, the DP attempted to carry out its campaign promises, launching an ambitious program of economic development financed in large part with American aid, and liberalizing various restrictive laws. Furthermore, the DP was aware of the importance of rural support and did its utmost to maintain the favor of the villagers by a partial relaxation of religious restrictions; the call to prayer could once again be chanted in Arabic and religious instruction became a regular school subject unless the parents requested that their children be excused.

Its economic development program led to the growing integration of the villager into the national economy. The rural areas became increasingly market-oriented and the inhabitants' way of life began to be less self-sufficient and more dependent upon the market. The highway construction program and the availability of transportation meant that the peasant could easily migrate to the cities and make frequent visits to market towns where he was exposed to new ideas, attitudes, and values.

When villagers found it easy to travel to urban centers, large numbers did so, and many of them settled there permanently. Increased urbanization was caused by both push and pull pressures: the attraction of city life and the opportunities perceived therein, as well as population pressures in rural areas and increased consolidation of landholdings as a result of mechanization. Thus, many villagers now developed ties with urban centers through trade, travel, or relatives who had migrated there, and the rural areas came increasingly into contact with the outside world.

Even the peasant who was disinclined to travel was exposed to new concepts via radios, which were now to be found in every

---

[1] The material in this section is adapted from Joseph S. Szyliowicz, "Political Participation and Modernization in Turkey," *Western Political Quarterly*, 19 (June 1966), 266–284.

coffeehouse or party local. The number of sets, for example, increased from 46,230 in 1938, to 362,466 in 1950, to 1,341,272 in 1959. In these places, groups of villagers would gather to pass the time of day and discuss local problems or occasionally political issues. The army, reorganized with American support, proved to be an important means of reinforcing the changes taking place in the rural areas. The peasant draftees became part of a new social environment where they were given technical training and exposed to modernism.

All these factors led to the transformation of rural life and to the emergence of the peasantry as an important factor in the political arena. Although unorganized and unable to articulate its demands consistently, this stratum became politically conscious and aware of its potential power. Increasingly it began to apply pressure upon the existing administrative organization with the result that traditional negative notions of government, the master-servant relationship between the administration and the peasantry, were transformed, and the villager began to view the bureaucracy and the government as institutions that he could manipulate for his own benefit.[2]

Not surprisingly, the DP was overwhelmingly re-elected in 1954 with 56.6 per cent of the vote and 503 assembly seats out of a total of 541. The CHP won 35 per cent of the vote and only 31 seats. Encouraged by this evidence of popular support, the Menderes government embarked upon an ambitious program of economic development which it proved unable to complete owing to haphazard planning, adverse terms of trade, large defense expenditures, and a shortage of capital. The result was a drastic inflation and a scarcity of consumer items. Affected most by this economic crisis were the urban elements, especially the salaried classes, who began to criticize the administration more and more frequently.

The government proved highly sensitive to opposition, and many restrictive measures were adopted to limit the rights of free speech, assembly, campaigning, and the autonomy of the universities. The electoral law was also amended to make coalitions difficult, and as the elections approached, the DP amended it once again to prevent the formation of a united opposition. As a result, fewer people went

[2] For a study of these changes in one specific community, see Joseph S. Szyliowicz, *Political Change in Rural Turkey: Erdemli* (The Hague: Mouton, 1966).

to the polls in 1957 (77 per cent of the electorate), and the DP was again victorious. Despite its diminished support (48 per cent of the vote), it elected 424 deputies out of a total of 610 as compared to 41 per cent and 178 seats for the CHP.

These results served to increase ill will between the various segments of society, many opposition leaders charging that the DP's victory was due to its manipulation of the electoral system. The growing bitterness between the two major parties—which by 1960 had become so severe that many observers believed the country to be on the verge of systemic change—was aggravated by shifts in the socioeconomic structure which had been occurring since 1946. Groups that had traditionally enjoyed high social status and a near monopoly of political power, such as the intellectuals and the bureaucracy, saw their positions seriously threatened by new groups (including, for example, landowners and businessmen) that had assumed leadership positions in the DP and had successfully mobilized the peasant electorate.

Nor did the former political elite approve of the economic and fiscal policies of the Menderes government. The peasantry's exemption from direct taxation placed a heavy burden upon the salaried classes, while their living standard was lowered owing to the inflation caused by the government's development program. And, as social status became more closely correlated with economic power, the prestige of the bureaucrats, the intellectuals, and, above all, the military, began to drop.

These developments were reflected in the changing composition of the membership of the Grand National Assembly. The official group (military and bureaucratic) which had been dominant diminished and was replaced by the representatives of such occupational categories as "trade," "agriculture," and the "free professions." This change has been described in the following words: "Along with the provincial lawyer, the small-town merchant or tradesman seems to typify the changed Assemblies of the Democratic Party's decade of control, just as the official and the officer typified the Kemalist epoch." [3] In other words, the reforms of Ataturk and the developments of that era led to the multiplication of elites and to latent

[3] Frederick W. Frey, *The Turkish Political Elite* (Cambridge: M.I.T. Press, 1965), p. 183.

competition between these elites, resulting, once the rules of the game were amended to permit open competition, in the victory of those who had hitherto played but a minor role in the national decision-making apparatus.

Unfortunately, the character of the country's leadership during this period did not permit these new patterns to evolve smoothly or be absorbed easily within the existing system. The government's lack of sensitivity extended to all aspects of modernization. Its priorities were not based on developmental requirements so that policies were often adopted solely on the basis of their popular appeal. Thus, though the DP government sought to develop the country and integrate the society, it actually polarized the populace to such an extent that systemic change became inevitable. For these developments, the opposition party, especially the traditional elites, also bear responsibility since their tactics contributed greatly to the erosion of democratic processes.[4]

Educational Developments in the DP Era

All these developments led to greatly increased demands for educational expansion throughout rural areas though the concern for education did not become evident overnight—as late as 1952 about half of all villagers were either indifferent or hostile to modern schools, and in terms of rural priorities, education was considered less important than improvements in agriculture, health, and credit facilities.[5] Such attitudes, which indicate the limited impact of the Ataturk reforms upon village life and the continuing strength of traditional values, soon began to change as economic, political, and social change came increasingly to characterize rural society. Not all parts of the country, however, were equally affected by these developments and some areas, notably eastern Turkey, continued to be characterized by a highly traditional way of life. Nevertheless, for the first time in the country's history an awareness of the importance and utility of education became widespread.

Besides spurring the growth of new demands in hitherto static

[4] Richard D. Robinson, *The First Turkish Republic: A Case Study in National Development* (Cambridge: Harvard University Press, 1963), p. 196.

[5] OECD Country Reports, *The Mediterranean Regional Project: Turkey* (Paris: Organization for Economic Cooperation and Development, 1965), pp. 61ff.

areas, the establishment of a competitive multiparty system also provided the structures through which these demands could be articulated and satisfaction obtained. No longer were townsmen and villagers at the mercy of a hated and despised administration; now they possessed the ability to make their voices felt and increasingly demanded schools as well as roads, clean drinking water, and mosques. As a result, this period witnessed a spectacular increase in the number of students enrolled in all schools.

Expansion at the middle and high levels occurred at a faster rate than at the primary; the number of primary students increased from 1,616,626 in 1950 to 2,866,501 in 1960 while the number of middle school students rose from 68,187 to 291,266, the number of *lycée* students from 22,169 to 75,632, and the number of college and university students from 24,815 to 65,297.[6] These impressive increases, however, obscure three serious weaknesses that characterized educational developments in this period. First, the political motivation of this expansion and the intrusion of political considerations into educational affairs did not permit the adoption and implementation of a systematic policy of educational expansion; second, the rise in student enrollments did not keep pace with the country's rapidly growing population or with manpower requirements; and third, expansion outstripped the expenditures that were devoted to education with unfortunate consequences for quality.

Political factors tended to dominate educational developments, and little evidence of any attempt to develop a coherent or pragmatic policy is available. None of the four persons who served as ministers of education in the fifties were primarily educators, and they were shuffled in and out of office rather frequently without providing the kind of strong leadership that education had enjoyed earlier. Moreover, the decision to open schools was often political and not based on objective criteria. To cite but one example, a secondary-level commercial school was not opened in the planned location owing to the personal intervention of the minister of finance who wanted the school located in another community.[7] Indeed, speed and lack of

[6] Andreas Kazamias, *Education and the Quest for Modernity in Turkey* (Chicago: University of Chicago Press, 1966), p. 271.

[7] Lester I. Bruckner, "History of Accounting Education in Turkey, 1923–60" (Ph.D. diss., New York University, 1965), pp. 304–305.

planning characterized educational policy. In 1953 twelve new middle schools were to open immediately, even though the school year had already begun. In 1959, four days before schools were to open, thirteen more schools were suddenly scheduled to be opened immediately. Similarly, on many occasions, *lycées* were opened after the school year had started in buildings already used by other schools and without adequate teachers or other facilities. A final indication of the planlessness of the government is provided by an analysis of the speeches and statements by government officials (including the minister of education), which reveals few indications of any coherent educational policy; most were limited to announcements of the number of schools to be opened.[8] In effect, as these illustrations indicate, the government merely reacted to whatever pressures were placed upon it; when demands were generated for more educational facilities new schools were opened, but the lack of a coherent philosophy and the absence of any advance planning seriously handicapped the educational expansion that did take place.

In three other matters involving education the government also reacted to popular pressure; it closed the village institutes, reintroduced religious teaching in the schools, and no longer enforced compulsory attendance requirements. These measures were to contribute to the alienation of many urban dwellers from the DP, which was attacked for having made concessions to reactionary elements. The question of religious instruction was, of course, a sensitive one, although after 1946, when opposition parties were established, the CHP government, in order to broaden its base of support, had relaxed somewhat the restrictions on religious teachings in the schools. In 1949–1950 a course on Islam was included in the fourth and fifth grades on a voluntary basis, and practically every primary school student took this course. After coming to power, the DP changed the regulation so that students could opt out of the course and opened secondary-level schools for training religious leaders—there were nineteen by 1958–1959—and established a Faculty of Theology in Ankara. In 1956 a course on Islam was introduced into the first two grades of the middle school, again on an opt-out basis.[9] All these

[8] Richard E. Maynard, "The Lise and Its Curriculum in the Turkish Educational System" (Ph.D. diss., University of Chicago, 1961), pp. 121; 192–194.

[9] *Ibid.*, pp. 72–73.

steps aroused much concern among intellectuals and others who viewed such policies as betraying Ataturk's principle of secularism and as disseminating values and orientations that were dysfunctional for modernization.

A second educational matter which aroused widespread indignation among the intellectuals and which also contributed greatly to their alienation from the DP government was the future of the village institutes, which were also considered a vital part of Ataturk's reforms. We have already pointed out (Chapter IV) that this experiment, which represented an imaginative and innovative way of dealing with rural education, contained significant deficiencies, but in the ideological ferment that swept Turkey after World War II, no serious consideration of its educational value or of the ways in which it could be strengthened was possible. In place of rational analysis, the populace rapidly polarized into two camps that hurled epithets at each other. On the one hand were most of the intellectuals who regarded the institute movement as a means whereby the Ataturk reforms could be extended to the rural areas. Opposed to them were many villagers who did not appreciate being forced to build schools without compensation and many members of the new groups that had coalesced in support of the DP, especially small-town professional and business elements. They regarded the experiment as a threat to a valued way of life and feared that their position in the rural areas would be undermined. In the eyes of many, the institutes were part of a Communist conspiracy designed to subvert the country and its heritage.[10] The result of this debate was that the institutes were merged in 1954 into the regular teachers' schools, thus closing the gap that had formerly existed between the graduates of the two types of institutions and at the same time destroying the unique characteristics and dynamism of the institutes.

A third decision that indicates the government's approach involved the relaxation of attempts to enforce compulsory attendance. The natural result was a sharp decline in the percentage of village girls enrolled in school as many families welcomed the opportunity to maintain a traditional way of life. In many cases parents viewed the education of women as morally undesirable, others were unwilling to

[10] Kemal H. Karpat, *Turkey's Politics: The Transition to a Multi-Party System* (Princeton: Princeton University Press, 1959), p. 372.

incur the expenses involved or to lose the work contribution of the child, and some did not recognize the utility of a terminal primary education.

Such policies indicate quite clearly the extent to which the government was responsive to rural opinion and was willing to sacrifice educational objectives, if necessary, to maintain popular support. Such calculations, however, proved to be very shortsighted, for the consequences of these decisions were most damaging in political, social, and economic terms, as well as for the educational process. Teacher morale dropped precipitously in the fifties, and the entire climate within the schools changed markedly. Many rural teachers, especially the graduates of the village institutes, had been truly dedicated and idealistic, but the government's educational decisions led to a growth in feelings of cynicism and self-aggrandizement with adverse consequences for the quality of education.[11]

At the same time that the government was following policies that were alienating intellectuals and teachers, it was attempting to meet the demand for education, but partly because of lack of planning, the increase in educational opportunities did not match the population growth. This marked the second major weakness of educational development in the fifties. Although the percentage of literates increased sharply from 33.5 per cent in 1950 to 43.7 per cent in 1960 (from 42 to 62 per cent for men, from 19.4 to 25.4 per cent for women), the total number of illiterates actually rose from 11,335,000 to 13,283,000 in the same period. Similarly, despite the rapid increases in primary school enrollments, the percentage of boys attending school rose but slightly from 81 to 84 per cent while the percentage of girl students actually dropped from 54 to 52 per cent. And, while the percentage of students continuing their studies rose sharply, from 21 per cent in 1948–1949 to 44 per cent ten years later, the primary school still provided a terminal education for well over half of all students enrolled (about 65 per cent of all girls).[12]

Thus, despite this unprecedented expansion at all levels, educational opportunities remained very restricted and only a small per-

[11] Robinson, *op. cit.*, pp. 196–197

[12] M. Nuri Kodamanoğlu, *Education in Turkey, 1923–1960* (Istanbul: Ministry of Education Printing Press, 1965), Graph 16, p. 34; Graph 21, p. 46; Table XVI, p. 48.

centage of the populace reached the pinnacle of the educational pyramid. The situation has been vividly summarized by one scholar: (a) Of 100 primary school students about thirteen can expect to enter a middle-level institution; fewer than 3 can expect to enter a *lycée,* about one can expect to enter a university. (b) Of 100 middle school students, about twenty-six can expect to enter a *lycée,* about fourteen can expect to enter a university. (c) Of 100 *lycée* students, about fifty-five can expect to enter a university, about eighty-six an institution of higher learning.[13] Nevertheless the 1950's did witness the opening of educational opportunities for large segments of the population which heretofore had not enjoyed them. This was especially true at the secondary level, which until now had been concentrated in Istanbul. In 1943–1944, 42 per cent of all *lycée* students were studying there, and a further 17 per cent in Ankara and Izmir. By the late 1940's, the percentage of students attending *lycées* in Istanbul had dropped to 33 per cent, and in the 1950's it declined even more markedly. Overall, the number of general secondary schools rose between 1950 and 1960, from 88 enrolling 21,440 students (of these 18,057 were attending the 59 public *lycées*) to 182 schools and 59,300 pupils (of these 52,400 were enrolled in the 130 public *lycées*).[14]

Unfortunately the expansion of educational opportunities was not related in any way to the country's manpower requirements. The percentage of students who took academic subjects in middle schools so as to prepare for a *lycée* education rose from 67 per cent in 1949–1950 to 84 per cent in 1959–1960. A similar tendency was apparent at the *lycée* level where the percentage of students preparing to continue their studies increased from 51.5 to 55.4 per cent; at the same time the percentage of students enrolled in technical and vocational fields dropped correspondingly.[15] Thus, although enrollments expanded rapidly, they did so in an unbalanced way, and the previous efforts to develop technical and vocational education were largely undermined.

The regular academic institutions also suffered during this period

---

[13] Kazamias, *op. cit.,* p. 171.

[14] Maynard, *op. cit.,* pp. 185–186; Kodamanoğlu, *op. cit.,* Graph 27, p. 72; OECD, *op. cit.,* Table 46, p. 143.

[15] Kodamanoğlu, *op. cit.,* Table XIX, p. 52; Table XXVI, p. 63.

because of the third major deficiency of the educational policy followed by the DP: Inadequate fiscal resources were allocated to education; expenditures rose by 35 per cent while enrollments were growing by 84 per cent. Not surprisingly, educational standards dropped precipitously. Thus, while middle-school enrollments quadrupled (the percentage of the 12–14 age group attending school rose from 7 per cent in 1949–1950 to 17 per cent in 1959–1960), the number of teachers did not begin to keep pace and the size of the classes rose significantly. Split shifts were commonplace, and even though heavy reliance was placed upon part-time teachers, the teacher-student ratio deteriorated from 1:20 in 1955 to 1:26 in 1962. *Lycée* education also suffered. While the number of students increased about threefold, the number of teachers only doubled, and output, as measured by the ratio of graduates to new entrants, fell from 84 to 64.[16] This period also witnessed a rapid expansion in university facilities from three universities in 1950 to six in 1960, but once again, as we shall see, expansion was not commensurate with the need as the number of students enrolled far exceeded available resources.

This period also witnessed another major change in Turkish education as close relations developed between the United States and Turkey, and American educational views, which were widely disseminated through both private and governmental sources, supplemented the existing European (especially French) heritage. Through numerous advisors assigned to the Ministry of Education by AID, interinstitutional cooperation with American universities, and support from the Ford and Rockefeller Foundations, a new stream of educational philosophy was introduced into the country, a stream that in many cases conflicted sharply with the views of administrators and educators who had been trained along European lines. Consequently a new cleavage was created among the staff in many bureaus and schools.

Under these conditions, the quality of education, which had improved during the Ataturk era, deteriorated rapidly in the 1950's, a situation that was obvious to all. One American educator, for example, after visiting a large number of schools, reported overcrowding in almost all primary schools. Many of them were operating on

[16] OECD, *op. cit.*, pp. 123, 78; Kodamanoğlu, *op. cit.*, Table XXII, p. 55, Table XXX, p. 68.

double or even triple shifts so that classroom periods had to be shortened, many school activities omitted, and teachers overworked. Not only were existing facilities badly strained, but most buildings were poorly designed and inadequately heated and lighted. Because heating was usually provided by one stove, the pupils near the stove tended to be too warm, the others too cold. Illumination was usually provided by one or two light bulbs dangling from the ceiling. No shades were utilized so the available light tended to be concentrated, thus subjecting students to great eyestrain.

Teachers, however, complained most, not about these physical deficiencies or the inadequacy of teaching materials and textbooks, but about their low salaries and status which limited their effectiveness in rural communities. Their income was not sufficient to provide them with an adequate standard of living, and most village teachers looked eagerly toward the possibilities of obtaining more lucrative employment elsewhere. Many did succeed in finding such positions, it being estimated that 50 per cent of the graduates of rural teacher-training programs did not become teachers. In urban areas, many teachers taught additional classes or secured outside positions to supplement their low salaries.

The situation at the secondary level was equally unsatisfactory. These facilities, though better than the primary schools, were also poorly heated and lighted and possessed inadequate equipment and libraries, especially for science instruction. The severe shortage of qualified teachers resulting from the rapid expansion had led to the employment of local professional persons on a part-time basis and the hiring of primary teachers, with obvious consequences for educational standards.[17]

All these deficiencies were also noted and severely criticized by Turkish educators and intellectuals who made such problems a matter of growing public concern. Severe charges were leveled by the political opposition to which the government, as in other areas, reacted with increasing sensitivity. As the political atmosphere grew steadily worse, the government published fewer data concerning education, especially from 1955 onward, and suppressed the em-

[17] George E. Hutcherson, "Report on Visit to Schools," typewritten (Ankara: AID, March 1959), *passim*.

barrassing report prepared by the National Commission on Education which had been established in 1958 with Ford Foundation support. Its text, which was not published until after the 1960 revolution, censured practically all aspects of the educational system. It discussed primary education as follows: "In order that our primary schools may better educate pupils, the size of the classes must be reduced and the system of two, three, or four teaching shifts, practiced at present in some places because of lack of buildings and teachers, must come to an end." Secondary education (first and second cycle) was criticized even more severely:

secondary educational institutions are most in need of attention and speedy reform. Most of these schools are inadequate as far as buildings, furniture, equipment and all kinds of teaching aids are concerned. Above all, teachers and administrative staff of these institutions are generally inadequate in quality and in numbers . . . it is also a fact that children finishing school under these conditions are well below the desired standard.

Similar criticisms were made of technical and vocational schools:

The buildings, workshops, laboratories, and even more so the teachers and teaching aids of some schools were not satisfactory. The existing administrative staff and teachers . . . were not of the desired number and quality . . . the schools were grossly overcrowded and . . . because of lack of space in the workshops the pupils were unable to gain the required degree of technical proficiency. The relationship between lessons in general subjects and technical lessons was not maintained, the study courses were inadequate, and there were no textbooks and lesson books suitable for these syllabuses. No advice and vocational guidance services had been set up in these institutions, and there was no cooperation with local industry.[18]

Higher Education and Student Activism

The most important consequence of the DP's educational policy, however, was not the precipitous decline in quality, but the alienation of the intellectual elite, including the university students, whose agitation led directly to the 1960 revolution.[19] To understand this

[18] *The Report of the Turkish National Commission on Education* (Istanbul: American Board Publication Department, 1961), pp. 49, 52, 59.
[19] The discussion and the data contained in this section are adapted from

development, it is necessary to review the changes in higher education which took place after World War II. Developments within the Turkish polity and society during this period had their counterparts in academia, and the Universities Law of 1946 granted autonomy to the universities; apart from some powers reserved to the minister of education, they were now free from government control. The management of university affairs was entrusted to academic bodies, and the universities were organized around independent faculties consisting, as in Germany, of a number of "chairs" in specific subjects. Unfortunately, the "chair" system and the process by which a faculty member was hired and advanced up the academic ladder proved extremely rigid and concentrated power in the hands of a few individuals within the faculties so that personal considerations came to be dominant factors in almost all aspects of university life. The administrative and control machinery which had been established soon proved ineffective in controlling the abuses that developed, since power and responsibility was vested within the individual faculties with the unfortunate result that the universities soon faced serious problems of morale and discipline with obvious consequences for the scholarly atmosphere so vital to the successful functioning of any institution of higher learning.

The administrative and organizational weaknesses were greatly aggravated by the explosion in enrollments which took place during this period. The government took the position that every *lycée* graduate was entitled to a university education and since, as we have seen, there was a great expansion in the number of *lycées,* great pressures were generated for increased admission to the universities. As in other countries of the Middle East, the natural sciences were able to resist the pressures for additional enrollments far better than the social sciences and the humanities, and though the total number of students increased from 20,000 in 1945 to over 53,000 in 1960, there was a marked imbalance in the growth of various fields. The percentage of students enrolled in the social sciences increased from

Joseph S. Szyliowicz, "Students and Politics in Turkey," *Middle Eastern Studies,* May 1970; and from my "A Political Analysis of Student Activism: The Turkish Case," *Sage Professional Papers in Comparative Politics,* vol. 3, no. 01–034, 1972).

44 per cent in 1949 to 50 per cent in 1959, whereas the percentage of those enrolled in scientific and technological fields declined from 44 per cent to 40 per cent of the total.

This unbalanced growth was due to two principal factors. First, since science education necessarily involved laboratory work and access to equipment of all sorts, a shortage of physical facilities was considered to be much more of a handicap to expansion than in other fields where the common medium of instruction is the lecture. Equally important, however, was the high prestige accorded to the social sciences, especially law, and the limited opportunities and low salaries available to graduates in basic scientific and technical fields.

The pattern of enrollments was also shaped by the vast discrepancies in quality between the different *lycées*. Students who graduated from those located in Ankara and Istanbul, especially the private ones, stood the best chance of gaining admission to the faculty of their choice. Thus the faculties with the greatest prestige, such as political science, received the best prepared students, largely children of educated, well-to-do, urban dwellers. This bias still largely exists. By and large the great majority of university students are recruited from middle- and upper-class parents who live in towns and cities. This is owing, of course, not only to the greater educational opportunities that exist in these places, but primarily to the fact that the demand for university education is still mainly derived from the "modern" segments of Turkish society.

The available data are limited, somewhat contradictory, and subject to varying margins of error, but they reflect this trend; from 34 to 54 per cent of the students at the University of Ankara are children of bureaucrats and army officers, and from 6 to 14 per cent are the children of professionals. Seventy per cent of those enrolled in the Political Science Faculty have a similar background. In Istanbul University, 29 per cent of the students are children of bureaucrats and army officers, 18 per cent of professionals. The remainder are primarily children of businessmen, merchants, and landowners.

It was precisely these groups who were most affected by the consequences of the government's policies. Not only were they opposed on ideological grounds, but the income of all on fixed salaries, especially government officials, army officers, and many intellectuals, declined greatly owing to inflation. Simultaneously their prestige also dropped as the new groups that were emerging within Turkish society quickly gained positions of power and influence. That these developments should have reinforced the antigovernment stance of the students who regarded the DP as endangering the economic development of the country, its democratization, and the Ataturk reforms is not surprising. Furthermore, many of the students were aiming for careers in the civil service, and they could see the prestige and financial rewards attached to such positions decline rapidly while the competition for the available posts was increasing as enrollments in the faculties swelled.

The expansion of teaching staffs did not nearly keep pace with the growth in the number of students, particularly in the social sciences. In this field the number of professors rose from 199 to 484 during this period, but the number of students per teacher climbed from 37 to 50. In the arts and sciences it dropped from 1:14 to 1:18, in the fine arts from 1:1 to 1:3, and in higher agricultural education from 1:7 to 1:10. In higher technical education and in health education it improved from 1:9 to 1:6 and from 1:15 to 1:6, respectively.

Many of the available staff members devoted a considerable amount of time to positions outside the university, despite a legal limitation on the time that can be devoted to supplementary positions. They did so mainly because of economic pressures (salaries of professors remained unchanged during the inflation which characterized the period from 1955 onward), but partly because prestige is gained most easily, not through teaching, but by nonacademic pursuits.

The lack of teaching staffs was also a major factor which hindered the attempt to develop new institutions at Izmir (Ege University, opened in 1955) and Erzerum (Ataturk University, opened in 1958) to cope with the growing enrollments. Not only was there an unfilled demand for faculty at the existing universities, but established faculty members were reluctant to move from Istanbul or Ankara and to leave the prestige of Istanbul University, Istanbul Technical University, or the University of Ankara. This problem was particularly acute, as we shall see, for Ataturk University, which experienced major staffing difficulties.

Another serious problem was the shortage of such physical facilities as classrooms and libraries. Despite the growth in law school enrollments, for example, from 4,217 in 1945 to 14,531 in 1960, the largest auditoriums, at Ankara and Istanbul universities, held only a few hundred persons, thus making it impossible for the majority of the students to attend any one lecture.

Throughout the universities, methods of instruction were formal and traditional and emphasized memorization—lectures often consisted merely of the exposition of a professor's book without any interpretation or opportunities for questions and discussion—in preparation for the examinations which were the only basis of success or failure. Three months out of the nine-month academic year were devoted to these examinations, which were often oral and in which the student was expected to demonstrate that he had memorized a certain set of facts contained in the lecture notes. Such a system rarely inspired even the serious student to attend classes or to study at any time except prior to the examinations, if then, because students were not required to take final examinations and were free to repeat a course as often as they wished. Nor was there any personal contact between teachers and students. Even if a faculty member had the inclination and time to meet with his students, there were few places where he could do so and usually there were far too many students to allow any genuine relationships to develop.

The limited emphasis upon written work by the student meant that libraries were seldom used. Here, too, facilities were inadequate both in terms of the number of books, their accessibility, the training of librarians, and the physical plant. To give but one illustration, the library of Istanbul University was housed in a building which was declared unsafe several years earlier, and only members of the academic staff could check books out, though senior students were allowed to make use of its facilities. In most libraries subject indexes were lacking and the filing was done by date of acquisition, thus making it very difficult for even the most dedicated researcher to locate needed materials.

Two other factors served to lower the quality of the universities during this period. First, the expansion of educational opportunities at the secondary level had similar unfortunate consequences, for the standard of *lycée* instruction was of very low quality in many schools, particularly the newer ones in remote areas. Thus, the universities found—and continue to find—that many students arrived ill-prepared for college work.

Second, the great demand for a university education was not always motivated by the desire of a student to obtain a degree. Many persons enrolled in whatever faculty happened to have space available, regardless of the subject, in order to avoid military service or to qualify for the many benefits a university student received. These included a 25 per cent discount for admission to movies, theatre, opera; a discount of from 33⅓ to 75 per cent for local transportation; and a 50 per cent reduction for all rail and sea travel within Turkey. In addition to these financial benefits must be considered the high prestige accorded to a university student, and many youths, especially from Anatolia, were eager to gain this status in the eyes of their families and friends.

Under these conditions it is not surprising that very few students graduated in four or five years, and the situation deteriorated considerably from 1946 onward. It was estimated, for example, that in 1946, 26 per cent of the students enrolled in the Law Faculty at Istanbul University successfully completed their course of study within five years, but by 1958 the figure had dropped to 8 per cent. The percentage of serious and successful students in the Faculty of Letters was even lower. It was estimated that between 1950 and 1958 only 15 per cent of the freshmen became sophomores and only 6 per cent of these graduated within five years. Even the elite Political Science Faculty suffered, the percentage of students passing without delay dropped from more than 75 per cent in 1955 to less than half in 1964.

Thus, being a university student became more than ever a frustrating experience. Only a very small number of youths became aware of the true meaning of higher education or developed an interest in genuine intellectual achievement. For the majority, being a student came to represent a way of life that had little relationship to the pursuit of knowledge, and as conditions within the universities deteriorated, so feelings of resentment and alienation became more and more prevalent. Students were also affected by the deteriorating economic and social conditions of student life which served to reinforce the general feeling of discontent and frustration generated by the academic environment. Very few students worked their way through college and only a small number of very inadequate fellowships were available. The great majority were totally dependent upon their families for their income and as a result of the inflation many families found themselves unable to provide their children with an adequate allowance, and the standard of living of most students, never high, dropped sharply.

As a result of such factors, university students, especially those in faculties with the worst academic climate and with the most gloomy perceptions of opportunities for future success, became politically active. Their activism was stimulated by the low legitimacy of the government and by their elitist training and orientation which led them to believe that they were the ones who, by a rigorous process of selection and training, were responsible for resolving the nation's problems. Further strengthening their strong feeling of elitism was the legacy of Ataturk. Every student was familiar with the conclusion of the famous seven-day speech in which Ataturk declared, "Turkish youth, your primary duty is ever to preserve and defend the National Independence, the Turkish Republic." Thus, all students considered themselves—and were considered by many to be—the guardians of the Ataturk revolution, a feeling which enhanced the legitimacy of student activism within the country.

The political scene continued to deteriorate as relations between the DP and the CHP became increasingly acrimonious. In mid-1959 a series of incidents raised the specter of civil war, and it began to appear as though the government were actually planning to eliminate all opposition to its rule. The natural result was to heighten further the opposition of students and faculty, and in mid-1960 the students were involved in an incident that precipitated the revolution of May 27. On April 28 and 29 at Istanbul and Ankara universities, student demonstrations against the policies of the government resulted in violent clashes with police. Although few students were actually injured, rumors swept like wildfire through both cities and martial law was declared immediately. The universities were closed, a step which merely served to disseminate news of these events throughout the country as students returned to their homes. With the country on the brink of civil war and the army forced into politics by a government seeking desperately to maintain itself in power, revolution was inevitable.

Rationalization, Planning, and Politics

The 1960 revolution marked a turning point in Turkey's educational development since the new military leaders all recognized that education was one of the major problems (most felt it to be the single most important problem) confronting the country. Different officers focused on different aspects; many were concerned with problems of rural education and most suggested that the village institutes be reopened, others emphasized the high rate of illiteracy that still prevailed, others problems of higher education, but all agreed that educational reform was essential and should be given a high priority.[20]

One of the first measures taken by the new government was the publication of the report of the National Commission on Education discussed earlier. A second was the establishment of the Reserve Officers Teaching Program to deal with the problem of rural education. Facilities were totally inadequate and a serious teacher shortage prevailed; Teacher-student ratios were estimated at 1:55 as compared to 1:42 in towns and cities in 1960. Dropout rates were also far higher in the villages; overall between 40 and 50 per cent of all students did not graduate from primary schools. In urban areas about 70 per cent of the first-year male students enrolled in the fifth class; in village schools only about 35 per cent did so.[21]

The program was designed to meet the teacher shortage by sending graduates of *lycées* and *lycée*-level technical and vocational schools into primary schools throughout the country. It also served to provide meaningful employment for graduates who could not easily be absorbed into the Reserve Officers Corps. To assess its utility, the participants were surveyed and the published results serve not only to provide insights into the effectiveness of the program, but also to highlight the educational problems confronting rural areas and the attitudes of the inhabitants toward education in general.[22]

[20] Walter F. Weiker, *The Turkish Revolution, 1960–61* (Washington: The Brookings Institution, 1963), pp. 118–120.

[21] OECD, *op. cit.*, p. 93; Kazamias, *op. cit.*, pp. 166–167.

[22] İbrahim Özgentaş, *Yedek Subay Öğretmenlere Uygulanan Anket Sonuçları* (Ankara: Milli Eğitim Bakanlığı, 1966), *passim*.

Few of the officers had any village experience, about two-thirds coming from towns and cities, but the vast majority, 82 per cent, were assigned to rural schools. Eighty per cent of the officers were under twenty-three years of age and none were trained teachers. Despite the fact that they would be engaging in a new profession in a strange environment, the officers were given little or no formal preparation, the average course lasting for a week or even less.

Such completely inadequate training clearly meant that totally unprepared persons were serving as rural teachers, but the quality of the educational experience that the officers were able to transmit was also indirectly affected, since more thorough preparation might have enabled them to integrate themselves into their communities more easily than proved to be the case in most instances; 40 per cent encountered frustrations in adjusting to rural life, 67 per cent experienced difficulties in dealing with the people.

Besides inadequate preparation, the actual facilities that were available created many problems for the neophyte teachers. Sixty-five per cent of the officers were located in a one- or two-room school, and 22 per cent held classes in the mosque, a village house, a room, or even a hut. Twenty-nine per cent of the teachers reported they had had less than half of the desks and chairs that they needed, and half of the instructors lacked the most basic teaching aids and equipment. And between 25 and 47 per cent did not receive the brochures, books, and pamphlets that were supposedly sent to all teachers by the Ministry of Education's in-service training department. As we shall show later, problems of administration and supervision comprise a major bottleneck hindering the development of education in Turkey today.

Despite such frustrations, the officers' responses to the survey were also indicative of the demand for education in rural areas. Sixty-eight per cent reported that the villagers were considerably interested in the schools' activities. When discussing dropouts, only 5 per cent attributed this problem to the fact that parents did not believe in the utility of the school, 75 per cent said it was due to the family's need for the child's labor, another 5 per cent attributed it to poverty.

It seems safe to conclude, therefore, that, like most programs of its kind, this experiment had its greatest impact outside the educational sphere. Though it is obvious that the educational benefits to rural Turkey were not particularly great, the side effects of this program should not be underestimated, notably its contribution to the further narrowing of the rural-mass gap. A large number of urban youths were exposed to the realities of village life in general and to the problems of rural education in particular. Though the results of such exposure are difficult to measure, one study has pointed out that following their experience about half of the reserve officers indicated that they would like to remain teachers, whereas only about 15 per cent of all *lycée* graduates selected teaching as a career.[23]

Of more lasting significance was a third policy decision of the military government: to systematize planning. A planning board was established within the Ministry of Education and an agreement signed with OECD in 1961 to establish an educational planning group as part of the Mediterranean Regional Project. This was placed within the newly established State Planning Organization. In 1962 a national convention met to discuss the report of the National Commission on Education and the activities of the planning board.[24]

The fundamental approach of both the Mediterranean Regional Project and of the two five-year plans that followed, the first for 1963–1967, the second for 1968–1972, was one of manpower projections. Future requirements for skilled personnel in various fields were estimated and the output of the educational system was then examined to determine the extent to which professional and technical manpower requirements would, in fact, be met by the existing institutional arrangements. These studies quickly revealed the fundamental imbalances, weaknesses, and limitations of the existing structure. Secondary-level training could provide only one-third of the graduates required by 1977, and universities and colleges only one-half of the estimated demand. Administratively and structurally, the major constraints were:

the lack of mobility between the various branches of the system. The shortage of places in primary and lower secondary education, and the

---

[23] Leslie L. Roos, Jr., and George W. Angell, Jr., "New Teachers for Turkish Villages: A Military-Sponsored Educational Program," *Journal of Developing Areas,* 2 (July 1968), 530.

[24] Nuri Eren, *Turkey Today—And Tomorrow* (New York: Praeger, 1963), p. 189.

rigid distinction between the professional and the general branches in secondary education, restricted a potentially beneficial flow between the two. There is also a lack of terminal choice inherent in the present system. In higher education, pure and applied sciences, health and agriculture lag behind the social sciences.[25]

The educational section of the first five-year plan, which made projections for a fifteen-year period, was designed to correct such weaknesses and to gear the schools to the manpower needs of the country. In the drive to modernize, education was assigned the fundamental role, and the plan established two priorities: the universalization of primary education by 1972 and the improvement of technical and vocational training at the secondary and higher levels. The percentage of students at the secondary level who were studying technical and vocational subjects was scheduled to rise dramatically and a similar shift was envisaged at the university and college level. Qualitatively the plan sought to give priority to a reduction in the high student-teacher ratios at all levels and to various efforts designed to upgrade the quality of education.[26]

The decision to expand primary education so as to enroll every child in that age group by 1972 was established on social and political grounds. It was felt that primary education was a fundamental requirement for all people in a democratic society and that primary schools represented an important channel for disseminating modernity throughout the country. To solve the problems of rural communities with too small a population to support a school (about 13.5 million people live in more than 22,000 such settlements) and to overcome the marked disparities between urban and rural, east and west, and male and female enrollments, the policy of establishing regional boarding schools was adopted.[27]

Such a priority, though justifiable on the grounds of social justice

[25] OECD, *op. cit.*, pp. 20, 21.

[26] *First Five Year Development Plan, 1963–1967* (Ankara: Republic of Turkey, Prime Ministry State Planning Organization, 1963), pp. 411ff; hereafter referred to as *First Plan*.

[27] Kodamanoğlu, *op. cit.*, Table VII, p. 12. *Second Five Year Development Plan, 1968–1972* (Ankara: Republic of Turkey, Prime Ministry State Planning Organization, 1969), p. 182; hereafter referred to as *Second Plan*.

and equal opportunity, could be severely criticized in terms of the resources that would have to be allocated thereto and the dangers of further decline in an already low quality of education. Specifically, the decision to universalize primary education meant that the number of students enrolled at this level would rise from 3.4 million in 1962 to 6.8 million in 1977, that an estimated 140,000 additional primary teachers would be required, that primary-teacher-training institutes would have to increase their output by 78 per cent from 1963 to 1977, that an additional 81,300 classroom units would have to be provided (though in 1963 a shortage of 25,000 classrooms already existed) and that 37 per cent of the total educational budget would be diverted to this level.[28] These resources would have to be provided merely to accommodate the projected expansion and would not affect existing patterns in any way.

The political consequences of the program, however, may prove quite significant in view of the marked regional imbalance—the availability of schools decreases rapidly as one moves from the western to the eastern part of Turkey, where a large percentage of the population is not of Turkish background. The greatest educational opportunities exist in the eleven northwestern provinces; the lowest in eleven eastern and southeastern areas. These differences are qualitative as well as quantitative; the best-qualified teachers, the greatest staff ability, the highest salaries, are generally to be found in the western section of the country; the least-qualified teachers, the highest turnover, the lowest salaries, in the eastern region. Yet it is the east that is least endowed with facilitators of good schools as determined by such indexes as percentage of urban population, density of population, and percentage of population with Turkish as mother tongue.[29] To provide equality of opportunity under these conditions requires larger investments than in other parts of the country, but these may contribute greatly to the process of national integration.

Nevertheless, serious questions remain concerning the costs of universalizing primary education. In view of the existing qualitative

[28] *Ibid.*, Table 362, p. 406; OECD, *op. cit.*, pp. 109–110.
[29] Jefferson N. Eastmond, *Educational Opportunity in Turkey, 1964* (Ankara: Ministry of Education Research and Measurements Bureau, June 1964), Table 27, p. 48; pp. 5a, 6a.

problems confronting rural education, the benefits to be gained, educationally and developmentally, are likely to be small since it is likely that the planned expansion will merely provide the opportunity for more youngsters to partake of a low-quality educational experience with little relationship to their needs. Thus, the political gains that may well be derived from the universalization of a low-quality, nonfunctional educational experience are not likely to offset the considerable expenditures involved, expenditures which could well have been allocated to programs designed to upgrade and revitalize the existing primary system and to implement the Report of the National Commission on Education which had recommended an emphasis upon middle and higher educational opportunities for rural children to alleviate the low rate of functional literacy among the graduates of the village schools.[30]

Furthermore, without such an emphasis, one could easily foresee that new, irresistible demands would be generated for expansion of the higher levels beyond projected targets. Hence the more successful the government proved to be in achieving its quantitative goals for primary education, the smaller the possibility of maintaining the already low standards of the higher levels, since great political pressures would be generated to force the abandonment of enrollment targets for the middle schools and the *lycées*.

Such pressures could be controlled only by a strong government confident of its legitimacy and strength within the country, but the political scene following the revolution was not conducive to that kind of leadership. The decision by the military to return power to civilian hands after a frustrating year-and-a-half of attempting to legitimize the coup and deal with the many serious problems confronting the country occurred in a society that remained split along essentially the same lines as in the late 1950's. On one side were the groups who had supported the DP and who now voted for the AP (Justice party), essentially a continuation of the former party; on the other those who had welcomed the revolution. Several coalition governments were formed, characterized by lack of cohesion and leadership, and in the 1965 election the AP swept into power with 53 per cent of the vote

[30] *Report of the Turkish National Commission on Education,* pp. 45ff.

as compared to 29 per cent for the CHP.[31] Thus, from 1960 onward, weak coalitions that tended to be inactive on the major problems confronting the country were the norm. And the success of the AP in winning a majority of the deputies, 240 out of 450, did not result in the emergence of the kind of strong, positive leadership that was so vitally needed.

Headed by Suleyman Demirel, a former engineer, the AP consisted of a heterogeneous coalition of conservative and liberal elements with conflicting goals and aspirations for control of the party. For several years Mr. Demirel was able to balance these forces and to retain the confidence of the military. The country enjoyed a fairly rapid rate of economic growth and much progress was made in expanding and diversifying the economy. At the same time a genuine spirit of democracy flourished and all shades of opinion were freely expressed.

Despite these advances, the country did not enjoy the kind of dynamic, farsighted leadership that was required if rapid development were to be achieved within a democratic framework. Pragmatic considerations over the position of different groups within the polity and the acquisition and retention of political power became dominant, often at the expense of the requirements of modernization. Seeking to maintain and strengthen its position the government neglected various important problem areas that represented constraints upon development because of the political costs involved in challenging existing patterns and entrenched interests. Despite their accuracy such calculations proved to be shortsighted, and Mr. Demirel found himself increasingly subject to criticism, not only from his opponents, but from former supporters as well. Conditions deteriorated rapidly, aggravated by a steady inflation and other economic difficulties, and concern with the pace and direction of development became more and more widespread and opposition more and more radical.

In this environment student activism once again emerged as a major political force. Students had remained active following the 1960 revolution, for the factors making for student frustration and alienation

---

[31] See J. S. Szyliowicz, "The Turkish Elections: 1965," *Middle East Journal,* 20 (Autumn 1966), 473–494. For later developments see J. M. Landau, "Turkey from Election to Election," *World Today,* April 1970, pp. 156–166, and M. Hyland, "Crisis at the Polls: Turkey's 1969 Elections," *Middle East Journal,* 24 (Winter 1970), 1–16.

which we have already discussed remained unresolved. Demands for university reform continued to be raised by students through this period, and in 1968 a series of strikes, boycotts, and demonstrations affected all the universities. The students demanded reforms in various areas and spokesmen for a variety of faculties expressed their dismay at the gloomy future prospects that they faced upon graduation. The sixties, however, witnessed a basic change in the character and orientation of student activism, for as political tensions rose and cleavages within the polity became ever deeper, the democratic character of the society ensured that these cleavages would be reflected among the students. They became ever more polarized and radicalized and questions of university life were soon supplemented by ideological issues. One observer who is well acquainted with the Turkish educational system has suggested that it contributes to predilections for ideological solutions:

The graduates of Turkish schools are not discriminating in their approach to facts. . . . The tendency to seek simple black-or-white answers to complex questions, instead of recognizing that truth is frequently gray, seems to be [a] consequence of the oversimplified right-or-wrong approach followed in Turkish instruction.

The present appeal of Marxism to Turkish youth, although partly due to youthful idealism and partly due to the circumstance that it was for a long time taboo and therefore seems especially daring, is also in part attributable to the fact that it claims to provide authoritative black-or-white answers to all the problems of society.[32]

Whatever the reasons, by 1968 students were not only highly politicized and polarized but relied increasingly upon violence to achieve their ends. Both extreme leftists and rightists, organized with the support of various political actors, often engaged in violent confrontation. One bloody incident occurred on February 16, 1969, in conjunction with the scheduled visit of the United States Sixth Fleet to Istanbul when a massive demonstration, organized by radical students and trade unions, collided with right-wing elements. Several persons were killed and over 200 wounded, many seriously. This tragedy had a

---

[32] E. J. Cohn, *Turkish Economic, Social, and Political Change,* Praeger Special Studies in International Economics and Development (New York: Praeger, 1970), pp. 110–111.

sobering effect upon everyone concerned, but the approaching general election made it inevitable that violence would erupt once again, and by the end of the year eight youths had been killed in a series of incidents involving extremist student groups.[33]

The 1969 election and its aftermath did not ease the tense political atmosphere. Though the AP was returned to power with a majority of the seats in the Assembly, it won only a minority of the popular vote and shortly thereafter Suleyman Demirel, for personal and political reasons, formed a cabinet without the representation of any members of the right wing of his party. A governmental crisis ensued as forty-one AP deputies voted against the budget. Mr. Demirel, after a one-month hiatus, was able to form a new government with the support of some minor parties and independents, but the political scene remained highly unstable as the government's majority shrank from 259 seats out of 450 to 234. Students contributed greatly to political turmoil, and in the first seven months of the year thirty were killed or injured in various clashes, demonstrations, boycotts, and strikes. Agitation and violence were not limited to students, however, and numerous strikes by other groups, including the police, took place. The unrest reached a climax on June 16, 1970, when a riot in Istanbul involving an estimated 70,000 leftist students and workers who were taking part in a demonstration against proposed labor legislation left four persons killed and over 100 injured before the army could restore order. Martial law was imposed for three months.[34]

In early 1971 the government moved to halt the anarchy by introducing stringent new legislation designed to curb revolutionary activities by students and others, but in March, confronted with increasing pressures by radical elements within and without the armed forces, senior officers decided that if Turkey were to remain a democratic society and to achieve its potential, new civilian leadership was required. They issued an ultimatum calling for the resignation of the Demirel government, and shortly thereafter the first, in what proved to be a series of coalition governments, was formed by Nihat Erim.

Educational factors played a major role, directly and indirectly, in

[33] All papers, Feb. 17, 18, 19, 1969; Newsletter #4, p. 1.
[34] *New York Times,* Aug. 5, 1970; all papers, June 17, 18, 19, 1970.

the downfall of Prime Minister Demirel. The universities were strong-holds of opposition and even of revolutionary activity, and despite some signs that fragmentation, violence, and extreme politicization resulted in the diminished effect of student activism, different factions helped create, once again, a political situation where military inter-vention became inevitable. Moreover, education represented one of the many social and economic sectors where the necessity for funda-mental change was ignored for far too long; as a result many dysfunc-tional aspects were further entrenched, the pace and direction of change was deeply affected, and the legitimacy of the government was seriously weakened. Particularly condemned by many intellectuals was the emergence of a separate school system to train religious leaders. The proliferation of these institutions (by 1967, 30,159 students were receiving a religious education),[35] was widely regarded as a betrayal of the principle of secularism and served to sharpen cleavages within the society. Not surprisingly one of the first specific educational re-forms announced by the Erim government was the elimination of this educational dualism.

Ultimately the reluctance of the government to confront the many aspects of its policy in education and other fields that strained the social fabric in this manner is attributable to the primacy of political over developmental requirements which characterized the Demirel government, though it must be noted that positive leadership was not always forthcoming from other groups or forces either. The most ob-vious manifestation of this situation is to be found in the way in which planning was carried out. Despite the emphasis upon rationalization, the expectations and goals of the planners often remained on paper, for, as the authors of one study pointed out: "The State Planning Or-ganization is not deeply enough involved in the political and policy structure . . . to give effect to the many changes suggested to increase efficiency and improve resource allocation." [36] The resulting ineffi-

[35] "Report on Educational Development in 1967–1968," presented to the XXIst Session of the International Conference on Public Education, mimeo. (Ankara: Ministry of Education, National Council of Education, July 1968), p. 20; hereafter referred to as "Report, 1967–1968."

[36] Lester B. Pearson, ed., *Partners in Development* (New York: Praeger, 1969), p. 322.

ciency and waste aggravated serious social and economic problems and contributed greatly to heightened criticism, opposition, and tension within the country and ultimately to the decision of the military to intervene.

Educational policy reflected such considerations, and serious concern with the functioning of the system or with the character of the changes that were occurring did not become evident among policymakers until the end of the decade. Throughout the sixties quality was again sacrificed for quantity as governments proved unwilling to deny schooling to anyone and acceded to popular demands with little regard for the consequences or the calculations of the planners. This was particularly true of postprimary academic institutions where, as we shall see, standards fell markedly at all levels. At the primary level the goals of the first five-year plan were reached, 90 per cent of all children from seven to twelve years of age, about five million students, being enrolled by 1968. Subsequently, however, the rate of increase slowed below projected targets; in 1971–1972, 5,120,000 students were enrolled instead of the anticipated 5.78 million. Here, too, the natural corollary of quantitative success was qualitative failure. Between 1960 and 1965, for example, the teacher-student ratio changed from 1:46 to 1:48 in rural areas, and from 1:41 to 1:45 in towns and cities, even though the production of teachers rose by 30 per cent and 40 per cent respectively in the same period.[37]

Contributing greatly to the dysfunctionality of primary education was an obsolete, rigid, irrelevant, and impractical curriculum which was condemned by the second plan in the following words: "The curricula at the primary school level do not conform with environmental conditions, the basic principles of education or the objectives of work and play. The village primary schools do not have the characteristics of an educational and cultural centre." [38] To remedy these defects a new curriculum, based on modern educational principles, was introduced. Major changes include the addition of seventy minutes more of instruction daily, the adoption of the concept of block

[37] *Second Plan*, p. 178; The data for 1971–1972 were provided by the Turkish Educational Attaché in New York from figures prepared by the Ministry of Education; hereafter referred to as "Educational Attaché."

[38] *Second Plan*, p. 178.

time replacing the fixed period so as to make the program more flexible in terms of topics and children's needs, the consolidation of topics so as to eliminate the previous pattern of too many isolated subjects (fourteen lessons have been collapsed into five groups), and the provision of a general outline within which the course of study can be related to the particular environment of the school so as to adjust the curriculum to local characteristics. In fact, primary education now begins with a study of the environment. Improved teaching methods are emphasized throughout, particularly observation, experimentation, and group activities. The authors of the new program have also attempted to utilize published materials for in-service training. The teachers' guide carefully elaborates the purposes of the program, its general principles, the methods and techniques to be used, and includes a section on child psychology and its relationship to education. The new program also provides specific guidance to teachers in one-room schools and those on double shifts.[39] That the new curriculum with its emphasis upon modern, rational, and scientific principles is a vast improvement over the previous one is unquestioned, but it is unlikely that its adoption will lead to significant changes, since qualitative improvements are dependent upon many interrelated factors which remain to be tackled. Nevertheless, if teachers conscientiously read the guide and attempt to follow its principles—a difficult task for many in view of their poor training—some upgrading in primary education may be evident.

The problems that characterized education at the higher levels are similar to those of primary education, but they were aggravated by the very success of the government in achieving its quantitative goals for primary schooling. Inexorably additional strains were placed upon the postprimary academic institutions as thousands of graduates sought admission. Given the character of the polity, enrollments simply could not be limited to planned targets and the number of students continuing their education rose sharply.

Education at the first cycle of the secondary level has traditionally consisted of two types: the general, which prepares students for further academic training, and the vocational and technical, which pro-

---

[39] *İlkokul Programı* (İstanbul: Milli Eğitim Basimevi, 1968), pp. 265ff.

vides students with some practical training. The number of students in the vocational stream has always been very small, though the percentage rose from 7 per cent in 1939–1940 to 17 per cent in 1959–1960. As in Egypt, it became evident that a meaningful vocational training could not be provided at this level, and it was decided to transform the vocational schools into general middle schools (except for the village midwives' school and the first level of the religious schools). All other vocational schools accepted no new students in the 1968–1969 academic year and are being phased out.[40]

Most students have always enrolled in the general middle school, which is almost the only channel for further academic training and which, as a result of the explosion in enrollments in the fifties, had already experienced a precipitous decline in quality. To prevent the further erosion of this level, the first plan proposed that the number of students rise slowly; the percentage of the age group attending was to climb by only 1 per cent during the period and enrollments by about 100,000 in each plan period to 480,000 in 1967 and 593,000 in 1972. In fact, these targets were greatly exceeded, total enrollments reaching 682,000 by 1968. The second plan revised all projections sharply upward, and planners now anticipate that the percentage of school age children enrolled will increase to 50 per cent by 1972 (instead of the earlier projected 20 per cent) and that the actual number of students will reach 1,331,000 by 1972. As at the primary level, however, these projections are not being met; in 1971–1972 enrollments totaled 946,592.[41]

Such a slowdown in enrollments may be a healthy sign, for in the sixties soaring enrollments were again accompanied by dropping standards as already crowded facilities were strained more than even before. The number of students per teacher rose from 26:1 in 1962 to 42:1 in 1966. Similarly, the percentage of students successfully completing each year's schooling fell sharply from 70 per cent in 1960 to 50 per cent in 1965.[42]

The experiences of the middle schools were essentially replicated

[40] OECD, *op. cit.*, p. 77; *Second Plan*, p. 184.

[41] *First Plan*, Table 359, p. 404; *Second Plan*, Table 86, p. 183. The percentages are calculated from data in *First Plan*, Table 359, p. 404, and *Second Plan*, Table 86, p. 183; "Educational Attaché."

[42] *Second Plan*, p. 178; OECD, *op. cit.*, Table 40, p. 140.

at the high school level. Attempts to expand vocational and technical training were not particularly successful, whereas the projected enrollment targets in the academic institutions were greatly surpassed. The plan had emphasized the restructuring of education to favor technical and vocational education at the expense of general training. Specifically it was intended that the number of students studying vocational and technical subjects at this level would rise from 38 per cent of the total in 1963 to 54 per cent in 1967 and 61 per cent in 1972, but these targets simply could not be met in view of the continuing strength of traditional social and cultural factors which emphasized the attraction of academic training and downgraded vocational and technical education. As a result, the targets of the second plan had to be revised drastically downward. It was anticipated that the percentage of students receiving such training in 1972 would amount to 40.8 per cent of the total, and this goal was in fact reached.[43]

Although these schools never operated at full capacity, few efforts were made to deal with their many weaknesses; of every 100 graduates from the girls' technical schools, for example, twenty-four continued their education, forty-one were not employed, and most of the thirty who did obtain a position were "working in jobs unrelated to their vocation." This situation was typical of all technical and vocational schools. In the words of the planners:

Problems . . . are the inability of the graduates to adapt themselves to working life even though they have acquired the proper theoretical knowledge, the lack of facilities which would prepare them for working life during academic years, the inability of schools to follow developments in industry because of the lack of a specialty of ties between industry and education, the lack of confidence of employers in the capability of these graduates, the uncertainty about wages and the extent of authority and responsibility of these employees. The . . . productivity rates among the various branches of technical institutes is between 30 and 55%. . . . In vocational schools of high school level (agriculture and hygiene) the productivity is satisfactory. However, the graduates of agricultural schools generally become white collar workers and this is not the purpose of

---

[43] *First Plan*, Table 360, p. 405; *Second Plan*, Table 98, p. 194; "Educational Attaché."

these schools. The quality of high level technical schools is not different from that of technical institutes.[44]

To increase the attractiveness of vocational and technical schools, existing restrictions that keep graduates of these institutions from continuing their education are scheduled to be lifted. Accordingly, under the second five-year plan, graduates will be encouraged to continue in their specialty after a training period to upgrade their skills to the college level. To improve quality, new programs are to be developed, and a closer working relationship will be established with industry.[45] How successful these efforts will be remains to be seen. Even if quantitative targets can be met, however, it is doubtful whether adequate human and physical resources will be available to prevent further qualitative difficulties.

While the enrollment targets for vocational and technical schools could not be achieved, those for the academic secondary institutions were vastly exceeded. The number of students, which was supposed to amount to 107,000 in 1967, actually reached about 170,000 in that year, and once again the projections of the planners had to be increased to 360,000 in 1972, more than double the previously anticipated figure of 168,000. Once again the rate of growth slowed and enrollments in 1971–1972 amounted to only 282,000. Here, too, such a trend is promising, for in the sixties the inability of the government to resist popular pressure produced a marked decline in standards as classrooms became more overcrowded and inadequately trained teachers were recruited. As a palliative, institute and college graduates without formal preparation for teaching are used, and it would be helpful to study the effectiveness of this approach in the other countries that have resorted to similar devices.[46]

Such fields as modern languages, mathematics, and the natural sciences remain especially in need of teachers, and there are many statistical indications of the ways in which quality in all fields has declined. To cite only two, the teacher-student ratio dropped to 1:33 in

[44] *Second Plan,* pp. 178–179.
[45] *Ibid.,* p. 191.
[46] *First Plan,* Table 359, p. 404; *Second Plan,* Table 88, p. 184; "Educational Attaché."

1966, the percentage of students passing each class fell from 62 per cent in 1960 to 49 per cent in 1965. To reverse this trend the second plan envisages a decrease in the number of students per class and an increase in the number of teachers and programs of in-service training. The extent to which these improvements were realized while the number of students increased from 170,000 in 1968 to 282,000 in 1971–1972 is not clear.[47]

Even if these qualitative targets were met, however, it is not likely that secondary education will be functional to development until it is restructured along modern lines.

One vitally needed reform involves curriculum revision. The present scheme, as elsewhere, is based on memorization, with little relevance to either individual or societal needs. Among the most criticized areas is science instruction, which is one of the weakest fields at the secondary level. To remedy this deficiency, a project for science education was funded by the Ford Foundation in 1963 to make preparations for the opening of a pilot science *lycée* where modern methods would be utilized to train selected students. New textbooks and teaching materials were prepared by a team of science teachers and introduced in the new school beginning in 1964. On the basis of these experiences, the mathematics text in general use was subsequently revised and a series of conferences on mathematics teaching were held. A modified version of this program was adopted in 1967 in a number of schools and a five-week course was held for the teachers who would be involved. Responsibility for the further refinement and implementation of the science-teaching project has been vested in the Scientific Commission for the Development of Science Teaching in Turkey, which has sponsored a number of research and publication projects in this field. It is anticipated that the new science curriculum that is developed will, in the coming years, be applied in all secondary schools in the country. The remaining parts of the secondary curriculum, as well as the entire middle school program, are also to be revised.[48]

Curriculum reform was but one of the areas of educational change

[47] *Second Plan,* pp. 178, 185; Table 88, p. 184.
[48] "Report, 1967–1968," pp. 32ff.

that came to occupy policy-makers by the end of the sixties as dissatisfaction with the existing system became more and more marked. Student activism and teacher militancy further emphasized the need for change, and toward the end of the decade the government undertook a review of the entire educational enterprise. In July 1970 the minister of education stated that secondary education, first and second cycle, would be restructured so that its function would no longer be, as it had always been, to prepare students for the university, but rather to train students in a variety of useful skills. This change included channeling students away from the academic stream into secondary technical and vocational schools. In this manner it was hoped that students who did not continue their education after middle school would be able to integrate themselves more meaningfully into the society, that the demand for middle-level manpower would be met, and the pressures for admission to *lycée* and university reduced.[49]

The impact of this particular innovation is unclear, but there are hints that educational reform is being accorded a high priority by the military leaders, who used stringent measures to end the anarchy in the universities and throughout the country. They have made it quite clear that they expect the civilian leadership to sponsor major changes in various fields, but to secure agreement on specific reform proposals has not been an easy matter and has led to continuing political maneuvering and the breakup of several coalitions. Nevertheless the military appears committed to the enactment of appropriate legislation and to the maintenance of democratic processes, and it appears that changes in education and other areas will be forthcoming before the elections scheduled for October 1973. The kinds of educational reforms that are envisaged are indicated by the program of the first coalition government formed after the military intervention, which stated that "the system based on separate religious education will be terminated and it will be integrated into the secular educational system. The situation of university teachers will be improved, technical education will be broadened, and experimental schools started with the aim of eventually extending compulsory education to eight years." [50] Other areas in which reforms are projected include the state

[49] *Cumhuriyet,* July 11, 1970.

[50] *Turkish Digest* (published in Washington, D.C., by the Turkish Embassy, 1971) VII (1971), nos. 1, 2, 3.

economic enterprises, land ownership patterns, taxation and finance, the judicial system, and the administration.

The Administrative Context

The concern evidenced with administrative reform is highly promising, for the changes outlined above cannot be implemented successfully unless change is forthcoming in the existing administrative structure. The centralized nature of the educational system requires that any change be initiated by the Ministry of Education, which is responsible for establishing curriculae, selecting and publishing teaching materials and texts, appointing and supervising teachers and administrators, and financing the entire enterprise. The minister of education is assisted by three undersecretaries: one for general education, one for cultural affairs, one for technical and vocational education. Under their direction are a very large number of directorates-general responsible for various aspects of education.

Despite its expansion and its imposing new quarters, the Ministry today functions much as it did in earlier times when the lack of educational progress could be largely attributed to its deficiencies. In the late 1950's, for example, the National Commission stated:

Today the educational and executive departments of the central organization of the Ministry of Education, instead of being concerned with their proper task, namely the basic problems of implementing the country's education, are occupied and often overwhelmed with individual problems such as appointments, transfers, promotion, and discipline and day to day questions.[51]

Similarly, the Mediterranean Regional Project pointed out that the Ministry had simply grown over time without any attempt at functional rationalization. Thus the delegation of authority was not clearly defined and authority was not commensurate with responsibility. Overall, the Ministry was so highly centralized that even routine decisions had to be approved at high levels, a practice resulting in marked delays.[52]

Despite such criticisms, no significant changes had taken place by the late sixties, and the author of a recent study concluded that: (1)

---

[51] *Report of the Turkish National Commission on Education,* p. 127.
[52] OECD, *op. cit.,* pp. 100–101.

structurally the Ministry is top-heavy and is characterized by rigidity, duplication, and competition between various practically independent units. (2) All authority is concentrated in the hands of the Minister and the undersecretaries who are appointed, not on the basis of professional or administrative experiences, but usually on political grounds. (3) Decision-making and policy-implementation and termination are not rational procedures. (4) The two advisory bodies to the Ministry, the National Council of Education, which meets once every four years, and the permanent Board of Education, are weak and ineffective bodies. (5) The Ministry is characterized by inertia, a tendency to defend the status quo, and "various pathologies of authority, such as authority without competence, overemphasis, exaggerated aloofness, and insulation from criticism." [53]

That these deficiencies characterize a highly centralized system means that it is impossible to innovate in any school. Not only are problems of communication practically insurmountable (three weeks are required for a Ministry directive to reach an urban school, four weeks to get to a rural one, and even longer for a message to travel from a school to the Ministry), but all changes must be approved at the highest levels. To attempt change in a particular school without obtaining formal consent is impossible since principals possess only limited decision-making powers and inspectors enforce established patterns.

Nor are the personnel policies of the Ministry conducive to the development and maintenance of a highly qualified and dedicated corps of teachers. Decisions to transfer teachers from rural to urban areas or to retain one in a particular location are frequently determined in terms of rewards and punishments. The most important criterion affecting promotions and assignments is seniority, and inadequate recognition is given to ability or quality of training. Because most teachers naturally prefer the comforts of towns and cities, they teach in rural areas only when compelled to do so. In some cases favorable locations have been sold at a profit. Thus the newest,

[53] Ziya Bursalioğlu, "The Need for Reorganization in the Turkish Educational System," in *Education as a Factor of Accelerated Economic Development* (Istanbul: Economic and Social Studies Conference Board, 1966), pp. 314–321. On the functioning of the bureaucracy in general, see Cohn, *op. cit.*, pp. 85–99; on the Ministry of Education see pp. 107–108, 113–114.

youngest, and most poorly prepared teachers are to be found in rural areas.

Inspection, supervision, and evaluation are carried out by poorly trained personnel, and their numbers are far too limited to provide any significant inputs for the classroom teacher. At present, about 1,000 elementary school supervisors work, on an average, with about 100 teachers each. Most of these are located in urban centers, some in villages. In most provinces, however, only one or two vehicles are available to the director of education for all purposes, so that even when access is possible (and in the east many communities are often isolated in the winter for extended periods) the supervisor has difficulty in reaching the community.[54]

When an inspector or supervisor does arrive, his visit is regarded with fear and trepidation. Most of his time is taken up, not in an evaluation or guidance, but in acting as an accountant, supervisor, and coroner, so that most are viewed as a "hatchet man or a persona non grata." Provincial inspectors, though better trained, are not effective either. Under these conditions, it is not surprising that principals and directors are unable to provide educational leadership, to organize urgently needed programs in such fields as teacher improvement, to adapt instructions to the needs of the community as well as to individual pupils, to program teacher time and school facilities efficiently, or to avoid poor school maintenance and unsanitary, unattractive buildings and grounds.[55]

Nor is it surprising that a considerable amount of dissatisfaction exists among teachers and administrators in the system, especially in the rural areas, or that these administrative and supervisory weaknesses have aggravated the critical teacher problem in the country. Questions of teacher recruitment and training have also received widespread attention, and in 1964 a commission established by the Ministry of Education concluded that the existing state of affairs was attributable to: (1) the multiplicity of teacher-training institutions, which led to the division and truncation of the profession; (2) the fact that no institutions prepared teachers for the primary and secondary teacher-training institutes, which have therefore to utilize

[54] Carol D. Anderson, "End of Tour Report," typewritten (Ankara: AID, 1966), *passim.*

[55] Bursalioğlu, *op. cit.,* pp. 324–325; Anderson, *op. cit.*

their own graduates, thus perpetuating existing standards and practices and lessening the possibility of qualitative improvements; (3) the neglect of advanced teacher training and of the qualitative aspects of teacher preparation in general; and (4) the neglect of new subject areas and teaching methods and the absence of research in these fields. To alleviate these problems, the commission recommended that faculties of education be established within the universities, and three were subsequently opened. From these faculties should come the trained administrators, curricula and research specialists, and guidance personnel who are so urgently needed. But whether they will be able to achieve meaningful change in the absence of reforms designed to remedy the many administrative deficiencies discussed above is doubtful.

Thus the problem of the teaching corps will undoubtedly remain a crucial one for many years. Recruitment and retention represent major problems, and serious shortages, as discussed earlier, exist at all levels. Morale in the profession, because of poor personnel procedures, limited prestige, and low income, is extremely low. The financial plight of teachers has been vividly attested to in a recent series entitled "Can You Manage?" run by *Cumhuriyet,* a prominent Istanbul newspaper. One middle-school teacher wrote:

I am not able to marry. . . . I am a teacher for two years. I receive in my hand 575 TL [per month, less than $40]. I live in a room of the Turkish Teachers' Federation and thus I do not pay rent. If I get married and have to pay rent how can I manage? . . . I do not read except for newspapers and books that are in the hands of my friends.

A *lycée* teacher wrote:

I am married with three children. I receive 600 TL. If I could give private lessons I would receive 1,000 TL, we would rejoice. For one and a half years I have been in Adana but I have been unable to bring my wife and three children. Because in any event, in the village she has relatives who look after her. . . . If you ask about my rent it is 200 TL. And that is for a bachelor's room.[56]

Because of such considerations, the alienation and frustration of teachers has risen markedly and their mood has become increasingly militant. In February 1963, teachers organized a mass meeting and

---

[56] These quotations are from the Sept. 25, 1968, issue.

demonstration in Ankara; another meeting six years later attracted 34,000 persons. In December 1969, the two major unions sponsored a four-day strike by 50,000 teachers and published a manifesto with the following demands: (1) education should be freed from foreign influence and reorganized to serve the people; (2) teachers should cease being punished for advocating change; (3) teachers who have lost their positions because of unfair decisions should be reinstated; (4) partisan considerations should cease to influence educational policy; (5) unions should be consulted when educational plans and programs are drawn up; (6) teachers' persons and property should be safeguarded; and (7) teachers should be provided with an income adequate to let them lead a civilized life.

The Ministry reacted by claiming that the boycott was illegal and suspending several thousand teachers. Most were subsequently reinstated and the remainder, supported by the unions, will probably win reinstatement through the courts.[57] Thus the prospect is for more militancy by the teachers and greater tension with and within the Ministry and the government—a state of affairs that will not facilitate educational transformation.

Higher Education

Even though the universities are not under the control of the Ministry of Education they too were plagued by questions of administration and coordination and it proved as difficult to achieve the planned qualitative and quantitative goals here as at lower levels. Most of the changes inaugurated after the 1960 revolution did not resolve the major problems confronting the universities, and in some cases, such as Law 117 which summarily dismissed 147 faculty members (they were later reinstated, thus further aggravating existing cleavages and hostilities within the institutions), the result was positively harmful.[58] Other attempts to remedy administrative and institutional weaknesses also produced few benefits. The traditional "chair" system was amended somewhat and junior faculty granted more rights, and most importantly, total autonomy was accorded to the universities, which largely served to further hinder attempts at innovation.

[57] Frank A. Stone, "Perspectives on Education," *Current Turkish Thought* (Istanbul: American Board Newsletter) n.s. #4 (March 1970), p. 2.

[58] For details of this incident see Weiker, *op. cit.,* pp. 52–56.

Nevertheless, the process of differentiation in Turkish higher education continued, and these years witnessed the establishment and further development of universities that differed from the traditional pattern. In the 1960's there were seven universities in the country, three of which—Ataturk University, the Middle East Technical University, and Hacettepe University—possess unique characteristics that we shall discuss below. The others include the University of Istanbul, the oldest and largest, the Technical University of Istanbul, the University of Ankara, the Aegean University, and the Black Sea Technical University, which opened in 1963 and consists of faculties of engineering and architecture. Recently Robert College became the eighth Turkish university and was renamed Bosphorus University.

The expansion and differentiation of the university system did not prove adequate to accommodate the thousands of additional secondary school graduates seeking to continue their education, and a national examination to control pressures upon the universities was established. This test represents a formidable hurdle—in 1970 only 17,500 students out of about 70,000 applicants passed—but its introduction did not diminish the pressures upon the universities because enrollments could not be held to levels desired by planners or academicians as political considerations proved irresistible. Though the first five-year plan provided for an increase in total college and university enrollments from 63,000 in 1963 to 88,000 in 1967, 126,000 students were actually scheduled to attend institutions of higher learning in 1968. Enrollments were then expected to exceed 182,000 within five years. In contrast to the situation at the lower levels, however, the new goal is being surpassed; in 1971–1972, 179,818 students were attending institutions of higher learning, whereas the plan anticipated enrollments of only 164,500 in that year.[59]

Nor is the examination system itself free from serious defects. No minimum standards were established, so that even those who do pass may not possess the aptitude or qualifications for university-level work. Furthermore, there is a built-in class bias. Successful students

[59] Ömer Celal Sarç, "Higher Education in Turkey," in *Education as a Factor of Accelerated Economic Development* (Istanbul: Economic and Social Studies Conference Board, 1966), p. 109; Cumhuriyet, July 11, 1970; *First Plan,* Table 359, p. 404; *Second Plan,* Table 97, p. 194; "Educational Attaché."

tend to be graduates of the best secondary schools, notably private ones and those in the major cities; the products of the smaller schools, especially those in the eastern provinces, do not do nearly as well, thus emphasizing a serious cleavage within the society.[60] Another drawback is that since quotas are established by each faculty, only limited correspondence exists between the students who are interested and the numbers who can be admitted. This is especially true of science and engineering where many students who desire to study these subjects because of their high prestige in contemporary Turkey could not be accommodated. As always, such faculties as law and letters have, on the other hand, established relatively generous quotas. Hence, only a minority of students gain admission to the faculty of their choice; many are either temporarily or permanently studying subjects in which they have little interest, since the important thing is to be enrolled at any cost in an institution of higher learning, a situation that exists in many countries of the Middle East.

While such pressures led to a rapid increase in the numbers of students enrolled in higher academic institutions this expansion took place with but limited consideration of the country's manpower requirements, a point to which we shall return below, and with inadequate inputs of physical and human resources. All fields have been adversely affected, including the natural sciences, which suffer from inadequate facilities and great shortages of qualified staff. Moreover these fields are among the weakest subjects in the secondary schools, so that as the number of students admitted to these faculties expanded, standards inevitably declined markedly. A similar situation existed in all other specialties. A recent study showed that since 1960 only about 19 per cent of the students enrolled have graduated from the Istanbul University Law Faculty and that of every 100 students who register in the Faculty of Letters, only fifteen continue their studies and only six ever graduate. Overall, it has been estimated that only 35 per cent of all students at Istanbul University ever obtain a degree.[61]

Despite overcrowding in all faculties, the explosive growth in de-

---

[60] Cemal Mihçioğlu, *Üniversiteye Giriş Sınavlarının Yeniden Düzenlenmesi* (Ankara: Sevinç Matbaası, 1962), pp. 65ff.

[61] Mediko-Sosyal Merkezi, "1964 Yili Çalişma Raporu," multilithed (Istanbul: Mediko-Sosyal Merkezi, 1965), p. 13.

mands for higher education could not be accommodated by the existing institutions, and private colleges proliferated rapidly to take advantage of the popular demand for a diploma. By the end of 1967 there were nineteen private schools offering training in such fields as engineering, dentistry, pharmacy, architecture, and commerce. They enrolled 25,596 students, about 20 per cent of all students attending institutions of higher learning in Turkey. This development led to a considerable controversy within the country. Students in the state universities objected that their education was hampered because their professors, who had been recruited to teach in these colleges, were devoting less time to their regular duties. Questions of quality and elitism were also raised by many critics who argued that the goal of these institutions was primarily to make money for their owners and that all students who could afford the high fees were therefore uncritically accepted and passed. An inquiry by a Senate committee into this issue did find that the overwhelming majority of the private schools possessed inadequate facilities. In response to these charges, the Association of Private Schools claimed that the deficiencies had been exaggerated, that inadequate conditions had in some instances been corrected, that private colleges represented a legitimate means of meeting the demand for higher education (in fact, the principle of private higher education had been recognized by all major parties, and the first permit to open such a school was granted by the coalition government following the 1960 revolution), and that some fellowships were available for qualified students who could not afford to pay tuition. According to their figures, 35 per cent of all advanced students were enrolled in private institutions, of these 7 per cent were receiving full scholarships.[62]

The announcement that a private law school was to be opened in 1968 led to a major confrontation as students of the law schools of Ankara and Istanbul universities, with faculty support, staged a strike and professional associations declared they would not accept private school graduates as members. As the question of the future of the private schools became more urgent the government moved to extend controls over these institutions, but this most troublesome political issue was resolved when the Turkish Supreme Court ruled

[62] *Pulse,* Nov. 9, 1967; *Cumhuriyet,* Dec. 13, 1968.

that private colleges were unconstitutional and all these schools were subsequently nationalized. Nevertheless important issues remain to be resolved. Their faculty is still essentially drawn from the staff of the regular universities, a situation with obvious implications for the quality of education at each institution. Moreover, most colleges prepare students for fields that are already overcrowded.[63]

At the same time that these students and university graduates in nontechnical specialties face difficulty in finding positions, the country's development is seriously hampered by shortages of doctors, scientists, engineers, and technicians. Despite the introduction of manpower planning and the increased educational demand, enough technical manpower is simply not being produced to meet present needs, and even more critical shortages are forecast by experts. Major imbalances exist in the ratio between highly skilled and ancillary personnel in such fields as medicine, which forces highly trained personnel (doctors) to spend valuable time performing routine activities that could be handled by others. In 1955 there were two technicians for every engineer; by 1960 there were only 1.5 technicians for every engineer. Similarly, there were 72 artisans per engineer in 1955, and 56 artisans per engineer in 1960. This situation improved somewhat in the sixties, but major bottlenecks remain. The ratio of health personnel to doctors was also very unsatisfactory: 0.44 nurses, 0.41 midwives, 0.18 pharmacists, and 0.17 dentists per doctor. In the field of general administration a similar shortage exists. The number of managers in Turkey is 1.4 per hundred workers, in other countries approximately 4.6 per hundred. Furthermore, the educational background of Turkish managers is not very impressive; only 53 per cent have completed some sort of higher education. Moreover, when projections of anticipated supply and demand curves for high-level manpower are made, even more acute imbalances are uncovered in all technical fields. The shortage of engineers, for example, will rise from 8,600 in 1967 to 55,800 by 1982; that of scientists and technicians from 6,700 to 189,200 and that of doctors from about 900 in 1972 to 13,500 a decade later.[64]

[63] *Pulse*, Dec. 4, 1968; İlter Turan, "Educational Developments," *Current Turkish Thought*, n.s. #10 (October 1971), p. 8.

[64] *Second Plan*, pp. 162–164; the estimated shortages are computed from Tables 74, 79, pp. 165, 169.

Aggravating this situation is the flow of engineers and physicians overseas. Between 1962 and 1966 the ratio of emigrating to graduating scientists and doctors stood at about 15 per cent, of engineers, at about 11 per cent. The financial loss has been calculated at over $11,500,000 annually for training these persons plus another $54 million per year in lost earnings. The causes of migration are similar to those for the rest of the region. In addition to poor salaries, engineers are frustrated by such factors as isolation from the international mainstream, lack of concern with research by their colleagues and superiors, and difficulties in applying their skills in an innovative manner owing to the rigid and traditional context in which many of them work. Doctors are additionally frustrated by the limited opportunities in urban areas, where two-thirds of all the country's physicians practice, and by the lack of resources and support available to those willing to serve in rural areas.[65]

Government officials and planners are attempting to stem the brain drain and are also placing renewed stress upon scientific and technical training in colleges and universities; enrollments in these fields are scheduled to rise from 42 per cent of all students in 1968 to 67 per cent in 1973.[66] Even if such a switch does prove possible a marked expansion of educational facilities will also be required, and a rapid growth in enrollments is projected through 1982. To increase capacity as envisaged by the planners will be no easy matter, particularly in scientific fields. Staff shortages constitute a major hindrance to the projected expansion of the university system in every field, but the most acute situation exists in the sciences.

Nor has it proven a simple matter to eliminate this bottleneck. To meet the need to expand the number of faculty, the first five-year plan provided for 3,000 fellowships for foreign study for graduate students preparing for an academic career. This program, however, proved to be a dismal failure—an experience that does not bode well for the anticipated expansion of university and college facilities—as only 500 persons were recruited by the end of 1966. The lack of interest in these fellowships was due primarily to the diminished at-

[65] Peter G. Franck, "Brain Drain from Turkey," in *The International Migration of High-Level Manpower*, Praeger Special Studies in International Economics and Development (New York: Praeger, 1970), pp. 201, 310, 343–344.
[66] *Second Plan*, Table 96, p. 193.

traction of academic life, a phenomenon that is attributable to the fact that the structure of the academic profession in most universities remains highly traditional and that the situation of the *asistan* (assistant), the lowest rung of the academic ladder, is especially unrewarding. Even those possessing a Ph.D. are notoriously underpaid and have to serve for several years in that rank before becoming eligible for promotion to full faculty status as a doçent—a rank somewhere between the American assistant and associate professor. Moreover, in some cases, the returning Ph.D. has not received a faculty appointment because of the inbreeding that characterizes higher education.[67] We shall discuss patterns of academic appointment and promotion and their relevance to university reform in more detail later.

Moreover even if the supplementary educational capacity can be developed according to the ideal timetable of the planners (a very big *if*) it is not expected that the new facilities will be able to meet the demand in the near future, and serious shortages of manpower are projected until the 1980's. It is anticipated, for example, that 3 per cent of the net shortage of engineers will be met through new facilities by 1972, 36 per cent by 1977, and 93 per cent by 1982.[68] Thus, even under the most optimistic projections, development will be hampered by serious shortages of skilled personnel for many years.

To some extent, especially at the lower levels, this shortage will be met by the military establishment. Though not discussed in the development plans, thousands of draftees receive technical training of all sorts in the extensive network of military schools. It has been estimated that the skills of about 100,000 men annually are upgraded significantly during their military service. Furthermore, the officer corps, numbering approximately 40,000, is an important source of managerial talent for the country.[69]

Nevertheless, even with such an input critical shortages of skills will remain. How critical these shortages will actually be is difficult to foresee, for the manpower projections which underlie all calcula-

[67] *Ibid.*, p. 190; Turan, *op. cit.*, p. 9.

[68] *Ibid.*, Table 83, p. 173.

[69] Richard D. Robinson, *High-Level Manpower in Economic Development. The Turkish Case* (Cambridge: Harvard Middle Eastern Monographs, No. 17, 1967), pp. 62–63.

tions are themselves based on assumptions of doubtful validity including: (1) that the ratio of high-level manpower to total labor force obtaining in the early 1960's was adequate to sustain the projected 7 per cent growth rate; (2) that the efficiency of high-level manpower would remain constant; and (3) that the labor force as a percentage of the total population will remain essentially the same. However as one scholar has pointed out:

> The first assumption is open to debate. The second is open to even more serious question. The efficiency of high-level manpower is a function of (1) the degree to which the supply of specific skills are matched with those needed; (2) the extent to which associated jobs requiring lesser skills (e.g. subprofessional, middle management) are performed by other than high-level manpower; (3) the extent to which those receiving high-level skills possess creative personalities . . . intelligence, and physical energy. . . . Surely several if not all these factors will shift in value.
>
> The third assumption . . . is likewise unjustified in the face of the massive shift off the land and into the city, from the farm to the industrial labor market.[70]

Regardless of the validity of this assessment or of the projections which underlie educational planning it is widely felt by most observers that Turkey does face a shortage of skills and that existing imbalances and practices within higher education represent a major obstacle to the country's future development. When to such considerations is added the fact that the universities were bastions of antigovernment sentiment and major sources of political instability it is not surprising that questions of university reform became matters of national debate. In 1970 a Commission on University Reform prepared a draft bill, but in the highly politicized environment of the day any attempt at reform was bound to be viewed by many as an attempt by the Demirel government to eliminate opposition.[71] Thus, political and ideological considerations have, in the past, greatly complicated the important question of university reform, but the new governments of Nihat Erim and his successors are giving priority to transforming higher educational institutions into centers of intellectual activity.

To do so in view of the many deeply entrenched interests and

[70] *Ibid.*, pp. 111–112; see also Peter G. Franck, *op. cit.*, pp. 333ff.
[71] Stone, *op. cit.*, p. 4.

traditional orientations will not be easy, but if the universities are to provide the wide variety of services that are needed by the country —extension work, summer programs, evening courses, directed research, and the like—and if they are to be metamorphosed so as to produce the kinds of graduates necessary for development, fundamental changes in the structure and functioning of these institutions are essential. As one astute and experienced professor and administrator has remarked:

The present university system, composed on one side of old-established universities, which are extremely large and cumbersome, attached to their own *status quo* and showing little capacity even to paper over their internal differences with agreed common proposals for change, and, on the other side, of new universities which have not all yet found their balance and sense of direction, has to be closely and critically examined.[72]

Many reform proposals have in fact been forthcoming in recent months including the introduction of tuition, full-time obligations by the faculty, the use of credit hours, greater centralization of administration, the establishment of a central planning and coordinating council with government and university representatives, and a mandatory retirement age for faculty.[73] Such innovations, though useful, are not likely to bring about the drastic revision of existing practices or the transformation of the very ethos of these institutions that are required to make them truly functional to the requirements of modernity. To achieve the needed renewal of intellectual life and vitality, new staff must be trained and dedicated modern educators placed in positions of responsibility within the existing and the projected institutions. Furthermore, new faculty are vitally needed if the goals of the planners concerning the creation of new institutions are to be realized.

Since recruitment and training of faculty is a major hindrance to the development of higher education, the existing framework for graduate work in Turkey will have to be reorganized drastically and more effective means of selecting students and preparing them for an academic career developed. The present system is essentially the traditional European one with its emphasis upon legalistic rules and

[72] Osman Okyar, "Universities in Turkey," *Minerva,* 6 (Winter 1968), 228.
[73] Turan, *op. cit.,* p. 12.

requirements. In most universities faculty rank consists of two grades, the doçent and the professor. To become a doçent the graduate student assistant starts to work on a Ph.D. degree, but without structured instruction or supervision. Seldom is any formal course work required. The supervision that he receives depends upon the faculty member to whom the young student is, in effect, apprenticed. Often the student is neglected and left largely to his own devices and the thesis which he ultimately produces seldom consists of an original piece of research or represents any contribution to knowledge. The lack of thorough training in the discipline or in research methodology tends to perpetuate the existing system as does the fact that the graduate student is essentially at the mercy of one man whose whim will ultimately determine his failure or success. Even after obtaining the degree, however, the student is still not qualified (in the traditional universities) for faculty rank. He must now repeat the process by writing another thesis and passing another examination on both subject matter and the thesis to qualify as a doçent. All in all, about ten to twelve years are required to become a full-fledged faculty member. To qualify as a professor, the doçent must learn a second foreign language, prepare another thesis, and demonstrate evidence of other scholarly accomplishments.[74]

Such a procedure is clearly wasteful and, as we have noted, discourages many persons from entering the academic world. Furthermore, this long, arduous, socializing process produces individuals who are integrated into the existing system and accept its norms and values. Deviants do not often successfully complete the requirements, so that the procedure tends to produce precisely the kinds of individuals who will continue to perpetuate existing patterns and who will not be able, or willing, to undertake the kinds of innovative behavior that will be necessary to produce the needed radical changes in higher education. The static character of the existing system is perhaps most vividly illustrated by the fact that many persons who have earned a Ph.D. abroad have been unable to obtain an appointment because many faculties prefer to prepare their own staff in their own way.[75]

[74] Okyar, *op. cit.*, pp. 226–227.
[75] Turan, *op. cit.*, p. 9.

Many dedicated and able faculty are, of course, to be found throughout the system, and these men have made determined attempts to eliminate some of the worst abuses of existing procedures. In some cases, such as the Political Science Faculty at the University of Ankara, notable reforms have been achieved, but by and large the judgment that "arrangements for the Ph.D. degree tend to perpetuate enfeebling, archaic practices derived from the past and thus contribute markedly to the continuation of formalized, repetitive and impersonal teaching in universities" is only too valid a criticism of the contemporary scene.[76] Until changes can be wrought in this area, it would be unrealistic to expect the transformation of higher education in Turkey.

The New Universities: Problems and Prospects

That such changes are possible is indicated by an examination of the development of the nontraditional institutions of higher learning —Ataturk University, the Middle East Technical University, and Hacettepe University. Their history also highlights the difficulties inherent in attempting to create universities that do not conform to existing patterns. From the outset a major conflict developed within the country between representatives of the older institutions and their allies who felt that a uniform system of higher education was most desirable and proponents of differentiation who argued in favor of a diversity and flexibility of structures and functions geared to the varied needs that each institution is expected to meet. Having won the initial battle the latter are also hopeful that the new institutions, which are very different, will serve as models of reform and change for established universities.[77]

One specific model was to be provided by Ataturk University which, though a young institution, possesses a history dating back to 1937 when Ataturk suggested that a university be opened in eastern Turkey to complete a network of higher educational institutions within the country. Istanbul University, which had been reorganized in 1933, would serve the western region, the newly established University of Ankara the central part, and a new university at Van,

[76] Okyar, *op. cit.,* p. 227.
[77] *Ibid.,* pp. 231–232.

the eastern area. The eruption of World War II postponed the implementation of this project, but in the early 1950's the new DP government established a commission to prepare a report on location, structure, and functions. In 1953 the government contacted the U.S. aid mission to determine whether assistance would be available for the project, and in 1954 President Celal Bayar, during a visit to the United States, obtained the support of the government for a new university to be based upon the American land-grant pattern. The University of Nebraska was selected as the sponsoring institution, and appropriate enabling legislation was passed after a three-year delay caused by strong disagreements between Turkish and American scholars as to the structure of the new university. The conflict was resolved by a weak compromise that essentially provided for the replication of the existing Turkish university pattern. Why such a change in the Turkish government's position took place is not easy to understand, but two suggestions have been advanced. Firstly, as we have already indicated, the era of the DP was not marked by any coherent developmental philosophy or attempts at systematic planning. Under these conditions the creation of an institution purposefully structured to stimulate regional development was most unlikely. Perhaps more important was the opposition of the existing universities, whose representatives argued strenuously and effectively against any deviation from the academic status quo.[78]

Classes eventually started in temporary quarters in Erzerum in 1958 with about 135 students, of whom 125 were enrolled in the faculty of agriculture, the remainder in science and letters. In 1962, 759 students were enrolled (662 in agriculture, 97 in science and letters), and in 1966, 1,650 students (of whom 800 were studying agriculture, 800 science and letters, and 50 medicine in a new faculty opened that year).[79]

From the outset, the new institution was confronted with serious problems of physical facilities and, especially, qualified staff. The former problem has been largely resolved by the erection, on 10,000 acres of land, of a new campus with buildings that provide adequate

[78] Osman Okyar, "The University and Regional Development," in *Science and Technology in Developing Countries,* Claire Nader and A. B. Zahlan, eds. (Cambridge: Cambridge University Press, 1969), pp. 368ff.
[79] *Ibid.,* p. 375.

classroom, office, and laboratory space. Student housing, however, remains inadequate as do facilities for students' social and recreational needs. More serious was, and is, the question of staffing the University. No faculty member from Ankara, Izmir, or Istanbul was willing to transfer to this desolate, underdeveloped, and relatively isolated region, especially since salary schedules were the same for all universities. In 1966, however, new legislation provided a 75 per cent salary advantage, which was increased in 1967 to 100 per cent. Better staff housing and airline connections to Ankara and Istanbul were also expected to raise local morale and further enhance the desirability of joining the institution.

These changes, however, have not sufficed to attract able and dedicated faculty to the university, for few academicians enjoy living in the kind of environment that Erzerum represents. Similar problems have also been encountered in attempting to staff the new Black Sea Technical University located in Trabzon, and one observer has concluded that a critical variable making for successful university development is location in an area that has reached a particular social, cultural, and economic level.[80]

During the early years it was necessary to use University of Nebraska staff, and to provide permanent faculty, new graduates were recruited and sent to the United States for training. In return for each year spent abroad the participant incurred a two-year teaching obligation at Erzerum. For such a program to be successful, able and dedicated students had to be selected, but the first participants possessed a weak academic background and limited knowledge of English; the effort to provide English-language instruction was never fully satisfactory. Thus some students proved unable to meet the standards of the American universities and even those who were able to do so were not sent abroad to earn M.A.'s or Ph.D.'s. Subsequently the selection process was improved; altogether about sixty persons have been sent to the United States: two have earned Ph.D.'s and eighteen have received M.A.'s.[81]

In the late 1960's, Ataturk University had 222 staff members,

[80] Turan, *op. cit.,* p. 9.

[81] D. G. Hanway, "End of Tour Report: Ataturk University, An Experiment in Institution Building to Serve Eastern Turkey," in *Turkish University Program,* mimeo. (Lincoln, Neb.: University of Nebraska, 1967), p. 55.

about a tenth of whom were studying abroad or were on temporary leave. Only 25 members, however, were of academic rank (doçent or professor): 122 were assistants, 75 were assistants who have earned a Ph.D. In short, only 25 persons were officially qualified to lecture and conduct classes for the entire student body of about 1,650. In addition to a heavy teaching load they were also involved in the administration of the institution and were responsible for training and supervising the junior staff. In 1965 the University estimated that 267 faculty members would be required in 1970 but that only 80 could be produced from within, leaving a gap of 187 that would have to be filled from outside sources. Even these figures, however, were probably optimistic, since the projection of internal production was based on an intensive recruitment and training program which was never initiated. Nevertheless, by 1970–1971, 2,671 students were enrolled and the number of staff members was officially given as 481, so that some improvement may have taken place.

Institution-building has also been severely hindered by the faculty appointment and promotion process common to all Turkish universities, which has served to encourage persons to concentrate upon degree requirements at the expense of teaching and administrative responsibilities. Furthermore, the absence of senior staff within the institution has forced reliance upon faculty from other institutions to serve on examining committees, so that Ataturk University has as yet played practically no role in its own degree-granting process. In other words, the institution has been unable to reward those individuals who make the most effective contributions to the university, and indeed those persons who have been the most concerned with its development have tended to be penalized. As a result of these considerations, one American observer has concluded that, "the system of staff advancement . . . has such obvious weaknesses from both academic and institution development considerations that it alone will preclude development of Ataturk University as a modern university with high standards of excellence of staff productivity." [82]

Under these circumstances, little research or practical work has been carried on at the University though, because one of the primary functions of the institution was to promote the development of east-

[82] *Ibid.,* p. 50.

ern Turkey, at least one observer has argued that "the test by which the University stands or falls is whether it succeeds in setting up and applying an original and independent research program of its own." By this test the University has been a failure. The reasons for this state of affairs are many. Some are to be found in the general social and cultural environment within which Turkish universities function; other, more specific, reasons include the lack of recognition by the government of the importance of research and extension work and the concomitant absence of any incentives to promote such activities, which actually hinder the personal advancement of the faculty. The efforts of a few dedicated men have not been sufficient to overcome these handicaps which stem from what is perhaps the single most important hindrance to the development of the institution, the system of administration.[83]

The University has never enjoyed the kind of strong, dynamic leadership that was so obviously necessary to the creation of a modern institution. Since 1957, eleven different persons have served as rector, nine as dean of agriculture, eight as dean of science and letters. Responsibility for appointing a rector is vested in the Ministry of Education, but the Ministry has "seemed to accept little or no active responsibility for defining the role of the university, guiding the activities of the university or fostering its development along the lines of a service-oriented modern institution as originally proposed." [84] As a result, there has been neither continuity of leadership within the institution itself nor systematic and continuing support from the Ministry. The existence of these two factors serves, in very large part, to explain why Ataturk University has, despite very large inputs of American material and human assistance, never developed as originally anticipated.

The pattern was not replicated in the development of the Middle East Technical University (METU) which was administered by one man, Kemal Kurdaş, from 1961 to 1970. Under his leadership the University witnessed rapid development and is today one of the best equipped in terms of both physical facilities and faculty in Turkey.

The concept of METU dates back to 1954 when a United Nations

---

[83] Okyar, "The University," p. 377.
[84] Hanway, *op. cit.,* p. 51.

mission concerned with the neglect of training in architectural and urban planning in the Middle East suggested that a new type of university be established in Ankara to meet these needs. The Turkish government proved amenable to the idea of an international institution which would attract students from all over the Middle East, and in 1957 the Grand National Assembly passed a provisional law defining the goals and scope of the new institution; a unique charter was subsequently drawn up and ratified.

The structure of the university is radically different from that of the traditional Turkish universities. The law provided for an independent board of trustees appointed by the Council of Ministers. The nine members of this board possess final authority over all university matters and appoint the rector, who must be of Turkish nationality, for a three-year period. Academic affairs are largely delegated to the Academic Council, the members of which are elected by the faculties. Faculty rank is similar to that in the United States and all members of the teaching staff are appointed on a contractual basis, first for one year, then for two years, three years, and five years.

METU differs functionally as well as structurally from the conventional patterns of Turkish universities. The faculty consists of young Turks, practically all of whom possess a Ph.D. from an American or a European university, supplemented by a significant proportion of foreign professors. The language of instruction is English. The ethos of the university resembles an American institution of higher learning; the faculty stress discussion and critical analysis in their classes, and student-faculty relations tend to be informal and close. The original emphasis upon technical subjects has been supplemented by the inclusion of training in the natural sciences, the social sciences, and the humanities.

The University actually dates back to 1956, when a program of instruction in city planning was established with forty students and three teachers. In 1963 it moved from a temporary campus in the center of Ankara to a new modern campus with excellent facilities of all sorts on the outskirts of town. In the mid-sixties the number of students had climbed to about 5,000 enrolled in faculties of arts and sciences, administrative sciences, engineering, and architecture; the teaching staff numbered about 500.

Despite its impressive growth, METU has been confronted with serious problems of staffing and, in its early years, of equipment. The latter needs were met, to some extent, through the cooperation of various foreign governments, international organizations (the UN, CENTO) and private foundations, notably the Ford Foundation. Nevertheless, some shortages of equipment have remained, especially in engineering fields, and the library, which was not expanded at a fast enough rate, is also inadequate.[85] More serious, however, has been the question of staffing. From the outset it proved difficult to find qualified Turkish scholars who could teach in English and who believed in the philosophy of the new institution, especially at senior ranks. Thus the University has had to rely upon young Ph.D.'s and upon foreign professors. The foreign faculty and visiting staff (in 1966, 107 out of 504), carry an extremely heavy load within the institution, which probably could not function without them. Such reliance, however, has created several problems. First, the foreign faculty have often been made available to METU without consideration of the actual needs of the institution, and secondly, it is obviously not possible to create a first-rate university unless measures are taken to develop an indigenous staff.

This has, in fact, been done by sending a large number of graduate students abroad, but the result has been to create an institution staffed almost completely by very junior faculty. The absence of senior staff, both Turkish and foreign, is evidenced by the fact that in 1968, of the 397 Turkish staff members, 12 were professors, 10 associate professors, and 77 assistant professors. The rest are instructors, graduate assistants, and part-time instructors. Of the 107 foreigners, 4 are professors, one an associate, 5 assistants; the bulk of the remainder are instructors. This imbalance between the higher and the lower levels of the academic hierarchy has created many difficulties. Though the young faculty are eager, well-trained, able, and energetic, they have often tended to lack the maturity and experience that is so vital a part of university training, especially at the graduate level. Nor can leadership be exercised easily in such a context since few senior men are to be found in any faculty and the new Ph.D.'s are competing anxiously with each other for recognition and advancement.

Perhaps partly as a reaction to this situation, Rector Kurdaş cen-

[85] Carol V. Newsom, "Report on Middle East Technical University, Part II," mimeo. (Ankara: AID, 1966), pp. 16–17.

tralized all decision-making into his own hands. Though the result was to produce a period of spectacular growth, he unfortunately was not an educator, and his policies, which often neglected important aspects of university life, antagonized many faculty members. As a result, curricula did not always provide systematic training from the freshman to the senior year in particular fields, the content of many courses overlapped, the subject matter seldom related adequately to local and regional problems, research was not continually emphasized, and cooperation within and coordination between faculties was not promoted actively.[86]

Questions of leadership have, however, proven less important than questions of ideology. From the outset METU has represented an attempt to create an American-type institution in Turkey. Though, as we have noted frequently, serious problems are encountered in transplanting institutions from one context to another, the most fundamental question in regard to METU has not been social or cultural but political—that is, at the same time that the attempt was underway to create a university modeled along American lines, the mood of the intellectuals was shifting steadily toward a violent anti-American position. In this context the other factors making for student unrest were supplemented by pressures upon both students and faculty to become *plus royaliste que le roi,* and the overall temper of the institution became increasingly militant and anti-American.

Perhaps the most obvious indication of this trend was the incident involving the burning of the United States ambassador's car in January 1969. While Ambassador Robert Komer, who had been invited, perhaps unwisely, by the rector, was eating lunch on the campus, a group of students gathered around his limousine and after a few moments of indecision, embarked upon a wrecking spree. Ambassador Komer was especially unpopular with leftist students and intellectuals because of his previous connections with the CIA and the pacification program in Vietnam. This incident was followed by continuing widespread student disturbances, including boycotting of classes and occupation of the university in the spring of that year. Though the university was ultimately closed and Rector Kurdaş resigned, not until the military intervention could a normal educational atmosphere be

[86] *Ibid.,* Part I.

restored. What this legacy of intense politicization holds for the future of METU, which possesses such promise as a center of higher learning, remains to be seen.

One institution which does not need reform and which enjoyed an almost total absence of student unrest for many years until it, too, was engulfed by the developments elsewhere is the third Turkish university to be established in the fifties, Hacettepe. Its strength derives essentially from enlightened leadership which has created a modern university that has not suffered from METU's identification with the United States—even though in spirit and in functioning this institution closely resembles any good American institution of higher learning.

Hacettepe University was the creation of a distinguished Turkish physician and administrator, Dr. İhsan Doğramacı, who, shortly after his graduation from an American medical school, began to concern himself with ways of restructuring medical education and the practice of medicine in Turkey. In 1954 he was named head of pediatrics in the faculty of medicine of the University of Ankara and soon established a small clinic and a foundation to support this facility. Dr. Doğramacı proved to be an able fund raiser (he secured, among others, a grant of $100,000 from the Rockefeller Foundation in 1955) and he used these resources to provide the nucleus of skilled manpower that he would need to achieve his vision by selecting twenty-five bright graduates of the medical faculties and sending them abroad for postgraduate work. In 1958, Dr. Doğramacı became the director of an Institute of Child Health within the University of Ankara. This institute rapidly proliferated new functions and programs, and within a few years plans called for the establishment of a major medical center consisting of a general hospital, a children's hospital, a nursing school, and programs in psychotherapy and medical technology. In 1962 these were supplemented by the establishment of courses in arts and sciences so that by 1963 what had once been a pediatric clinic had evolved into the nucleus of a new university. These developments clearly raised serious questions concerning the project's relationship to the University of Ankara in general and to its existing faculty of medicine specifically. Acrimonious debate resulted in the incorporation of the Hacettepe Medical Faculty together with its numerous related programs (including, by now, dentistry) as a separate faculty of the university. This arrangement proved to be shortlived as Dr.

Doğramaci continued to strengthen and expand his institution. In 1965 the Turkish Grand National Assembly gave legal recognition to "Hacettepe Science Center" and in 1967, by mutual consent, the faculty attained its independence from the University of Ankara and became Hacettepe University. Appropriate legislation was passed in the summer of 1967.

It was planned that by 1972 the new campus would consist of a thousand-bed general hospital and a 300-bed children's hospital, schools of medicine, dentistry, physical medicine, and nursing, facilities for instruction in the sciences, the social sciences, and the humanities, a library, research institutes, a graduate school, and staff and student housing. A large percentage of the funds for this complex have been provided by U.S. governmental and private agencies.[87]

The spirit of the new institution represents a radical departure from conventional methods of medical instruction in Turkey. The traditional faculties admit from 200 to 600 *lycée* graduates annually for a six-year program which about one-third complete successfully. As in the other fields, attendance is usually not taken, students are allowed to repeat examinations, most of the faculty is part-time, the usual medium of instruction is the lecture, and the emphasis is upon memorization of theoretical learning. There is little coordination between different professors so that much unnecessary duplication occurs and the primary focus is often not upon educating students systematically and well, but upon considerations of personal prestige and power. As a result of such practices, medical education, too, despite its high prestige, has been characterized by high rates of attrition—only 56 per cent of the freshmen enrolled in the medical faculties in 1947 ever acquired a degree, and less than half of these did so in the normal six years.[88]

From its inception, Hacettepe was designed to avoid these weaknesses. The entire faculty is on a full-time basis and cooperation and integration is a *leitmotif* of the institution. Curricula are drawn up by elected committees and are based on the principle that "teaching in the basic medical sciences is integrated in that the subject matter

[87] Carol V. Newsom, "Report on Hasettepe University," mimeo. (Ankara: AID, 1967), pp. 13–16.
[88] Carl E. Taylor *et al., Health Manpower Planning in Turkey* (Baltimore, Md.: Johns Hopkins University Press, 1968), p. 112.

is not divided according to the various departmental topics, but according to a system which starts from the simplest and smallest functional and structural unit, and evolves gradually into the teaching of the more complex functional and structural systems of the human organism." [89] Practical and laboratory work account for about two-thirds of the total and emphasis is placed upon the development of critical abilities and research skills. Close student-teacher relations are encouraged and feedback from the students concerning the program serves as one factor in its modification and improvement.

The development of the School of Arts and Sciences was guided by a similar orientation to that of the medical faculties and stresses the communality of faculty and students, the continuing development and revision of the curriculum, and the encouragement of extracurricular activities. Its original function was to provide a foundation for medical and dental students as well as to provide training in such areas as biochemistry, biophysics, and biomathematics, which contribute directly to practice and research in medical fields. Since then, however, the program has evolved into areas that are not directly related to medicine. These new areas have not yet developed the strength of the other departments and possess far more serious weaknesses of one sort or another, especially inadequate staffing.

Despite these deficiencies, which are aggravated by an inadequate administrative structure and overcentralization, Hacettepe University by and large represents a striking and successful departure from traditional patterns of higher education. It has introduced a dynamic factor into the Turkish educational system that could well serve as a model for the newer universities that are to be opened in the country. What is especially striking is that this institution has avoided the mistakes that have characterized the other two institutions discussed above—the lack of leadership at Ataturk University and the extreme politicization of METU. Most of the credit for the success of Hacettepe must certainly be attributed to its farsighted rector, who has managed to create an American-style institution while at the same time avoiding the obvious and close identification with the United States that has proven so fatal to METU. Whether Hacettepe will deeply influence the existing and the projected universities remains to

[89] Cited in Newsom, "Hacettepe Report," p. 20.

be seen, but it has already developed a close working relationship with the medical school of Ataturk University which could serve as a model for the further development of the kinds of interinstitutional linkages that are so necessary for the development of higher education in Turkey.

Whether this experience can be replicated on the scale that is required remains to be seen, particularly in view of the existing political uncertainties. Nevertheless the concern with reform within a democratic framework evidenced by the military augurs well for the future. Only if this concern is actually translated into the rapid and systematic restructuring of many aspects of Turkish life, especially education, however, will Turkey be able to fulfill the promise of its rich heritage and achieve the high rate of qualitative and quantitative growth that lies within its grasp. This is the opportunity and the challenge that confronts one of the few democratic countries in the non-Western world today.

VII

Iran: Toward a
Modern Educational System
in a Reformist Monarchy

In 1941 British and Soviet troops marched into Iran in order to ensure a supply line to the U.S.S.R. and forced the abdication and exile of Reza Shah, who had followed a pro-German policy. Mohammed Reza Shah, who was then 21 years old, replaced his father on the throne and began a royal career that was to span, within a few short years, dramatic changes in the country's political configurations and his own role therein. The vacuum created by the deposition of Reza Shah and the Allied occupation which lasted until 1945 (the Russians did not withdraw until 1946, a delay which precipitated one of the first major confrontations of the Cold War) created severe economic and political dislocations within the country. In these years most governmental powers were usurped by the Allies who divided the country into two zones which they administered as they pleased. The relaxation of tight government control and the disruption of existing institutions led to a new distribution of power within Iran as numerous political groups representing individual cliques, resurgent traditional forces, and modern elements emerged within the polity. The most important of these were the Tudeh party, a tool of Soviet policy, which advocated radical social and economic change and which quickly gained a large following, and the National Front headed by Dr. Mohammed Mossadegh, a conglomeration of modern and traditional groups that coalesced around the banner of a resurgent Iranian nationalism.

In this context, survival was the primary consideration of the young Shah, who was often forced to play a passive role in the interaction between the various groups. Utilizing his limited political resources with great acumen, he exerted pressure only on those occasions when he was in a position to do so, established temporary alliances with whatever groups in the country were willing to support him on various issues—the ulema, the military, landowners, aristo-crats—and manipulated the shifting coalitions expertly to maximize his own power.

Survival entailed, above all, the rebuilding of the demoralized military establishment, which, so carefully built up by Reza Shah, had collapsed together with the other institutions of his regime in 1941. To strengthen the army, to erase the memory of that debacle, and to make it the pillar of his rule, was the key element in the Shah's policy, and he gained an important psychological advantage when the Russians decided to withdraw from northern Iran, although another decade was required for a sense of pride to be instilled in the military. How decisive was the reoccupation of Azerbaijan in the Shah's masterful attempts to consolidate his own position cannot be over-emphasized. When asked why he was able, after 1949, to exert so much greater influence in domestic politics than before, he replied: "Well, I think that our recovery of Azerbaijan helped since I was responsible for that as Commander in Chief of the Armed Forces as well as being a king with a following among the people. After this I was projected more 'in lights.' " [1]

By 1949 he felt secure enough to institutionalize his power by convening a Constituent Assembly, a move facilitated by an unsuccessful attempt on his life which created a popular reaction in his favor. The 1906 constitution was amended to provide for the creation of an upper house, half of whose members were to be nominated by the Shah, half of whom were to be elected through indirect elections. A second amendment granted the Shah the power to dissolve the two houses at any time.[2]

Despite these gains, however, his position remained relatively weak, as was vividly demonstrated by the challenge to the monarchy during the crisis of 1951–1953. A dispute between Iranian nationalists and the Anglo-Iranian Oil Company over the distribution of profits quickly led to cries for nationalization of the country's oil resources and to the coalescence of all modern elements around the figure of Mossadegh, who seized control of the state apparatus in

---

[1] E. A. Bayne, *Persian Kingship in Transition* (New York: American Universities Field Staff, 1968), pp. 185–186, 142.

[2] John Marlowe, *Iran* (London: Pall Mall Press, 1963), p. 90.

1953. Although the Shah fled to Rome, Mossadegh's triumph was short-lived; his tactical mistakes had undermined the bases of his support, his policies had alienated important segments of the military. Three days later a military coup restored the Shah to power and enabled him to emerge as the leading political actor in Iran.

The roots of the crisis and, indeed, of the instability that characterized Iran during these years can be traced directly to educational developments of the thirties and forties and to the consequences of foreign occupation. Iran became integrated with the international economy, a process that was facilitated by the improvement of communications and transportation spurred by the occupation. The competitive propaganda efforts of Great Britain and the U.S.S.R. also served to arouse the populace. As a result of such factors, the demand for education which had been generated by Reza Shah's policies accelerated greatly during the war years and after. School enrollments grew rapidly at all levels; the number of primary students more than doubled between 1940 and 1951, rising from 287,245 to 650,355. To accommodate the flood of students, existing facilities were strained greatly, and in the major cities a half-day program had to be introduced. Private schools offering a high-quality education to those who could afford it proliferated rapidly. At the secondary level, enrollments rose at an even faster rate, climbing from 28,196 to 83,507 in the same period. A similar expansion occurred at the college level. New universities were formally opened in several provincial centers in 1949 and the number of students rose from 3,385 in 1940 to 5,502 in 1951.[3]

[3] All enrollment figures are drawn from data published in the *Report on Seven Year Development Plan for the Plan Organization of the Imperial Government of Iran* (New York: Overseas Consultants Inc., 1949), II, Exhibit B-7, and the *UNESCO Statistical Yearbook, 1969* (Paris: UNESCO, 1970). These figures essentially conform to those given by Marvin Zonis, "Higher Education and Social Change in Iran: Problems and Prospects," paper delivered at the conference, "Iran in the 1960's: A Consideration of Problems and Prospects," Columbia University, Nov. 7–9, 1968, mimeo. (New York: Columbia University, 1968), Tables I, III, pp. 12, 19, though according to his figures 101,100 students were attending secondary schools in 1951. The paper was subsequently published in *Iran Faces the Seventies*, Ehsan Yar-Shater, ed., Praeger Special Studies in International Development (New York: Praeger, 1971), pp. 217–259. According to data cited by Reza Arasteh, *Education and Social Awakening in Iran* (Leiden: E. J. Brill, 1962), pp. 57, 58, however, primary enrollments soared from 457,236 to 831,933 in this period.

This expansion of secondary and university enrollments created major problems of absorption. Economic opportunities were very limited at this time, and though most graduates entered the administration, few were able to obtain the kinds of employment to which they aspired. Often they were forced to take a second position in order to make ends meet. The resulting frustration led quickly to alienation, and at least one scholar has identified the problem of absorption as one of the primary causes for the unrest in the early 1950's:

Each successive year added its quota of hundreds of new graduates. Their feeling of being ready, willing and able to provide their services, but of finding virtually no congenial, stimulating opportunities, gradually produced a widespread atmosphere of frustration and rebellion, and a conviction that there must be a change. All that seemed to be needed was leadership; and since that was not forthcoming from the groups in political power, it came from the outside—notably from the Soviet-sponsored Tudeh party and from the Iran (National Front) party.[4]

Disaffected students, however, were only one of many elements that supported Dr. Mossadegh and his policies. From Reza Shah's schools had been graduated thousands of young, educated Iranians who, possessing new goals, values, and ideals, wished to see the emergence of a new social order within the country.

Most prominent among these elements, whose numbers and importance had been swelled by economic and political developments during those years, were the intellectuals, professionals, and bureaucrats, many of whom were frustrated by a system in which opportunities were declining while nepotism, favoritism, and similar traditional considerations continued to determine career mobility. Also aroused by the nationalist aspirations of Dr. Mossadegh were more traditional elements within the society, as well as less-educated ones, such as businessmen, tradesmen, and industrial workers.[5]

Ultimately, however, power still remained with the army, which by choosing to remain loyal to the monarchy enabled Mohammed

[4] Joseph Upton, *The History of Modern Iran: An Interpretation,* Harvard Middle East Monograph Series (Cambridge: Harvard University Press, 1960), p. 95.

[5] T. Cuyler Young, "The Social Support of Current Iranian Policy," *Middle East Journal,* 6 (Spring 1952), *passim.* See also Upton, *op. cit.,* pp. 102ff.

Reza Shah to regain his throne. From 1953 onward the Shah ruled with a strict hand and successfully consolidated his power, destroying or neutralizing actual and potential threats to his rule within the universities and elsewhere. Extensive U.S. support permitted him to strengthen the army, to develop an extensive internal security force, and to undertake various development programs which were to lead to significant changes within the country.

The Background of the Third Plan: Educational Development in the Fifties

As part of this effort, a seven-year plan was adopted in 1955, actually the second such plan. Planning in Iran dates back to the period immediately following World War II when the government decided to prepare a development program and asked an essentially American consortium to draw up a comprehensive plan. It was never implemented, however, owing partly to the many administrative problems of establishing such a pioneering and far-reaching innovation within the society, but primarily to a lack of financial resources, and, in fact, its preparation may have hastened the crisis of 1953.[6] Following unsuccessful attempts by the Shah during his visit to the United States in 1949 to obtain commitments for the necessary massive financial support, his government considered the possibilities of financing the plan by increasing the income available from oil revenues. A supplementary agreement providing for substantially greater revenues was negotiated with the AIOC in 1949, but the new agreement was widely regarded as inadequate and the banner of nationalization was easily raised by Dr. Mossadegh's National Front.

Following Mossadegh's overthrow, the United States provided significant amounts of economic and technical assistance and American influence grew rapidly. Numerous advisers soon permeated the Ministry of Education and the impact of American ideas was deeply felt in all aspects of the educational process. Many American universities accepted contracts to help develop specific projects in teacher training (Brigham Young University), agricultural education

---

[6] George B. Baldwin, *Planning and Development in Iran* (Baltimore: Johns Hopkins Press, 1967) provides a thorough and insightful analysis of developmental planning in Iran.

(Utah State), public administration (University of Southern California). Private foundations, such as the Near East Foundation, were also active in many fields, as were experts from many international agencies.[7]

One result of this activity, as in other Middle Eastern states, was to aggravate existing cleavages between graduates of foreign institutions and to introduce new sources of conflict. The most conspicuous arena where such feuding took place was the University of Teheran. There faculty educated in France attempted, unsuccessfully, to prevent the centralization of power and the infusion of American practices by a chancellor trained in the United States.[8]

Despite such negative aspects, foreign assistance helped to maintain the great expansion of the educational enterprise which continued during this period. Vast sums were allocated to this field, and primary enrollments rose from 650,355 in 1951 to 1,436,169 in 1960; secondary enrollments rose even more rapidly, from 83,507 to 295,869, during these years. Overall it was estimated that about 40 per cent of all children of primary school age and 13 per cent of all children of secondary school age were now attending school. The number of university students increased at the fastest rate of any level, from 5,502 to almost 20,000 students.[9]

Beginning in 1954 the Ministry of Education, ostensibly to meet the great demand for education and to raise existing standards, encouraged the opening of private schools through subsidies. The income from such subsidies and from the fees charged to the parents enabled these schools, which proliferated at both the primary and secondary level and which were attended mainly by children of upper-class parents, to enjoy greater resources and to attract better teachers

[7] *Ibid.,* pp. 145–146.

[8] Zonis, *op. cit.,* pp. 22–23.

[9] George Baldwin, "Iran's Experience with Manpower Planning: Concepts, Techniques, and Lessons," in *Manpower and Education,* Frederick Harbison and Charles Myers, eds. (New York: McGraw-Hill, 1965), p. 158. Our primary and university figures are in agreement with those cited by Zonis, *op. cit.,* Table III, p. 19, but according to his data secondary enrollments rose from 101,000 to 381,400 during these years. According to Baldwin, "Iran's Experience," p. 158, on the other hand, primary enrollments stood at 1,327,000 in 1960, secondary and university enrollments at 253,000 and over 30,000 respectively.

and to maintain higher standards than the public institutions.[10] In essence, what amounted to a dual system of education was established within Iran thus maintaining and strengthening the existing social stratification pattern.

Despite the rapid increase in enrollments at all levels, however, the size of the educational establishment remained relatively small, and the educational opportunities that did exist were distributed unequally throughout the country. Rural educational facilities were extremely sparse; only 17 per cent of the villages, primarily those located near major towns and cities, possessed schools. One-quarter of all schools were to be found in and around the capital, and these enrolled two-thirds of the children of primary school age in Teheran Province. In more isolated areas such as Kurdistan and Baluchistan, only about 15 per cent of the school-age population was actually enrolled. Overall, in the early 1960's, 85 per cent of urban children were attending primary school as compared to 25 per cent of rural children. A similar pattern obtained at the secondary level, the largest proportion of high school students being found in Teheran Province. The distribution of female students was essentially the same. Girls from Teheran Province constituted the overwhelming percentage of all female students, from Baluchistan the smallest. In Teheran province inhabitants of the capital accounted for the largest proportion of persons enrolled at all levels. Thus, 42.3 per cent of the male city dwellers and 62 per cent of the females were illiterate, as compared to 63 and 79 per cent of the male and female villagers of the province.[11]

As the educational enterprise expanded, it became increasingly obvious that existing attitudes governing goals of education had to be amended, and a change was evidenced in the philosophy guiding the policies of the Ministry of Education during the fifties away from the concept that the purpose of education is to teach certain facts to students and toward the belief that the purpose of education is to prepare students to function effectively in the society. In accordance with this new emphasis the objectives of secondary education were

[10]Mohamad Ali Naghibzadeh and Arthur J. Lewis, "Education in Iran" (Teheran, 1960), p. 6.

[11] Reza Arasteh, "The Struggle for Equality in Iran," *Middle East Journal*, 18 (Spring 1964), pp. 201ff.; Baldwin, *Planning and Development*, p. 144.

now defined as being "to train capable, competent and faithful individuals, in a manner to develop well rounded individuals, with both spiritual and physical powers, and to give them moral and social virtues." To further this goal, the implications of which will become evident when we relate education to its cultural environment, various changes were introduced. In theory some decentralization took place and teacher training, curriculum content, teaching methods, and the system of examinations were modified to some extent. Previously the curriculum had contained a large number of unrelated courses; now some were discontinued, others simplified, and some new subjects introduced. In 1959 the curriculum for the first cycle was rewritten, and an attempt was made to integrate the subject matter by grouping the twenty-one separate subject fields into ten major categories.[12]

All attempts at reform, however, inevitably foundered upon the inability of planners to resolve the most acute problem confronting the educational enterprise: the quality and quantity of teachers. In few provinces were there enough trained personnel to meet the need, and untrained persons were often recruited with obvious consquences for the quality of education. To resolve this problem, legislation to upgrade the attractiveness of teaching as a profession was passed; the weekly load of the teacher was reduced and higher salary schedules adopted. But neither of these steps had the desired effect. The critical shortage forced abandonment of the provision that the teaching load be reduced as the teacher became more experienced, and elementary teachers were required to teach at last twenty-eight hours per week, secondary teachers twenty-two hours per week. The attempt to raise salaries was also abandoned because of administrative and financial considerations. The failure of these efforts was, of course, disastrous for the profession. The economic position of teachers continued to be eroded as the cost of living increased steadily during the decade. Practically no teacher could support a family adequately and almost all were forced to take on additional employment. The change in the policy on teaching loads made the holding of a second position difficult, and large numbers of teachers chose to resign.

[12] Naghibzadeh and Lewis, *op. cit.*, pp. 11, 14.

As a result, the attractiveness of a teaching career declined even further, and the shortage of teachers became ever more acute; by 1960 the average class size was between forty and sixty students. To fill the need, any available personnel had to be hired, even though they often did not meet the legal requirements specifying that elementary teachers have completed the first cycle of the secondary school (middle school) plus two years of normal school, and that secondary school teachers be graduates of secondary schools with at least three years of college training. In many cases, elementary teachers who possessed only six years of formal education were appointed, and experienced elementary teachers were used to fill the vacancies at the first cycle of the secondary level. Overall, it was estimated that only 25 per cent of the 40,500 elementary teachers and less than 40 per cent of the 11,298 secondary teachers were qualified.[13]

In this period renewed attention was also paid to the expansion of vocational training and the number of vocational schools expanded greatly. At the same time, however, the number of students enrolled actually decreased owing to the irrelevance of the curricula, the very low quality of the teachers, the lack of adequate facilities and equipment, and the difficulties of finding appropriate employment after graduation. Not only were middle-level positions with adequate salaries very few, but most graduates sought desperately to avoid the kind of positions for which they had supposedly been trained and to obtain a white-collar job in the administration instead.[14]

This situation was attributable to the strength of traditional factors and to the lack of systematic attention paid to vocational education. A UNESCO team which surveyed this field pointed out that it was difficult to obtain accurate information on technical education, that official data and estimates varied widely, and that no one could ascertain precisely what the plans of the government were in this field or determine the extent to which these plans met the real needs of the country. In their report they emphasized the need to remedy these deficiencies: "We have but one comment to make on all the

[13] *Ibid.,* pp. 8–10.
[14] A. Page, H. J. Evers, and W. Mohler, "Technical Training and Economic Development in Iran," mimeo. (Paris: UNESCO, April 27, 1961), *passim.*

figures. . . . the enormous variations in the estimates clearly show the need for a special planning section of technical education in the Ministry. This recommendation has been made before, and we hope that it will be followed in the near future." [15]

Lack of systematic planning extended, of course, to all aspects of the educational system and was due partly to the traditional lack of communication and coordination between different agencies, so that "each educational body operated on an ad hoc basis, outside the framework of any predetermined plan and independently of other sectors, regardless of any relationship which existed between different educational levels," [16] and partly to the fact that serious educational planning was dependent upon a manpower plan which in turn could not be prepared until a national manpower survey was carried out in 1958. Not until the time of the Third Plan (1962–1967), therefore, was an attempt made to relate the output of educational institutions to manpower requirements in various fields. The Fourth Plan (1968–1972) further refined these projections.

Because of faulty planning and administrative deficiencies (which we shall discuss in more detail below) the attempts at reform discussed above were not based on any coherent policy and did not deal with the many serious problems confronting Iranian education in any organized way. The obvious result was that the changes that were inaugurated had but little effect upon Iranian schooling, which continued to function largely as before.

The Shah was fully aware of the serious shortcomings of his country's educational system. In 1960 he discussed primary education in the following words:

we must change the prevailing outlook. In our primary schools . . . many . . . teachers have . . . never had the advantage of a proper education, either in subject-matter or in methods. . . . Learning by rote is still stressed, rather than training the child to think for himself, to take responsibility, and to tell the truth. Our teachers . . . find themselves handicapped by poor equipment. Their salaries are low, and often they have housing problems.

---

[15] *Ibid.*, p. 18.
[16] *Education in the Third Development Plan* (Plan Organization of Iran, February 1968), p. 7; hereafter cited as *Third Plan.*

At the secondary level:

Each student should learn to love the truth and search for the truth and tell the truth. In the past the curricula and methods of our secondary schools have been very poorly adapted to this end. As in their earlier training, students learned mainly by rote; they were regarded as foolish or impertinent if they asked questions or challenged statements or thought for themselves. . . . In the Persian language we have a word *dastan,* which commonly implies something that is neither fact nor fiction but lies somewhere in between. In the past much of our teaching of history and other subjects was in that spirit, and the student learned nothing of modern natural or social science. . . . too much of the old *dastan* spirit lingers on even today; furthermore, we still over-emphasize uncritical memorization.[17]

The Third Plan

The educational provisions of the Third Plan, which represented the first comprehensive educational program in the country's history, were designed to resolve these problems and to integrate the quantitative expansion of the system which had taken place in the preceding decade. A better balance was to be sought between rural and urban facilities, between vocational and academic training, between the institutions of the metropolis and those of outlying districts.

The plan, which was regarded as the first part of a twenty-year program to modernize education and to relate it to the country's manpower requirements, was based on data whose reliability was questioned by foreign observers. A UNESCO mission on planning found that the existing information was inadequate as a basis for manpower projections. It pointed out that only 60 per cent of the births and 35 per cent of the deaths in the country were ever reported and concluded that "labor statistics, employment market information, and manpower planning are far from sufficient at present to meet the requirements of economic and social development planning. Statistical data on existing conditions are scarce and collecting, processing, analysis and publishing such data have only recently

[17] Mohammed Reza Shah, *Mission for My Country* (New York: McGraw-Hill, 1961), pp. 249, 255.

been initiated in many fields." [18] Although certain refinements and revisions were made for the Fourth Plan, such problems remain important.

Regardless of the accuracy of the statistical base, the plan specified the long-range goals that were to be achieved as qualitative improvements in the existing system and expansion of free and compulsory educational opportunities to all Iranians between seven and twelve years of age. The stress at all levels including the primary was upon upgrading the quality of education and upon measures to gear education more closely to the needs of the labor market. The plan identified several major areas of concern if the long-range goals were to be achieved, including: the expansion of the teaching staff and the upgrading of its qualifications; the improvement of educational facilities; the rewriting of curriculae to reflect the new educational philosophy which de-emphasized memorization; the preparation of new teaching materials to enable teachers to apply the new teaching philosophy; and an increase in financial resources to be obtained by tapping local funds.[19]

Priority was given to the expansion of primary education, and a target of providing educational facilities for 60 per cent of children from seven to twelve years old, or 681,000 new students, was established. Altogether 2.25 million pupils were to be enrolled in primary schools by the end of the Third Plan period, and 61 per cent of the total sum allocated to education was devoted to this level. These quantitative goals were, in fact, exceeded by about 675,000 students.[20]

At the secondary level, which consisted of two cycles, the plan proposed to emphasize qualitative improvements by limiting further expansion to about 6 per cent annually so that the number of secondary students would reach 400,000 by the end of the plan period.[21] The philosophy underlying secondary education was to be trans-

---

[18] "Report to the Government of Iran on Manpower Planning," mimeo. (Geneva: International Labor Office, 1965), p. 19.

[19] Baldwin, "Iran's Experience," pp. 160–161.

[20] *Third Plan*, p. 16. According to Baldwin, "Iran's Experience," p. 159, no clear-cut priorities were established; *Fourth National Development Plan, 1968–1972* (Teheran: Plan Organization, 1968), p. 260, n. 1; hereafter referred to as *Fourth Plan*.

[21] *Third Plan*, p. 27.

formed; no longer was this level to be viewed solely as a preparation for entrance into a university, rather

Secondary education will be regarded as a preparation for economic and social life as well as a preparation for university studies for the minority which can benefit from higher education. Secondary graduates will be ready to make a living at the end of their course, as well as having a general education. . . . There is no goal, now or in the future, to allow into academic secondary school all whose parents want them to go there no matter what their suitability. . . . The first cycle (ninth grade) will be regarded as the natural termination of secondary education for a large proportion of the pupils.[22]

These expectations proved to be totally unrealistic. Not only were the educational aspirations of the graduates of the expanded primary schools far greater than had been anticipated, but their demands were translated into pressures for admission to the secondary schools that simply could not be resisted for political reasons. This had two consequences. First, all attempts to achieve the qualitative goals established by the plan had to be postponed. Such specific projects as the improvement of foreign language instruction, the organization of supplementary summer courses, the establishment of educational and vocational guidance programs and in-service teacher-training programs simply could not be implemented in the face of the numerous urgent problems created by the vast increase in the number of students.

Second, the fact that student enrollments expanded at a rate of growth triple that envisaged in the plan (the total number of students attending secondary schools reached 658,000 by the end of this period), further aggravated two of the chronic problems confronting education: the inadequacy of physical facilities and of human resources. While the number of pupils increased by 68 per cent between 1961 and 1965, the number of secondary schools increased by only 31 per cent and the number of teachers by 34.5 per cent. And, since "secondary schools were not established and equipped in proportion to the increase in demand for secondary education . . . an increase in the volume of activities [took place] . . . thus leaving little time for teachers to control the work of the pupils."[23] The natural result

---

[22] Cited in Baldwin, "Iran's Experience," pp. 161–162.

[23] *Third Plan*, pp. 32–37; the quote is from p. 37.

was that the already low quality of secondary education declined even further as physical and human resources were stretched well beyond tolerable limits. By 1965 secondary education was considered as perhaps the most important problem area confronting the country's planners.

The crisis in teacher recruitment was aggravated by the failure to meet the goals of the Third Plan. To alleviate the already severe shortage, enrollments at existing teacher-training institutions were to be expanded and such measures as reliance upon the Literacy Corps (which will be discussed below) and one-year emergency courses in the two-year normal schools were to be emphasized. Altogether it was estimated that to meet the projected increase in student enrollments, 46,848 teachers would be needed between 1963 and 1967. In actuality only 34,620 teachers were trained through all programs, thus widening the gap between the supply and the demand. Most affected was the secondary level, where fewer than half of the estimated number needed were available.[24]

Furthermore, most of the new teachers were of poor quality, having been produced by emergency programs, and already low standards were diluted even further. Even those who graduated from the regular normal schools were not especially well prepared. A UNESCO study of teacher-training institutions revealed that the great majority were producing low-quality teachers because their facilities were inadequate, their staffs limited and poorly prepared, and their curricula extremely weak. How inadequate is the preparation of most teachers is indicated by the fact that 20 per cent of all primary teachers in 1965–1966 were untrained, and 27 per cent of the remainder did not possess the equivalent of a high school education. Thus the average teacher is poorly trained and poorly paid, and teaching remains a profession with very low status that attracts largely persons who hope that it will prove a channel to higher education.[25]

[24] *Fourth Plan*, p. 261.

[25] One analyst has suggested that the strategy of using short-term programs is more economical and reasonable than attempting to expand teacher-training facilities rapidly. The cost of training primary teachers through the one-year course was estimated as one-third the cost of later retraining to raise their standards at only 10–15 percent of this figure (Baldwin, "Iran's Experience," p. 164); R. A. Dickie, "Iran: Teacher Training," multilithed (Paris: UNESCO, October 1967), p. 8.

Despite its seriousness, the area of teacher recruitment and training was not the most glaring deficiency of the system. That distinction was granted to school construction, which was officially identified as "a worse problem than the quality of the teachers themselves." [26] Because of the lag in building new facilities, it became necessary even in large cities to introduce a split-shift system in the primary schools.

A corollary of the failure to limit enrollments to planned targets was the inability to achieve the projected expansion of vocational education. According to the Third Plan, a total of 25,000 to 30,000 persons were to be graduated from technical and vocational schools, but in practice only about 9,000 graduates were produced, about the same number as before—even though the number of students enrolled in these institutions almost doubled from 9,000 to 17,000. Increases in enrollments were not reflected in output because of the very high dropout rate, a symptom of the serious deficiencies which characterized the entire field of technical and vocational education. These have been summarized officially as:

the shortage of qualified teaching staff, the lack of proper teaching programmes for the branches of study required, poor co-ordination between existing technical and vocational schools and interested manufacturing organizations [and the fact that] the limited number of students graduating from such schools were not easily absorbed by the labor market.

The increase in the number of students was also limited by the failure to open projected new evening vocational institutes and technical colleges for women.[27]

The authors of the Third Plan also envisaged improvements in the quality of higher education, which was not marked by especially high standards. Quality had deteriorated even further during the 1950's as enrollments rose rapidly. The oldest, largest, and most prestigious of all institutions of higher learning was the University of Teheran. Modeled after nineteenth-century French universities, it consisted of practically autonomous faculties, each controlling its admissions, library resources, appointments, and promotions. Coordination between them was practically unknown, and no person or body could

---

[26] *Fourth Plan,* p. 29.
[27] *Ibid.,* pp. 30, 261.

provide leadership for the institution as a whole. More basic than these organizational handicaps, however, was the philosophy and ethos that prevailed within the institution. Few faculty were able or dedicated teachers; most instruction was by lecture, many of which were repeated year after year without change, and the student was expected to memorize the content of these lectures in order to pass the examinations that were administered at the end of each year. Salary levels were low, and raises and promotions were determined by rigid hierarchical factors that ignored ability and experience. Many instructors were only part-time and devoted most of their energy to nonacademic positions, an arrangement that was facilitated by the fact that classes at the university were scheduled in the morning. Few professors had offices where they could meet with students, and when they did they were far too busy to devote any appreciable time to developing meaningful relationships with the student. Nor did the majority of the faculty engage in research.[28]

The Shah had a very unflattering opinion of the average faculty member:

some of our professors still regard themselves as little gods whose opinions must not be disputed and whose time must not be wasted upon the students. Such a professor may march into his classroom, deliver his lecture, and march out again. . . . without any advance notification the professor may repeatedly fail to come to his class. . . . A great university professor is essentially research-minded. He possesses an attitude of deep humility. . . . But upon the slightest provocation certain of our professors will tell you what distinguished men they are. . . . Their intellectual arrogance betrays their lack of the scientific spirit. Some of them conduct no real research . . . but copy their lectures from foreign works, with or without credit being given to the original authors; or they originate some writing which they support with no scientific evidence; they deliver the same lectures year after year without ever bothering to bring them up to date.[29]

Conditions at the five provincial universities established after World War II were even worse. One American professor who spent a year

[28] Baldwin, "Iran's Experience," p. 167.
[29] Mohammed Reza Shah, *op. cit.*, pp. 258–259.

teaching at the University of Tabriz in the early 1960's has described his experiences there in the following way:

I had been warned to expect the worst, but I could not hold back a rising sense of dismay when I took up my duties at the Faculty of Letters. The building itself was a crude brick structure set between shops. . . . The dark, dirty, raw brick interior, unheated and opening upon an inner court, reminded me mostly of a stable. . . . Dim, weak-watted light bulbs dangled down into the rooms like coils of flypaper, and in order to read the text in my hand, I regularly brought along a flashlight, since most of my classes were in the late afternoon or evening. . . .

At first I attributed the bewildering quality of disorganization to the absence of the dean. . . . Classrooms kept getting mixed up; I could not find my students; they could not (or rather, did not) find me until half the hour had elapsed. School would be recessed unexpectedly; holidays were frequently declared, at the slightest pretense, . . . the students . . . soon became accustomed to me and lapsed into their usual abominable classroom behavior; whispered, made mischief while fellow students recited, and wriggled in their seats like unruly sixth graders. The general buzz was usually so loud I had to shout to be heard. . . .

Deviousness, lying, cheating and mischief were the daily lot, all transpiring in an atmosphere of hectic gaiety and excitement. . . .

The conscientious students would memorize the entire assignment, but most of them postponed this arduous work until spring, at which time they committed to memory the entire year's reading—feverishly goading themselves to the task. . . . Of course, I tried to tell them I did not wish them to memorize. . . . but to them, studying meant memorizing.

. . . As for the term papers, most of the students copied a few paragraphs from encyclopedias or books of criticism; others turned in no paper at all. Ignoring me, they were confident that the registrar of the school would only record the final mark. . . . They felt reasonably secure, since the examination papers became the permanent property of the university, locked in a safe. There *had* to be a proportionate number of high grades, middle grades, low grades and failures, so that no matter how I marked the papers, the school officials could "adjust" the marks. . . . Functionaries of the school lived partially on bribes, and students whose families were rich and powerful made their wishes felt. . . .

Corruption of the universities was only an expected part of the way things were everywhere else. Many of my students could not understand my indignation. . . . Cynics that they were, they pointed out that cheating and stealing went on everywhere, all the time, and even the most exalted were guilty of it; hence, I should not be surprised to discover it in my classes.[30]

This vivid description of the character of higher education is, of course, important not only for its portrayal of the qualitative problems but also because of the insight it provides into the nature of socializing processes. Whether such institutions, which are functionally related to the existing cultural framework, can be restructured to turn out the kinds of graduates who are needed if modernization is to take place is a fundamental point to which we shall return below.

That changes had to be inaugurated in this system was, of course, obvious to the planners, and various projects and measures to improve the quality of higher education were enunciated in the Third Plan. Of these the most important was the proposal to place all faculty members on a full-time basis. The appropriate law was adopted in 1961 and some progress was achieved, including the extension of the number of years required to earn a degree from three to four, and improvements in student-teacher relationships and in the quality of teaching in general. These changes, however, did not lead to any significant improvements in the quality of higher education, partly because the number of university students expanded rapidly, from 22,849 at the start of the Third Plan period to 38,096 in 1966.[31] This expansion, however, lagged behind the rapid increases at the secondary level, from whence an ever larger flood of graduates with one primary goal, to gain admission to a university, continued to burst forth.

Not only could most of these graduates not be accommodated but the fields of study of those who did enroll in a university bore little relationship to manpower requirements. Until now little attention had been paid to the distribution of students in various fields, and no attempt had ever been made to relate the number of students in any specialty to the projected needs of the society. Hallowed and pres-

---

[30] From *Persian Lions, Persian Lambs* by Curtis Harnack (New York: Holt, Rinehart and Winston, 1965), pp. 42–46. Copyright © 1965 by Curtis Harnack. Reprinted by permission of Holt, Rinehart and Winston, Inc., and Curtis Harnack.

[31] *Third Plan,* pp. 39–40. According to the *UNESCO Statistical Yearbook, 1969,* however, university enrollments in those years stood at 19,815 and 29,683 respectively.

tigious fields like law had always attracted large numbers of students, a trend that was accelerated by the rapidly growing enrollments of this decade, since Iran, like so many other countries, found it easier to expand the size of the student body in the liberal arts than in the sciences. Thus, in 1959, 55 per cent of all university students were studying social sciences, humanities, and theology, and only 45 per cent were enrolled in scientific fields of any kind. During the plan period, however, efforts were made to emphasize training in technological subjects, and according to official data, this program was successful: by 1965, 53 per cent of students were studying such subjects, as compared to 47 per cent in the traditional fields. To what extent such a change actually took place, however, remains uncertain because other data indicate that from 1950 to 1965 the percentage of all university students enrolled in law, the humanities, and the social sciences remained constant at about half of the total. Furthermore, it should be noted that enrollment figures are a poor indication of the actual production of any faculty. Not only do many students enroll in faculties simply because of the functioning of the admission examination, but many graduates do not pursue the career for which they have been trained, especially in technical fields, preferring to obtain a white-collar position. As we have seen, this is a common feature of other Middle Eastern countries as well.[32]

Thus the goals of the Third Plan were, at best, only partly met, and serious deficiencies continued to characterize the Iranian educational system, deficiencies that were officially described as follows:

Although relative progress has been made during the Third Plan period . . . about 40 per cent of all primary and secondary school teachers still do not hold the qualifications required for teaching at their respective levels. . . .

Teaching methods are still old-fashioned and inadequate, and academic text-books, other than those used at the primary school level, do not conform to modern scientific and educational progress. . . . A large number of school buildings are not suitable for their purpose, . . . a considerable number of schools still operate on a two-shift system. . . . The number of drop-outs, especially in vocational and technical schools, is high, and the average number of hours that the teachers actually work is less than the desired level. These and other factors have resulted in the

[32] *Third Plan,* p. 41; Zonis, *op. cit.,* Table VI, pp. 46, 47.

per capita cost of education being very high, particularly in vocational and industrial schools. . . . about 40 per cent of children of primary school age and about 80 per cent of adolescents are at present not receiving education.[33]

Education and Politics

From a political viewpoint, the most important weakness of the Third Plan was the failure to limit expansion of schooling to the planned levels. The flood of graduates had to be absorbed and, as always, the bureaucracy was the major goal of most students. The obvious dangers of political unrest led once again to the enlargement of the bureaucracy to accommodate the students' expectations, and between 1956 and 1963 the number of civil servants with higher education rose from 12,000 to 53,000, from about 8 per cent to more than 21 per cent of the total. Overall it has been estimated that the total number of professionals, bureaucrats, and intellectuals increased by about 60 per cent between 1956 and 1966, from 332,000 to 513,400. The ability of the graduates to find such positions served to encourage other prospective students, and the question of absorption became an increasingly serious one. Similar problems existed for high school graduates, only a small fraction of whom (between 11 and 16 per cent from 1963 to 1966) were able to gain admission to a university,[34] and only a small proportion of the remainder could obtain gainful employment.

Problems of absorption spurred the continuing alienation of educated elements from the regime for, although the Shah had been able to consolidate his rule, the cost of success was the neglect of many serious problems confronting the country. The disaffection of this group, whose numbers had increased tremendously as a result of the educational expansion of the fifties and sixties, is evident in the size of the brain drain. It was estimated in the early sixties that about 30,000 Iranians lived abroad, of whom at least 60 per cent had no intention of returning home.[35] Discontent could not be siphoned off in this

[33] *Fourth Plan*, pp. 262–263.

[34] James A. Bill, *The Politics of Iran* (Columbus, O.: Charles E. Merrill, 1972), p. 65.

[35] Marvin Zonis, "Educational Ambivalence in Iran," *Iranian Studies*, Fall 1968, p. 143.

manner completely, however, and the underlying frustration with the country's stagnation erupted into student demonstrations in the early 1960's. Student dissatisfaction was nationwide and many incidents occurred at all institutions of higher learning, but the most violent took place at the University of Teheran, where armed force was ruthlessly used by the government in January 1962 and June 1963 to suppress the students, an estimated 90 per cent of whom were supporters of the National Front. Altogether eleven major violent demonstrations, usually involving students, took place within the country between 1960 and 1963.[36] Nor was discontent limited to students; the thousands of new graduates represented a tremendous increase in the membership of those groups which had proven most receptive to the programs of Dr. Mossadegh and of the Tudeh party, and in 1965 an attempt was made to assassinate the Shah.

Under these conditions, the status quo could no longer be maintained, and the Shah moved astutely to stabilize the situation by launching a broad reform program known as the "White Revolution." The program, adopted by a referendum in 1963, called for land reform, the nationalization of forests, the sale of shares in government-owned factories to finance the land reform, the participation of workers in the profits of private enterprise, and the establishment of a Literacy Corps. Subsequently other projects were added, including a Health Corps, a Rural Development Corps, educational and administrative reforms, and the nationalization of waterways. Essentially the strategy evolved by the Shah was to create a modern state without transforming existing value and power configurations. To do so, he sought to establish a direct linkage with the peasantry while simultaneously neutralizing or co-opting dissatisfied elements within the country so as to gain the freedom of action necessary to implement his reform program.[37]

It may well be a mistake, however, to regard this ambitious program as merely a reaction to pressures generated by discontented

[36] On these events and subsequent developments see the articles by James A. Bill, "The Social and Economic Foundations of Power in Contemporary Iran," *Middle East Journal,* 17 (Autumn 1963), 400–418, and "Modernization and Reform from Above: The Case of Iran," *Journal of Politics,* 32 (1970), 36.

[37] In my analysis of the White Revolution, I have drawn on Marvin Zonis, *The Political Elite of Iran* (Princeton: Princeton University Press, 1971), and Bill, *The Politics of Iran.*

elements within the society. In a sense, the White Revolution can be viewed as a continuation of the strategy that Mohammed Reza Shah pursued throughout his reign. Since his accession to the throne he had been concerned with fulfilling the goals of his father and creating a strong modern nation. First, however, he had to consolidate his own power, and to do so he had to rely upon traditional elements. Thus he ran the obvious risks of undermining the bases of his regime without gaining the allegiance of new groups. With the White Revolution the Shah attempted to strike a delicate balance, to initiate sufficient development so as to maintain popular support, yet to do so without weakening the bases of power of his regime.

The continuing strength of traditional elements within the country should not be underestimated. When the Shah sought to emancipate Iranian women by giving them the right to vote in 1963, large-scale riots in the major cities resulted. Contributing to the unrest was the Shah's attempt to include some of the large religious estates in his land reform program. Since that time he has moved cautiously but steadily to reduce the power of the religious institution (very few students receive a madrasa education today), while at the same time seeking to enlist the ulema as supporters of his reform program. Under these conditions, therefore, his policy will not be easy to carry out and involves political risks.

To minimize such dangers and to safeguard his position against all potential opposition, the Shah has developed a sophisticated strategy which has at its core absolute control of the institutions of state power. The Shah has assumed personal direction of all security agencies and has placed men of unquestioned loyalty in all strategic positions within the bureaucracy and the military. Moreover, he has endeavored to implement his reform program without arousing the opposition of any large group within the society. The land reform program illustrates this point clearly. Most landowners were members of the ruling class but the reform did not alter their position. From a purely economic viewpoint landholdings were not vital, and all important families had previously diversified their interests by investing heavily in urban real estate and business enterprises of all sorts. Furthermore, the structure of the reform itself did not entail a significant loss of wealth for many, so that the economic basis of their power remains. Most importantly, however, their political base has been eliminated. They no longer exercise political control over vast areas, and the autonomy that they formerly possessed has been replaced by dependence upon the government's economic decisions. Thus, the Shah effected the redistribution of landholdings so as to begin to deal with the urgent problems of the peasantry, and he destroyed existing linkages between landlord and peasant, but he did so in a manner that did not alienate the ruling class.[38]

The Shah has also ensured that they, as well as formerly dissatisfied elements, benefit from his policies, a strategy which has been facilitated by the remarkable rate of economic growth (about 10 per cent a year) that, thanks largely to its vast oil revenues, Iran has achieved since the mid-sixties. As a result the Shah has effectively eliminated opposition to his rule and has seldom had to resort to the application of force. He has permitted supporters of Mossadegh to return to educational and other posts and has deliberately coopted many opposition leaders into important administrative offices. Although ascription remains of great importance, loyalty to the ruler has become a more important criterion for high office, as have education and ability, for the Shah sought not only to neutralize opposition and consolidate his position but to achieve his reform goals, and for this purpose needed to recruit technocrats in various fields, especially those related to economic development. Thus, by and large, the past of any individual is irrelevant if he possesses the requisite skills and is willing to change his behavior. The rewards for doing so are extremely high, and few former activists have refused to accept the power, wealth, and responsibilities that political subservience makes available. The most important consequence of this policy has been to render virtually insignificant the opposition, which has split into two groups: those who support the Shah's efforts at social change and those who view it as a device to maintain the existing system and therefore oppose it. The latter group, however, is demoralized, leaderless, and impotent.

At the same time, however, traditional patterns of social stratification and of social core group and elite composition have been maintained. Persons in key positions tend not only to be well-educated, often abroad, but also to be scions of important established families.

---

[38] See Zonis, *Elite*, pp. 27–28.

Thus, though education has become an important criterion for elite membership, persons who meet this criterion tend to be affilated with the ruling class, which has maintained and indeed strengthened its position. Empirical evidence for this point has been recently supplied by an insightful and detailed analysis of the political elite which found that the great majority had fathers who were themselves wealthy, well-educated, and powerful. Recruitment into the political elite, however, is not monopolized by the upper class and many individuals of middle- and lower-class origins have emerged in important administrative posts. Overall about 25 per cent of the present political elite come from such backgrounds. Moreover, it appears as though present social and political configurations will be maintained by the control that is being exercised over access to higher education. Not only does the system function in such a way as to eliminate many along the way but applicants for entry to a university are carefully screened; one influential personage remarked to an interviewer, "I have been instructed to restrict opportunities to those who have the most at stake in the system." [39] Thus in this area too the Shah has struck a delicate balance between stability and change and has preserved existing stratification patterns while ensuring that the bureaucracy is staffed by technically skilled persons.

At the same time, however, power considerations intrude here also, and only a degree of rationalization is permitted. Overlapping jurisdictions, diffusion of authority, lack of responsibility, and the continuing prevalence of such traditional behavioral patterns as bribery, corruption, reliance upon personal influence, and a concern with private gain characterize the bureaucracy and permit the Shah to maintain control over all aspects of administration.[40] How widespread are such patterns of administrative behavior has been attested to by the Empress Farah Diba, who recently complained about the

lack of coordination and cooperation between the different ministries and government agencies which resulted in a slowing down of progress in the country. Often a project is started without true deliberation and study and, as a result, there is chaos and confusion in the end. "Why must there be so much quarreling among these bodies?," the Empress asked emo-

[39] *Ibid.*, pp. 36–37; pp. 155ff.
[40] *Ibid.*, pp. 90ff.

tionally. "Why all this lack of cooperation? . . . No organization can succeed if it goes its own independent way. Why so much opposition from any branch against another? . . . Even in my own position, to get things done, I have to suffer so much anguish; God help those in the lower positions!" [41]

This interview should also probably be interpreted as an indication of the Shah's concern with the functioning of the bureaucracy, for the costs of the present system are extremely high and may well prevent the achievement of his reform goals. To increase administrative efficiency the Shah has made bureaucratic reform an integral part of his program and has sponsored a number of meetings to discuss ways of bringing about change in the practices discussed above. Whether fundamental improvements can be brought about, however, ultimately depends, as in other areas including education itself, upon the Shah's willingness to accept the risks to his position that would flow from the kind of policy required to create a rational and efficient administration, for, as we shall see, these behavioral patterns are deeply embedded in the cultural context.

Nevertheless the country is developing economically and remains remarkably stable. The government is so confident of its position that it has sponsored a major effort to reduce the brain drain. Efforts to stem the flow of students abroad have been supplemented by a major recruiting drive, the "brain gain," to persuade Iranians who have hitherto preferred to remain abroad for ideological reasons to return home.[42] Large numbers have, in fact, done so and occupy important technical, scientific, and administrative positions of all sorts. At the same time, Iran continues to suffer from a serious shortage of high- and middle-level manpower of various kinds, especially in the private sector, so that problems of absorption of educated persons may no longer be an important source of dissatisfaction and unrest, especially if the proposed restructuring of the educational system toward scientific and technical fields can be carried through.

Despite these impressive evidences of growth and stability, however, serious problems still confront the Shah, especially the extent

[41] *Iran Tribune,* August 1969, p. 8.
[42] On the brain drain, see George B. Baldwin, "Four Studies on the Iranian Brain Drain," in *The International Migration of High-Level Manpower* (New York: Praeger, 1970), pp. 374–396.

to which continued development can be achieved without a direct assault upon those traditional patterns and values which remain deeply embedded and which, though conflicting with the needs of modernization, legitimize the existing distribution of power and serve to maintain political stability. From an educational viewpoint, the problem is the extent to which the schools, colleges, and universities, which continue to transmit traditional values and orientations, can be restructured so as to produce graduates with the kinds of perspectives that are vital if modernization is to be achieved. Such a policy, as we shall show, not only would be most difficult to implement, but also involves important political considerations; most obviously the creation of a modern university system would produce precisely the kinds of graduates who would be most unlikely to accept the ideological and cultural foundations of the present system.

Ultimately, however, the success of the White Revolution will depend upon the commitment of the technocrats and other modern elements in Iranian society to its implementation. Although to date the Shah has, with considerable acumen, succeeded in maintaining the stability of the country and has launched many imaginative programs, he has done so essentially without sponsoring the kinds of changes that are vital if his own goals are to be achieved, and it may well be that existing configurations which we shall discuss below make it impossible for such reforms to be implemented.

The Literacy Corps

One of the most widely publicized educational projects in recent years, domestically and internationally, has been the Literacy Corps, which is regarded as fundamental to the success of the rural revolution. Since the essence of the Shah's program was to restructure rural society and to mobilize the peasantry into an effective base of support for his policies, far more than a redistribution of land was necessary. The Iranian peasant has traditionally been one of the most isolated, backward, and oppressed in the world, and to remove the burden of centuries and transform him into a modern farmer entailed the complete reorganization of rural life and the provision to the new landowners of credit, technical information, and technological assistance.

The Literacy Corps was originally viewed as a means of eliminating illiteracy in the rural areas and of promoting rural development in general. An analysis of the functioning of this program can therefore serve to provide insights into this approach as well as an evaluation of what is indeed a most significant experiment aimed at transforming rural society.

The Literacy Corps has apparently achieved significant results. By the end of the Third Plan period, 35,000 persons had been trained and about 238,000 primary school students and 106,000 adults a year attended classes taught by the corpsmen. Numerous community development projects, including the construction of 11,000 primary schools and the repair of 7,600 other schools, were also undertaken. The impact of the Literacy Corps has been officially assessed: "After land reform and other major changes, the literacy corps program has been the chief motivating factor in rural society and has been responsible for mobilizing human resources and directing them towards desirable ends." [43]

The corpsman is viewed officially as a "multi-purpose village-level worker" whose primary task is to achieve change in the education, economic condition, health, and political orientations of the villagers. In preparation for carrying out this task the corpsman undergoes a four-month training course at the end of which, if he passes an examination, he receives the rank of sergeant in the army, is outfitted with a special uniform, and is sent to a village for a fourteen-month tour of duty. Those who fail the final examination serve in the regular army. Besides the fundamental task of teaching all children six to twelve years old who have not hitherto attended school, the corpsman is expected to engage in the following educational activities: teaching adults in evening classes, starting village libraries, organizing youth and recreational groups, and supervising physical education programs. In the economic area he is expected to sponsor measures to improve the health and the sanitation of the community; among other things,

drinking water should be purified. Construction of shower baths, or changing the old pools to showers, is necessary. Changing the open latrines to sanitary ones, construction of desirable mortuaries, separating livestock from living quarters, introduction of better housing, and con-

[43] *Fourth Plan,* p. 260.

ducting special classes for village midwives for teaching sanitary methods are all of vital importance.

The corpsman is also expected to assist in the transformation of a peasant into a farmer, who

should be acquainted with the organization and functions of the Ministry of Agriculture. He needs to know the procedures for obtaining help from various sections of the Ministry of Agriculture . . . and . . . new information on insecticides, fertilizers, agricultural implements, soil studies, livestock breeding, and the like. Proper marketing methods should be taken to the farmer. New vegetables which make staple foods should be introduced. The recipient farmer needs to be prepared to assimilate all this information.

In the social sphere, the corpsman is supposed to see to it that the vacuum created by the elimination of the landlord's leadership is "filled by means of a democratic election of new leaders, and these leaders must be trained in new principles and practices of leadership." Special attention is to be paid to women, who "should be educated to take an active interest and to participate in social, economic, and political affairs." The involvement of the villagers in their own affairs is also stressed, "group action and group participation in village affairs must be promoted and encouraged, and various groups must organize to promote the village economy. Solving disputes and misunderstandings through peaceful negotiations is desirable." [44]

The Education Corps also has political objectives:

In order to inculcate the spirit of national unity, the people in the isolated villages and of the migrating tribes who speak different dialects and who have different customs and mores, should be led to the feeling that they belong to the nation. The national ties must be strengthened. Knowledge of the past national contributions to a development of world civilization and visions of the future participation in national and international development are important facets of the Education Corps training.[45]

In assessing the impact of the Literacy Corps and its effectiveness, however, certain reservations should be kept in mind. Unfortunately, precise data concerning the actual functioning of the Corps are not

[44] Amir Birjandi, *The Education Corps Project in Iran: A Work Plan for Rural Development* (Teheran: Ministry of Education, 1964), pp. 15, 16–18.
[45] *Ibid.*, pp. 18–19.

available, but several observers have commented upon various problems inherent in its concept and in its implementation.

The first concerns the adequacy of the training program. Four months is a short period in which to prepare a youth as a village teacher and change agent, but only a small part of the training program deals with practical and theoretical subjects relevant to the tasks of the corpsman. The overwhelming percentage (484 out of 708 hours) of the schedule is devoted, not to courses in teacher training and rural development, but to military subjects.[46]

The objectives laid down for the corpsmen are impossible to realize —even if the youth were to spend the entire four months in preparing himself for his role, it is obvious that few eighteen-year-olds could ever perform all the tasks assigned to him. It should be added, however, that the new Health and Rural Development Corps that were established in 1965 should lighten the load of the corpsman and will reinforce his efforts at rural development. Nevertheless, the disparity between the training program and the objectives of the Corps remains a major area of concern.

The effectiveness of the corpsman, however, is limited by factors other than poor preparation. Above all, he operates in an isolated traditional community where communications, transportation, and living conditions are primitive. He must function in a culture where age is venerated and the outside world regarded with suspicion. Though this problem is to some extent obviated by the fact that the villagers must request that a corpsman be stationed in their community (and in some cases have apparently received him enthusiastically),[47] adjusting to such an environment and functioning effectively therein is no simple matter. Other problems include the lack of physical facilities and the supervision of thousands of poorly trained instructors so as to maximize their effectiveness. A project was established to train supervisors, but one expert closely associated with the program identified the following difficulties in its implementation: "an overcrowded and irrelevant curriculum, inadequate faculty, accommodations, teaching facilities, financial resources, and ad-

---

[46] Ben M. Harris, "Literacy Corps: Iran's Gamble to Conquer Illiteracy," *International Review of Education,* 9 (1963–1964), 432.

[47] Lawrence M. Brammer, "Iran's Educational Revolution—Military Style," *Comparative Education Review,* X (October 1966), p. 497.

ministrative difficulties of various sorts." [48] Thus few corpsmen can expect to receive much useful assistance or counseling from their supervisors.

Even if the corpsman can integrate himself into the community, receive adequate guidance and support, and function ably and energetically as a teacher, many educational questions remain to be answered. The program essentially provides a two-year course in the villages; of 365,813 students enrolled in this program in 1965–1966, 52.8 per cent were attending the first grade, 26.6 per cent the second, 14.0 per cent the third, and 6.6 per cent the fourth, fifth, and sixth.[49] These figures indicate an extremely high dropout rate and it remains to be seen what degree of literacy can be achieved in this manner. Even if two years or so of schooling prove adequate in producing literacy, the question of reinforcement will become acute; that is, assuming that a child does become literate, how is that level of literacy to be retained in an isolated, traditional community where reading matter is almost never available.

In a sense, the more successful the program, the greater the problems, one of the most important being how to channel and cope with the demands for further educational opportunity that will inevitably be raised in newly stimulated rural areas. Existing facilities at all levels are already severely strained, but only limited attention has been devoted to the problems that would be created by a rise in the educational aspirations of the peasantry. It is expected that the two-year curriculum will be extended to correspond to the primary cycle and that former corpsmen who decide to become permanent teachers will receive additional training to enable them to teach this curriculum, but the question of absorbing these new graduates into the middle and higher levels of the system has not yet received adequate consideration. Because such questions reflect a lack of systematic planning and a failure to relate the program to the overall educational needs of the country, at least one observer has concluded that "serious deficiencies in this program would appear to make it a questionable approach for other countries to pursue." [50]

[48] Dickie, *op. cit.*, p. 6.
[49] Zonis, "Educational Ambivalence," p. 141.
[50] Harris, *op. cit.*, p. 433. For an optimistic assessment of the value of the corps, see Richard Blandy and Manyer Nashat, "The Education Corps in

This gloomy prognosis, however, overlooks the important non-educational dimensions of the Literacy Corps, which represents an important milestone in Iranian history. The impact of the Corps will, in fact, be considerable, though its influence will be felt primarily outside the educational sphere. In the first place, thousands of unemployed graduates were provided with meaningful positions and a potentially explosive group siphoned off from the urban centers where they would be most troublesome. Thus a dangerous political and economic problem has been alleviated, at least temporarily, and large numbers of young Iranians will become acquainted with the realities of village life. The vast majority of urban dwellers have heretofore been abysmally ignorant of rural conditions, and the experiences of the Literacy Corpsmen (and those of the other corpsmen) may well promote a new awareness of village realities among the intellectuals; the hardships they encounter may instill a sense of the difficulties involved in rural development. It is, of course, possible that this exposure to rural life will lead, not to a positive appreciation of the problems and difficulties of rural development, but rather to the further radicalization of already discontented students. As a result of his experiences the corpsman might easily become far more critical of the government and its policies than he had been. What the results of this important experiment, therefore, turn out to be for systemic stability remains to be seen.

Another important byproduct of the program may well be an increase in the number of rural teachers, for many corpsmen might decide to enter the teaching profession after their tour of duty. Here, too, the available evidence does not permit any clear conclusions to be drawn. One study, for example, indicated that 94 per cent of the corpsmen were willing to remain as teachers in their communities.[51] On the other hand, according to one expert interviewed by the author in 1969, only 16,000 out of a total of 52,000 Literacy Corpsmen have, in fact, remained teachers. Though even this figure represents an important increase in the number of teachers, few individuals were willing to return to rural areas and the majority have been assigned to towns and cities. Furthermore, it has been pointed out

---

Iran: A Survey of Its Social and Economic Aspects," *International Labor Review,* 93 (May 1966)

[51] Brammer, *op. cit.,* p. 496.

that only those who cannot obtain better opportunities elsewhere have been and are likely to be tempted to remain in the profession. Since the new recruits will not be any more highly motivated or qualified than the average poorly trained elementary teacher now active, the already low standards of the teaching staff will be diluted even further unless adequate remedial measures other than the present practice of holding summer camps are adopted.[52] Thus educational quality in rural areas will remain a serious issue for the foreseeable future.

Perhaps the most important aspect of the Literacy Corps and of the related programs will be in terms of nation-building. For the first time in Iran's history, the government is demonstrating an active interest in the peasants' welfare. The rural areas have received more attention in the past few years than in the previous millennium, and changes in peasant attitudes toward a more positive conception of the government have apparently already been identified.[53] Furthermore, the program may well serve to provide Iran with a unity it has never hitherto possessed. Farsi, the language being taught, may well replace the many different languages and dialects that now exist within the country and become the national language. In this area too, however, the implications for political stability and development are not clear. We have already noted the educational problems that will result from increased expectations by the peasantry. Similar problems will inevitably occur in other areas, for the expectations of an aroused peasantry will not be limited to increased educational opportunities but will include all aspects of their existence.[54] A heavy demand load will be placed upon the political system, but how effectively such demands can be processed and the consequences that will flow therefrom remain to be seen. For these reasons, it is suggested that though its educational impact may be limited, the psychological and political consequences of the Literacy Corps are likely to be of great importance. Unfortunately, such conclusions can only be considered tentative, since no serious research has yet been carried out on this most important experiment. That it has fulfilled the expectations of the government, however, is indicated by the establishment of a

[52] Dickie, *op. cit.*, p. 7.
[53] Brammer, *op. cit.*, pp. 495–496.
[54] Bill, *Politics of Iran*, p. 154.

women's counterpart, the Girls' Literacy Corps, in 1968 and the decision to expand its activities further the following year.

A second interesting, though far less publicized, educational innovation designed to eliminate illiteracy in a hitherto largely neglected group is the "White Tent" program which provides educational opportunities to the numerous nomadic tribesmen in Iran. This project dates back to the early 1950's when eighty teachers were trained with American assistance and dispatched to various tribal groups. They lived with the tribe and taught the children reading, writing, arithmetic, geography, history, and language. These early efforts encountered various difficulties. The nomads were displeased because they had to provide the teacher's salary from their own resources, the teachers because they were paid a lower sum than regular teachers, and to extort even this amount on a regular basis from tribal chiefs was no easy task. Subsequently forty new teachers were sent by the Ministry of Education, but it soon became apparent that the problems of adjustment and interaction between teacher and nomad required a new approach. Accordingly it was decided to recruit and train nomads as teachers for the tribes, and in 1956 a school specifically designed for this purpose was opened in Shiraz. Students from various nomadic groups were selected and entered the program. The goal was to graduate sixty teachers a year; by 1961, 127 teachers were serving in the field with various tribes. The program continued to thrive and by 1969–1970, 1,179 students had graduated. In 1970, 230 more were added to this total. The success of the program is also evidenced by the fact that only about 10 per cent of the graduates have resigned; more than a thousand, including 100 women, continue to serve as teachers in the field. Another indication of the popularity of the program is that now, with the sole exception of the Turkmen, all the different tribes are represented in the school.[55]

The Fourth Plan

The extension of educational opportunities represented but one of the many problem areas that were of concern to political decision-

[55] Clarence Hendershot, "White Tents in the Mountains: A Report on the Tribal School of Fars," mimeo. (Teheran: AID, 1965); I am grateful to Professor Pierre Oberling for making available to me data on this topic from his forthcoming book, *The Qashqai Nomads of Fars* (The Hague: Mouton, 1973).

makers as evidenced by the widespread debate that occurred in the sixties over the shortcomings of Iranian education. This state of affairs represented a radical departure from a time when school and teachers were, according to the minister of education, "the most neglected sector" in Iranian society. Because of such neglect, education retained the many dysfunctional features discussed earlier. A seminar held in 1969, for example, heard speakers condemn practically all aspects of the existing system, including its administration, emphasis upon examinations and rote learning, the poor quality of teachers, inadequate texts and other teaching materials, and weak curricula. One speaker, summarizing these deficiencies, charged that the secondary schools were "wasting the time of our young people in the meanest way possible. . . . the system puts the emphasis on quantity rather than quality. Our young people are expected to learn as many subjects as possible; in fact, they learn nothing." What is noteworthy, however, is that all these failings of Iranian education have received such widespread publicity in the past decade that one editor commenting on the seminar wrote: "but these are problems which are so well known that by now they should hardly bear repeating. It is the means of dealing with these nagging problems that should be attracting the attention of teachers and authorities." [56]

The most important attempt to remedy such nagging problems of the educational system is embodied in the provisions of the Fourth Plan (1968–1972), which aim to eliminate the lack of resonance between educational outputs and the country's manpower requirements and to raise existing standards. The new plan envisages the total reorganization of the system from a 6-6 structure to a 5-3-4 one; that is, the primary period will be reduced from six to five years and the six-year secondary cycle will be broken down into a three-year academic and guidance period and a four-year secondary stage. In the five-year primary course, which is compulsory and free for all children, the student will study Persian, religion and morals, arithmetic, geometry, social studies, science, health education, arts, manual work, physical education, and music. Upon completing his fifth year, the student will take an examination to determine whether he should be permitted to continue his studies.

[56] *Tehran Journal*, July 28, 1969; *Kayhan International*, July 30 and 31, 1969.

The aim of the three-year intermediate period is to identify the talents and aptitudes of youngsters who wish to continue their education and to determine their interests and abilities so as to channel them into the kinds of positions and educational institutions for which they are best suited. Since educational and vocational guidance is a fundamental objective, the curriculum includes courses designed to provide practical knowledge about technical and vocational education as well as practical training in a workshop or on a farm. Instruction in Persian, religion and morals, mathematics, experimental science, social science, foreign language, art, physical education, and safety is provided.

After completing the three-year cycle, students will sit for an examination to determine their future schooling. Those who pass will continue their education in either academic or practical fields, depending upon their abilities and interests. The remainder will be guided toward appropriate employment. Special entrance examinations will be available for students wishing to enter a field for which they have not qualified.

Secondary education will be divided into two branches, an academic four-year program and a practical course of from two to four years depending upon the nature of the study and the level of specialization required. The academic stream, at this level, will probably consist of two stages, the first three years being devoted to general subjects, the last year permitting specialization in science, physics and mathematics, social science, or literature and fine arts. Students who complete the first three years will be guided into the branch that is most appropriate to their inclinations and abilities. Eighty per cent of the courses in each branch will be compulsory, 20 per cent elective.

The technical and vocational cycle will be divided into two streams, the first consisting of a two-year course designed to train skilled workers and farmers, the second a four-year course designed to train middle-level technicians and administrative personnel. Students who enroll in the four-year technical branch are expected to possess higher qualifications than those who study in the two-year vocational cycle.[57]

Specific targets call for an increase in the number of primary school students from 2.9 million to 3.7 million; that is, 93 per cent

[57] "Educational Aims and the New System of Education in Iran," Publication No. 57, mimeo. (Teheran: Ministry of Education, May 1968), pp. 9, 10.

of urban school-age children and 55 per cent of rural children will be enrolled in primary schools by the end of the Plan. Enrollments in the new guidance cycle are expected to reach 737,000 at that time. At the general secondary level, the goal is to enroll 376,000, but the continuing elitist orientation of educational goals is reflected in the fact that only 20 per cent of these students will be attending public schools; the remaining 80 per cent are to be enrolled in private institutions. An additional 80,000 students will be taking combined theoretical and vocational courses designed to produce middle-level manpower. The total number of secondary school graduates in this period is estimated at 290,000 (244,000 from the academic cycle, 46,000 from the vocational and technical one). It is anticipated that these graduates will be absorbed in the following manner: 50,000 will enter universities and colleges, 42,000 will become teachers and Literacy Corpsmen, 23,700 will go into private industry, and 112,000 into the services sector. The largest proportion of the remainder— 62,300—are girls, who, it is expected, will not wish to obtain employment.[58]

The stress on vocational and technical training that is so evident in the restructuring of the educational system will also be felt by the institutions providing industrial, agricultural, technical, and vocational training. The capabilities of the middle-level vocational schools (*honarestans*) are extremely limited in capacity, quality, and range of subjects. Even in fields of emphasis, less than half the needed manpower can be produced, and many specialties such as metallurgy, industrial chemistry, and industrial designing are not offered at all. Hence a general shortage of middle-level technicians is anticipated, and the Plan urges the implementation of decisions designed to expand and restructure the existing system of *honarestans*. These measures include steps to coordinate training with actual employment opportunities, to upgrade the status of the institutions and the general quality of the training they provide, and to diversify the curriculum to include new specialties. If these measures do lead to improvement in training, the number of dropouts, presently 30 per cent, will decrease, and it is estimated that 8,000 graduates, two-thirds of the needed technicians, can be produced without any addi-

---

[58] *Fourth Plan,* pp. 266–268.

tional investments.[59] In view of the magnitude of the problems hindering the development of vocational and technical education and the experiences of the Third Plan in this regard, it remains to be seen whether the new emphasis upon the production of middle-level manpower will lead to appreciable quantitative and qualitative results.

Vocational and technical fields are also emphasized at the college and university level. Overall the plan provides for a 60 per cent increase in the number of such students, from 37,500 to 60,000. Of these, 55 per cent will receive training in scientific and technical fields. Graduates are expected to number about 35,600, and no problems of absorption are foreseen in view of the great demands for high-level manpower, especially engineers. On the contrary, a shortage of about 7,580 is envisaged.[60]

Educational Reform and the Administrative Context

Although the provisions of the Fourth Plan represent an important and thoughtful attempt at educational reform, one must reserve judgment concerning the degree to which these programs will actually be put into practice or the extent to which their implementation will lead to significant improvements. One reason for this reservation is the dubious reliability of the data upon which the manpower projections are based. This aspect, however, is closely linked to more fundamental questions concerning the administrative context in which planning occurs. We have already analyzed this problem, but its practical consequences should not be underestimated. As one analyst of the country's planning efforts has pointed out:

Public policies, administrative decisions, and national development plans all have to be made with few statistics, with unreliable statistics, and with few other forms of organized information. . . . To anyone working in this milieu it seems next to impossible to get things done, to learn what has already been done or is about to be done, to prevent things from getting undone, to learn who is doing what and the what who is supposed to be doing. Nearly everything the planner weaves by day somehow becomes unravelled by night.[61]

[59] *Ibid.*, p. 74.
[60] *Ibid.*, p. 272.
[61] Baldwin, *Planning and Development,* p. 4.

Similar considerations inevitably apply to educational activities as well. It has become commonplace in Iran for plans to be announced with great fanfare and quietly shelved owing to patterns of administrative behavior and to the lack of continuity and stability. Any new minister of education arrived with his own staff and, during his term of office, attempted to implement his own educational ideas and projects. The inevitable result, unless the Shah demonstrated a personal interest, was that few innovations were ever inaugurated on an appropriate scale or were allowed to develop over any extended period of time.

Even when a particular reform is implemented, however, many difficulties arise, for the traditional administrative tendency is to change formal aspects of different educational sectors without adequate attention to the dynamics involved or to actual conditions in classrooms. The outcome of the educational provisions of the Third Plan (and of earlier reform programs) illustrates this deficiency aptly. That meaningful change cannot be achieved by attention only to structures is also exemplified by the dysfunctional results of the new emphasis on scientific and technological subjects in the academic schools. This reform aroused the ire of many speakers at a seminar held in 1969 on the teaching of the social sciences who condemned, perhaps not unnaturally, the neglect of those subjects. At the secondary level, history, geography, and social studies are accorded two hours a week each, and to pass the student needs a grade of only 25 per cent which he can obtain by memorizing one chapter from each text. What is most important, however, is not that this arrangement has produced graduates who lack any understanding of their society, but that most are equally deficient in the sciences, since these fields continued to be taught in the traditional way. In other words, the emphasis upon science has merely meant that the student memorized more works in those subjects.[62]

For this and other reasons, many experts regard the most important proposal of the Fourth Plan, the restructuring of the educational system to include a "guidance" cycle, with skepticism and anticipate numerous problems when the attempt is made to implement it. Though the objective of diverting students into technical and voca-

[62] *Kayhan International,* July 30, 1969.

tional specialties is clearly necessary if the country's manpower needs are to be met and the pressures for admission to the universities reduced, serious doubts have been expressed concerning the desirability, feasibility, and practicability of the idea. Given the continuing attraction of white-collar positions in general and of the university degree specifically, its implementation is bound to create serious difficulties even under the most favorable conditions. Moreover, little evidence of systematic planning is apparent and many critics have argued that the 5-3-4 concept has never been analyzed in terms of practicality, costs, and benefits; that this may indeed have been the case is suggested by the postponement of the project from 1967 to 1971 because no counselors had been trained or other preparations made. It has also been pointed out that in many respects the project represents a luxury for a country whose educational problems are so great and so evident. Its success will depend upon heavy inputs of specialists who can guide students and administer sophisticated, evaluative tests such as personality and psychological examinations, but such skills are scarce and could probably be used more profitably elsewhere. The new program will also place heavy demands upon the classroom teacher, and it is unlikely that the quality of the average teacher is adequate to permit the successful application of the new principles. Thus the structure may change but content and application will probably remain essentially the same.

Besides such practical obstacles, the very concept of a "guidance" cycle can also be criticized. Essentially the goal is to steer more students into technical fields and away from academic careers, but this goal could probably be achieved much more easily by relying upon far simpler devices such as well-planned examinations or even the record compiled by the student in his school career. For these reasons many have argued that, given the present level of Iran's educational system, the program, even if it does prove workable, will represent a waste of time, energy, and resources that could have been utilized more fruitfully elsewhere.

If meaningful educational change is to be achieved in this context, therefore, an efficient educational bureaucracy that can not only stress structural reform but also consider the functional variables involved in the implementation of different programs is vital. To create such a perspective within the existing context of Iranian administration, however, represents a complex challenge because, as we have seen, prevailing patterns of coordination, implementation, cooperation, and planning represent major bottlenecks to efficient administration throughout the bureaucracy and these patterns are closely linked to the political and cultural environment.

Nevertheless, structural reforms have been implemented in the field of educational administration, most notably the breaking up of the former unwieldy Ministry of Education, which hold some promise of amelioration. Many observers have commented on the very limited coordination, integration, and cooperation, both vertically and horizontally, within the Ministry, and on a general level of efficiency which has been considered poor even by standards in other ministries. The cost to Iran has, of course, been tremendous; one indication of the wastage is that only five out of 136 countries spent more for central educational administration than Iran (14.6 per cent of the total education budget).[63] Now the original Ministry is responsible only for primary and secondary education, the new Ministry of Science and Higher Education has jurisdiction over educational planning, and there is a third new Ministry for Cultural Affairs and Fine Arts.

To staff the new ministries with qualified educational, administrative, and supervisory personnel, the Institute of Planning and Educational Administration was established in 1969 according to the provisions of the development plan. The aim of the Institute is to provide in-service training in planning and educational administration to personnel in ministries dealing with education. Plans call for a series of courses ranging from one week to several months for central and local administrators in various specialized fields such as budgets, personnel administration, and the like. Whether the graduates of this institution will be able to transform educational administration in Iran and whether reorganization of the Ministry of Education will lead to greater efficiency remains to be seen. Indeed, some observers have argued that its fragmentation may complicate all aspects of educational decision-making, since the division of functions and responsibilities among different bodies will increase problems of coordination and cooperation.

Another important administrative reform that may well encounter

[63] Zonis, "Higher Education," p. 224.

similar difficulties involves the decentralization of education within the country. The Ministry of Education plans to delegate authority and responsibility to the local chiefs of education in each province. The Ministry will take the role of supervisory leadership and will establish and enforce general standards concerning curriculum, teacher training, and other matters. Implementation and local adjustments, however, will be the direct responsibility of the local authorities. The objectives of this program are to encourage widespread recognition of the need for modern education; to find ways to gain the confidence of the populace by enabling them to participate actively in planning and to obtain their financial support for the expansion of educational facilities; and to reorganize educational administration at the provincial level so as to increase the authority of chiefs of education in administrative and financial matters. Although this reform is vitally needed, it will not be easy to alter existing practices because, among other things, "school officials are so overburdened with paper work that they have no time for the real job of running the schools." [64]

Culture, Politics, and Higher Education

Even though the new-found attention that is being accorded to education and the administrative changes that have been made and are being discussed are promising, it will not be easy to overcome the administrative, cultural, and educational traditions that mitigate against the transformation of the existing system. Further complicating the issue are the political factors we have already discussed, which inexorably intrude into decision-making and often conflict with the requirements of educational rationalization. This is most obvious at the university level, which of all levels has probably been accorded the most attention in recent years. Thus the fate of university reform may well serve as an indication of the degree to which the educational revolution will achieve its goals.

Because of its political, economic, and social importance, the Shah has taken a personal and continuing interest in the many problems which continued to characterize Iranian higher education, and the Fourth Plan anticipates qualitative improvements to alleviate the

[64] *Tehran Journal,* July 28, 1969.

chronic intellectual deficiencies we have already discussed. Suffice it, therefore, to point out that a 1968 study revealed that only 7 per cent of the students at the University of Teheran used the library, and that the head of the new Social Research Center of the University declared: "Students do not listen carefully during lectures. I have told them to listen many times during my lectures but unfortunately they have not paid attention . . . students are not in the habit of taking notes during lectures. . . . It is not enough to give them mimeographed sheets . . . it is quite possible that professors would mention new things." Subsequently the chancellor forbade the distribution of mimeographed lecture notes to the students, since students merely collected these notes and memorized them for exams without ever attending classes. He pointed out that not only should students take their own notes at lectures, but that they should be encouraged to study books rather than confining themselves to memorizing lecture notes. As for providing an intellectual environment where research could be carried out, a UNESCO consultant who made a study of the organization of scientific training in Iranian universities and colleges called for the total reorganization and rationalization of this field. He concluded that "scientific research does not yet exist in Iran except for a very few, rare, instances." [65]

The absence of a rational intellectual climate within institutions of higher learning does not mean that the students are receiving a dysfunctional education, if functionality is viewed in terms of preparation for the existing social order. Indeed, Iran's colleges and universities, like the other parts of the educational system, are solidly embedded in the sociocultural milieu and functionally related to it, a phenomenon which has been described as follows:

Although this academic environment sounds grim on the basis of abstract educational theory, it is no different from the environment or society into which the student will have to enter after he leaves school. Consequently, the educational system may be said to be well adapted to preparing the students to live and work effectively in their society, and as such, the Iranian educational system may be said to be a success. It only is a failure

[65] *Kayhan International,* Feb. 22, 1968; the study is reported in the issue of Jan. 24, 1968; *Tehran Journal,* March 25, 1968; M. Soutis, "Iran: Organisation de l'enseignement supérieur scientifique," multilithed (Paris: UNESCO, 642/BMS/RD/AUS., July 1968), p. 64.

if, it is argued, its role is to *change* and not to *adapt* to the occupational environment that the student enters. For the system incubates the "educated man" who primarily, although not exclusively, is a political animal, who is a good memorizer, who speaks well, but not concretely, who is quick to copy and serve those in authority, who tends to talk rather than to act, who hates to make decisions, who is not utilitarian, who is not objective, who cannot operate effectively in a critical environment, who does not necessarily understand what he accepts, who cannot analyze his responsibilities, who is not adaptable as far as the work and the positive environment are concerned (but only as far as maneuvering people is concerned), and finally, who basically is insecure and maladjusted to any of his occupational demands and consequently, unproductive—in brief, an individual who is the very antithesis of the kind of educated or sophisticated individual required to participate in, let alone create and develop, a rational, self-generating economic system.[66]

That these traits are, in fact, characteristic of university and college graduates has been corroborated by a study of the "modern middle class," which indicated that they possess an orientation that is a positive impediment to modernization, and that they can best be characterized as traditional men. They believe that man is evil and irrational and always changing, that today's friends are tomorrow's enemies, that man is not to be trusted, that achievement depends upon the manipulation of people, that they are morally and intellectually superior to the rest of the people, and that government is the enemy of the people. The respondent in this study tolerates lies to a remarkable degree, regards the telling of truth as a sign of stupidity, and uses emotional prose and exaggeration in his communication with others.[67]

Such values and attitudes, of course, have a direct bearing upon the patterns of administrative behavior that we have discussed, and one scholar who has analyzed Iranian culture in terms of its administrative practices has singled out similar traits and values as most relevant. These include the total absence of any feeling of community beyond the family, and an extreme individualism unaccompanied by feelings of personal integrity, responsibility, or initiative, so that individual relationships are based on distrust, suspicion, pessimism, cynicism, jeal-

[66] Norman Jacobs, *Sociology of Development* (New York: Praeger, 1966), p. 159.
[67] Raymond D. Gastil, "Middle-Class Impediments to Iranian Modernization," *Public Opinion Quarterly*, 22 (Fall 1958), *passim.*

ousy and envy, and behavior is rigid and compulsive. As a result, subjectivity and traditionalism dominate decision-making at all administrative levels and the process of making decisions is characterized by illogical and irrational communications, a lack of planning, fatalism, and highly ritualized, absolute deference to authority, which is highly centralized and never delegated.[68]

The degree to which these traits continue within the society can readily be appreciated from a speech by Empress Farah Diba, who severely criticized the extreme sycophancy and flattery to which she was constantly subjected by all classes. The speech naturally elicited widespread comment, and, most significantly, the educational system was singled out as one of the most important contributing factors by at least one editor. He wrote, "Our schools are still organized in such rigid ways as to train our children in a totally outdated tradition as far as social behavior is concerned." [69] To restructure a system which, though it socializes students into patterns of behavior that are "totally outdated" and dysfunctional to modernization, is fully integrated into and supportive of the existing sociocultural environment and also facilitates the Shah's policy of cooptation and division would be no simple matter under the most favorable circumstances. In the present context, the orientation of the political elite itself, whose members, according to a recent study, share the attitudes of insecurity, mistrust, and cynicism that we have analyzed, complicates the issue. Though they are extremely well-educated and have traveled extensively abroad, they are by no means committed to the creation of a modern educational system. Their views on education are highly traditional, stressing elitism and a strong belief in the uniqueness and efficacy of existing cultural patterns. Thus their feelings can best be viewed as ambivalent: On the one hand they are fully convinced of the need to develop the country's educational system qualitatively and quantitatively; on the other, they possess highly traditional views of the scope, character, and purpose of education. Moreover such attitudes are strongly held by all members of the elite, young and old, those with advanced degrees and those without. As a result:

---

[68] Richard W. Gable, "Culture and Administration in Iran," *Middle East Journal,* 13 (Autumn 1959), 407–421.

[69] *Kayhan International,* June 30, 1969; Amir Taheri, "The High Gate," *ibid.,* July 1, 1969.

There is no reason to expect . . . that the increasing influence of the younger and currently less powerful of the political elite (and also the better educated ones) will result in any marked attitudinal shifts in the governing group. Those who must make and implement future decisions which will affect the Iranian political system in general and its educational system in particular are as likely as the present elite to be prisoners of their own attitudinal ambiguities.[70]

Under these circumstances any decision to restructure higher education involves considerable difficulties and obvious political risks, but the pressures for change simply could not be ignored and the Shah apparently decided to accept some of these risks in 1968. Confronted with a system that was not producing the kinds of "modern men" who were vitally needed to implement the White Revolution, with the dissatisfaction of many students with the status quo, and with the continuing and growing pressures for admission to the universities, the Shah resolved the struggle that was underway between proponents of reform and advocates of the status quo by proclaiming an educational revolution aimed at transforming colleges and universities so as to make them a dynamic component of the country's drive to modernity.

To implement the new revolution a conference was convened at Ramsar which drew up a charter calling for fundamental reforms in existing practices. Traditional abuses were to be eliminated, and the university staffs and administrations were to earn salaries sufficient for a reasonable standard of living and ideally would be willing to devote their lives to the service of knowledge and the pursuit of truth. Those who took advantage of their association with the universities to increase their income or social standing were to be replaced by chancellors, heads of faculties, and staff who were familiar with modern educational practices and who would devote full time to their academic responsibilities. In the selection and promotion of academic staff, such criteria as age and length of service were to be replaced by such qualifications as a willingness to devote oneself full-time to academic pursuits, familiarity with modern methods and practices, ability to conduct genuine research, and willingness to cooperate with colleagues and to devote time to students. In short, every effort would be made to develop the quality of research and teaching and to relate

[70] Zonis, "Educational Ambivalence," p. 145.

the activities of the universities and research centers to national needs.[71]

To ensure that these reforms would be implemented, the Shah accepted the resignations of all university chancellors. Of the eight, only two were reappointed, and these positions are now filled by highly educated young technocrats, predominantly with graduate degrees from European or American universities. The Shah has continued to demonstrate his personal interest in this topic and convened a conference in Shiraz one year later (1969) to evaluate the progress that had been achieved to date. Among the gains noted were: (1) the atmosphere in the universities had improved, owing to new student-teacher dialogues and student participation in decisions involving them; (2) increased attention was being paid to provincial universities hitherto neglected; (3) 150 young professors had been recruited from abroad as faculty for the provincial universities; (4) Aryamehr Industrial University had successfully enlisted the assistance of the private sector; and (5) Pahlavi University was serving as a model in raising standards.

Although these achievements appear impressive, the many weaknesses characterizing Iranian higher education could obviously not be resolved in such a short span of time. To alleviate serious deficiencies that remained, various resolutions stressed that (1) all research work be original and not duplicate that previously carried out in the West; (2) all aspects of administration be improved; (3) objective standards for the promotion and the appointment of faculty be adopted; (4) interuniversity cooperation be improved; (5) medium- and long-term programs be drafted by the Ministry of Science and Higher Education in cooperation with the universities; (6) wider use be made of night classes and TV; and (7) greater attention be paid to teaching Iran's cultural heritage.[72]

The importance of university reform in Iran today and of coordination and cooperation was also indicated by the establishment of a new body, the Central Council for State Education, comprising the ministers responsible for education, science, culture and arts, the di-

[71] "Charter of the Educational Revolution," mimeo. (Ramsar, Aug. 7, 1968), *passim;* on the causes and consequences see Zonis, "Higher Education," pp. 208ff.

[72] *Kayhan International,* May 10, 1969.

rector of the plan organization, the head of the Institute for Scientific Research, Planning, and Education, and all the university chancellors. This council was assigned supreme responsibility for dealing with all aspects of higher education, including planning and coordination, the harmonization of laws, administration, financial and employment procedures, the establishment of priorities for the disbursement of funds, credits and grants, criteria to evaluate faculty and students, and minimum standards for admission.[73]

Essentially this council has been charged with supervising the educational revolution but its task is not a simple one, for, despite the positive measures that have been adopted and the Shah's concern with university reform, educational issues, as we have emphasized, are inextricably linked to fundamental political and cultural questions, and educational decisions involve calculations of costs and benefits in terms of power and the future shape of the society. The inevitable result is ambivalence toward the restructuring of higher education, for such a policy would have to be implemented in the face of opposition from various groups who approve of the status quo, including as, we have seen, members of the political elite itself as well as many administrators and faculty. Moreover, the consequences might well be the transformation of an educational system that supports existing patterns into one that destabilizes them.

Any fundamental change would inevitably affect the position of students who, in the early sixties, vividly demonstrated their alienation and opposition to the regime. The Shah effectively applied the same policy toward them that he utilized in dealing with other opponents; he gained effective control over all university affairs and defused potential causes of unrest by carefully screening applicants, meeting some of the student demands concerning fellowships, examinations, physical facilities, and the like, by coopting leaders, by guaranteeing students who remained politically reliable access to positions of power and prestige, and, when necessary, by resorting to intimidation.

How such considerations influence the functioning of higher education can be vividly illustrated by an examination of the development of Pahlavi University in Shiraz; although it was hailed as a

[73] *Ibid.*, May 29, 1969.

model for the other institutions of higher learning at the 1969 conference that evaluated the progress of university reform, it actually serves as a case study of the complexities involved in implementing an educational revolution in contemporary Iran.

In 1959 the Shah, on a visit to the United States, indicated his interest in establishing a modern American-type university in Iran, an indication that soon resulted in the arrival of a team from the University of Pennsylvania. Following an examination of the existing higher educational facilities, the team recommended that the University of Shiraz, which dated back to 1949 when a small medical school was established and which by 1959 had faculties of science, literature, and agriculture, be metamorphosed into a new institution. Pahlavi University was legally established on June 30, 1962, under principles radically different from those that prevailed in the other Iranian universities. Although the Ministry of Education was the principal source of financial support, the University was an autonomous institution administered by its own board of trustees and all matters relating to staffing and student affairs were vested in the University itself.[74]

The University signed an AID contract for advisory services, and important accomplishments that resulted from the efforts of the Pennsylvania team and local Iranian administrators and faculty included the rapid growth of physical facilities, the development of an American type of liberal arts curriculum, the establishment of fundamental library holdings in several fields, the organization of a lecture and seminar series, the institution of faculty meetings, the opening of a biological museum, and the carrying out of University-sponsored archaeological excavations. Minor achievements (though significant ones in terms of the environment) included the publication of a bulletin for the College of Arts and Sciences and of a faculty directory and the preparation of class schedules prior to the actual beginning of classes.

These accomplishments, however, must be balanced against the size of the human and material resources that were provided and the shortcomings that today characterize the institution:

[74] Arthur Doerr, "An Assessment of Educational Development: The Case Study of Pahlavi University, Iran," *Middle East Journal,* 22 (Summer 1968), *passim.*

Pahlavi University is rich in prospects, but the prospects remain un-realized. The faculty, with notable important exceptions, is not distin-guished. The students, though carefully selected, bring backgrounds of intellectual achievement, personal discipline, and cultural mores which are inimical to creative thinking, perception and cognition essential to real academic excellence. . . . The faculty, students, and administration ap-pear unable to communicate effectively with each other. The student is being shortchanged by inadequate instruction in many areas, and . . . stifled by an arid intellectual climate and an unimaginative program to fulfill the needs of the inner man. The student is considered a kind of automaton who should follow instructions, regurgitate pre-digested ideas and follow slavishly a pattern of concern set for him in high school. Pahlevi officials, rather than feeling a sense of destiny, appear to drift with the tide. . . . Personal ambition seems to consume many, and self-seeking not infrequently overrides the needs and demands of the institu-tion.[75]

Thus, although the structure of a modern institution has been created, the content remains elusive and Pahlavi University is functioning along traditional Iranian lines.

The essential reason for this state of affairs is to be found in the character of the environment within which the institution has always functioned, especially the cultural and political aspects discussed ear-lier. Pahlavi University was conceived by the Shah as a means of creating a first-class center of higher learning. Such a move would have important advantages politically and educationally. Firstly, the University of Teheran had been the scene of much antiregime activity. The creation of a new university far from the capital, with high standards, would lessen the importance and prestige of the older in-stitution and would also serve as a spur to academic reform. Further-more, such a university would stop the brain drain and provide a powerful incentive to many Iranians to return home by offering them the opportunity to participate in the development of a modern pres-tigious institution. Its establishment would also increase the number of students who could be admitted to higher education, and its remote location would lessen the dangers of student unrest.[76]

Counterbalancing these advantages were the political dangers in-

---

[75] *Ibid.*, pp. 322–323.
[76] Bill, "Politics," pp. 78–87.

volved in creating a modern institution of higher learning. To minimize the risks, the Shah sought to maintain control by appointing persons loyal to the regime to positions of administrative power. The faculty, on the other hand, was composed largely of persons who had hitherto been alienated from the existing culture and who had chosen to remain abroad rather than return to what they regarded as a hostile environment. Their expectations that the situation would be different at Pahlavi University were soon disspelled, for the essential consideration affecting all educational decisions was the maintenance of stability and the prevention of unrest. Thus the faculty rapidly found itself enmeshed in the traditional context and subject to the normal blandishments utilized to maintain the status quo. As a result the faculty rapidly fragmented, some cooperating with the administration, some working to produce change. The students represented the third force, and various strategies were utilized to maintain their allegiance to the status quo, including the administration's support against the faculty over such issues as grades, generous fellowships, and excellent physical facilities. Quite naturally, "it is considered more important to keep the students happy . . . than to see to it that they are getting an education characterized by real excellence." [77]

Hence, conflict rapidly ensued between faculty, students, and the administration, and often among factions within each group, all of whom possessed different perceptions of the functioning and purpose of the university and their role therein. It is for this fundamental reason and not because the "de facto head of the University is himself an uneducated man who . . . has no concept of the purposes, structure or function of the University" that "the priorities of the University are all askew." [78]

Recent events at the University of Teheran provide further insights into the complexities of academic reform within the present context. In late 1970 student demonstrations led to the temporary closing of the school. Trouble centered around the Faculty of Law, whose dean, Dr. M. Ghanji, an able young scholar trained abroad, had been appointed by the Shah in 1968 in accordance with his policy of placing reformers in important university positions. Dr. Ghanji promptly

[77] *Ibid.*, pp. 199–200; Doerr, *op. cit.*, pp. 320–321.
[78] Doerr, *idem.*

moved to introduce the kinds of changes provided for in the Ramsar Charter including the introduction of new and relevant courses in the curriculum and the establishment of linkages with various ministries to make it easier for graduates to find employment. He also moved to transform the faculty and its orientation by insisting that professors hold only one position and that they be in their offices every morning, replacing several staff members with young faculty, and generally attempting to exercise control over the content of specific courses to prevent abuses. As a result of these changes Dr. Ghanji aroused much opposition in various quarters, and before long trouble erupted over a minor issue, how long students should be allowed to prepare between different parts of the annual examination. Originally they were allotted forty days, a practice which permitted students to do little during most of the school year; it was reduced to twenty in 1969 and to eight in 1970. Law and literature students protested, and when Dr. Ghanji took a firm position a disturbance broke out and police were called in. Some students were arrested, others drafted into the army, others expelled from the university. Passions continued high, violence erupted again in several locations, the university was closed, and Dr. Ghanji's position severely shaken.[79]

Under these circumstances it should not be surprising that the Shah's reform program has had but little impact upon Iranian higher education. What is particularly noteworthy, however, is that pressures may be building up among even moderate students for further steps to implement the promised reform. In May 1971 a hundred students, all of whom were members of the Iran-i Novin party (the Shah's party, which had scored an overwhelming victory in the 1970 municipal elections) met with the editors of *Kayhan*, a major Teheran newspaper, to discuss the causes of student unrest and conditions within the universities. The students felt that activists comprised only a small minority, but emphasized that practically all students were concerned with political issues even though they had no opportunities to acquire knowledge on these questions, to learn how to analyze and discuss political affairs in a meaningful and sophisticated manner, or to express their views through legal channels—a fact which, in their

[79] David Housego, "Dean's Innovations Outrage Teheran Students," *The Economist,* Dec. 11, 1970.

eyes, represented a major reason for student agitation. They strongly complained of existing teaching practices, pointing out that some professors were teaching courses in which they had no expertise, many were still teaching from thirty-year-old notes, few carried out any research, and classes were still conducted in a highly traditional manner. As a result the students felt that they were acquiring a useless and outdated education and argued for greater relevance, especially for training in political and social science. They also appealed to the government to implement the Ramsar Charter, particularly in the area of student-faculty relationships. They sought closer contacts between faculty and students, the opportunity to express and defend their viewpoints, the right to question professors and to receive a reasonable answer instead of an abrupt dismissal, a greater role for students in university life, and the replacement of administrators who were not comfortable with the provisions of the charter with new men.[80]

The dismal picture painted by these students demonstrates the degree to which traditional patterns remain unchanged despite the Shah's evident concern with the state of higher education and his efforts to ensure that the provisions of the Ramsar Charter be carried out. As we have pointed out, given the conditions within the universities and the existing interaction with the social, cultural, and political milieu, the Shah's strong support is required, for the transformation of education at any level will require far more than an imperial decree. Without his personal, continuing, intervention the changes that are necessary will not be forthcoming, but even if the appropriate decisions are made many serious obstacles remain. If the Iranian educational system is ever to modernize, a prolonged, comprehensive, and determined effort, administered by able and dedicated officials at all levels and supported continuously by the ruler, will be required. Whether the Shah would be willing or able to mobilize such resources and whether such a policy is possible given the existing political configuration remains to be seen. Yet even a commitment of this magnitude may not suffice, for it is doubtful that such a basic change in educational practices can be achieved without at the same time promoting a policy of modernization in all aspects of Iranian life and culture, a

[80] *Kayhan* (Air Mail Edition), May 13, 1971 (in Persian).

policy that would involve even higher costs of all kinds. Thus Iran today confronts a fundamental dilemma involving conflict between cultural, political, and developmental considerations. Such conflict has characterized Iran for the recent past, and the ways in which this tension is resolved will, in the last analysis, determine the future of the educational system, and indeed of the country itself.

VIII
Conclusion

In the preceding chapters the historical development and present condition of education in the Middle East have been critically analyzed and evaluated. Now it is appropriate to apply systematically the analytical scheme elaborated in Chapter I and to bring together the various findings that emerge from this study. One basic finding is that not only do the educational systems of Turkey, Iran, and Egypt share a common heritage and similar patterns of development but the communalities are so striking that it is even possible to delineate parallel stages of educational development. In each case educational reform was initially equated with military strength, was born out of military necessity, and dates back to an era when indigenous elites, confronted with powerful external challenges, came to the realization that their aspirations, whether survival or aggrandizement, depended upon revitalized military establishments. Among the varied reforms adopted to strengthen the armed forces was the opening of new schools for officers to learn European methods of warfare. It was soon apparent, however, that military strength was derived from a varied and interrelated complex of technological skills, and other schools were soon developed to provide cadres trained in the many specialties needed by a modern army. Thus the number and types of technical military schools proliferated, and an independent system of nontraditional educational institutions came into being.

Closely related to these innovations was the awareness that European skills and knowledge were applicable to civil affairs and that reforms were also needed here to provide the infrastructure vital to the successful functioning of the military. Before long, additional schools were opened to provide the relevant civilian sectors with persons trained in administration, technical subjects, and foreign languages. Here, too, higher institutes proliferated, so that within a relatively short period a more or less comprehensive system of modern education at the higher levels had sprung up in all three countries.

All these schools were designed to provide the armed forces and the bureaucracy with persons trained in specific skills, but to fulfill this function proved to be no simple matter since qualified instructors, appropriate instructional materials, and adequately prepared students were not available. To remedy such deficiencies various solutions were attempted, including hiring European instructors (as costly and inefficient a method then as now), sending students abroad, and establishing preparatory courses, but such expedients quickly proved inadequate. Nor were the traditional institutions able to assist in meeting these demands, so that the need for a comprehensive modern educational system free from religious control became ever more apparent. The resulting pressures led inevitably to the opening of additional modern schools, first at the secondary level and later at the primary level, to supply the new system.

This phase can be considered as the third stage in the development of modern educational systems (the first being the opening of higher schools to serve the military, the second the establishment of higher institutions to provide manpower for the bureaucracy). The number of modern schools at all levels proliferated, though in different decades in each country, and in time a more or less comprehensive system of education from the primary to the university level was established. Thus, by the end of the nineteenth century the Middle Eastern states possessed a significant number of competing and unintegrated modern schools, some of which were public, others foreign, still others private, which paralleled and rivaled the traditional religious schools organized along medieval lines. These had successfully resisted all attempts at reform, and by the end of the nineteenth century the only major change was the addition of new subjects such as science to some of their curricula.

Subsequent developments represent a fourth stage. The process of diversification, differentiation, integration, and centralization continued in each country. At the same time, educational opportunities expanded greatly and roles became more professionalized. Nevertheless, the focus remained upon structural rather than functional change, upon ad hoc improvements rather than upon the elaboration of a systematic and coherent set of policies based on a careful analysis of the strengths and weaknesses of the system in terms of national needs. Even when national plans have been drawn up, their impact upon educational practices and processes have been limited.

Within this general framework, however, important variations in such dimensions as the rate, scope, and intensity of these developments resulted from differences in the nature and timing of the stimulus for change and particularly from the orientation of a specific society. These orientations are associated with particular types of political systems, four of which—the adaptive, the radical, the reformist, and the competitive—were identified in Chapter I. Egypt and the Ottoman Empire during the nineteenth century are examples of the reformist category, Iran of the adaptive, and Turkey under Ataturk of the radical; the marked variance in the degree to which a modern educational system was introduced and accepted within the Ottoman Empire and Egypt on the one hand and Iran on the other as well as the kind of educational policy followed by Ataturk are due to the different orientations toward modern education common to each type. In Egypt and the Ottoman Empire great progress was made in developing a network of modern schools at all levels, and questions of educational reform and change became a topic of major concern to many intellectuals. Though a similar pattern occurred in Iran, in all stages Iran lagged far behind the Ottoman Empire and Egypt in terms of both the scope and intensity of the changes that were inaugurated. Only a very limited number of schools was actually established, and the number of persons who were affected by modern education remained very small.

Thus, in an adaptive system only limited change takes place in education. Most educational opportunities are within the traditional system and only a small number of modern schools are established. These are highly elitist and characterized by various devices that filter out most students at low levels. The curriculum emphasizes traditional subjects such as religion and languages and only limited attention is paid to science and technology. Throughout the system the approach is formal and legalistic, quality is low, and wastage high. Those who reach the higher stages are mostly related to the ruling class.

In a reformist system the process of establishing new schools at all levels accelerates and a modern educational system is created. Rapid expansion of educational opportunities occurs particularly in postcolonial polities where the common neglect of education by the colonial power coupled with the inevitable politicization of the populace increases popular pressures for schooling, but where expansion is organized in such a way as to maintain existing social and cultural patterns within the society. The educational structure is also characterized by imbalances and blockages which limit access to the upper levels of the system. Depending upon the specific character of the regime, religious schools are discriminated against or reformed and a more or less coherent modern system developed. Attention may also be given to bringing about improvements in the quantity and quality of education available to the populace and, through planning, to harmonize educational output with economic goals. Concern with maintaining the existing value system, however, places important parameters upon the degree to which the kinds of changes that are required to transform schools into institutions compatible with the requirements of modernity can be implemented, and little attention, at best, is paid to restructuring traditional aspects of the cultural and social environment which shape the functioning of the educational system.

Such limitations do not obtain in a radical system where the goal is modernization and appropriate policies are adopted to restructure all aspects of the society including education. Here quantitative expansion of the educational system is accompanied by structural reorganization. Not only are more and more new schools of various types established to meet the manpower needs of the society and the pressures toward egalitarianism, but at the same time imbalances and bottlenecks are eliminated and the different levels—higher, secondary, primary—are integrated into a diversified, unified system. Certain ideological orientations also have a direct and marked impact upon the schools; a policy of secularization is implemented; curricula are revised to reflect the ideological orientation of the regime and to make them more applicable to the problems of the society; and the emphasis upon modernity is reflected in a concern for planning educational change systematically and implementing whatever reforms in structures and functions are necessary to relate the educational system more appropriately to national developmental needs. Such changes are reinforced by and reinforce changes that are made in informal educational and other institutions and processes.

Competitive polities (such as modern Turkey's) are also characterized by a concern for educational expansion and rationalization. They already possess a developed system of modern schools, which is usually expanded rapidly owing to the desire of at least one of the competing elites to maintain or enhance its position by satisfying popular demands. Efforts are also made at rationalization, but the lack of unitary and cohesive leadership and the existence of organized interest groups complicates the process of aggregating differing views concerning education as well as the implementation of whatever policies may be decided upon. In such a context dynamic and able leadership is necessary to remedy whatever weaknesses and dysfunctionalities may characterize formal and informal educational processes.

That this is the case suggests that the relationship between each of these polities and their educational systems is not necessarily as close and direct as delineated above. Many variables such as priorities, resources, leadership, the international environment, and the like deeply affect the kinds of educational policies that are, in fact, implemented in any society. A competitive system such as Turkey may not enjoy such leadership and a radical system such as Egypt under Nasser may also fail to deal adequately with major educational weaknesses. We shall return to this point below.

Similar considerations are relevant to the second dimension of our analytical framework, the impact of modern education upon the region. A delicate and often subtle interplay of groups, values, personalities, and institutions is involved here too, and the process of change and innovation is, as we have attempted to show, far more complex than is generally believed. That the introduction of modern educational practices has had profound consequences for all countries cannot be denied; in fact the emergence of the different types of political systems that we have discussed is itself an indication that educational systems are not only objects of change but also agents of change. The new schools were a major channel for the transmission of new ideas, and their graduates played important roles in the modernization process though, once again, important distinctions can be made on the basis of the internal political and social configurations within a particular society. Moreover, the usual equation between modern education and reform is, at best, an oversimplification, and it is erroneous to view change in the Middle East as the result of a struggle between the reformist graduates of the modern institutions and the reactionary graduates of the traditional religious schools. Similarly, the particular contributions made by specific modern schools vary greatly, and it is important to differentiate carefully between them. This distinction is most obvious in regard to the role of the American and the French missionary schools in promoting the development of Arab nationalism. Not only has the overall contribution of these schools been greatly exaggerated, but important differences characterize the relationship of specific institutions to this movement.

Our primary concern, however, is with the ways in which the introduction of modern education has affected the character and composition of social core groups and elites within different societies. In this regard, one fact stands out: Educational achievement became increasingly important as a criterion for recruitment into elite positions, and the links connecting status, mobility, and education became tighter and tighter. Here too, however, the centrality of the schools as determinants of power and status within any society varies according to the society's social and political configuration. Before the introduction of modern education, Egypt, the Ottoman Empire, and Iran could all be characterized as feudal societies whose social core group consisted of a ruling class, though in the case of the Ottoman Empire this pattern represented a shift away from the recruitment of functional elites on the basis of achievement criteria which had characterized the Empire at its zenith.

During the course of the nineteenth century educational developments led to important changes in the social-core-group pattern within Egypt and the Ottoman Empire. Although Egypt retained a ruling class, the reforms of Mohammed Ali and his successors led to the displacement of the Turco-Circassian ruling class by a new one, most of whose members were native Egyptians. This pattern remained until 1952, when modern elements seized power, established a radical political system, and forged a new social core group—a political elite consisting of officers and technocrats. In the Ottoman Empire the ruling class structure was also retained but its composition changed drastically as many persons of non-ruling-class background realized the opportunities created for persons with nontraditional skills and acquired a modern education plus a knowledge of Western languages and thus gained access to positions of power and importance. These persons were co-opted into the ruling class within a relatively short period of time and a fairly rigid stratification pattern re-emerged and lasted until the 1908 revolution. By that time the demand for modern skills was so great that many persons had acquired a modern education, and in the political changes that followed, a series of functional elites, within which members of the upper class were well represented, began to emerge. This process accelerated during the reign of Ataturk, and by the end of World War II competition between various elite groups was so keen that the political framework was transformed into a multiparty system. In Iran, no change took place in the social-core-group configuration during the nineteenth century or even during the reign of Reza Shah, who retained traditional stratification patterns despite his commitment to reform and change. The modern schools proliferated but maintained a highly elitist orientation that facilitated the retention by the ruling class of its traditional position. Nor has the reform program inaugurated by Mohammed Reza Shah in the sixties yet led to fundamental change, though many technocrats have been co-opted into ruling class membership.

Thus, from these three cases one fundamental point emerges: the establishment of a modern educational system does not automatically create channels of mobility for persons of lower or even middle class backgrounds unless the advancement of such elements is deliberately promoted by the ruler or the political elite. If no such policy is pursued, then students for the new schools are drawn from groups that are already prominent within the society. Depending upon the cultural and social environment, they can be persons of upper-class backgrounds (as in Iran in the nineteenth century) or persons who hold office at the center and utilize opportunities that are not monopolized by scions of the upper class (as in the Ottoman Empire in the first half of the nineteenth century). It does not take long, however, for most members of an upper class to recognize the importance of a modern education and to ensure that its offspring acquire appropriate modern knowledge and skills. Given their wealth and other perquisites, the result is often continuity in patterns of composition of social core groups and elites, a continuity that can be reinforced by controlling access to higher education.

To what degree such policies are followed is also determined by the character and functioning of the political system. In an adaptive polity, concern with the status quo ensures continuity in the composition of social core groups and elites. In a reformist or competitive system, such continuity is also marked, though to a lesser degree, since the expansion of educational opportunities creates possibilities for mobility that can be utilized by persons of nonelite background, and policies designed to promote the advancement of particular groups may also be undertaken. Radical polities are even more likely to adopt such policies so that it is in these societies that one can differentiate most sharply between past and present patterns of social core groups and elites.

Patterns of continuity and change are also evidenced in the pattern of educational development itself. Though the processes of integration, differentiation, diversification, expansion, and centralization have taken place everywhere in the manner we have described, the functional aspects of modern schools exhibit a remarkable continuity with traditional orientations. Whether one looks at the role of the teacher or the behavior of the student or the values and attitudes of students, teachers, and administrators, one is struck by the remarkable degree of continuity with traditional practices. Islamic customs have everywhere proven able to resist innovation, and antiquated approaches have been grafted so successfully onto new institutions that many provide a modern equivalent of a madrasa education.

Reinforcing this heritage was the imprint left upon the modern schools by nineteenth-century European practices as what once represented radical change proved remarkably compatible with established practice. Particularly influential was the French model. The native elites of all three countries looked to France for their inspiration, and the French, eager to expand their influence in the Middle East, provided advice and encouragement as well as services and facilities of all kinds so that the new military and civilian schools in Iran, Egypt, and the Ottoman Empire were usually based on French models; French officers, teachers, and experts helped establish and administer them and dozens of military and educational missions were sent to France. Nineteenth-century French schools, like all other European schools of that age, were not noted for flexibility and individuality, and instruction by rote and the memorization of accepted factual data soon came to characterize modern and religious school alike.

Thus we come to the third dimension of our analysis: To what degree are the educational systems of particular states producing persons who possess modern orientations, values, and attitudes? The answer is critical and tragic. In every country of the Middle East, though more so in some cases than in others, the structure of a modern educational system has been created, but in every country the functioning of that system at all levels possesses many aspects that are dysfunctional for modernization. That is, despite differences in the character of social core groups and political systems, Turkey, Iran, and Egypt are characterized by similar patterns and processes that serve to hinder the achievement of modernity.

The fundamental reason for this state of affairs is to be found, perhaps paradoxically in view of the distinctions that we have drawn between political systems, within the polity itself. Since World War II none has accorded a high priority to education or proved willing or able to sponsor the kinds of transformation in educational patterns and processes that were so desperately required by changing conditions, so that in each state the emphasis remained essentially upon educational expansion rather than qualitative change. In short, despite variations in such factors as political costs and benefits, the magnitude of the task, the resources available, and the very different nature of the polities themselves, it is because the educational policy outputs of Turkey, Iran, and Egypt have been so similar that their school systems are in such profound need of radical change.

To understand this seeming paradox it is necessary to return to our typology and to look at the governments of Turkey, Iran, and Egypt from that perspective. That Iran was unwilling to transform its schools is not surprising. Historically, polities whose social core group consists of a ruling class or a political elite with a strong class orientation have been reluctant to adopt policies to promote technological change of any magnitude. Their desire to preserve the status quo and their realization that a rapid rate of growth could unleash forces that might displace them combine to produce conservative policies. The creation of a middle class has often resulted in a direct challenge to the foundations of the power of a ruling class. In other cases a growing middle class has accepted the leadership of the existing social core group, but the very process of technological innovation and development has changed existing criteria for mobility to favor persons who can apply the new technology, many of whom achieve elite status, thus altering the composition of the social core group indirectly.

The case of contemporary Iran illustrates this pattern well. Mohammed Reza Shah, despite great concern for his country's welfare and his commitment to reform, has avoided implementing programs that would adversely affect existing authority and value patterns within the society. Seeking to achieve rapid economic development without fundamental social, cultural, or political change, he has attempted to restructure many aspects of Iranian life and has sponsored reforms designed to ameliorate many of the major weaknesses of the educational system. Yet, despite their imaginativeness, these programs constitute only an ad hoc response to various problems. They do not—and within the present context cannot—involve the total functional reorganization of an education system that is not adequate even in terms of the Shah's aspirations for his country. In short, though Iran possesses tremendous potential for modernization, the character of the political system ensures that, despite the adoption of various reforms to remedy the most glaring weaknesses, education will essentially continue to function as in the past, reinforcing those values, attitudes, and social characteristics that maintain traditional social, cultural, and political patterns.

The case of Turkey is different. As we have suggested, for modernization to take place in any competitive system, positive, sophisticated, and dynamic leadership is required to overcome the problems created by the dispersal of power and authority. Since 1950, however, Turkey has not enjoyed that kind of leadership. The difficult task of harnessing the energies of the populace to the achievement of Ataturk's vision of a powerful modern state was never tackled in any systematic and coherent way. On the contrary, the past twenty years have been marked by a reluctance to sponsor the kinds of fundamental changes in many areas that, though unpopular in the short run and perhaps even longer, were vital for modernization. In such a context, educational priorities remained with quantity rather than quality, and the urgent task of educational transformation was never seriously tackled.

Egypt since 1952 represents a third type of political system, the radical. Many radical regimes, though ideologically committed to rapid change in all aspects of the social order, have often been noted more for their rhetoric than for actual policies. Here, too, the question of leadership is vital, and few such systems have enjoyed the kind of dynamic, charismatic, and sophisticated direction that is necessary if rhetoric is to be transformed into reality. In many ways Nasser was a great leader and possessed such qualities, but his commitment to radical change within Egypt did not extend to all aspects of the society. Thus, though genuinely concerned with modernization, he never sponsored the kinds of changes that were necessary in many areas of the culture and never resolved fundamental and complex problems of mobilization and institutionalization. In this context it is not surprising that education and many other domestic problem areas received a low priority, and when to this is added the lack of ideology and program that characterized the revolutionaries and the expenditure of time and other resources first on the consolidation of power and then on such external issues as the Suez crisis, the Yemeni civil war, and the 1967 war, it is obvious that even during the "socialist phase" many aspects of Egyptian life would remain unchanged.

Thus the educational systems of Turkey, Iran, and Egypt are all characterized by similar dysfunctionalities. Seldom did governments evidence a commitment to educational transformation, though many suggestions have been advanced and specific projects implemented in an effort to resolve various deficiencies. All countries have also turned to formal planning in an effort to deal with these problems but the results to date have not been particularly inspiring. Most reforms either have dealt with peripheral issues or have involved the introduction of one or, at best, a group of interrelated changes within an existing framework that inevitably negates these efforts. Furthermore, plans are usually based on inadequate data and most projections concerning enrollments in academic institutions have been vastly exceeded, whereas those for technical and scientific fields have seldom been achieved because of the lack of appropriate accompanying change in the societal context. Hence, few qualitative improvements have been evident despite the inclusion of numerous projects to upgrade teacher qualifications, to reform vocational training, or to alter administrative practices as social attitudes and cultural values combine to negate the wishes of the planners.

Explosive demands for education resulted in mushrooming enrollments and qualitative decline throughout the region as governments, for ideological or political reasons, proved unwilling or unable to cope with this unprecedented pressure and did not erect effective barriers to prevent unmanageable numbers of students from flooding all levels of the system. Accompanying this permissive attitude was the inadequate allocation of resources to provide the required new facilities to accommodate expanded enrollments. Since even before the explosion in social demand the schools of the Middle Eastern countries were not noted for high standards, this devaluation resulted in even more serious qualitative problems in all parts of the educational system of every country in the region.

As a result, the educational systems of Turkey, Iran, and Egypt all produce thousands of badly prepared students at all levels. Poorly trained and motivated instructors teaching large numbers of students along traditional lines (regardless of the formal nature of the curriculum) has become the norm everywhere. One reason for this state of affairs is that teachers, especially in technical and scientific fields, are in very short supply. All areas, however, suffer from unqualified personnel resulting in very high dropout rates, large numbers of repeaters at all levels, and a flood of ill-prepared graduates with high expectations.

From the perspective of political development the present situation is extremely serious. Thousands of graduates cannot find any opportunity for meaningful employment and additional thousands seek admission to universities and colleges in the hope that a degree, any degree, will enable them to obtain the rewards to which they aspire. They, too, are doomed to disillusionment, frustration, and alienation, for the problem of graduate unemployment is already acute in many countries. Nevertheless each year a new wave of university graduates with nonmarketable skills is produced while, ironically, most countries face serious shortages of skilled personnel of all types. This represents one of the most important consequences of the establishment of modern educational systems: the production everywhere of a new group which continues to grow at a pace far too rapid for its members to be absorbed in any productive way. The knowledge that they face dreary futures, often occupying a position of no importance that has been artificially created to provide them with some sort of income, has served to aggravate student unrest, and student activism, latent or overt, remains a potent force everywhere. To what extent the political systems of the Arab Republic of Egypt, Iran, and Turkey possess appropriate institutions and resources to process satisfactorily the ever increasing demands placed upon them by discontented students and frustrated graduates remains one of the fundamental variables that will determine their future political development. Every other state in the region faces the same problem.

In short, explosive population growth, rising unit costs of instruction, shortages of qualified teachers, growing gaps between needed and available manpower, and escalating requirements for advanced technological skills have conspired to create staggering pressures on traditional educational methods throughout the Middle East. Everywhere the present educational systems have already revealed their failure to respond to these pressures and it is no exaggeration to state that education has reached a state of intellectual and financial insolvency and can only be expected to deteriorate even more.

This situation represents a crisis in the eyes of many observers, a crisis which must inevitably deepen since social demand will inexorably grow faster than the financial and human resources that are likely to be available for investment in education. Little educational advancement is possible at a time when unit costs are expected to rise, inflation will probably continue apace, and increasing numbers will wish to obtain ever more schooling unless the cost of providing instruction can be reduced. One immediate way is to eliminate promotion barriers to avoid the waste involved in having students repeat several grades prior to graduation. Repeaters, however, represent but a fraction of the wastage that exists in the Middle Eastern educational system; dropouts, inadequate curricula, ineffective administration, all contribute to the dissipation of a significant proportion of all monies invested in education. Hence it is unlikely that significant savings can easily be achieved within the present context to meet the demand generated by explosive population increases and rising expectations, and further deterioration in an already desperate situation is widely anticipated.

Clearly such a situation is not functional to the requirements of modernization. Not only does an educational experience featuring traditional methods and emphasizing traditional values not produce the kinds of flexible and innovative types who are necessary if modernization is to be achieved, but a vicious cycle has been created as thousands of students continue to be crippled by an increasingly outmoded and useless education. Moreover, the longer present educational systems continue to operate along these lines the more difficult it will be for these states to achieve modernity as ever increasing numbers of graduates are socialized into attitudes and values which do not contribute to—and indeed positively hinder—the achievement of a sufficiently rapid rate of growth to create new positions to absorb an ever growing flood of newcomers with similar orientations.

If education is to be rescued from this impasse a totally new approach is required, and there are many signs that an awareness of this is spreading throughout the Middle East. A UNESCO-sponsored working group, for example, concluded that "a total reform of the system of education in all its aspects" was necessary if the numerous problems confronting education in the Arab world were to be overcome.[1] This view found support at the 1970 Marrakesh conference where a feeling was voiced that "if any change was to occur in respect of education whether along the lines of the Marrakesh Conference or other-wise, it should, and indeed must, come through revolutionary measures . . . annihilating the existing institutions with all vestiges of the past and building new ones."[2] Illustrations of similar attitudes in Turkey and Iran could also be given.

To suggest that such a strategy represents the only meaningful way to deal with the educational problems confronting the countries

---

[1] "Problems of Children and Youth in National Planning and Development," paper presented to the Third Regional Conference of Ministers of Education and Ministers Responsible for Economic Planning in the Arab States, Marrakesh, Morocco, 12–20 January 1970, mimeo. (Paris: UNESCO/MINED-ARAB/Ref. 5, 1970), p. 10.

[2] Mohammed A. El-Ghannam, *Education in the Arab Region Viewed from the 1970 Marrakesh Conference,* Educational Studies and Documents, no. 1 (Paris: UNESCO, 1971), p. 31.

of the Middle East is not to minimize the awesome difficulties and problems that will have to be overcome. The educational enterprise in every country has demonstrated a remarkable ability to withstand efforts at reform and to absorb the impact of major external forces without changing. One expert has described this situation as follows:

There is a near consensus in all Arab countries that the expansion of education in past years has not, in general, been accompanied by a corresponding improvement in quality and has even been achieved at the expense of the latter. Conventional criteria of quality—such as teacher-student ratio, teacher qualifications, class size, cost per pupil, school building and equipment specifications, textbook standards, examination results —if applied to education in Arab countries would lead in many cases to disturbing findings. Much more serious and disturbing, however, is the lack of adaptability of education in Arab countries. During the last ten or twenty years, education in these countries has increasingly ceased to be for a privileged few, at least at the first level. Arab societies have been changing and aspiring to further change. The international scene has also been changing, with more emphasis placed on science and technology. In consequence, the aims, content, methods, concepts, administration and structure of education should also have been changed, but, unfortunately, inertia still prevails.[3]

In the face of such rigidities it would obviously be rather naïve to expect the instant radical reformation of educational systems and practices. Nevertheless it is even more naïve to ignore the fact that in recent years the components to facilitate the transformation of dysfunctional educational systems have in fact become available, that further advances are continually being made in their elaboration and development, or that an educational revolution has occurred in an Islamic society even without the application of this knowledge.

The Central Asian case illustrates both the difficulties and the potentialities inherent in educational transformation.[4] Through a process of trial and error that lasted for twenty years the Soviets successfully established a modern educational system in a traditional

[3] *Ibid.,* p. 19.
[4] The role of education in Central Asia is insightfully analyzed in the sophisticated study by William K. Medlin *et al., Education and Development in Central Asia: A Case Study of Social Change in Uzbekistan* (Leiden: E. J. Brill, 1971). See also Harry Lipset, "Education of Moslems in Tsarist and Soviet Russia," *Comparative Education Review,* 12 (1968), 310–322.

Muslim society. Education was viewed as one of the most important channels for social change, and the schools played a vital role in the modernization of the region. Throughout, however, the activities of the school system were integrated with and supplemented by other agencies and institutions designed to promote modernization, an experience that strongly supports the proposition, advanced throughout this work, that for educational transformation to take place it is necessary for other complementary social, political, and economic institutions to be simultaneously changing in the same direction. Moreover, the fact that educational transformation in Central Asia occurred without the utilization of the kinds of technologies that have since been developed means that not only is it possible to replicate this model in other Islamic societies but that it is possible to do so even more effectively and rapidly, if appropriate commitments are made, leadership exercised, and resources mobilized.

As a result of scientific and technological developments and the greater understanding of human behavior which has been achieved, powerful tools which can bring about significant changes in the educational process have been created in recent years. The chief developments which are directly relevant to education have taken place in four interrelated areas: advances in educational technology, which includes hardware and associated curricula useful to the teaching process and tools that can be applied to management and administrative problems as well; greater understanding of behavioral psychology and the learning and teaching process; studies in innovation and in the introduction of new concepts into society including the fields of mass communications; and new advances in management and planning, which include systems analysis and related techniques.

These advances provide the means to spark an educational revolution of unparalleled scope and intensity. Such a revolution would involve the total restructuring of the educational experience in terms of courses, curricula, and teacher capabilities so as to render it functional in terms of the requirements for achieving modernity. It would consist of the reallocation of inefficient and ineffective expenditures of human and material resources on the basis of comprehensive planning and modern management techniques; the abandonment of continuing and proliferating traditional and outmoded teaching methods; and the overcoming of resistance to the introduction of new and innovative teaching concepts and materials based on the application of the fundamentals of learning psychology and the learning environment. Nor would its impact be limited to the formal educational system. Whatever other arrangements can best be used to disseminate appropriate skills, values, and orientations, such as in-service training programs, would also be organized according to these principles.

To provide appropriate leadership at all levels, able and committed persons must be recruited. No fundamental change is possible unless a critical mass of teachers and administrators with the knowledge, skills, and ability to administer and implement an educational revolution is assembled. Unfortunately education is not noted for efficient administration or flexible and innovative managers and teachers. In very few cases have ministers of education provided vigorous leadership or demonstrated sensitivity to the problems of introducing new methods within an existing system. Nor have most teachers received the kind of preparation necessary for successful innovation. Such practices cannot produce educational transformation, and if the educational system is to be brought into harmony with the requirements of a modernizing society a dynamic, committed administration with the appropriate skills in management and a strong sense of innovation is required.

At the core of this strategy lies the power of the new technology, though it must be stressed that piecemeal or ad hoc efforts directed toward the solution of immediate and defined educational weaknesses will not produce the needed educational transformation. Such an approach—even if it involves glamorous innovations such as satellite broadcasting—inevitably makes little impact upon fundamental problems and is, in reality, self-defeating to the creative and innovative use of available knowledge and technology. If real change is to be achieved, a comprehensive and integrated program based on a systems approach and designed to create a totally new educational experience marked by dynamism, flexibility, intellectual vigor, and continual self-renewal is essential. Only from such an educational system can come the kinds of persons who possess the attitudes and values that characterize modern man. Thus all aspects of education must change —administration, methods of teacher training, curricular content, and the relationship between teachers and students—and must be brought into a coherent and integrated whole. Innovation in all areas must become the accepted norm and the new hardware and software that are available must constantly be applied to all aspects of the learning process and integrated therein.

Technology is stressed because, given the existing conditions of school systems in the Middle East (or in the United States, for that matter), it is unlikely that radical change can be achieved without the application of such techniques. Programmed instruction provides controlled procedures designed to train students to think rather than to memorize. Educational media can be used to supplement existing teacher skills in thousands of classrooms and thus to retrain numerous teachers who are presently relying on traditional methods because of inadequate preparation as well as to transform the education now available to masses of students. That such approaches can be effective—if properly applied—has been demonstrated in many instances, though much research remains to be carried out on various aspects.[5]

That the new technology holds the key to an educational revolution of unparalleled scope and intensity is evidenced by the results of projects that have involved educational television, notably in American Samoa, where since 1964 this medium has been used to bring about fundamental change in education. Furthermore, plans have already been drawn up to utilize communications satellites to reach millions of people at relatively low cost. The most advanced of these projects is designed to beam educational television to India's numerous villages, and present plans call for 5,000 television receivers to be located throughout rural India by the mid-1970's when broadcasting by satellite would be inaugurated.

As we have stressed, however, educational transformation involves far more than the application of a particular innovation, and it re-

[5] See, for example W. Schramm, P. H. Coombs, F. Kahnert, and J. Lyle, *The New Media: Memo to an Educational Planner* (Paris: UNESCO, International Institute for Educational Planning, 1966); *New Educational Media in Action: Case Studies for Planners* (3 vols.; Paris: UNESCO, International Institute for Educational Planning, 1967). An excellent analysis of the current "state of the art" is S. Tickton and S. McMurrin, eds., *To Improve Learning: An Evaluation of Instructional Technology* (2 vols.; New York: R. R. Bowker, 1970).

mains to be seen whether all the critical areas that are involved will be adequately developed and integrated into the kind of overall program that is required. If appropriate software is utilized, if planning and management are sophisticated and flexible, and if proper attention is paid to problems of implementation, integration, and reinforcement, however, then truly significant change may be forthcoming in the Indian system of education.

To argue that a strategy which incorporates the new technologies, as defined above, possesses unique potential and unsurpassed promise, if utilized appropriately, is not to be guilty of unsophisticated scientism but rather to recognize potentialities. The successful implementation of such a strategy would, in the short run, serve to reduce waste and thus contribute greatly to the financing of an educational revolution, in the medium term permit an economic growth rate to accommodate graduates in all fields, and in the long run make possible the creation of a modern state. No other strategy holds similar promise.

Nevertheless it must be recognized that this great potential may not often be realized because of the magnitude of the obstacles that must be overcome. Which societies possess the imagination, the drive, or the leadership to mobilize needed resources and to implement such a strategy successfully remains to be seen. Many others will simply be unwilling to adopt a policy with the profound implications that flow from the required commitment to modernization. As we have stressed, if education is to be restructured in consonance with the principles described earlier and if the school is to achieve its potential for social change, educational transformation must be accompanied by societal transformation. The schools can produce modern men only if informal educational structures and other institutions reinforce, continue, and expand the changes taking place within the classroom. In the last analysis, therefore, the degree of commitment to modernization evidenced by a particular social core group and its ability to implement successfully a program to achieve that goal will determine whether educational reforms are to be merely restatements of old values or changes involving fundamental transformation.

The U.A.R., Turkey, and Iran have reached a turning point in their efforts to modernize. How much further they will progress toward this goal depends largely upon the responses that their political systems—the radical, the competitive, and the reformist, respectively—will make to urgent educational and related needs. An educational process functioning in ancient ways cannot promote change, serve the needs of citizens, or permit these states to fulfill the destiny of their rich heritage. Today knowledge is available for the required educational revolution. Whether the political will and the political capability to utilize the new technology appropriately also exist awaits the judgment of history.

Appendix Tables

Appendix 1. Percentage enrolled of corresponding population of school age as defined for each country (figures in parentheses indicate the appropriate age group), 1967

Country	First and second levels combined		First level		Second level	
Algeria	(6–18)	40	(6–11)	68	(12–18)	8
Bahrain*	(6–16)	89	(6–11)	118	(12–16)	46
Iraq	(7–18)	49	(7–12)	69	(13–18)	24
Jordan*	(6–17)	70	(6–11)	96	(12–17)	39
Kuwait	(6–17)	74	(6–9)	93	(10–17)	60
Lebanon	(6–17)	67	(6–10)	111	(11–17)	28
Libya†	(6–17)	59	(6–11)	90	(12–17)	19
Morocco	(6–17)	32	(6–10)	55	(11–17)	12
Qatar	(6–17)	63	(6–11)	96	(12–17)	24
Saudi Arabia	(6–17)	18	(6–11)	29	(12–17)	6
Sudan	(7–18)	16	(7–10)	33	(11–18)	6
Syrian Arab Republic	(6–17)	58	(6–11)	81	(12–17)	30
Tunisia	(6–18)	65	(6–11)	106	(12–18)	19
United Arab Republic	(6–17)	52	(6–11)	71	(12–17)	30
Yemen	(6–17)	5	(6–11)	8	(12–17)	0.6

Source: Mohammed A. El-Ghannam, *Education in the Arab Region Viewed from the 1970 Marrakesh Conference*, Educational Studies and Documents, new series no. 1 (Paris: UNESCO, 1971), p. 53. Reproduced by permission of UNESCO.
* 1966.
† Public education only.

460

Appendix 2. Total enrollment by level of education in the Arab states, 1960, 1967 (in 000s)

Country	First level		Second level (general)		Second level (vocational)		Second level (teacher training)		Third level		Total	
	1960	1967	1960	1967	1960	1967	1960	1967	1960	1967	1960	1967
Algeria	867.6	1485.4	83.3	116.1	34.7	38.9	1.7	5.4	7.2	9.7	994.5	1655.5
Bahrain	18.9*	35.2*	1.1	9.2	0.2	0.8	0.1	0.2	–	0.1	20.3	45.5
Iraq	760.5	991.0	136.0	246.0	8.0	10.0	8.2	10.0	11.3	35.0	924.0	1292.0
Jordan	212.5	340.0	57.0	110.3	1.6	3.5	0.08	–	1.0	3.4	272.18	457.2
Kuwait	26.9	54.0	12.1	42.0	0.2	1.1	0.08	2.4	–	0.9	39.28	100.4
Lebanon	265.2	401.8	45.5	109.8	0.8	1.8	0.5	2.2	7.5	29.1	319.5	544.7
Libya	126.2	247.5	12.3	34.3	1.5	1.9	2.2	6.0	0.7	2.9	142.9	292.6
Morocco	795.9	1105.2	59.0	248.7	17.2	17.8	1.1	1.2	4.7	9.0	877.9	1381.9
Qatar	5.7	11.9	0.2	2.0	0.1	0.4	0.02	0.1	–	–	6.02	14.4
Saudi Arabia	115.0	329.2	9.5	49.2	2.0	1.2	3.5	4.7	1.3	4.8	131.3	389.1
Yemen (People's Democratic Rep. of)	26.4	56.3	7.6	17.7	0.4	0.3	0.1	0.3	–	–	34.5	74.6
Sudan	317.7	518.3	69.2	142.0	2.8	5.7	1.1	2.2	3.8	8.7	394.6	676.9
Syrian Arab Rep.	527.0	767.9	84.8	213.6	7.5	5.9	2.0	8.0	14.4	33.1	635.7	1028.5
Tunisia	440.5	826.3	40.7	81.7	14.2	45.6	1.2	6.2	2.6	6.8	499.2	966.6
UAR	2610.2†	3471.3†	389.6	925.9	108.0	162.7	18.2	34.9	106.8	173.9	3232.8	4768.7
Yemen	61.3	66.8	1.1	2.7	0.03	1.3	0.06	0.2	–	–	62.49	71.0
Total Arab States	7177.5	10708.1	1009.0	2351.2	199.23	298.9	40.14	84.0	161.3	317.4	8587.17	13759.6

Source: El-Ghannam, op. cit., p. 52. Reproduced by permission of UNESCO.
* Public education only.
† Not including Al-Azhar primary schools with 31,797 pupils in 1967 and language schools with 3,298 pupils in 1967.

Appendix 3. Educational development in the Arab Republic of Egypt, 1930–1969

Level	1930	1936	1939	1945	1950	1955	1960	1965	1966	1967	1968	1969
Primary												
Schools	8,894	8,687	8,558	7,947	1,537	2,593	3,335	3,720				
Teachers					44,753	48,585	67,688	87,390	87,144	90,773		
Students	809,000	1,203,000	1,447,000	1,222,000	1,310,169	1,869,493	2,663,247	3,450,338	3,445,627	3,506,429	3,553,100	3,618,751
% Female students					36	37	39	39	39	39	38	39
Student-teacher ratio					29	38	39	39	40	39		
Secondary (1st cycle)					(1953)			(1964)				
General												
Teachers						16,018	14,125	19,783				
Students					349,000	328,478	253,737	472,568		757,604	775,511	793,891
% Female students							28	30			32	32
Vocational												
Teachers						564	1,980	3,847		8,273	5,531	4,272
Students					3,000	8,218	41,422	43,248				
% Female students						15	15	17			34	20
Secondary (2nd cycle)		(1935)	(1940)									
General												
Teachers						8,238	9,105	10,493				
Students	15,816	15,985	22,889	38,823	92,000	107,612	132,161	174,246		275,091	276,339	293,144
% Female students	6	8	8	9	14	15	22	28			31	32

Vocational*												
Teachers	14,030	19,495	17,400	18,463	43,000	4,858	5,490	9,173				
Students	5,962	7,613	8,263	15,791	33,595	50,088	67,186	91,252		153,648	197,054	241,590
% Female students	0.4	2	4	5	7		12	19			29	30
Higher education												
Teachers						3,266	4,251		8,840	9,841		
Students						70,056	106,780	177,123	179,100	174,614	180,243	196,077
% Female students						14	17	21	22	23	24	26
Students per 1,000 inhabitants	58	59	69	116	165	305	413	598	594	565		

Sources: The data for 1930–1945 are from *World Survey of Education*, Vols. II, III, IV (Paris: UNESCO, 1958, 1961, 1966). The data on secondary education, first and second cycle, 1953–1955, are from *The Increase of Population in the U.A.R. and Its Impact on Development* (Cairo: Central Agency for Public Mobilisation and Statistics, September 1969). The data on primary and higher education, 1950–1967, are from *Statistical Yearbook, 1969* (New York: United Nations, 1970). The data on secondary education, first and second cycle, 1960–1965, are from "Survey of Educational Progress Achieved in Arab States since Ministers and Directors of Education Met in Beirut in February 1960" (Paris: UNESCO/MINED/ARAB STATES/8, 1966) mimeo. The data for 1969 are from "Report on the Development of Education in the United Arab Republic in the School Year 1969/1970" (Cairo: United Arab Republic Ministry of Education Documentation Centre for Education, May 1970), multilithed.
  * Includes teacher training.

Appendix 4. Educational development in Turkey, 1923–1972

Level	1923–1924	1927–1928	1930–1931	1935–1936	1940–1941	1945–1946	1950–1951	1955–1956	1960–1961	1965–1966	1970–1971	1971–1972
Primary*												
Schools	4,894	6,043	6,598	6,275	10,596	14,010	17,428	18,724	24,398	30,466	38,227	39,112
Teachers	10,238	15,194	16,318	14,949	20,564	27,317	35,871	42,169	62,526	85,653	132,577	
Students	341,941	461,985	489,299	688,102	955,957	1,357,740	1,616,626	1,983,668	2,866,501	3,924,326	5,011,926	5,164,119
Male			315,072	454,128	661,279	865,860	1,016,915	1,238,327	1,800,026	2,360,250		
Female			174,227	233,974	294,678	491,880	599,711	745,341	1,066,475	1,564,076		
Students as % of children aged 7–11				32	37	52	68	69	71	92		
Graduates			21,179	37,700	97,836	150,883	165,132	198,407	311,426	451,504‡	753,536	
Student-teacher ratio												
Urban schools				43	47	48	43	44	43	43	43	
Rural schools				54	61	62	51	52	49	48		
Secondary* (1st cycle)												
Schools	72	78	83	191	238	252	406	573	745	939	1,848	1,831
Teachers	796	791	1,068	2,403	3,867	3,931	4,528	6,385	12,080	15,024	22,301	
Students	5,905	19,858	27,093	52,386	95,332	65,608†	68,187†	133,217	291,266	433,210	810,893	869,251
Male		15,674	20,148	38,497	69,097	46,074	50,262	97,576	220,486	317,375	593,415	
Female		4,184	6,945	13,889	26,235	19,534	17,925	35,641	70,780	115,835	217,478	
Graduates	1,857		3,999	8,248	16,089	12,389	11,508	21,167	42,686	73,896‡	142,000	
Secondary* (2d cycle)												
Schools	23	19	22	66	82	83	88	123	190	240	518	454
Teachers		791	1,068	2,403	3,867	3,931	4,528	6,385	12,080	15,024	22,515	
Students	1,241	3,819	5,699	13,622	24,862	25,515	22,169†	33,412	75,632	114,641	253,742	282,050
Male		2,748	4,333	10,691	18,881	20,411	17,526	25,237	56,016	84,543	180,940	
Female		1,071	1,366	2,931	5,981	5,104	4,643	8,175	19,616	30,098	72,802	
Graduates		398	1,093	2,172	5,081	6,236	5,568	8,024	11,977	23,227‡	42,200	

	1923–1924										1970–1971	1971–1972
Vocational and technical (1st and 2d cycle)												
Schools		44	59	64	103	244	326	415	530	787	917	825
Teachers		698	815	679	1,355	3,826	4,488	5,294	8,333	11,236	15,039	
Students	6,547	7,718	9,101	8,187	24,641	54,248	53,289	72,675	108,221	182,476	244,144	247,082
Male		4,896	5,859	5,404	18,162	43,724	41,663	56,960	75,495	122,250	161,328	
Female		2,822	3,242	2,783	6,479	10,524	11,626	15,715	32,726	60,226	82,816	
Graduates		972	1,277	1,818	2,998	8,271	12,487	13,918	23,507	33,608‡	47,415	
Higher education												
Teachers	328	451	526	743	967	1,388	1,950	2,453	4,071	5,836	10,628	11,000
Students	2,914	3,918	4,186	7,277	12,844	19,273	24,815	36,998	65,297	97,308	155,358	179,818
Male		3,477	3,646	6,162	10,262	15,688	19,953	30,764	52,290	77,187		
Female		441	540	1,115	2,582	3,585	4,862	6,234	13,007	20,121		
Graduates		627	574	1,009	1,678	2,440	3,107	3,124	6,025	9,238	23,426	
Students per 1,000 inhabitants	422		118			155				235	313	

Sources: The data for 1923–1924 are from İ. Başgöz and H. E. Wilson, *Educational Problems in Turkey 1920–1940*, Uralic and Altaic Series, No. 86 (Bloomington: Indiana University Press, 1968), pp. 233ff. The data for 1927–1966 are from *Milli Eğitim Hareketleri 1927–1966* (Ankara: Devlet İstatistik Enstitüsü, 1967). The figure for students per 1,000 inhabitants for this period is from *Statistical Yearbook, 1969* (New York: United Nations, 1970). The data for 1970–1971 are from *Milli Eğitim İstatistikleri, Öğretim Yılı Başı, 1970–1971* (Ankara: Devlet İstatistik Enstitüsü, 1971). The data for 1971–1972 and the figures for the number of graduates at all levels and the number of teachers at the secondary (2d cycle) level for 1970–1971 were supplied by the Turkish educational attaché in New York City.

* Public and private schools.
† Decline in number of students is attributable primarily to emphasis upon vocational and technical education.
‡ 1964–1965.

Appendix 5. Educational development in Iran, 1922–1969

Level	1922	1930	1935	1940	1945	1951	1955	1960	1965	1966	1967	1968	1969
Primary													
Schools	440	1,048	1,336	2,336	2,531	5,400	6,724	9,809	15,135*	14,740*	15,429*	15,556*	15,776*
Teachers		5,601	6,805	9,269	11,710	22,204	32,801	42,541	72,867	75,502	81,127		
Students	43,025	126,052	170,077	287,245	287,905	650,355	823,983	1,436,169	2,208,671	2,411,505	2,575,537	2,753,132	2,916,266
% Female						26	30	32	34	34	34		
Student-teacher ratio						29	25		30	32	32		
Secondary (1st and 2d cycle)													
Schools	46	150	180	351	288				1,711	1,865	2,098	2,332	2,585
Teachers		1,180	1,396	2,249	2,723				18,827		24,516		
Students	3,308	11,452	16,294	28,196	29,047	83,507	146,208	295,869	561,567	658,467	696,991	806,625	930,053
% Female							24		31	31	33		
Higher education													
Teachers		52	203	566	690	487†	543		2,486	2,772	3,382	3,432	
Students	91	830	1,645	3,395	4,218	5,502	10,097	19,815	29,683	36,742	46,987	59,143	
% Female							9		24	24			
Students per 1,000 inhabitants						34	55	92	121	145			

Sources: The data for 1922–1945 are from *Report on Seven Year Development Plan for the Plan Organization of the Imperial Government of Iran* (New York: Overseas Consultants, Inc., 1949), II, Exhibit B-7. All data for 1951–1967, except the number of schools at the secondary level and the higher education figures, are from *Statistical Yearbook, 1969* (New York: United Nations, 1970). These data and all figures for 1968–1969 are from *Iran* (Teheran: Ministry of Information, 1971).

* Does not include Literacy Corps schools.

† 1950.

Appendix 6. Secondary education, first and second cycles, in Iran, Turkey, and Egypt, 1951–1967

Level	Iran						Turkey						Egypt					
	1951	1955	1960	1965	1966	1967	1950	1955	1960	1965	1966	1967	1953	1955	1960	1965	1966	1967
General																		
Teachers	4,451	6,336	11,797	18,598	21,771	22,534		8,703	16,299		23,458	27,823	17,181	24,256	23,230	36,304	39,650	43,958
Total students	82,097	142,113	281,928	556,829	636,819	674,059	89,614	165,195	373,285	514,338	655,251	755,671	440,636	436,082	408,041	840,649	958,582	1,031,820
Female	17,140	34,022		169,708	196,396	217,973	22,373	42,902	90,966		174,374	200,581	85,365	90,334	110,839	244,418	283,944	309,851
Male	64,957	108,091		387,121	440,423	456,086	67,241	122,293	282,319		480,877	555,090	355,271	345,748	297,202	596,231	674,638	721,969
Vocational																		
Teachers				1,274	1,159	1,620	3,729	5,258	7,416	9,415	9,484	10,867	3,103	3,321	8,441	10,082	9,696	10,800
Total students	1,410	1,614	9,348	15,160	15,956	16,239	36,702	71,497	85,028	133,750	138,466	146,235	21,615	30,691	118,278	130,626	131,073	162,656
Female		542		2,517	2,685	2,974	10,029	15,500	26,272	39,292	40,136	41,191	495	5,371	25,473	27,263	32,956	44,157
Male		1,072		12,643	13,271	13,265	26,673	55,997	58,756	94,458	98,330	105,044	21,120	25,320	92,805	103,363	98,117	118,499
Teacher training																		
Teachers				229	463	362	742	745	1,248	1,689	1,868	2,040	1,721	2,137	2,067	4,531	4,111	3,585
Total students		2,481	4,593	4,738	5,692	6,693	16,306	16,400	23,315	57,926	54,469	57,788	23,908	27,795	19,922	49,448	42,549	34,894
Female		212		310	304	244	1,527	3,100	6,295	20,710	23,869	25,609	11,267	11,680	10,551	20,552	18,181	15,604
Male		2,269		4,428	5,388	6,349	14,779	13,300	17,020	37,216	30,600	32,179	12,641	16,115	9,371	28,896	24,368	19,290

Source: Statistical Yearbook, 1969 (New York: United Nations, 1970).

Index

469

**Education and Modernization
in the Middle East**

Designed by R. E. Rosenbaum.
Composed by The Colonial Press Inc.,
in 10 point linotype Times Roman, 3 points leaded,
with display lines in Optima Semi-bold.
Printed letterpress from type by The Colonial Press.
Bound by The Colonial Press
in Columbia book cloth
and stamped in All Purpose foil.

Library of Congress Cataloging in Publication Data
(For library cataloging purposes only)

Szyliowicz, Joseph S
  Education and modernization in the Middle East.

  1. Education—Near East. 2. Education—Egypt.
3. Education—Turkey. 4. Education—Iran.
I. Title.
LA1045.S99   370.19'3'0956   72–12292
ISBN 0–8014–0758–3